Occasional Religious Practice

Occasional Religious Practice

Valuing a Very Ordinary Religious Experience

SARAH KATHLEEN JOHNSON

OXFORD
UNIVERSITY PRESS

Oxford University Press is a department of the University of Oxford.
It furthers the University's objective of excellence in research, scholarship,
and education by publishing worldwide. Oxford is a registered trade mark of
Oxford University Press in the UK and in certain other countries.

Published in the United States of America by Oxford University Press
198 Madison Avenue, New York, NY 10016, United States of America.

© Oxford University Press 2025

All rights reserved. No part of this publication may be reproduced, stored in a retrieval system, transmitted, used for text and data mining, or used for training artificial intelligence, in any form or by any means, without the prior permission in writing of Oxford University Press, or as expressly permitted by law, by license or under terms agreed with the appropriate reprographics rights organization. Inquiries concerning reproduction outside the scope of the above should be sent to the Rights Department, Oxford University Press, at the address above.

You must not circulate this work in any other form
and you must impose this same condition on any acquirer

CIP data is on file at the Library of Congress

ISBN 9780197806548

DOI: 10.1093/9780197806579.001.0001

Printed by Marquis Book Printing, Canada

Contents

Acknowledgments   ix

Introduction   1

PART I. UNDERSTANDING OCCASIONAL RELIGIOUS PRACTICE

1. What Is Occasional Religious Practice?   17
2. Occasional Religious Practice in Context   38
3. Who Are Occasional Practitioners?   66
4. Why Practice Occasionally?   91

PART II. OCCASIONAL RELIGIOUS PRACTICE AS SELECTIVE PARTICIPATION IN RITUAL SYSTEMS

5. Ritual Systems   133
6. Selective Participation in Ritual Systems   172
7. Harmony and Dissonance Among Ritual Systems   189

PART III. DOING THEOLOGY WITH OCCASIONAL PRACTITIONERS

8. The Necessity of Doing Theology with Occasional Practitioners   217
9. Lived Liturgical Theologies of Occasional Practitioners   254
10. Occasional Practitioners and the Concerns of Ritual Experts   294

Conclusion   317

*Appendix A: Methodology: Ethnography as Theology, Religion as
    Practice, and the Relationship between Liturgical Studies and
    Sociology of Religion*   325
Appendix B: Research Methods   343
Appendix C: Interview Guides   365
Bibliography   373
Index   383

Acknowledgments

My gratitude goes first to the participants at the center of this study. This qualitative research was made possible by the clergy and congregations who welcomed my presence as a researcher and by participants in baptisms and funerals who shared their stories. This research is ultimately for these collaborators—and the many other dedicated clergy, occasional practitioners, and ordinary congregations like them—that we might learn to worship well together as people who relate to religion in different ways.

I am grateful for the many people who read and provided feedback on this manuscript at various stages of development, especially Kimberly Belcher, as well as Maxwell Johnson, Christian Smith, Todd Whitmore, and Nina Glibetić. I appreciated the opportunity to workshop this project with colleagues at the University of Notre Dame in the Department of Theology, especially the Liturgical Studies area and the Theology and Ethnography Group, as well as in the Department of Sociology, especially in the Center for the Study of Religion and Society and the Research and Analysis on Sociology of Religion workshop, and at the University of Toronto through the Toronto Mennonite Theological Centre at the Toronto School of Theology. Presentations and conversation at the North American Academy of Liturgy with the Critical Theories and Liturgical Studies Seminar, Societas Liturgica, the Institute of Liturgical Studies, the American Academy of Religion, the Society for the Scientific Study of Religion, the Association for the Sociology of Religion, the European Sociological Association, the Toronto School of Theology Liturgy Seminar, the Canadian Theological Society, Ecclesiology and Ethnography Canada, the Centre for Christian Engagement at St. Mark's College, and the Christian Congregational Music Conference helped refine and deepen my thinking.

Funding for this research was provided by a Social Sciences and Humanities Research Council of Canada Doctoral Fellowship (752-2015-0120), a Louisville Institute Doctoral Fellowship, and the Toronto Mennonite Theological Centre A. James Reimer Award. Costs associated with transcription and compensating participants were covered by research grants from the Institute for Scholarship in the Liberal Arts, the Center for the Study of

Religion and Society, and the Center for Liturgy at the University of Notre Dame. Editorial work on the manuscript was supported by an Explore Grant from the Saint Paul University Social Sciences and Humanities Research Council of Canada Institutional Grant program. I am grateful to editors Ulrike Guthrie and Anne Louise Mahoney. Many thanks to Theo Calderara and the team at Oxford University Press.

Carl Bear has been my closest companion and colleague at every stage in the development of this project and its publication. Thank you.

Introduction

I arrive at the Cathedral Church of St. James, the Anglican Cathedral in downtown Toronto, fifteen minutes before the 7:30 p.m. Christmas Eve Choral Eucharist is scheduled to begin. The soaring neo-Gothic space already feels full, including the overflow chairs set up on either side of the central box pews. It is a dramatic contrast to any of the four services celebrated at the Cathedral each Sunday. I am not the only one aware of the difference. The bishop begins his homily with an expansive welcome, explicitly welcoming those who are "faithful and doubting" and those who are "here by choice or by coercion." "There is a place for you," he says, "although there may not have been a place for you at 4:30!"—suggesting that the earlier service was even more crowded.

The following year, I attend the 4:30 p.m. Christmas Eve Lessons and Carols at the Cathedral. Many seats are filled when I arrive—a solid forty-five minutes before the service begins. I slide past an older couple and settle into a box pew five rows from the back. The pew fills quickly. An elementary school–age child ends up sitting on the lap of a parent at the far end; the family had to split up to find seats. By 4:15 p.m., every seat is filled, and worshipers line the walls at the back and sides. There are many more children and teenagers than on an ordinary Sunday. Most younger people appear to be part of multigenerational families—grandparents, parents, and grandchildren attending together.

I return to the Cathedral later that week on the Sunday after Christmas. The church building is still adorned for Christmas, with gleaming gold fabrics and an abundance of red poinsettias. The service includes many of the same familiar Christmas carols. However, in a stark juxtaposition to four days earlier, there are six empty pews in front of me, six empty pews behind me, and only a couple of people in the same section across the center aisle. One family with a child briefly sits at the back—they appear to be tourists—but otherwise the congregation is composed only of adults. The contrast is striking (Figure I.1).

Occasional Religious Practice. Sarah Kathleen Johnson, Oxford University Press.
© Oxford University Press 2025. DOI: 10.1093/9780197806579.003.0001

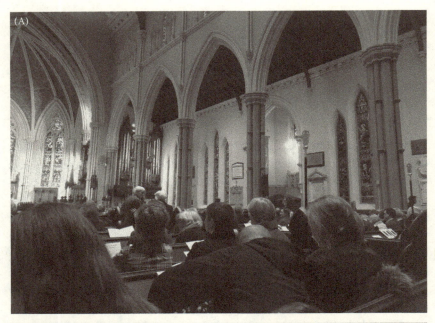

Figure I.1 Worship on Christmas Eve (A) and the Sunday after Christmas (B) at the Cathedral Church of St. James.

for Carl

Although these services took place at the Cathedral, my participant observation and interviews, along with diocesan statistics and common knowledge, suggest that they represent patterns present in many Anglican parishes in Toronto, the site of the ethnographic research that anchors this study. Quantitative data indicate that these patterns are widespread in Canada. International comparison points to parallels in the United States and Europe. What I am calling *occasional religious practice*—participation in religious practices occasionally rather than routinely, often in connection with certain types of occasions, such as holidays, life transitions, and crises—may be the dominant way in which people relate to Christianity in Canada, the United States, and beyond in the twenty-first century. To understand the roles of religion in contemporary societies and to do liturgical theology that connects with experiences of Christian worship today, it is crucial to take occasional religious practice seriously.

The Argument in Brief

Declining participation in religious institutions, increasing uncertainty about matters of faith, and a growing proportion of the population who identify as nonreligious all characterize the North American religious landscape. Nevertheless, people continue to turn to religious practices at critical moments in their lives, such as the birth of a child or the loss of a loved one, holiday celebrations, and times of personal or communal crisis.

Part I: Understanding Occasional Religious Practice

Part I of the book introduces and describes the concept of occasional religious practice, primarily within the sociological literature on definitions of religion and religious change. To begin, Chapter 1 *defines the concept of occasional religious practice* using sociological definitions of religion as practice. I then identify four types of occasions associated with occasional religious practice—holidays, life transitions, crises, and incidental circumstances—and illustrate them ethnographically. Chapter 2 situates the concept of occasional religious practice in historical context by pointing to early Christian, medieval, early modern, and modern instances of occasional religious practice. I also consider the literature on religious change in Canada, the United States, Europe, and Australia, and examine the prominence of occasional religious practice in contemporary contexts.

The identities, motivations, and experiences of *occasional practitioners* are the focus of the following two chapters. Chapter 3 explores the diversity of religious and nonreligious identities claimed by participants in baptisms and funerals in the Anglican tradition, as well as why they claim these identities, and how the same religious identity may be understood in very different ways. Chapter 4 addresses the frequently asked question: Why do people participate in religious practices occasionally? Based on motivations for occasional practice, I develop a typology of occasional practitioners with three broad categories—initiators, supporters, and catalysts. I also identify subcategories of initiators, including those motivated by cultural heritage, relational connection, and desire for spiritual connection, as well as those who are invisibly routine in their practice, or involuntarily occasional. Subcategories of supporters include advocates, inner-circle supporters, and outer-circle supporters. In addition, I consider how occasional practice changes over time—annually, over the life span, and in response to turning point events. Finally, I examine how occasional practitioners experience the occasionality of their practice and note that most are very content with this way of relating to religion, which they often describe as being "not very religious."

Although there is an abundance of literature on nonreligion and strong religion, relatively little of it explores the substantial space between these extremes. Sociological studies of the contemporary religious landscape tend to group occasional practice with a variety of other factors, such as affiliation and belief, in ways that obscure the presence and internal diversity of occasional practitioners. The concept of occasional religious practice provides insight into two key areas of the study of religion. First, it explores how religious practices may be very important to practitioners on certain occasions, even if they consider themselves "not very religious" and do not engage in religious practices routinely. Second, it reveals the vast diversity of participants present at religious practices on certain occasions, including analysis of their wide-ranging religious and nonreligious identities and the complex social and spiritual motivations for their religious practice.

Part II: Occasional Religious Practice as Selective Participation in Ritual Systems

The second part of the book shifts from a focus on people who are occasional practitioners to an emphasis on the *ritual practices themselves*, and does so in conversation with ritual theory drawn from the discipline of religious studies. Greater awareness of the diversity of participants present at religious rituals challenges the common assumption in religious studies that rituals are practiced in relatively cohesive and comprehensive systems.

Chapter 5 outlines and develops Catherine Bell's theory of *ritual systems*. I emphasize how people positioned differently in ritual systems may define the same ritual system in different ways, and how ritual systems are often interpreted through overlaps with other ritual systems. In Chapter 6, I apply ritual systems theory to occasional religious practice, defining occasional religious practice as *selective participation in a ritual system that some practice routinely*. I integrate ritual theory with theory from sociology of culture to explain how occasional practitioners select practices based both on deeply held internal cultural models and as a flexible and strategic response to specific situations. Separating a practice from a ritual system and interpreting it through overlapping systems has the potential to contribute to the always ongoing transformation of ritual systems. Chapter 7 presents an *extended case study of the overlaps between the Anglican and Roman Catholic ritual systems*. I examine five specific baptisms as examples of the diversity of ways that occasional practitioners thoughtfully and intuitively negotiate these overlaps. The example of the occasional practice of baptism is a focus throughout Part II.

Introducing the concept of occasional religious practice makes it possible to consider the consequences of particular rituals being separated from the larger ritual systems of which they are part. In addition, it makes it possible to explore how rituals within a specific system may be interpreted through overlaps with other, quite different, ritual systems. This includes the likelihood that ritual participants positioned differently within a ritual system will understand the same ritual system in very different ways. The concept of occasional religious practice invites a re-examination of the meaning and function of religious ritual in contexts characterized by selective participation and diverse overlapping ritual systems. Part II serves as a bridge between the social scientific core of the book in Part I and its theological heart in Part III.

Part III: Doing Theology with Occasional Practitioners

Theologically, this study challenges the common liturgical theological assumption that all participants in Christian worship are formally affiliated, fully believing, actively practicing, and morally compliant with the tradition in which they practice.

Part III is the most explicitly theological portion of this volume. Framed by a case study of photography as a liturgical theological expression, Chapter 8 makes a theological argument for *why it is necessary to attend to the experience and insights of occasional practitioners* when doing liturgical theology by means of three distinct yet interconnected approaches. The first engages scripture, specifically the stories of Zacchaeus and the woman at the well; the second draws on classical liturgical theology, declaring the death of Mrs. Murphy—the archetypal routine practitioner—and also the occasional presence of her great-granddaughter; and the third takes inspiration from liberation theology in a call to attend to the liturgical and theological margins as a way to start where it hurts, think at the borders, and engage in dialogue through praxis. Doing liturgical theology with occasional practitioners requires openness to changing how ritual experts do theology yet has the potential to enrich the theology and practice of all participants.

Chapters 9 and 10 explore the *lived liturgical theologies of participants* in this research without claiming that their perspectives represent occasional practitioners more broadly. I begin in Chapter 9 by presenting three themes that run deeply through interviews with non-expert participants: liturgical experience as material more than linguistic, including space, clothing, and objects; emotional more than conceptual, including overall mood and specific moments; and relational more than personal, in terms of the meaning of baptisms and funerals. In Chapter 10, I consider how non-expert participants speak to themes that are significant for ritual experts: God, whom many participants describe as "something more"; tradition, which participants frame positively as a source of history, continuity, and stability; and the relationship between worship and ethics, which is reflected in participants' desire to be "good people" and in their sense that occasional participation in Christian worship is a resource for this.

Theologically, this study recognizes that many occasional and routine participants in Christian worship are not formally affiliated, fully believing, actively practicing, and morally compliant with the tradition in which they practice. Setting aside this fiction invites greater awareness of who is actually present in Christian worship. In the context of centuries of liturgical theology dominated by clergy and professional theologians, it raises the question of what theological insights those on the theological and liturgical margins may have to offer and provides encouragement to engage these potentially prophetic perspectives. Awareness of occasional religious practice invites consideration of how people who relate to religion in different ways can do liturgical theology together and better engage in religious practices together.

In short, this research takes occasional religious practice seriously as a substantial way of relating to religion. It recognizes the vast diversity of occasional practitioners. It acknowledges the power of occasional practice to shape ritual. It invites theological collaboration with occasional practitioners. It thoroughly investigates who is present in Christian worship on occasions such as baptisms, funerals, and holidays, and takes the diversity of participants present as a starting point for understanding religion and religious ritual and for doing liturgical theology.

Case Study and Methods

This interdisciplinary research at the intersection of sociology of religion and liturgical studies builds on recent developments in each discipline, especially a turn toward ethnography as theology that creates new space for engagement with the social sciences, and a turn toward sociological definitions of religion as practice that invites dialogue with liturgical studies. This study addresses two specific concerns held in common across disciplines: (1) who has a voice in determining liturgical theology and practice; and (2) what gaps exist (a) between prescribed practices and observable patterns of worship, and (b) between official teachings and participants' interpretations of their experience. It does so by listening deeply to stories about occasional religious practice.[1]

Case Study

This book examines big questions about what Christian worship is meaning and doing in increasingly nonreligious and religiously diverse social contexts and thus contributes to our understanding of religion in the twenty-first century, religious ritual, and liturgical theology. At the same time, it is a close examination of how particular individuals experience particular events in particular communities during a narrow window of time. As ethnographic

---

[1] Appendix A outlines a robust interdisciplinary methodology.

research, it claims that "a case study that pays close attention to a specific experience—even an exceptional one—reveals patterns and designs that pervade the larger picture as well."[2] Therefore, as a way into these broad theoretical and theological themes, I examine baptisms and funerals in the Anglican Church of Canada in Toronto, Ontario, between 2017 and 2020 as a starting point for conversations about religious practice. Why these?[3]

The *Anglican tradition* has both Catholic and Protestant resonances, yielding results that are applicable to a wider spectrum of the Christian tradition, especially because the Anglican tradition is internally diverse, with Anglo-Catholic, mainline, evangelical, and intercultural expressions. At the same time, specific liturgical resources and theological approaches are associated with Anglican baptisms and funerals, which allows for consideration of whether and how official institutional approaches align with the experience and interpretations of participants.

This study is based in Christian churches affiliated with the Anglican Church of Canada, which is the primary expression of the Anglican Communion in Toronto.[4] The various church bodies that comprise the Anglican Communion today trace their origins to the sixteenth-century Reformation in England. Although the Anglican tradition has never been an established state religion in Canada, the Anglican church has had a politically, socially, and economically privileged role in public life in Ontario and Toronto.[5] While there have been various historical controversies and there are certain present-day tensions, the Anglican tradition in Toronto is now broadly progressive, both theologically and socially.[6] Since the 1960s, the Anglican tradition in Canada has been experiencing declining membership and participation.[7]

Theologically, Anglican religious identity is anchored in ritual practice more than doctrine or ecclesial structure, especially in the *Book of Common Prayer* (1962) and the *Book of Alternative Services* (1985), the latter of which,

---

[2] Lynn Davidman, *Tradition in a Rootless World: Women Turn to Orthodox Judaism* (Berkeley: University of California Press, 1991), 27.

[3] Appendix B describes in detail the case selection.

[4] Anglican Church of Canada, "Welcome to the Anglican Church of Canada," accessed December 11, 2023, http://www.anglican.ca. The Anglican Church of Canada is the equivalent of The Episcopal Church in the United States and the Church of England in England, for example.

[5] Alan Hayes, *Anglicans in Canada: Controversies and Identity in Historical Perspective* (Urbana: University of Illinois, 2004).

[6] Hayes, *Anglicans in Canada*.

[7] Neil Elliot, "Statistics Report for House of Bishops," *Anglican Samizdat*, October 5, 2019, accessed December 11, 2023, https://www.anglicansamizdat.net/wordpress/latest-anglican-church-of-canada-membership-and-attendance-statistics.

rather than being an alternative at this time, has become the primary prayer book in active use in Canada.[8] Grounded in the prayer books, Anglican liturgy is relatively fixed yet also somewhat flexible. This allows a range of institutional actions and interpretations to exist within a recognizable and coherent historical, theological, and liturgical tradition. Anglican baptisms and funerals are well established, clearly defined, historically mainstream religious practices in Toronto.

Baptisms and funerals, as religious rituals that mark birth and death, often involve participants with a range of relationships to religion, including those who, apart from these occasions, may rarely or never participate in Christian worship. As family events, baptisms and funerals often bring together multiple generations. As events in which diverse participants are personally invested, they provide common ground for conversations about religion.

Christian baptism is mentioned in scripture and, while some specifics of the ritual have shifted over time, water baptism in the name of the Triune God has been a universal norm since the earliest centuries of the Christian tradition.[9] Christian baptism has many layers of theological meaning, some of which are outlined in the World Council of Churches' *Baptism, Eucharist and Ministry*, and are quoted in the Anglican *Book of Alternative Services*: participation in Christ's death and resurrection; conversion, pardoning, and cleansing; the gift of the Spirit; incorporation into the Body of Christ, the church; and a sign of the Reign of God bringing new life in the present world.[10] In the Anglican tradition in Toronto, baptism is almost always practiced in the context of the primary assembly of the Christian community, usually Sunday morning worship, and therefore participants in baptism experience a regular Christian worship service as part of the baptism.

---

[8] *The Book of Common Prayer* in its various forms is foundational for Anglican identity. The Anglican Church of Canada has two prayer books in active use: the 1962 *Book of Common Prayer* (General Synod of the Anglican Church of Canada, *Book of Common Prayer and Administration of the Sacraments and Other Rites and Ceremonies of the Church According to the Use of the Anglican Church of Canada* [Toronto: ABC Publishing, 1962]); and the 1985 *Book of Alternative Services* (General Synod of the Anglican Church of Canada, *Book of Alternative Services of the Anglican Church of Canada* [Toronto: ABC Publishing, 1985]). Clergy may also borrow liturgical resources from other communities within the Anglican Communion. Anglican Church of Canada, "Liturgical Resources," accessed December 11, 2023, https://www.anglican.ca/faith/worship/resources.

[9] Maxwell Johnson, *The Rites of Christian Initiation: Their Evolution and Interpretation*, rev. ed. (Collegeville, MN: Liturgical Press, 2007); Kenneth Stevenson, *The Mystery of Baptism in the Anglican Tradition* (Norwich: Canterbury Press, 1998).

[10] World Council of Churches, *Baptism, Eucharist and Ministry* (Geneva: World Council of Churches, 1982), 1–3.

Christian funerals and other practices associated with Christian dying, death, and burial, as well as the remembrance of the dead, also have their origins in the earliest years of the Christian tradition and have evolved significantly over time.[11] Christian burial, however, has long been marked by the tension between grieving and healing in a time of human loss, and gratitude and hope in the resurrection of Christ. Unlike baptism, in the Anglican tradition in Toronto, funerals take place apart from the primary assembly of the congregation at a time that is suitable for the family and friends of the deceased. Multiple liturgical events may be involved, such as a liturgy in a church and a committal at the graveside. The church liturgy may take various forms, including a funeral or memorial service, with or without a eucharist, and may draw on either the *Book of Common Prayer* or the *Book of Alternative Services*.[12] Friends and family shaping the liturgy make choices about various elements, such as scripture readings, hymns, and prayers, many of which would also be found in Sunday worship.

From a liturgical standpoint, despite notable distinctions, baptisms and funerals are integrally connected to one another theologically and within the rites themselves, and to broader Christian liturgical practice.[13] Although an Anglican baptism or funeral is the starting point for the interviews that anchor this study, these conversations often address many other life transitions, as well as other services of Christian worship, in a range of traditions, in and beyond Toronto.

The fourth largest city in North America, *Toronto* is a global city characterized by tremendous religious and cultural diversity, yet where Anglicanism was once a dominant cultural force. The religious history of the region, diversity of the population, cultural cachet of the city, and abundance of ritual options make selecting an Anglican ritual a noteworthy choice. Canada is an understudied yet valuable case for implied comparison to both the United States and Europe.

---

[11] Geoffrey Rowell, *The Liturgy of Christian Burial: An Introductory Survey of the Historical Development of Christian Burial Rites* (London: Alcuin Club, 1977); Richard Rutherford and Tony Barr, *The Death of a Christian: The Order of Christian Funerals* (Collegeville, MN: Liturgical Press, 1980).

[12] General Synod of the Anglican Church of Canada, *Book of Common Prayer*, 591–610; General Synod of the Anglican Church of Canada, *Book of Alternative Services*, 565–605. In some cases, other resources may also be available, such as *Book of Common Prayer* texts with contemporary language replacing archaic language or resources in additional languages.

[13] Bruce Morrill, *Divine Worship and Human Healing: Liturgical Theology at the Margins of Life and Death* (Collegeville, MN: Liturgical Press, 2009).

Methods

At the heart of the study are sixty-one extended semi-structured interviews, including forty-one interviews with participants in Anglican baptisms or funerals that took place in three partner congregations, and twenty interviews with Anglican priests in the Diocese of Toronto.[14] Participant observation of eighty Anglican liturgies with a focus on baptisms and funerals supplement those interviews, as does archival research that provides a broader context and access to historical examples. This fieldwork took place between June 2017 and June 2020, and was disrupted by the COVID-19 pandemic in the spring of 2020.[15]

The volume weaves together descriptions drawn from fieldnotes and excerpts from interviews with participants and clergy with theoretical and theological analysis, with all unattributed quotations coming from interviews. In this weaving, the most ordinary of religious experiences—occasional participation in Christian liturgy on the occasion of holidays, baptisms, and funerals—as described by people who consider themselves "not very religious," becomes a resource for refining our understanding of religion and Christian worship today.

Situating Myself

All research is done from a specific perspective and within a particular context—including my own as the researcher. Reflexivity is always essential, especially in relation to ethnographic research, and there are many dimensions of my identity that are relevant to this study, four of which I highlight here.[16] First, I am an interdisciplinary scholar primarily based in the discipline of liturgical studies yet deeply engaged with the social sciences. I aspire to listen to and connect with multiple disciplinary audiences, yet religious practice and especially religious rituals most often capture my attention. Second, I am an intensive religious practitioner. I have deep and broad personal and academic experience in a range of Christian traditions,

---

[14] More information regarding the interviews is available in Appendix B; interview guides appear in Appendix C.
[15] Appendix B describes in detail the methods employed.
[16] Many other aspects of my positionality are relevant to ethnographic research. I explore some of these in greater depth in Appendix B.

including in leadership positions. While I have great respect for people who relate to religion in a range of ways, including those who are occasionally religious and those who never participate in religious practices, my own practice is intensive and always has been. Third, I am not Anglican. Although my relationship with the Anglican tradition has changed over the course of this research, especially when I started a job directing an Anglican Studies program in 2022, I remain an outsider to the Anglican tradition, and this shapes how I engage with occasional participants in Anglican practices and interpret their experience. Fourth, I am Canadian and from Ontario. While this research was originally completed as part of my doctoral studies at the University of Notre Dame in Indiana, I lived in Toronto for three years to conduct fieldwork. Thus, in this book I attend to my own context of origin and to the region and culture where I continue to live, work, and worship.

Clarifying Presuppositions

With an interdisciplinary audience in mind, at the outset of this study it seems important to articulate several presuppositions in an effort to address potential misunderstandings. Although these premises shaped this research from its inception, they were also reinforced and refined through the study itself.

The first presupposition is that this research prioritizes *dialogue* among those who relate to religion in different ways. This is somewhat analogous to interreligious dialogue among those associated with different religious traditions, or ecumenical dialogue among different Christian traditions. Dialogue in this sense is directed toward mutual understanding, including awareness of points of harmony and dissonance, as well as opportunities to collaborate on practical matters held in common. Dialogue recognizes the legitimacy of distinct positions and perspectives and, in this case, distinct ways of relating to religion. In other words, this research is explicitly *not* evangelistic. My goal is not to change how anyone relates to religion in terms of "converting" occasional practitioners into routine practitioners, although I do hope this research can facilitate more positive experiences of Christian worship for all involved on the occasions when they are present. However, I do not intend the use of the term *dialogue* to imply that this understanding, awareness, and collaboration is primarily verbal, discursive, or explicit.

Especially in the context of occasional participation in religious practice, dialogue may take more narrative, emotive, and embodied forms.

The second premise is that, as in any ethnographic study, *certain theoretical and empirical stories emerge in the foreground* while other equally reasonable stories recede to the background. The interpretation of the ethnographic data presented here foregrounds questions of religious change, religious ritual, and liberative liturgical theology. The same data could be used to interrogate religion and the family, religion and ethnicity, and religion in public life, among other possibilities. Scholars who specialize in these areas may find that these themes are present yet undeveloped. Future research, and even further analysis of this data, could amplify different stories. However, choices must be made, and the themes in the foreground of this analysis reflect both questions and theory I brought to the field as well as priorities that emerged in the research process itself.

Third, this research is intentionally *ecumenical* in its theological approach and practical implications. Although the study is anchored in the Anglican tradition, it addresses questions that face Christians across traditions who inhabit and navigate a shared religious landscape. The diversity of the participants in this research reinforces this ecumenical emphasis, especially the prevalence of Roman Catholics. It is also evident in the diversity of the theological sources engaged. Therefore, apart from the background necessary for the ethnographic case, this study is not primarily concerned with speaking into questions specific to Anglican theology and practice or the implications for Anglican communities, although the choice of case study means it may speak more directly to Anglican contexts. Instead, the intended theological audience includes a broad range of Christian traditions.

The final premise is theological. I assume that the *Spirit is at work within and beyond the formal and informal institutions of the church.* God is active in the lives of people, including occasional practitioners, in ways that are known, unknown, and unknowable to theologians and social scientists. However, in keeping with the liberative theological approach of this study, I also presuppose that God is present in a distinct way in places of pain and marginalization, including the theological and liturgical margins.

With these presuppositions in mind, I invite you to an encounter with a distinct, pervasive, and meaningful way of being religious—occasional religious practice.

PART I
UNDERSTANDING OCCASIONAL RELIGIOUS PRACTICE

1
What Is Occasional Religious Practice?

In 2016, when Rob Ford, the controversial former mayor of Toronto, died at the age of forty-six, an elaborate funeral at the Anglican Cathedral marked his passing. The drone of bagpipes and cheers of supporters accompanied the funeral procession to and from the Cathedral. Many prominent politicians filled the pews. Family members and others offered personal tributes to Ford before the Bishop of Toronto led an Anglican funeral liturgy. Ford was not a particularly religious person. He had been married at All Saints Roman Catholic Church, and his father had been buried at Westway United Church. But in a posthumous biography, his brother Doug Ford described Rob as "pretty easygoing about religion overall,"[1] while acknowledging that "I don't know what his spiritual or religious beliefs were really. That wasn't the kind of conversation we ever got into."[2] It seems that Ford and his family had had little connection to the Anglican tradition prior to his funeral.

Although the high-profile nature of Ford's funeral was exceptional, turning to religious ritual on the occasion of a death is not. Indeed, what I am calling *occasional religious practice* may be the dominant way in which people relate to Christianity in Canada, the United States, and much of Europe in the twenty-first century. In this chapter, I draw on interviews with participants in Anglican baptisms and funerals in Toronto to define and describe the concept of occasional religious practice.

Defining Occasional Religious Practice

Occasional religious practice is a way of relating to religion that is defined by occasional participation in religious practices—attending religious services occasionally rather than routinely and usually in association with specific

---

[1] Rob Ford and Doug Ford, *Ford Nation: Two Brothers, One Vision—The True Story of the People's Mayor* (New York: HarperCollins, 2016), 79.
[2] Ford and Ford, *Ford Nation*, 12.

occasions, such as holidays or life transitions. Occasional religiosity or occasional religiousness are other ways of describing such occasional religious practice.

Occasional religious practice contrasts with routine religious practice. There are also people who are more intensive in their practice, and others who never participate in religious practices (Figure 1.1). Context determines these relative categories. What one community considers routine another may consider occasional. Moreover, what a community or individual considers occasional or routine may change over time. For example, routine attendance does not necessarily mean weekly attendance. In settings where many participants attend Christian worship monthly rather than weekly, participants might consider monthly attendance to be routine attendance. Intensive religious practice is a more extreme level of practice that is beyond routine. This research does not presume that occasional, routine, or intensive practice is better or worse, or even more or less religious, than the others: these are simply different ways of relating to religion.

The following composite example points to common patterns in interviews: The mother of a newborn arranges for her child to be baptized at a congregation where, as a child, she attended Christmas and Easter services. Before marriage, the father of the infant had never attended a Christian worship service; he now attends funerals, weddings, and baptisms with the family. The grandmother of the child attended Sunday school and Sunday worship routinely until high school. Since that time, she attends on Christmas and Easter. At the time of the baptism, the parents and grandmother are therefore all occasional religious practitioners. The infant's great-grandparents attend Sunday worship together most Sundays, except for when they are at the cottage in the summer, or when they feel unsafe driving in the snow. The great-grandmother also attends mid-week Eucharist on Wednesday and prays morning prayer at home. The great-grandfather is

Figure 1.1 Types of religious practice.

routinely religious. The great-grandmother is intensively religious. The priest who officiates this baptism is also intensively religious. All participants join together in baptizing the child. The baptism is thus a religious practice that brings together participants who relate to religion in different ways.

How occasional religious practice is defined depends on *how religion is defined*. And religion is notoriously difficult to define. Is religion a chosen or ascribed identity? A set of beliefs? A source of social cohesion? A way of life? An ethical framework? Is it some combination of these, or something else altogether? To a certain extent, in this case study it is enough to simply agree that Christianity and Anglicanism are religion, and to move forward. At the same time, to describe and investigate occasional religious practice more broadly, a definition that serves the purpose of the study of occasional religious practice in other contexts is necessary.

Sociological approaches to the study of religion that define *religion as practice* anchor the concept of occasional religious practice.[3] Drawing on Christian Smith's theory of religion, which builds on the work of Martin Riesebrodt, I define religion in terms of practices—repeated religiously meaningful behaviors:

> Religion is a complex of culturally prescribed practices, based on premises about the existence and nature of superhuman powers, whether personal or impersonal, which seek to help practitioners gain access to and communicate or align themselves with these powers, in hopes of realizing human goods and avoiding things bad.[4]

Several aspects of this definition of religion are valuable when considering occasional religious practice.

First, religion is about *practice*. Not identity. Not belief. Not function. Religion is about actions people do that are concrete and observable. These practices are religious no matter what participants are thinking or feeling as they engage in them, and no matter what results they do or do not bring about. This is crucial because, while the practice of occasional practitioners appears remarkably uniform, such practitioners understand themselves in

---

[3] For more discussion of practice-centered definitions of religion, see Appendix A.
[4] Christian Smith, *Religion: What It Is, How It Works, and Why It Matters* (Princeton, NJ: Princeton University Press, 2017), 22; Martin Riesebrodt, *The Promise of Salvation* (Chicago: University of Chicago Press, 2010). Riesebrodt and Smith aspire to universal definitions of religion. My focus is instead on how these definitions are helpful for defining and refining the concept of occasional religious practice.

diverse ways. They identify as religious, nonreligious, somewhere in between, or even affiliate with religious traditions other than the one in which they are practicing at that moment. In short, they have a broad range of religious identities and motivations for occasional practice, as I will discuss in Chapters 3 and 4. A practice-based definition allows for this.

Second, religious practices are *culturally prescribed*. In Riesebrodt's terms, they are "institutionalized liturgies."[5] Such practices include official rites prescribed by religious institutions, as well as popular practices prescribed by local cultures. However, not just any idiosyncratic practice can be considered religious. This is important for distinguishing occasional religious practice from other ways of understanding contemporary spirituality as practiced independently or in loose networks.[6] Although occasional religious practice may be integrated alongside other spiritual practices, it necessarily occurs in relation to existing religious institutions and cultures.

Third, religious practices are connected in *complex systems*. Occasional practitioners may participate in one practice without participating in the rest of the system, as described in relation to Rob Ford's funeral and the family baptism above. This definition allows practices to be considered not only in relation to larger systems but also independently, as the second part of the book explores.

Fourth and finally, religious practices are *meaningful*. As Riesebrodt's version of the definition states, "Religion is a complex of meaningful practices—that is, of actions—that are situated in a relatively systematic web of meaning."[7] These practices are based on meaningful premises. They have prescribed meanings associated with superhuman powers, as described in the Introduction in relation to Anglican baptisms and funerals. At the same time, many other layers of meaning may also be at play, especially for participants who engage in religious practices only occasionally, as explored in Part III of the book.

To summarize, occasional religious practice is not about personal identity or belief. It is about participation in part of a meaningful system of observable, institutionally or culturally prescribed practices:

---

[5] Riesebrodt, *The Promise of Salvation*, 77.
[6] Nancy Ammerman, *Sacred Stories, Spiritual Tribes* (New York: Oxford University Press, 2014); Elizabeth Drescher, *Choosing Our Religion* (Oxford: Oxford University Press, 2016).
[7] Riesebrodt, *The Promise of Salvation*, 72.

What matters is not that every practitioner is aware of and truly believes in the culturally meaningful premises of every practice, but rather that *the practice itself* is institutionalized in a complex of repeated actions that are culturally meaningful in religious terms, that is, oriented toward gaining access to superhuman powers. That distinction is important.[8]

We can consider occasional practitioners to be occasionally religious regardless of their affiliation, their reasons for practicing, or their attitudes and experiences while practicing, although these are certainly important areas of research.

Participation in corporate worship is the most obvious form of occasional religious practice. It is the clearest application of Smith and Riesebrodt's definition of religion and is the primary focus of this study. However, corporate worship is not the only possible occasional practice. Participation in any institutionally prescribed practice would qualify, such as lighting a devotional candle in a cathedral, making a financial contribution to a religious organization, or occasionally praying the Prayer Jesus Taught at home before sleep. At the same time, it is crucial to note that, *by definition*, occasional religious practice only exists in relation to culturally prescribed religious practices that can be practiced routinely. Occasional religious practice depends on traditions, congregations, and clergy, and the concept of occasional religious practice depends on a clear definition of religion.

This research explores how occasional religious practitioners experience and understand religious practices and brings their accounts into dialogue with how particular religious institutions and cultures prescribe and interpret these practices. While Smith recognizes the potential for this theory of religion to prioritize the perspective of established authorities, he also articulates its capacity for critique—with which I agree:

> This tilt toward practices that are prescribed by cultural traditions—rather than religious people's thoughts and feelings about their religions, including their critical, alienated, and dissenting positions—is, I believe, justified. I realize, however, that it may seem to be biased toward the status quo, established orthodoxies, and authorities who have the power to determine "correct" practices and, therefore, who is in and out, acceptable or not. So I want to be clear that this book's theory need not privilege the

---

[8] Smith, *Religion*, 31.

religiously official and powerful. When understood and deployed well, it actually provides helpful tools for those who wish to critique established authorities and traditions.[9]

This study employs the critical capacities of defining religion as practice to interrogate established orthodoxies and authorities by listening to the voices of occasional practitioners and bringing them alongside established religious traditions as a valued source of valid critique, not as the object of criticism. In doing so, it asks the types of questions to which Smith points, but does not pursue:

> Who "owns" religious cultures and traditions and why? How is religious authority maintained, perhaps even at the expense of religious ethics? Where are boundaries of religious unacceptability and therefore exclusion drawn, why there, and how do they change over time? When and why might dissent from or transgression of dominant religious practices actually become a religious practice itself? How do religious communities negotiate dissonances between their official prescriptions and subjective dispositions of practitioners when the latter disagree with or do not fit easily into official standards? In short, how do power, authority, continuity, voice, inclusion, exclusion, alienation, critique, transgression, and dissent work in religions in the real world?[10]

This study privileges the voices and experiences of the occasionally religious, placing them in conversation with the presumed status quo, in relation to specific practices that are central to prescribing institutions as well as to people who practice occasionally.

Types of Occasions

Four types of occasions are associated with occasional religious practice: holidays, life transitions, crises, and incidental circumstances (Figure 1.2). Practitioners may focus on one type of occasion, or the same individuals or families may practice in connection with multiple types of occasions.

---

[9] Smith, *Religion*, 15.
[10] Smith, *Religion*, 15.

WHAT IS OCCASIONAL RELIGIOUS PRACTICE? 23

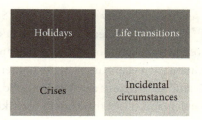

Figure 1.2 Four types of occasions.

Holidays

Some people engage in religious practices in relation to holidays, especially Christmas and Easter among Anglicans in Toronto. This is immediately obvious to the routine participant observer. The clergy who are providing liturgical leadership or preaching may even address this directly, for example in how they invite those present to participate in the liturgy. Some parishes even shape their communications with holiday occasional practitioners in mind. One congregation listed the Holy Week and Easter worship schedule on a newsletter distributed on Christmas Eve. Another advertised a Mother's Day Brunch in May on Easter Sunday in April.

Holiday attendance statistics gathered annually from congregations by the Anglican Diocese of Toronto support the idea of significant occasional participation. In 2018, there were 204 congregations in the diocese. About half are in the City of Toronto and its suburbs, and half are in surrounding rural areas and small cities. Attendance more than doubled on Christmas in the average congregation: Sunday attendance was on average 92 people; attendance on Christmas was on average 212 people. In some congregations, attendance on Christmas more than quadruples. The same is true of Easter attendance.[11]

These patterns in the Anglican Diocese of Toronto parallel patterns that Reginald Bibby tracked nationally. His research notes on "Christmas Onlys" in Canada in 2013 and 2014 show that in 2013, 37 percent of Canadians attended a "special Christmas service," 18 percent of those being "monthly-plus" routine attenders, and 19 percent being less frequent attenders—those whom I call occasional practitioners.[12] This gap is particularly striking among Anglicans: in 2013, 20 percent of those who identify as Anglican

---

[11] Anglican Church of Canada, Diocese of Toronto, Annual Statistical Returns, 2013–2018.
[12] Reginald Bibby, "A Research Note: The Christmas Onlys Revisited," Project Canada Surveys, December 22, 2014, accessed March 18, 2021, http://www.reginaldbibby.com/images/Release_2014_Christmas_Onlys_Revisited_Dec_24.pdf.

attended religious services monthly or more, and 53 percent attended Christmas services.[13] Christmas is clearly a significant occasion when considering occasional religious practice on holidays in Canada.

With this context in mind, it is unsurprising that interview participants in this study mention attending religious services for holidays. The consistency and clarity in how participants name this pattern is striking:

> My dad used to say, "Really good Anglicans—they go Easter and Christmas."

> I just feel there's just certain times of the year that you need to attend.... The celebration of Christmas, the celebration of Easter.

> I'm not a regular church goer. I show up at Easter and Christmas and things like that. Unlike my husband, I don't go nearly as often, and I'm not as involved. But that said, I do support church and there's certain times when those things are important to me.

> I think like baseline is kind of going to those big events, like Christmas and stuff like that. It's funny because I remember, when I was going to a youth group, like I was literally making fun of the people that only went at Christmas. I feel like there was a name for them—I just don't remember what it was. I feel like anytime you judge people it totally happens to you, like 100 percent of the time. So the universe kind of takes a while to give the punchline.... So it totally happened to me. Easter and Christmas are the two biggest for sure.

> We don't go to church weekly, we go to church when, like, I guess you can call it the "C and Es,"... Christmas and Easter.

In the statements above, participants in interviews describe their own occasional practice on holidays. At other times, participants describe the holiday practice of family members and friends:

> [My adult children] they don't go. You know, they go once in a while like a Christmas or if there was something special going on.

> It's been interesting to see [my brother] as a family man. Even at Christmas, they send pictures that they had gone to church together for Christmas.

---

[13] Reginald Bibby, "The Christmas Onlys: A Wakeup Bell for Canada's Religious Groups," Project Canada Surveys, December 23, 2013, accessed March 18, 2021, http://www.reginaldbibby.com/images/Release_2013_Christmas_Onlys_Dec_23_2013.pdf.

And in the past, I thought it would have just been [my sister-in-law] taking the kids. But that [my brother is] participating is really nice.

[The deceased] never, other than Easter, I don't even think at Christmas, went to services or anything. I think they went for Easter service. That's the type of faith stance.

I remember going to [name of parish] for the Christmas services and the Easter services and my father-in-law was there on some of the occasions, but not all of them. So I never saw him going, but I always do remember him—it's not that he said something—but his expectation was that his wife and children, it's their place to be there. I can't even say exactly how it was intoned... but it was an expectation that that's what they're supposed to do.

When I interviewed multiple members of the same family, their assessments of their own and one another's holiday religious practice matched closely, which suggests honest and accurate reporting.

While Christmas and Easter are the main occasions for holiday practice, participants also mention the largely secular civic celebrations of Mother's Day, Father's Day, and Remembrance Day:

I do admit, it's the Easter services. It's sometimes the Christmas services that I'm attending. When I'm back in [my hometown], if I'm there for Mother's Day or Father's Day, I go to church with my parents there. But it's more for occasions.

We like to go on the Mother's Day service and the Father's Day service. [My son] learns a lot from those. Christmas, Easter, Mother's Day, Father's Day. Yes. I would say those are the main ones.

I confess that I more or less dragged my grandpa out to Remembrance Day services, or he started going to them for me. I felt that they were important.

While interview participants mentioned these occasions less frequently, it is significant that, like Christmas and Easter, they are broader cultural events in Canada and are times when extended families often gather (less so on Remembrance Day). Unlike Christmas and Easter, however, these events are not specifically connected to the Christian calendar, although they are often marked in some way in Anglican congregations.

Holidays, especially Christmas and Easter, may be important occasions for *routine practitioners* as well as occasional practitioners. Some routine practitioners are more involved in their religious communities during these seasons, for example to help facilitate additional worship services, social events, or charitable endeavors. Two participants described eating meals at church on Christmas and Easter in order to help out with the multiple services taking place on those days. At the same time, there are also routine practitioners who do not attend on these occasions because of certain medical or social barriers, such as needing to avoid large crowds or requiring specialized transportation or personal support.

At the opposite end of the spectrum, these holidays remain significant for people who *never* attend religious services, as seen in one interview in which a father describes how much his nonreligious daughter loves Christmas, and in another in which a woman speaks of setting up the Christmas tree for her secular Jewish parents-in-law. Nevertheless, occasional religious practice on holidays is the most common form of occasional religious practice described in interviews, apart from participation in the baptism or funeral that is the starting point for the conversation.

Life Transitions

Life transitions, especially birth, death, and marriage, are important occasions for occasional religious practice. Rituals associated with adolescence, such as confirmation, may also be significant, although less so in the Anglican tradition in Toronto. While there are some who participate in religious practices in relation to both holidays and life transitions, there are also those who *only* practice in connection with life transitions. This includes attending events to support others, but also being the participant at the center of the practice—a parent of a child being baptized, a member of a couple being married, or the primary planner of a funeral. We see this pattern in national survey data, especially in relation to funerals. A 2015 Angus Reid Institute survey shows that 41 percent of Canadians want to have a religious funeral. Unsurprisingly, this includes 80 percent of people who embrace religion. More interestingly, it includes 34 percent of those whom Reginald Bibby describes as being in the "religious middle," and 28 percent of those who identify as "spiritual but not religious." Even 7 percent of those who reject religion outright expressed a desire for a religious funeral.[14]

---

[14] Reginald Bibby, *Resilient Gods: Being Pro-Religious, Low Religious, or No Religious in Canada* (Vancouver: UBC Press, 2017), 179.

Because of how I selected participants for this research, many interviews were with occasional practitioners at the center of life transition rituals: the parent or godparent of a child being baptized, or the partner or adult child of the deceased at a funeral, as well as family members and friends to whom they introduced me. Since those who are particularly invested in these events are more likely to agree to participate in an interview, it is unsurprising that participants often emphasize that these events are important for them and their inner circle, even though these events are among a small number of occasions on which they participate in religious practices:

> [My husband] is Anglican but not feeling he has to go to church every Sunday and be a part of that. He only goes strictly [for] weddings and funerals. But it was important for [him] that we christen [our son] as well.

> That's how we were raised. Your weddings, your funerals, your christenings and stuff all happening at the church.

> I was married there. We had [my father-in-law's] funeral there and we baptized our daughter there. The only reason I go there is because my wife belongs there. I think they're great. They're phenomenal. Honest to God, at [name of parish] they've been—I am not Anglican, I never go to church, I just go there when it's wedding, baptism, or a funeral—but they're super, super nice, super supportive.

> R: [My fiancée] has said that he did not like going to church and he doesn't like that you have to get dressed up to go. So, unless it was a baptism, I probably wouldn't have got him there.
> I: Are there other occasions when he would attend?
> R: Well, we're getting married next week, so he'll have to go. He'll have to be in attendance. But no, not for a service. Maybe for a formal occasion he will go if it's a baptism or a funeral.

> I'm pretty traditional. We got married there, and the kids are baptized there, and you know my grandma's funeral [was] there. She's buried there. I'm probably traditionally like the other women in my family.

> My dad won't go to church. My dad believes in the importance of marriage and the importance of baptism and he will go for those sorts of things. But if you ask him to go on a regular Sunday service, he will be in the parking lot in the car with a coffee and a paper. He will take you there. He will get you there on time.

> I don't remember my grandmother ever setting foot in a church for anything but a wedding or a funeral. My grandfather was the one who went to church. Every Sunday he would go to church and when he got home Granny was there with breakfast ready.

I was surprised that several participants who had initiated and planned baptisms had never previously attended another service at the church where their child was baptized, not even to get a sense of what to expect.

Participants who describe witnessing a pattern of occasional participation in practices associated with life transitions among their wider circle of friends and family are sometimes somewhat baffled by the intensity of commitment on these occasions:

> I have friends who . . . were not people that were churchgoers. But when it came time for rituals, for weddings and funerals, that was very important to them. So, that's interesting to me that that's part of the culture. That even though they didn't take part in church, that they had been formed at a young age like that was necessary for them to have that kind of ritual in their lives.

> It's funny they don't go to church, but if they are getting married, you can't get them [to] go to city hall. They have to be in the church, isn't that the strangest thing? . . . I'm thinking they don't go to church but if they're ever getting married, it will be in a church. No city hall for them.

> I mean it's funny how people you didn't think were religious suddenly want to get married in church. I have friends who—she married a Catholic and so she had to—before the priest would marry them, she had to be baptized, she had to go through confirmation, everything. And then I find out—I found out just a couple of years ago she doesn't go to church anymore. So, I thought that was odd to go through all that.

This level of personal investment is different from participants who describe occasional attendance at religious services focused on others where they do not have a significant role in initiating, planning, or leading in the event:

> I haven't found myself back in a church for anything other than a funeral, wedding, or a Remembrance Day in years. . . . What funerals are good for is to bring people together. And even if it were something like a wedding or

a baptism, confirmation, things like that. These are significant moments in people's lives. And if somebody said to me, "Would you come to my son's confirmation? Would you come to his baptism?" [I would say:] "Absolutely. I'll be there for you."

The time I go to the church now is for funerals or weddings or baptisms.

As these quotations imply, there is a pervasive pattern of occasional participation in connection with life transitions connected to a complex array of situations and motivations, which the following chapters explore in depth.

Crises

Some people turn to religious practices in times of crisis. These crises may be brief or sustained, and may even be separated in time from an associated ritual practice. Crises may be *personal*, such as a medical diagnosis, a move, or any number of other possibilities. There is a significant overlap between occasional participation connected to crises and *life transitions*. Death is often a time of crisis, especially if unexpected or tragic, and birth is as well. In the interviews, many of the stories about childbirth are marked by infertility, reproductive loss, unplanned pregnancies, or simply facing the unknown:

We had lost four children along the way. Four miscarriages. And then we were pregnant with my fifth. So, our first son that made it through.

We had gone through such a hard time trying to get [my daughter]. So my husband and I had to do IVF; I had to go through multiple surgeries. And the chances of having her for our scenario were so low. To me, [the baptism] was just a way to get back in . . . a way to start new again.

[My uncle] ended up having, we found out later, cystic fibrosis, and he died when he was, I think between 6 and 9 months old. He was a sickly baby. Anyway, that experience for my mother and watching her mother, my grandmother, deal with that and how that changed their family dynamic. Perhaps [this is why] religion came more into play in that family.

When we found out we were having another baby, my husband didn't want another baby. I really didn't want another baby. . . . We thought about our car, thought about finances, thought about our house. We seriously talked about termination.

While the baptism of a child is often a joyful celebration, the birth of a child is also a major turning point and brings a host of challenges.

Interview participants mentioned *medical diagnoses* and conditions as crises that prompt religious participation, whether it is the health of the individual or a close friend or family member that is in peril:

> I don't attend mass very often, but I've had some—as I mentioned—some serious health issues, and in the last few years [I've been] watching my mother die and caring for her. It's been a really difficult time. And the only thing that could ground me was combination of prayer and meditation, whichever you want to call it. And I didn't need to be in a church to feel that—although being in a church heightens, without question it heightens, the effect of prayer and meditation.

> I had a cousin who got in an accident and she got hit by a car. So I said I was going to go to church and do prayers for her. I went, and I did that at the beginning.

> I worked with a gentleman quite a few years ago who was a recovering alcoholic.... He said, "After AA, I just decided I had to pick a spiritual path." And so he went around to different churches and talked to them. I guess he went to the Anglican church and went to Catholic church, he went to interview the ministers ... and then he picked this one.

> I think that in times of difficult emotional situations, for example, in a time of mourning or in a time of sickness, I think the church is a great way to kind of— religion can be a conduit for a lot of those emotions, to help you navigate some of those emotions. So, I see a lot of value there.

One participant told the story of a powerful religious experience while in the hospital during an extended medical crisis, and specifically linked it to how she understood the baptism of her child. Her crisis occasional practice is connected to her life transition occasional practice:

> I remember at one point I had some clarity in the hospital. Everything became very clear. Like suddenly, and it was a weird, and I just remember thinking like, "Okay, if I'm going to die, I'm fine with dying. I just want

to see my son one more time. I want to put some things like in line, like organize some things." I basically looked in the mirror and I said that "If God is there and listening, I surrender. So, if this is my time to go, I completely surrender. If it is not my time to go, then I will certainly not take so much for granted, and I will start to understand the power of faith a lot more."

As soon as I went back into the bed and I laid down, they came in, and they said, "We think we have [a diagnosis], we're pretty sure, and we can treat you for that." . . . It's a pivotal moment for me, where I relied on faith, like really for the first time. The answer was so fast. It was very, that moment of clarity for me, was faith for sure. I know other people might be more like it's nature or it might be something else. But for me it was faith. That for me has brought me a lot closer to the church to, to faith in general. . . .

"Do you believe in God, will you continue to do, blah, blah, blah." [The response in the baptismal rite is:] "with God's help." I think it's this idea. Even though you are the parents, and you're going to do your best to guide the child in a way that is encouraging and that is nurturing, all of those things, but faith really, really says that you cannot do those things without God's help. You have to turn to him.

I think that's the part that for me—that pivotal moment in the hospital—I felt very much prior that I was going to be in control. That somehow, I was going to be able to change those circumstances for myself. That it was just going to the right hospital, or meeting the right doctor, that I was going to do the research to find this, or I was just going to get better. I don't know how, but in that pivotal moment, it was sort of like, I can only do those things with God's help. If I am vulnerable and if I am willing to relinquish some control that answers could be in front of me. Or I may be able to hear something that I couldn't hear when I was only listening to myself. It's this idea that you hope to be a good parent, but with God's help.

Crises may be turning point events in terms of how people relate to religious practices in addition to being events marked by religious practices.

To outsiders, crises may *appear relatively minor*, or even as more ordinary aspects of work or life. But to the individual, such a crisis may be significant and prompt religious participation:

I've been having some difficulties the past couple of months. So, it's when I'm feeling very low and I need to get new energy, that's when I go.

So, I would love to make it a practice to go every Sunday. I just—I can't commit to that right now. But it's when I need a little bit more energy in my life.

I work in a hospital environment where sometimes it's hard to keep that faith knowing the things that go on in the world. I fought with God for a long time. I had to go through this process of understanding how and why things happen, why bad things happen to good people. So I struggled a lot with my faith in the last couple of years. So I would go to the church and sit there and just pray to ask for guidance, because I didn't understand certain things.

As this example of struggling with the question of undeserved suffering suggests, times of crisis can also *draw people away* from religious practice:

During [my husband's] illness before his passing and after his passing, I guess I was a little saddened and probably didn't go to church for a while. Just upset that the fact that something so awful happened to somebody so wonderful and it was not fair. . . . And the same with my mom. Like when she passed away, I probably didn't go to church for a little bit because I don't know if I was angry or upset or whatever.

Personal crises of various forms are related to changes in religious practice that are specific to each individual and situation.

Communal crises may lead to occasional religious practice.[15] This could be part of what we see in the extravagance and collective response to Rob Ford's funeral, described at the outset of this chapter, and in community vigils in response to tragedies in Toronto.[16] The crisis prompting the practice may not be local. For example, even in Toronto, clergy reported an increase in religious participation following the terrorist attacks in New York on September 11, 2001.[17]

---

[15] Paul Post, Ronald L. Grimes, Albertina Nugteren, Per Pettersson, and Hessel Zondag, *Disaster Ritual: Explorations of an Emerging Ritual Repertoire* (Leuven: Peeters, 2003); Martin Hoondert, Paul Post, Mirella Klomp, and Marcel Barnard, eds., *Handbook of Disaster Ritual: Multidisciplinary Perspectives, Cases and Themes* (Leuven: Peeters, 2021).

[16] Community vigils involving religious and secular leaders and practices were held in response to violent acts in the city of Toronto, including a shooting in the Danforth neighborhood and an attack on pedestrians with a vehicle on Yonge Street, both in 2018.

[17] Although the COVID-19 pandemic occurred within the time frame of this study, it is difficult to determine its impact on occasional practice because corporate gathering was so limited during this time.

Incidental Circumstances

Finally, some occasional religious practice is simply due to incidental circumstances—being a tourist, providing transportation to an aging relative, a family member visiting for the weekend, or just feeling like going to church one Sunday. Stories of incidental participation come up in interviews:

> I will never understand how in all the churches I've been into in Europe, every single one just makes the hair on my arms stand up. There's just something about—even the shape of them.
>
> I took my grandfather to church there a number of times.
>
> R: We always say we're Anglican and that's fine. Nobody's taking attendance because there are other ways that you participate and [the priest] knows that. We all know that.... So, depending on people's interests and likes, there was many ways to participate. It doesn't have to be every Sunday at service.
> I: Are there certain occasions when it's more likely that you would go on a Sunday?
> R: I was going to say, whenever my daughter is home [from university or work in another part of the province], yes, we would go.

Incidental participation may intersect with holiday participation, as in this story of incidental Easter attendance by both holiday occasional practitioners with Anglican backgrounds and their Hindu classmate:

> I did go once to an Easter service when I was in my first year of university. It was Easter and I had an exam on Easter Monday, and I had an exam on the Saturday before Easter, so I couldn't come home for Easter that year. And it was my first year being away and I was kind of sad that I was missing Easter. And one of my friends in residence was also traditionally Anglican but also not a very regular churchgoer, kind of like me. And he said to me, he's like, "Well, there's a real big Anglican cathedral downtown." He said, "Do you want to go to Sunday service on Easter?" And I'm like, "Yeah, all right." And we went and it was much the same [as my home parish]. Much the same, the homily wasn't as good, very nice priest, but it wasn't as good. And then my friend, [name], who is Hindu, decided that he wanted to come along and see what it was all about, so he came along as well.

The combination of personal invitation and a certain mood prompting openness to incidental attendance also features in this description from an occasional practitioner who had negative experiences of religion in the past:

> I'm open to going. It doesn't have to be a special occasion. But I find I have to watch how I'm feeling. If I'm like, okay, today's a good day, I can handle the possibility of maybe getting an evil look. I'm sorry, that's a fear that's in the back of my head. Or can I deal with the guilt today? You know, it is a very emotional thing for me. But in all honesty, as of right now, it's fair to say that I attend church strictly on special occasions, or if someone wants to be there for some reason.

Sometimes having a minor leadership role, such as serving as an usher (which Anglicans sometimes call a sidesperson) prompts incidental occasional practice that may even become more routine:

> I'll be honest with you. We're not regular, crazy going every week. But my dad used to be sidesman, so every three or four months they would call and we'd go there.
>
> Later on in life [my father-in-law] got involved and again, I think it was because of my mother-in-law's influence. And he was involved a little bit through [name of parish] in helping with picking up collections. And so he started going on Sundays with my mother-in-law because he now had a little job to do.

While supporting aging parents or grandparents is a common context for incidental participation, one participant is especially clear that she is not open to this possibility and that life transitions are the only occasion when she could conceivably attend a religious service:

> I: Are there occasions other than baptisms and funerals when you might attend a religious service?
>
> R: I would never go to church. I occasionally thought if there would be any—okay so, when my mother was unable to go to church on her own—not that I was going to do this because I live [quite far away]—but I sort of like, oh, would I make an effort and go and take her to church? And then I would think no. I think it's going to be hypocritical. I can't do that. I just won't do that.
>
> I: What feels hypocritical about it to you?

R: It's just like, it's okay if she wants to do that. I don't want to give anybody the wrong idea that I'm interested [laughter].

While holiday and life transition practitioners may be open to attending incidentally on other occasions, this is not necessarily the case. Incidental occasional practice is not linked to significant personal or community events to the same extent as the other three types of occasions, and therefore is often not associated with the same sense of relational obligation.

Theorizing Types of Occasions

All four types of occasions—holidays, life transitions, crises, and incidental circumstances—are interconnected. Many individuals practice on some combination of these occasions. The four types of occasions also parallel theoretical models of understanding religious practices, and religion as practice.

Three of these four types of occasions parallel three of the kinds of "general practices" that sociologist Martin Riesebrodt identifies in his theory of religion as practice. Riesebrodt defines *general practices* as "interventionist practices in which virtually all members of a religious community can or should participate."[18] "*Interventionist practices*" include all practices aimed at establishing contact with superhuman powers, especially "symbolic actions such as prayers, chants, gestures, formulas, sacrifices, vows, or divination."[19] Riesebrodt contrasts interventionist practices with "behavior regulating practices" that relate to "the religious reshaping of everyday life with respect to superhuman powers,"[20] and "discursive practices" that refer to "interpersonal communication regarding the nature, status, or accessibility of superhuman powers" and how to associate with them.[21] It is interventionist practices that are the key to defining religion, according to Riesebrodt and Smith.[22] Christian liturgy is best described as an interventionist practice, although it may have discursive and behavior-regulating dimensions as well.

There are three types of general interventionist practices in Riesebrodt's framework. First, *calendrical practices* relate to "vegetative, astrological-cosmic, and salvation-historical" cycles.[23] The "salvation-historical" cycle

---

[18] Riesebrodt, *The Promise of Salvation*, 92.
[19] Riesebrodt, *The Promise of Salvation*, 75.
[20] Riesebrodt, *The Promise of Salvation*, 76.
[21] Riesebrodt, *The Promise of Salvation*, 75.
[22] Smith, *Religion*, 42–44.
[23] Riesebrodt, *The Promise of Salvation*, 95.

is dominant among Anglican occasional practitioners in the celebration of Christmas and Easter, although the dates of these occasions also have vegetative and cosmic connections, for example, to the solar and lunar calendars. Second, *life-cycle practices* "concern transitions in humans' social status" and are performed "on occasions such as birth, entry into the religious community, the affirmation of the latter by young adults (initiation, complete membership), marriage, dying, and death."[24] In the Anglican tradition, these practices take the shape of baptism, confirmation, marriage, ministry at the time of death, and funerals. Third, *variable practices*, are often "reactions to crises and misfortunes" that "seek either to avert impending misfortune and produce future blessings, or to give thanks for blessings already provided and cope with misfortunes already suffered."[25] Occasional practitioners may turn to Anglican practices at such times, for example, attending a Sunday liturgy or stopping by the cathedral to light a prayer candle. The three types of practices identified as central to defining and explaining religion for Riesebrodt parallel three types of occasional religious practices. Incidental occasional practice is a way to recognize and name exceptions to these common patterns.

Occasional religious practice both challenges and reinforces Riesebrodt's assumption that "virtually all members of a religious community can or should participate" in these general practices. On the one hand, these are the practices in which occasional practitioners choose to participate. On the other hand, specific general practices are often separated from the complex of general practices performed by practitioners to the extent that it is clear that "virtually all" members of the community are not participating in them. For example, in relation to life-cycle practices in the Anglican tradition, the largest number of people choose to participate in rituals associated with death, followed by birth, and then marriage.[26] Relatively few people, even routine practitioners, choose to participate in confirmation, and when they do, it may not be in association with adolescence. Furthermore, those who participate in one or several of these life-cycle practices may not engage in calendrical or variable practices. Nevertheless, Anglican occasional

---

[24] Riesebrodt, *The Promise of Salvation*, 108.
[25] Riesebrodt, *The Promise of Salvation*, 111–112.
[26] Anglican Church of Canada, Diocese of Toronto, Annual Statistical Returns.

practice in Toronto in the twenty-first century maps onto theory associated with definitions of religion as practice. Rob Ford's funeral, although exceptional in terms of the politics and media coverage surrounding it, in other ways reflects a very ordinary way of relating to Christianity in Canada, as is discussed in the next chapter.

2
Occasional Religious Practice in Context

The preacher looks across the small crowd gathered on the stone floor. The tall church walls reach up to the lofty ceiling, offering some protection from the summer heat. Perspiring nonetheless, the preacher shakes his head with dismay and rebukes his congregation:

> How am I distressed, think you, when I call to mind that on the festival days the multitudes assembled resemble the broad expanse of the sea, but now not even the smallest part of that multitude is gathered together here? Where are they now who oppress us with their presence on the feast days?[1]
>
> Can you imagine what distress and grief I suffer when I observe, that if a public holy day and festival is at hand there is a concourse of all the inhabitants of the city, although there is no one to summon them; but when the holy day and festival are past, even if we should crack our voice by continuing to call you all day long there is no one who pays any heed?[2]

The preacher dismisses the excuses of the absent and reprimands those present for failing to "forcibly drag them hither."[3] The reality of occasional religious practice was clearly a concern even in antiquity, in this case for the famous fourth-century preacher, John Chrysostom.

This chapter situates occasional religious practice as an ordinary way of relating to religion in two contexts. It first considers occasional religious practice in historical context through a series of brief vignettes, like the example above. It then provides a deeper look at the pervasive yet largely unexamined presence of occasional religious practice in sociological studies of the contemporary twenty-first-century religious landscape in Canada, the United States, Europe, and Australia. In conclusion, I summarize five key

---

[1] John Chrysostom, *In illud: Si esurierit inimicus*; translated in Philip Schaff, ed., *Nicene and Post-Nicene Fathers* (Edinburgh: T&T Clark, 1889), ser. 2, 9:224.
[2] Chrysostom, *In illud*, 9:226.
[3] Chrysostom, *In illud*, 9:224.

contributions of the concept of occasional religious practice to the study of religion.

Occasional Practice in Historical Context

Occasional religious practice has a long history. One barrier to recognizing occasional practice as a very ordinary way of relating to religion across time is the living memory of what routine religious practice in Canada and the United States was like in the mid-twentieth century. The vibrant growth, crowded Sunday schools, and frequent attendance in mainstream Protestant denominations in the 1940s and 1950s shaped the childhoods of a generation.[4] However, many of those same baby boomers have since "left the church en masse."[5] While in the United States this generation returned to the church to raise their children, in Canada "the baby boomers walked away from the church and didn't come back."[6] This experience formed some of the participants in this research, especially the grandparents of children being baptized and the adult children responsible for planning funerals. The religious transformation that they have witnessed, and to which they contributed, over the past sixty years has shaped their impressions of religion. This is also the case for many established church leaders and scholars of religion. A crucial step in engaging occasional religious practice is therefore unseating mid-century North America as the norm for religious participation by setting occasional religious practice in broader historical perspective.

Although Christian leaders have long desired routine practice of all Christians, for much of Christian history this has been the pattern only among the intensively religious, such as clergy and monks. In fact, we can interpret the near constant encouragement for more routine and intensive practice precisely as evidence of a persistent pattern of occasional religious practice:

> Regulations provide excellent evidence for what was actually happening in local congregations, not by what is decreed should be done but by what

---

[4] Brian Clarke and Stuart Macdonald, *Leaving Christianity: Changing Allegiances in Canada since 1945* (Montreal, QC and Kingston, ON: McGill-Queen's University Press, 2017), 37.
[5] Clarke and Macdonald, *Leaving Christianity*, 53.
[6] Clarke and Macdonald, *Leaving Christianity*, 224.

is either directly prohibited or indirectly implied should cease to be done. That such regulations were made at all shows that the very opposite of what they were trying to promote must have been a widespread custom in that period.[7]

When we look at past so-called golden ages of Christianity with this in mind, it becomes clear that routine participation in Sunday liturgies by ordinary Christians was not the norm. Although an in-depth historical analysis of occasional religious practice is beyond the scope of this volume, the following vignettes highlight the presence of occasional religious practice in often idealized eras and locales.

In the *late antique period*, ordinary Christians were more likely to participate occasionally in major feasts and the cult of the martyrs than to attend routine Sunday liturgies.[8] Participation in the cult of the saints included attending occasional celebrations in cemeteries and at tombs, especially anniversary commemorations—in essence, an ancient form of holiday occasional religious practice.[9] These patterns of religious participation are evident in numerous sermons by the fourth-century preacher John Chrysostom, as in the example at the outset of this chapter. In the two excerpts below, John Chrysostom observes greatly increased attendance at a martyr festival in Antioch,[10] and again at Easter, possibly in Constantinople:[11]

> For *who wouldn't wonder today at our assembly*, at the magnificent spectacle, the fervent love, the warm disposition, the unrestrained desire? *Virtually the entire city has transferred itself here.*[12]

---

[7] Paul Bradshaw, *The Search for the Origins of Christian Worship*, 2nd ed. (Oxford: Oxford University Press, 2002), 18.

[8] Sarah Kathleen Johnson and Nathan Chase, "Occasional Religious Practice in Early Christianity" *Questions Liturgiques* 104, no. 3-4 (2024): 129-154. (Note: This article was authored after the submission of this manuscript.)

[9] Paul Bradshaw and Maxwell Johnson, *The Origins of Feasts, Fasts, and Seasons in Early Christianity* (Collegeville, MN: Liturgical Press, 2011), 171-173; Peter Brown, *The Cult of the Saints* (Chicago: University of Chicago Press, 1981).

[10] Mayer and Allen confirm the location of this homily as a "suburban martyrium in the vicinity of Antioch." Wendy Mayer and Pauline Allen, *John Chrysostom* (London: Routledge, 2000), 93.

[11] John Chrysostom preached in both Antioch and Constantinople, and it is often impossible for us to know where he preached a particular homily. For further discussion of the provenance of Chrysostom's homilies, see Wendy Mayer, *The Homilies of St. John Chrysostom: Provenance—Reshaping the Foundations* (Rome: Pontificio Istituto Orientale, 2005).

[12] John Chrysostom, *Hom. in martyres*; translated in Mayer and Allen, *John Chrysostom*, 94. Emphasis added.

> *Easter comes, and then great the stir, great the hubbub, and crowding* of—I had rather not call them human beings, for their behavior is not commonly human. *Easter goes, the tumult abates*, but then the quiet which succeeds is again fruitless of good.[13]

In an era often looked to as an example of "Christian worship in its simplest and purest form ('the springtime of the liturgy,' as it has been called),"[14] there is clear evidence of occasional religious practice.

Two centuries later in the *early medieval* West, we can listen between the lines of sermons preached by Caesarius of Arles and hear how Christians in sixth-century Gaul also failed to live up to the hopes of leadership regarding the frequency and quality of their religious service attendance:

> Indeed can those *who hardly ever come to church call themselves Christians* and, when they do come, do not remain standing in order to pray for their sins but make excuses for themselves or while there incite quarrels or fighting?[15]

> I ask that you carefully carry everything you have heard, everything you have freely received under the Lord's inspiration from my preaching, that you carry it to wherever you go, to your neighbors and friends who *cannot come to church with you or, even worse, perhaps do not even wish to*.[16]

This encouragement toward more frequent attendance is evidence that the opposite was the case: that in fact many people who identified as Christian only occasionally attended Christian worship.

In the *medieval period*, the church developed specific regulations regarding minimal levels of lay participation, yet it was widely recognized that ordinary Christians rarely met even these minimums. As historians Norman Tanner and Sethina Watson describe, there was "a broad spectrum of responses to the medieval church, from the extravagant, intense and

---

[13] John Chrysostom, *In Acta apost. hom.* 29; translated in Schaff, *Nicene and Post-Nicene Fathers*, ser. 2, 11:186. Emphasis added.

[14] R. C. D. Jasper and G. J. Cuming, *Prayers of the Eucharist: Early and Reformed*, 3rd ed. (Collegeville, MN: Liturgical Press, 1987), 3.

[15] Caesarius of Arles, *Sermon* 16.3; translated in Lawrence Johnson, *Worship in the Early Church* (Collegeville, MN: Liturgical Press, 2009), 4:92. Emphasis added.

[16] Caesarius of Arles, *Sermon* 74.4; translated in Johnson, *Worship in the Early Church*, 4:105. Emphasis added.

devout on one end, to the distracted, apathetic, dismissive or hostile on the other."[17] Routine and intensive practice was the norm for those with a religious vocation, whereas ordinary people were held to a different minimum standard: it was a "multi-speed" system, to borrow terminology from philosopher Charles Taylor.[18] Even, and perhaps especially, at the height of Christendom, people related to religion in a range of ways.

Only in the *sixteenth-century Reformations* did church leaders extend the expectation of routine and even intensive religious practice beyond those who made monastic vows to all Christians, and even then, this was only successfully implemented in small pockets. Historian Miia Kuha, for example, describes how in Lutheran Eastern Finland in the seventeenth century, "the clergy repeatedly complained that, although their parishioners did not go to church regularly, nevertheless on certain holy days of the year, such as Christmas and Midsummer, many were eager to attend and take communion."[19] Historian Christopher Marsh describes how in Protestant England, "popular religion," the faith and practice of the majority of England's inhabitants, existed alongside official practices, especially in the form of holiday festivals, and that this eased the transition away from Rome and toward the Church of England.[20] The unofficial occasional religious practice in which the majority of the population participated was less affected by shifting religious and political alignments than the official rites of routine practitioners.

Several centuries later, occasional religious practice characterized *Victorian England*. Religious practice was divided along class lines, with the working class remaining invested in practices associated with life transitions:

> Large swaths of the working class in Victorian England had a more tenuous connection with organized religion. Many adults attended church irregularly or not at all, but they still thought it important that their children be baptized and attend Sunday School to learn the basics of the Christian faith.[21]

---

[17] Norman Tanner and Sethina Watson, "Least of the Laity: The Minimum Requirements for a Medieval Christian," *Journal of Medieval History* 32, no. 4 (2006): 409.

[18] Charles Taylor, *A Secular Age* (Cambridge, MA: Harvard University Press, 2007), 81.

[19] Miia Kuha, "Popular Religion in the Periphery: Church Attendance in 17th Century Eastern Finland," *Perichoresis* 13, no. 2 (2015): 18.

[20] Christopher Marsh, *Popular Religion in Sixteenth-Century England* (New York: St. Martin's Press, 1998), 7, 96.

[21] Clarke and Macdonald, *Leaving Christianity*, 214.

While participation in religious practices was occasional, historian Jeffery Cox also describes how "diffusive Christianity" characterized Victorian society, and that it "informed the outlook and moral sensibility of people who were not regular churchgoers."[22]

In the United States, sociologists Roger Finke and Rodney Stark trace the ebb and flow of various expressions of Christianity from the *American colonial period* to the present. They map a striking increase in religious participation between 1776, when 17 percent of Americans were "churched," to 1980, when 62 percent were adherents.[23] While their focus is increasing religious affiliation rather than religious practice, it suggests that the true baseline for religious participation should not be the routine attendance of the 1950s. Liturgist James White's discussion of the emergence of "Frontier Worship" in America in the eighteenth and nineteenth centuries is also anchored in the idea that the population was "largely unchurched,"[24] especially in terms of liturgical participation. Pragmatically driven worship practices developed that were accessible to those less familiar with established traditions, such as occasional camp meetings. Such practices were evaluated based on their "effectiveness in producing converts in a largely unchurched nation."[25] This approach to Christian worship is explicitly oriented toward occasional practitioners.

Perhaps it could even be said that throughout history *most* ordinary Christians have been occasionally religious. This resonates with sociologist of religion Christian Smith's concept of "default religious laxity":

> In the absence of other causal factors that influence it, religiousness in human life should tend to default to a "baseline" of a modest level of practice, to an "equilibrium" that maintains future opportunities to increase religiousness but invests only in modest religious practice in the meantime.[26]

---

[22] Jeffrey Cox, *The English Churches in a Secular Society: Lambeth, 1870–1930* (Oxford: Oxford University Press, 1982); cited in Clarke and Macdonald, *Leaving Christianity*, 237.

[23] Roger Finke and Rodney Stark, *The Churching of America, 1776–2005* (New Brunswick, NJ: Rutgers University Press, 2005), 22.

[24] James White, *Protestant Worship* (Louisville, KY: Westminster John Knox Press, 1989), 172. Ross offers a valuable critique of an oversimplified approach to "frontier worship" yet does not challenge the underlying presumptions regarding its roots in occasional religious practice. Melanie Ross, "New Frontiers in American Evangelical Worship," *Studia Liturgica* 51, no. 2 (2021): 159–172.

[25] White, *Protestant Worship*, 177.

[26] Smith, *Religion*, 198.

Naming religious laxity as a "default" acknowledges that what is "lax" is in fact common and is presumably serving well those who live this out. While the lack of strictness implied by "laxity" is apt, the connotation of a lack of care is not. Many practitioners who increase their religiousness on certain occasions care deeply about these practices. However, default religious laxity suggests that what needs to be explained is *not* why people practice occasionally rather than routinely, but instead why some people are routine or even intensive practitioners.

When we view occasional religious practice today in this broader historical context, such practice does not appear to be a striking departure from the past, but rather a contemporary manifestation of an enduring pattern. The primary shift between past and present religious practice may not be the frequency or even type of occasional practice, but instead the social context in which occasional practice unfolds. Occasional practice under the "sacred canopy" of Christendom, where Christian tradition and culture is largely assumed (although this could also be interrogated), is different than occasional practice in a modern, pluralistic, multicultural context like twenty-first-century Toronto.[27] While intensive practitioners may, through their practice, create and shelter under "sacred umbrellas,"[28] occasional practitioners engage in religious practices fully exposed to the winds of change that surround them. It is crucial to understand occasional religious practice today in the context of a changing religious landscape.

Occasional Practice and Religious Change

Occasional religious practice can be considered in relation to the abundant literature on religious change in Canada, as well as in the United States, Europe, and Australia. I draw out occasional religious practice as a common thread in sociological studies of the contemporary religious landscape.

Canada

Based on national survey data for Canada, Reginald Bibby claims that 44 percent of Canadians are "*low religious*—those in the "*religious middle*"

---

[27] Peter Berger, *The Sacred Canopy: Elements of a Sociological Theory of Religion* (New York: Anchor, 1969).
[28] Christian Smith and Michael Emerson, *American Evangelicalism: Embattled and Thriving* (Chicago: University of Chicago Press, 1998).

who "neither embrace nor reject religion." Intriguingly, Bibby describes this population primarily in terms of occasional ritual participation:

> They are often brothers and sisters, aunts and uncles, cousins and friends who were raised "in the church" and in other religious settings. They are expected to show up for funerals and weddings and baptism and the like. Many also make cameo appearances at seasonal services like Christmas or Easter. Many want to have religious funerals and burials.[29]

The "low religious" are the dominant group in *every* region, age, and gender category; 87 percent of the "low religious" continue to identify with a religious tradition, whereas 13 percent identify as having no religion. About one in four is associated with Mainline Protestantism, led by those who have connections to the United Church and Anglican Church. With 44 percent of the population in this category, occasional religious practice appears to be the most common way of being religious in twenty-first-century Canada when compared to the 30 percent of the population who routinely embrace religion, and the 26 percent who reject religion entirely.[30] It is more accurate to describe occasional religious practice as a *dominant and ordinary* way of being religious in Canada, rather than as a "low" or "marginal" expression of religiosity. However, quantitative survey data reveal little about what occasional religious practice looks like in practice.

Despite the pervasive presence of the occasionally religious in the Canadian religious landscape, Joel Thiessen observes that *"marginal affiliates"*—his term for this phenomenon—have been the subject of very little research. "Marginal religious affiliates," whom Thiessen argues make up 40–50 percent of the Canadian population,[31] are those who would likely respond affirmatively to the following survey question:

> Some Canadians suggest that they draw selective beliefs and practices from their religious tradition, even if they don't attend regularly. They indicate that they don't plan on changing religious traditions, but they will turn to religious groups for important religious holidays and rites of passage. How well would you say that this describes you?[32]

---

[29] Bibby, *Resilient Gods*, 84.
[30] Bibby, *Resilient Gods*, 65.
[31] Joel Thiessen, *The Meaning of Sunday: The Practice of Belief in a Secular Age* (Montreal and Kingston: McGill-Queen's University Press, 2015), 8.
[32] Thiessen, *The Meaning of Sunday*, 92.

Table 2.1 The Angus Reid Institute Spectrum and Attendance at Religious Services, 2017

	Attend Religious Services (Other Than Weddings or Funerals)			
	Non-Believers	Spiritually Uncertain	Privately Faithful	Religiously Committed
Once a month or more	3%	1%	14%	69%
A few times a year	2%	6%	25%	13%
Only rarely	15%	31%	36%	13%
Never	81%	62%	25%	5%

Adapted with permission from Angus Reid Institute, *Faith Continuum Groups Release Table* (Canada: Angus Reid Institute, 2017). http://angusreid.org/wp-content/uploads/2017/04/2017.04.10_FaithContinuumGroups_releasetables.pdf.

In this Calgary-based interview study, Thiessen identifies three motivations for ongoing occasional participation: tradition, family pressure, and connection to a higher power in a sacred space.[33]

In 2017, the Angus Reid Institute conducted a series of polls about religion in Canada to mark the national sesquicentennial. The results suggest a "spectrum of spiritual belief and practice": 19 percent of Canadians profess no faith and are named *Non-Believers*; 21 percent profess deep devotion and are considered *Religiously Committed*; and 60 percent of Canadians are in between, with 30 percent being *Spiritually Uncertain*, and 30 percent *Privately Faithful*.[34] Unsurprisingly, these categories map onto attendance at religious services (Table 2.1).[35] Twenty percent of Canadians routinely attend "religious services (other than weddings or funerals)" once a month or more. People across the spectrum attend occasionally—meaning a few times a year apart from life transitions—including 2 percent of Non-Believers, 6 percent of the Spiritually Uncertain, and 35 percent of the Privately Faithful. Since the polling question excluded key occasional practices, a wider portion of the spiritual spectrum may actually attend in connection with these events

---

[33] Thiessen, *The Meaning of Sunday*, 78–80.
[34] Angus Reid Institute, "A Spectrum of Spirituality," April 13, 2017, accessed December 11, 2023, http://angusreid.org/wp-content/uploads/2017/04/2017.04.12_Faith_Wave_1_Part_1.pdf; Angus Reid Institute, "Faith and Religion in Public Life," November 16, 2017, accessed December 11, 2023, http://angusreid.org/wp-content/uploads/2017/11/2017.11.15-Cardus-Wave-3.pdf; Angus Reid Institute, "Spirituality in a Changing World," May 17, 2017, accessed December 11, 2023, http://angusreid.org/wp-content/uploads/2017/05/2017.05.17-Faith-Wave-1-Part2.pdf.
[35] Angus Reid Institute, "Faith Continuum Groups Release Tables," April 10, 2017, accessed December 11, 2023, http://angusreid.org/wp-content/uploads/2017/04/2017.04.10_FaithContinuumGroups_releasetables.pdf.

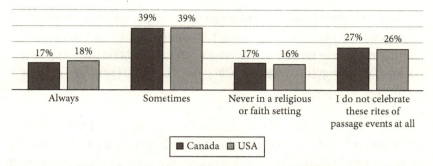

Figure 2.1 Millennial celebration of rites of passage in religious contexts. "How often have you ever celebrated, or plan to celebrate in future, your own rites of passage events with a religious or faith group?" Respondents 18–35 years old, MTS 2019.

Reproduced with permission from Sarah Wilkins-Laflamme, *Religion, Spirituality and Secularity Among Millennials* (London: Routledge, 2023).

than these numbers suggest. Nevertheless, even within the limitations of the poll, it appears that occasional practice is present across the spectrum.[36]

Sociologist Sarah Wilkins-Laflamme, in her research on millennials (people born between approximately 1986 and 2005) in Canada and the United States, likewise presents four well-defined categories that parallel those identified by the Angus Reid Institute: (1) religious and (2) nonreligious millennials, as well as (3) spiritual seeker and (4) cultural believer millennials.[37] Twenty-five percent of millennials attend religious services "at least once a year" but not one a month or once a week, which suggests they are occasional religious practitioners.[38] In addition, the majority of millennials in both Canada and the United States "always" or "sometimes" celebrate life transitions in a religious context (Figure 2.1).[39] Again, this shows evidence of widespread occasional practice. Unsurprisingly, these dynamics are especially evident among "cultural believer millennials":

> Belonging and belief remain somewhat important to most *cultural believers*, but contact with a place of worship usually only happens for special holidays or occasions, if at all: 34% of cultural believers in Canada and

---

[36] Angus Reid Institute, "A Spectrum of Spirituality."
[37] Sarah Wilkins-Laflamme, *Religion, Spirituality and Secularity Among Millennials: The Generation Shaping American and Canadian Trends* (London: Routledge, 2022).
[38] Wilkins-Laflamme, *Religion, Spirituality and Secularity*, 42.
[39] Wilkins-Laflamme, *Religion, Spirituality and Secularity*, 45.

25% in the United States attend religious services a few times or once a year; and 55% of cultural believers in Canada and 50% in the United States say they always or sometimes celebrate or plan to celebrate rites of passage with a faith group (marriage, birth/initiation/baptismal rites for a child or a funeral, for example).[40]

However, an important distinction between Wilkins-Laflamme's "cultural believers" and the Angus Reid Institute's "privately faithful" is that the millennials in Wilkins-Laflamme's category tend not to engage in private spiritual or religious practices.[41] Patterns among millennials can be set in a larger context.

In the context of a quantitative analysis of religious change in Canada since 1945, Brian Clarke and Stuart Macdonald acknowledge occasional religious participation with the term "*soft de-churched*" in reference to mainstream Protestants:

> As we have seen in the case of Canada's former mainstream Protestant denominations, some of these Census affiliates could be called cultural Anglicans, Presbyterians, and United Church people. They still identify as such, and may attend church at Christmas, or even Easter. But as they do not attend ordinary church services, they increasingly are not presenting their children for baptism or enrolling them in Sunday School. Call them "*soft de-churched.*" For all intents and purposes, they have left the church. Then there are those who have left the church and never attend. Call them the "hard de-churched."[42]

Clarke and Macdonald recognize an analogous dynamic among Catholics, naming them "fringe Catholics" and "nominal Catholics":

> In-between those who attend regularly and those who never attend are those who say they attend a few times a year and those who say they attend at least once a year.... We might describe those who attend a few times a year as *"fringe" Catholics*. They may attend from time to time, but their personal connection to a parish is tenuous. As for those 1.39 million Catholics who say they attend at least once a year, we consider them *"nominal" Catholics*. Notice that they won't say that they attend several times a

---

[40] Wilkins-Laflamme, *Religion, Spirituality and Secularity*, 110. Emphasis added.
[41] Wilkins-Laflamme, *Religion, Spirituality and Secularity*, 58.
[42] Clarke and Macdonald, *Leaving Christianity*, 203. Emphasis added.

year. But unlike those who say that they never attend, Roman Catholics are saying that they are possibly open to the ideal of attending at least once in a while. Perhaps they do attend at least once a year, likely at Christmas or on some other family occasion. Or perhaps they intend to do so, but the occasion may not arise in any given year.[43]

Clarke and Macdonald name occasional religious practice and helpfully articulate how widespread it is in Canada in the twenty-first century. However, Clarke and Macdonald have a high standard for what is considered "churched." From their perspective, occasional practice is not enough to make someone truly religious. This definition of what constitutes legitimate religious identity may be based on the unhelpful benchmark of the mid-twentieth century or may be motivated by a project which is aimed at quantifying how Christianity has declined in Canada. It is regrettable that they dismiss this occasional way of relating to religion as "cultural" or "nominal" and consider occasional practitioners to have "left the church" or to be on the "fringe," when many in these categories would not themselves name their relationship with religion in these terms, but instead express with sincerity that occasional religious practice is a meaningful and valuable part of their lives.

Importantly, Clarke and Macdonald acknowledge that occasional practice today is not the "diffusive Christianity" of the Victorian era. It is not only occasional religious practice that matters, but also the context in which it is practiced that is significant:

> Churches now function in a completely new cultural context, one in which Canadian culture no longer transmits and supports Christian beliefs and practices, as it once did. As a consequence, many have never been exposed to Christian beliefs and rituals and have no clue what they might be about.[44]

A Canadian religious landscape characterized by declining affiliation with and participation in the Christian tradition, growth in nonreligion to the extent that it is the second largest "religious" group, and an increasing number of people affiliated with non-Christian religions, shapes who practices occasionally and how they experience the religious practices they encounter.

Each of these analyses of the Canadian religious landscape and religious change in Canada—by Bibby, Thiessen, the Angus Reid Institute, Wilkins-Laflamme, and Clarke and Macdonald—points to a complex religious middle

---

[43] Clarke and Macdonald, *Leaving Christianity*, 207. Emphasis added.
[44] Clarke and Macdonald, *Leaving Christianity*, 26.

ground. While there are certainly people at the extremes of religion and nonreligion, many more Canadians exist somewhere in between. These studies suggest that occasional practice is an important characteristic of the middle ground, although some occasional practitioners can also be found at the edges. A better understanding of occasional religious practice can help nuance and complete this picture of the Canadian religious landscape. The exploration of religion in Canada is assisted by the consideration of comparable regions.

United States

The United States is an important point of comparison for religion in Canada, as Canada's closest neighbor and a dominant cultural influence, and as a region characterized by similar patterns of religious change.[45] Although there are significant differences between the two countries, especially in relation to religion, research on religion in the United States can inform the study of occasional religious practice in Canada, and vice versa.

One American development was the release of a new religious typology by the Pew Institute in 2018 that categorizes Americans as highly religious, somewhat religious, or nonreligious, using self-reported survey data on belief, identification, and practice (Figure 2.2).[46] These designations roughly parallel Bibby's Canadian categories of high, low, and no religion, the Angus Reid Institute spectrum, and Wilkins-Laflamme's classification of millennials. Although the typology draws on measures beyond participation in religious practices, it also points to patterns in occasional religious practice (Figure 2.3).[47] For example, only the most religious group, the "Sunday Stalwarts," attend religious services weekly:

> Outside of the Sunday Stalwarts, relatively few Americans—even those who otherwise hold strong religious beliefs—frequently attend religious

---

[45] David Martin, "Canada in Comparative Perspective," in *Rethinking Church, State, and Modernity: Canada Between Europe and America*, ed. Marguerite Van Die and David Lyon (Toronto: University of Toronto Press, 2000), 23–33; David Voas and Mark Chaves, "Is the United States a Counterexample to the Secularization Thesis?," *American Journal of Sociology* 121 (2016): 1517–1556.

[46] The typology was created based on a nationally representative survey of participants with a range of conventional religious affiliations, including those affiliated with a diversity of Christian traditions, non-Christian religious traditions, and the unaffiliated. No single typology group constitutes a majority of any Christian tradition. For example, Evangelicals, Mainline Protestants, Catholics, and members of historically Black Protestant traditions are spread out across several typology groups, showing that a range of beliefs and practices are present within each of these traditions. Pew Research Center, "The Religious Typology: A New Way to Categorize Americans by Religion," August 29, 2018, accessed December 11, 2023, https://www.pewforum.org/wp-content/uploads/sites/7/2018/08/Full-Report-01-11-19-FOR-WEB.pdf, 31.

[47] Pew Research Center, "The Religious Typology."

services or read scripture. About eight-in-ten Sunday Stalwarts attend religious services at least once a week—three times greater than the share of frequent attenders among God-and-Country Believers, and roughly seven times larger than the proportion of the Diversely Devout who are as observant.[48]

Source: Survey conducted Dec. 4-18, 2017, among U.S. adults. "The Religious Typology"

PEW RESEARCH CENTER

Figure 2.2 The religious typology: the highly religious, nonreligious, and in between.
Reproduced from Pew Research Center (2018). The Religious Typology. https://www.pewresearch.org/religion/2018/08/29/the-religious-typology/.

---

[48] Pew Research Center, "The Religious Typology," 9.

Eight-in-ten Sunday Stalwarts attend religious services weekly; among all other groups, no more than about a quarter say the same

% who say they attend religious services ...

	At least once a week %	Monthly/ yearly %	Seldom/ never %	No answer %
Full sample*	23	26	51	<1 = 100
Highly religious groups				
Sunday Stalwarts	82	15	2	1
God-and-Country Believers	27	41	32	<1
Diversely Devout	12	36	51	1
Somewhat religious groups				
Relaxed Religious	17	35	48	0
Spiritually Awake	8	35	56	1
Nonreligious groups				
Religion Resisters	2	11	87	0
Solidly Secular	2	12	87	0

* For a variety of methodological reasons (e.g., differences in weighting procedures, mode of survey administration, etc.), estimates of religious attendance and measures of some other practices for the full sample from surveys conducted on the American Trends Panel are not directly comparable to estimates from telephone surveys (including the Religious Landscape Studies).

Note: This question was one of the input variables used in the cluster analysis model to define the typology groups. See Appendix A for details. Figures may not add to 100% due to rounding.

Source: Survey conducted Dec. 4–18, 2017, among U.S. adults. Respondents were asked about their attendance at religious services in a previous wave of the American Trends Panel (ATP); nearly all respondents (n = 4,699) most recently answered the question about religious attendance in an ATP wave conducted May 30-Oct. 23, 2017, though a few respondents (n = 30) last answered the question in an earlier survey. The religious attendance question in the May 30-Oct. 23, 2017 wave was "Aside from weddings and funerals, how often do you attend religious services? More than once a week, once a week, once or twice a month, a few times a year, seldom, never?"
"The Religious Typology"

PEW RESEARCH CENTER

Figure 2.3 The religious typology and religious service attendance.

Reproduced from Pew Research Center (2018). The Religious Typology. https://www.pewresearch.org/religion/2018/08/29/the-religious-typology/.

Note that 2 percent of "Religion Resisters" and the "Solidly Secular" attend services weekly, suggesting they are "routinely religious" according to the definition in this study (Figure 2.3). On the other end of the typology, 2% of "Sunday Stalwarts" and 32% of "God-and-Country Believers" never attend religious services, suggesting they are "never religious" according to this definition. When religion is defined in terms of *practice*, a focus on believing in religious concepts or claiming religion is important is insufficient to qualify someone as being religious. It is significant that here, as in the Canadian Angus Reid Institute poll, the question asked about religious service attendance *specifically excludes* some of the most common occasional practices: "Aside from weddings and funerals, how often do you attend religious services?"[49] which again points to the significance of these events as occasions when people who relate to religion in a diversity of ways enter into religious practices together.

Sociological research on *nonreligion* has flourished in the United States over the past decade and is another important resource for reflecting on occasional religious practice, especially because some, and perhaps many, who identify as nonreligious are what I am calling occasional religious practitioners. Those who check the "none" box in response to survey questions about religious affiliation are internally diverse. For example, Christel Manning describes four types of worldviews among "nones" in her interview study of nonreligious parenting: "unchurched believer," "seeker spirituality," "philosophical secularist," and "indifferent."[50] Joseph Baker and Buster Smith likewise classify secular individuals according to four mutually exclusive yet blurry categories: "atheist," "agnostic," "nonaffiliated believers," and "culturally religious."[51] Baker and Smith link their category of *"culturally religious"* with occasional practice:

> We consider attendance at religious services twice a year or less to be evidence of a lack of public practice. That is, we consider "Christmas and

---

[49] Pew Research Center, "The Religious Typology," 39.
[50] Christel Manning, *Losing Our Religion: How Unaffiliated Parents Are Raising Their Children* (New York: New York University Press, 2015), 36.
[51] Joseph Baker and Buster Smith, *American Secularism: Cultural Contours of Nonreligious Belief Systems* (New York: New York University Press, 2015).

Easter" Christians or Jews who attend temple annually on a high holiday but do not pray to be culturally religious rather than actively religious.[52]

Joel Thiessen and Sarah Wilkins-Laflamme compare nonreligion in the United States and Canada and likewise recognize the internal diversity among those who identify as nonreligious, including "involved seculars, inactive nonbelievers, inactive believers, the spiritual but not religious, and religiously involved believers."[53]

Despite sporadic reference to practice, self-identification and belief are the primary focus of most typologies of nonreligion. Elizabeth Drescher offers a helpful corrective to this in her interview study of "the spiritual life of America's Nones," including the observation that:

> While Nones are characterized by the fact that they do not claim formal, membership-based affiliation with institutional religious groups, many of those I interviewed periodically—indeed, in some cases quite regularly—attended services in one or more church, shanga, synagogue, temple, or other religious community.[54]

This is particularly true of practices associated with life transitions and holidays:

> Rituals associated with life transitions such as births, graduations, marriages, and deaths, as well as seasonal celebrations and holidays, bring Nones and Somes into frequent spiritual proximity.[55]

As Drescher's research implies, in addition to situating occasional religious practice in the context of nonreligion, it is important to consider studies of spirituality.

Contemporary *spirituality* and its relationship with religion is the subject of an emerging body of literature. Nancy Ammerman's inventive research examines how religion is part of everyday life for Americans with a range of relationships to religion and spirituality. Her emphasis is squarely on the

---

[52] Baker and Smith, *American Secularism*, 17.
[53] Joel Thiessen and Sarah Wilkins-Laflamme, *None of the Above: Nonreligious Identity in the US and Canada* (New York: New York University Press, 2020), 171.
[54] Drescher, *Choosing Our Religion*, 9.
[55] Drescher, *Choosing Our Religion*, 8.

"everyday," not the occasional, yet occasional religious practice nevertheless emerges in a discussion of those "*on the margins of organized religion*": "They attend for holidays and rites of passage but do not think of regular weekend attendance as necessary."[56] There is also a growing literature about the so-called "*spiritual but not religious*," a slippery term that I am wary of applying to anyone who does not claim it for themselves,[57] but that nevertheless has certain points of connection with occasional religious practice, especially in terms of selective participation in complex systems.[58] However, an important difference between expressions of spirituality and occasional religious practice is that occasional religious practice depends on established religious institutions and practices.

Europe

Much of the sociological research with connections to occasional religious practice has centered on Europe, where occasional religious practice has been impossible to ignore, especially in relation to established state churches. David Voas provides a particularly vivid description of what I call occasional religious practice in his European cross-national comparison of "*fuzzy fidelity*," a term associated with an intermediate level of religiosity, a "casual loyalty to tradition":

> We know, though, that religious commitment is not dichotomous (so that people are either religious or non-religious). Despite dramatic shifts in the prevalence of conventional Christian belief, practice, and self-identification, residual involvement is considerable. Many people remain interested in church weddings and funerals, Christmas services, and local festivals. They believe in "something out there," pay at least lip service to Christian values, and may be willing to identify with a denomination. They are neither regular churchgoers (now only a small minority

---

[56] Ammerman, *Sacred Stories, Spiritual Tribes*, 116.
[57] Ammerman helpfully challenges the use of this term. Nancy Ammerman, "Spiritual but Not Religious? Beyond Binary Choices in the Study of Religion," *Journal for the Scientific Study of Religion* 52, no. 2 (2013): 258–278.
[58] Robert Fuller, *Spiritual, but Not Religious: Understanding Unchurched America* (Oxford: Oxford University Press, 2001); William Parsons, ed., *Being Spiritual but Not Religious* (New York: Routledge, 2018); Linda Mercadante, *Belief Without Borders: Inside the Minds of the Spiritual but Not Religious* (Oxford: Oxford University Press, 2014).

of the population in most European countries) nor self-consciously non-religious. Because they retain some loyalty to tradition, though in a rather uncommitted way, we can call the phenomenon fuzzy fidelity.[59]

Voas argues that "fuzzy fidelity" is a transitional phase between religion and secularity that rises and then falls, rather than a new and enduring way of being religious. He also observes significant variation in how this unfolds in different national contexts in Europe. Ingrid Storm further interrogates "fuzzy fidelity" and identifies four types: "moderately religious," "passively religious," "belonging without believing," and "believing without belonging."[60] The strongest common characteristic across groups in Storm's typology is choosing religious services for birth, marriage, and death.[61]

Grace Davie develops the concept of *"believing without belonging"* (that Storm later borrows) in the British context: "A large number of people continue to believe but have ceased to belong to their religious institutions in any meaningful sense.... Despite a lack of regular attendance, it is to the Church of England that most English people turn when the services of a religious institution are required," especially services associated with life transitions.[62] Davie later nuances this approach to allow for subtler and more complex relationships between believing and belonging, proposing instead the concept of *"vicarious religion"*: "the notion of religion performed by an active minority but on behalf of a much larger number, who (implicitly at least) not only understand, but, quite clearly, approve of what the minority is doing."[63] This includes the ongoing role of:

> churches and church leaders in conducting ritual on behalf of a wide variety of individuals and communities at critical points in their lives. The most obvious examples can be found in the continuing requests, even in a moderately secular society, for some sort of religious ritual at the time of a birth, a marriage, and most of all at the time of a death.[64]

---

[59] David Voas, "The Rise and Fall of Fuzzy Fidelity in Europe," *European Sociological Review* 25, no. 2 (2009): 171.

[60] Ingrid Storm, "Halfway to Heaven: Four Types of Fuzzy Fidelity in Europe," *Journal for the Scientific Study of Religion* 48, no. 4 (2009): 702–718.

[61] Storm, "Halfway to Heaven," 708. These terms draw from the work of Grace Davie.

[62] Grace Davie, "Believing Without Belonging," *Social Compass* 37, no. 4 (1990): 457. Day and Lövheim have adapted Davie's concepts of religion in Britain to explore religious change elsewhere in Europe. Abby Day and Mia Lövheim, *Modernities, Memory, Mutations* (New York: Routledge, 2015).

[63] Grace Davie, "Vicarious Religion: A Methodological Challenge," in *Everyday Religion: Observing Modern Religious Lives*, ed. Nancy Ammerman (Oxford: Oxford University Press, 2007), 22.

[64] Davie, "Vicarious Religion," 23. Elsewhere, Davie also references ongoing participation in what she calls "occasional offices" associated with birth, marriage, and death. See Grace Davie, *Religion in Modern Europe: A Memory Mutates* (Oxford: Oxford University Press, 2000), 61–81.

For example, in 2018 the Church of England still performed baptisms for 9 percent of the total number of births in England and Wales, and Anglican funerals for 25 percent of deaths.[65] In addition to life transitions, attendance at Church of England services on Christmas and Easter is significantly higher than average Sunday attendance, suggesting that holiday occasional religious practice continues in Britain.[66] Davie recognizes that these patterns have implications for the institutions that find themselves responsible for maintaining religious traditions, as explored in Chapter 6.[67]

Also based in England, Abby Day's research on *"Christian nominalism"* argues that "what is often dismissed as 'nominalism' is far from an empty category, but one loaded with cultural 'stuff' and meaning."[68] People often claim religious identities for significant social reasons:

> People who "believe in belonging" claim social and cultural identities to reinforce a belief in belonging to specific groups of people, particularly those with whom they have affective, adherent relations or those whom they recognize as having legitimate authority.[69]

"Ethnic nominalists" claim Christian identity as an expression of nationality and culture. "Natal nominalists" receive Christian identity from parents or grandparents (potentially through baptism). "Aspirational nominalists" associate Christian identity with goodness and respectability.[70] Across categories, participation in "weddings, funerals, and christenings" is one way that Christian identity is performed.[71]

Slavica Jakelic's approach to *"collectivistic religion"* has certain parallels to Day's typology. However, drawing primarily on Eastern European Christianities, Jakelic helpfully recognizes that there are cases where religion is not seen as a choice:

---

[65] Church of England Research and Statistics, "Statistics for Mission, 2018," 2019, accessed December 11, 2023, https://www.churchofengland.org/sites/default/files/2019-10/2018StatisticsForMission_0.pdf.
[66] Church of England Research and Statistics, "Statistics for Mission, 2018."
[67] Davie, *Religion in Modern Europe*, 33.
[68] Abby Day, *Believing in Belonging: Belief and Social Identity in the Modern World* (Oxford: Oxford University Press, 2011), 192.
[69] Day, *Believing in Belonging*, 194.
[70] Day, *Believing in Belonging*, 175.
[71] Day, *Believing in Belonging*, 181.

They experience their religion as ascribed to them rather than chosen by them, as fixed rather than changeable, despite *and* because of the fact that their religious identities are profoundly shaped by the historical and cultural particularities of their social location.[72]

Jakelic examines how collective identity brings individuals into a group around "values, ideas, historical narratives, symbols, and institutions."[73] Jakelic quotes Mikis Theodorakis, a Greek composer:

> The Church is the cradle of our nation, the cradle of our race, the cradle of Hellenism. In there we spend the dearest hours of our lives. There we baptize our children.... There we get married and there we say farewell to our beloved. *Whether we want it or not* we have spent in the Church the most moving moments in our lives... *whether we want it or not*, [the Church and Orthodox Christianity] constitute the core of our existence.[74]

Occasional religious practice may be one aspect of the unchosen formation of collective identity in collectivistic expressions of Christianity. Jakelic argues that collectivistic religion is and will remain a powerful force in modern Europe, while emphasizing that religious change unfolds in distinct ways in different regions.

Australia

Australia and Canada have an affinity as far-flung former British colonies, although there are also significant differences between them. One difference is that, thanks to the National Church Life Survey, more survey data is available on religion in Australia.[75] Clear patterns of occasional religious practice emerge in the 2016 wave of the survey. While 11 percent of Australians attend religious services weekly, and 7 percent attend monthly, 44 percent have

---

[72] Slavica Jakelic, *Collectivistic Religions: Religion, Choice, and Identity in Late Modernity* (New York: Routledge, 2016), 1.
[73] Jakelic, *Collectivistic Religions*, 43.
[74] Jakelic, *Collectivistic Religions*, 139.
[75] National Church Life Survey, "Research," accessed December 11, 2023, https://www.ncls.org.au/research.

attended "a special Christian service" such as a "wedding, funeral, Christmas service," at least once over the past twelve months.[76] Notably, the survey reports that Australians see the primary role of the church as to "conduct weddings, funerals, baptisms, etc." (56 percent). This is tied for the highest position with the role of the church to "encourage good morals" (56 percent) and exceeds roles associated with social service, meaning, social life, and public engagement.[77] The 2018 data also suggest a middle ground between the "practicing religious and spiritual" (26 percent) and the "'non-religious and non-spiritual" (35 percent) that takes two expressions: "non-practising religious and spiritual" (26 percent) and "spiritual but not religious" (1 percent),[78] which echoes the Pew typology in the context of the United States and the Canadian religious landscape studies.

Generational Religious Change

One striking pattern that pervades each of the regions discussed—Canada, the United States, Europe, and Australia—is generational religious change. In all of these regions, "each successive generation is slightly less religious than the one before."[79] Mark Chaves and David Voas make a compelling case for generational change based on affiliation, attendance, and belief. Although their focus is on demonstrating that this pattern is present in the United States, they also address religious change in Canada in terms of a decline in routine practice across generations (Figure 2.4).[80] A 2021 Statistics Canada report drawing on data from 1985–2019 reinforces this assessment, noting generational decline in religious affiliation and participation.[81] Although

---

[76] National Church Life Survey, "Infographics: Religion and Spirituality in Australia, 2016 Australian Community Survey," December 2016, accessed March 18, 2021, https://www.ncls.org.au/news/2016-acs-religion-spirituality-infographics.

[77] National Church Life Survey, "Infographics: Religion and Spirituality in Australia, 2018 Australian Community Survey," July 2018, accessed March 18, 2021, https://www.ncls.org.au/news/2018-acs-religion-spirituality-infographics.

[78] National Church Life Survey, "Infographics: Religion and Spirituality in Australia, 2018 Australian Community Survey."

[79] Voas and Chaves, "Is the United States a Counterexample?"

[80] Voas and Chaves, "Is the United States a Counterexample?," 1538. Of note, this research includes only respondents born in Canada. This is especially noteworthy at a time in which immigration is one of the primary factors shaping the Canadian religious landscape.

[81] Louis Cornelissen, "Religiosity in Canada and Its Evolution from 1985–2019," Insights on Canadian Society, Statistics Canada, October 28, 2021, accessed December 11, 2023, https://www150.statcan.gc.ca/n1/en/pub/75-006-x/2021001/article/00010-eng.pdf?st=sIvWsSbM.

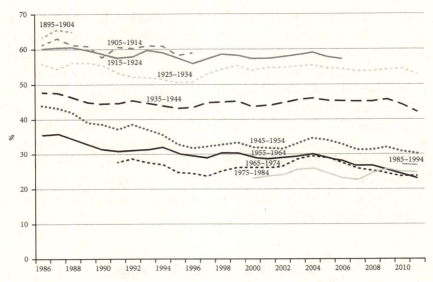

Figure 2.4 Generational religious change in Canada by monthly attendance, 1985–2012. Monthly attendance by decade of birth (religious affiliates only), Canada. Data are from the Canadian General Social Survey, 1985–2012. Includes only respondents with a religious affiliation who were born in Canada. Three-survey moving average.

Reproduced with permission from David Voas and Mark Chaves, "Is the United States a Counterexample to the Secularization Thesis?," *American Journal of Sociology* 121, no. 5 (2016): 1517–1556. https://doi.org/10.1086/684202.

these analyses do not directly address practices associated with occasional religious practice, such as life transitions and holidays, it is noteworthy that these are occasions that often bring together multiple generations within a family, which suggests that these are moments when individuals with different relationships with religion participate in the same ritual event. Occasional practices may also be moments for the transmission (or the failed transmission) of religion across generations.

Generational religious change is evident at the micro level in the interviews that I conducted for this study. Participants across generations describe generational change explicitly. A young mother in her thirties with an Italian Catholic background who practices in connection with life transitions depicts each generation of her family as successively less religious:

> My husband's grandfather is exactly like my grandmother—church every Sunday, practicing Catholic, there is no gray area. And then our parents, I'd

say are all religious but relaxed—they don't go church, but they're still like believers and have faith. And then it just trickles down. Like my sister is an example probably like me, but she's married to someone more religious. I think she has become more like I guess okay with the Catholic faith from getting married and going to marriage classes.

A young father who is nonreligious yet was raised in the Anglican church describes the lack of religious practice among his peers and his children compared to his own upbringing:

I don't think any of my cousins attend church. My sister doesn't. My wife was raised Catholic but she doesn't go to church or anything like that. She doesn't pray every night before bed. And I don't even think her parents do necessarily. So it's not—I can absolutely see sort of a dwindling of religion as time goes by with my children and everything. We don't—my daughter doesn't pray or anything. She doesn't—I don't even know if she understands what the idea of God is. She's small. She's four. And I remember when I was four, I said my prayers at night. You go to church. You go to Sunday school, things like that. So absolutely, I do see a dwindling of religion, religious faith as time goes by.

One younger participant who practices routinely recognizes that she is unusual in her congregation:

I go to a church. I go to Anglican church and a very small congregation. They're all dying. They're all just old. I think I'm the youngest person, one of the youngest people there. And I think that's interesting too, that it seems to be religion and going to church is an older person's thing.... And I think it's interesting that I'm 36, and that people my age aren't going to church, aren't spending their Sundays that way.

Younger participants tend to have a casual attitude toward generational religious change. It is a reality they observe, but about which they do not have particularly strong feelings.

Older participants also observe changing religious practice over generations, often with a hint of lament. A grandmother who identifies as Anglican and is occasionally religious, incidentally and in connection with holidays and life transitions, comments on these patterns in her family's experience:

Because my mother was such a strong Anglican, and getting us to go to church, and getting us to being a part of that. . . . And then we just felt it was important as we were getting married that we needed to be married in a church, felt that was the right way to do it. And then having children, having them christened, having them baptized and stuff. And then [my sister's] children, they all partake in religious ceremonies and stuff. But my children don't. My [other] sister, her kids don't. And same with my younger sister. None of her children. That's why it was really strange when we made sure that they came to grandma's funeral so that they could be a part of all that. Yeah. So maybe the next generation after ours, after our kids will connect better.

A Catholic grandmother who practices routinely likewise notices these patterns in her family and grieves that the younger generation, including her son and his family, rarely attend religious services:

One of my nephews, he's not baptized his children, so they never go to church. Whereas, once, I guess it's different. I don't know. Because we were baptized in church and we went to church every Sunday. And it's not to say that you'll have to go nowadays, every Sunday or whenever, but I think it's something that brings the family together.

Another Catholic grandmother who practices occasionally in relation to life transitions notices the changing relationship that the clients at her small business have with the Catholic tradition and worries that her children will also choose not to participate in occasional practices:

I wasn't sure how I would accept this new generation. The new generation of customers that I have [at my small business] don't feel that it's important to baptize, or introduce church, or Catholic school when the children are old enough to make their own choices. I am afraid that my children would meet somebody who thinks that this is not necessary. That would have disappointed me, even though I would have to accept it because we love our children and it is what it is, what they choose. I have another daughter and I would be afraid if her child is born, they don't baptize.

A younger baby boomer grandmother recognizes that this change already began with her generation:

> For me when my kids were born, we didn't baptize them. Lot of my friends' kids aren't baptized. I have some who are, but most—I'm in a different generation than my parents. With her they would have died if you didn't have the baby baptized. You had to do it.

Important to notice here is that it is *not usually the grandparents* of children baptized between 2015 and 2020 who are routinely religious, but rather the great-grandparents of the infant, who are often no longer living or no longer able to practice routinely. Grandparents and parents in this study both tend to be occasionally religious.

Generational change is also evident when I interview multiple generations within the same family. Although grandparents who are baby boomers are not necessarily routine practitioners, they tend to have more routine practice in their background, especially during childhood, than their own children. In contrast, many younger parents grew up as occasional practitioners and continue to practice occasionally as adults. It is also significant that occasional practice is a key marker of generational religious change for participants. They name and use occasional practices, especially life transition practices, to track generational religious change within their own families. This study sheds light on generational religious change in relation to occasional practices at the micro level.

Contributions of the Concept of Occasional Religious Practice

The concept of occasional religious practice as a way of relating to religion that is defined by occasional participation in religious practices—attending religious services occasionally rather than routinely, usually in association with specific occasions, such as holidays or life transitions—makes at least five contributions to the existing literature on religious change in Canada and comparable contexts.

First, introducing the concept establishes that *occasional religious practice is widespread*. Although the historical vignettes demonstrate that it is not a new phenomenon, giving a name to occasional practice highlights a common thread that runs through the literature on religious change and reveals the pervasive presence of occasional practice in contemporary contexts. While the precise combinations of characteristics these studies put forward reflect certain regions and time periods, the theme of occasional practice is clear in all of them. Occasional religious practice is a primary way in which people relate to Christianity in the Global North in the late twentieth and early twenty-first centuries. However, the existing literature tends to group occasional religious practice with other measures and markers of religiosity, such as affiliation and belief. Instead of considering occasional practice as one feature of a more broadly defined category, I show that examining occasional practice *in its own right* allows for careful consideration of the internal variation among occasional practitioners.

Second, naming occasional religious practice as a distinct way of relating to religion reveals that *occasional practitioners are diverse*. Examining occasional practice in the context of the literature on religious change points to unity as well as internal diversity; researchers interpret the same reported behavior or observable practice in a range of different ways. A broad range of theories link occasional practice to belief, culture, identity, motivation, and more. Therefore, it is crucial to *be cautious about making assumptions about occasional practitioners*. Occasional practitioners are a diverse group with a range of ways of relating to religion, shaped by a variety of religious experiences. Not all occasional practitioners are "spiritual but not religious" or "vicariously religious" or "nominally religious" or "nonreligious," but it is likely that some relate to religion in each of these ways. This raises the question of the nature of occasional practice in Canada. Is it "collectivistic" or "nominal," akin to "fuzzy fidelity," or "seeker spirituality"? Or perhaps, in the multicultural mosaic of Toronto, numerous patterns are present. Furthermore, a close look at Anglican occasional practice in Toronto may reveal patterns that are present elsewhere.

Third, *the use of the term occasional religious practice aspires to be value neutral*. The term aims to avoid presenting occasional religious practice as somehow irregular—"low," "fuzzy," "fringe," or "marginal"—or using language perceived as negative or critical about occasional religious practitioners, dismissing this form of practice as "nominal," "cultural," or "soft." Occasional religious practice is an ordinary way to be religious. This theory aspires to honor occasional religious practice as a valid and substantial way of being religious. It aims to acknowledge and engage occasional religious practice as a phenomenon in its own right—a different rather than lesser way of relating to religion.

Fourth, *taking occasional practice seriously raises theoretical and empirical questions about occasional practitioners.* While there is ample literature that gestures toward occasional practice, there is very little that delves deeply into how occasional practitioners understand and experience this way of relating to religion. How do occasional practitioners experience religious practices? What are these practices doing and meaning for them? Why do they choose to engage in religious practices occasionally? It also raises questions about others connected to the practices: How do routine and intensive practitioners who are present, especially clergy, experience the occasional practice of others? Do contemporary religious leaders respond with a similar dismay over occasional practice as did John Chrysostom? While many of these questions are best answered qualitatively, quantitative research and survey design would benefit from attending specifically to occasional religious practice rather than excluding participation in weddings and funerals from survey questions.

Fifth, *attention to occasional religious practice invites analysis of religious practices themselves.* By placing an emphasis on institutionally or culturally prescribed practices, religious rituals as well as religious practitioners can be considered in relation to religious change. How are practices adapted in response to occasional religious practice? How do interpretations of religious practices change? The concept of occasional practice invites reflection on religious practices from ritual theoretical and liturgical theological perspectives, as well as shedding light on religion in contemporary contexts and the religiousness of participants. It is to the religious identities of occasional practitioners that we turn in the next chapter: Who are occasional practitioners? How do they describe how they relate to religion?

3

Who Are Occasional Practitioners?

Five couples and almost a dozen godparents stand at the front of an Anglican church near a movable font. They have dressed intentionally for the occasion, whether for them this means crisp business casual wear or vibrant African fabrics. Parents, most of whom appear to be in their late twenties or thirties, cradle the children being baptized in their arms. A few older siblings cling to adult legs. Someone in each family group holds a thick cardstock printout of the baptism rite. The five families move through the words and actions of the rite together. They present each child for baptism by name. They make faith commitments on behalf of the child, affirming the ancient words of the Apostles' Creed. They make promises to live out this faith through participation in the Christian community and loving service in the world—"I will, with God's help," they chorus. They witness the children being welcomed into the church with water, oil, light, and prayer.

The parents and godparents speak the same words and go through the same actions. On the surface, the participants appear religiously uniform. But I have interviewed enough parents and godparents involved in baptisms to know that the participants in this service of baptism likely understand their religious identities in a diversity of ways.

The Religious Identities of Occasional Practitioners

Occasional practitioners, even those at the center of initiating a practice, who make formal religious commitments or provide significant leadership, have a range of relationships with religion that are expressed through claiming various religious identities. In this chapter, I outline the ways in which participants in Anglican religious practices in Toronto describe their religious identities, which include Anglican, Christian, Roman Catholic, and other specific Christian traditions, as well as identifying with non-Christian religious traditions, as spiritual, or as atheist or agnostic, among a range of nonreligious identities. In addition, I explore the variety of ways in which

Occasional Religious Practice. Sarah Kathleen Johnson, Oxford University Press.
© Oxford University Press 2025. DOI: 10.1093/9780197806579.003.0004

occasional practitioners understand these identities. This analysis provides a more complete picture of who is participating in occasional religious practices in the Anglican tradition in Toronto.

Anglican

It is unsurprising that many participants in Anglican baptisms and funerals identify as Anglican. However, there are many different ways to identify as Anglican. For some, religious background, current routine practice, and religious beliefs all align with the Anglican tradition. One routine practitioner in the Anglican tradition describes her husband, who also practices routinely, as "100% Anglican":

> I: It sounds like your husband would identify as Anglican.
> R: Absolutely, 100%. He grew up Anglican, he was raised Anglican, baptized Anglican. So he's Anglican. 100% Anglican.

An elderly woman, who practiced routinely for many years until old age became a barrier, describes her lasting Anglican identity:

> I was brought up and raised as Anglican ever since I was a little girl. My dad was a very Christian man and he raised us all as Anglicans. And I have gone to other churches just to visit, but my home church is Anglican.

These "100% Anglicans" are relatively rare. Even those who name an enduring connection to the Anglican tradition may not practice routinely. Some may even practice in a different tradition, such as the following lifelong Anglican who routinely attends a United Church of Canada congregation where his wife sings in the choir:

> I: How would you describe your religious identity at this point?
> R: I'll be Church of England till I die. [Laughs]
> I: Do you have English heritage?
> R: Yes. And it's interesting, a friend of mine over here is from ... Yorkshire which is where my family, my mother's family, is from, which is kind of interesting. And he brought me a DVD of the church [there]. . . . I realized that that was probably my family's church in England.

In short, strong claims to Anglican identity do not necessarily align with routine practice in the Anglican tradition.

Description of a connection to Anglican identity due to *cultural heritage or family background* is common among occasional practitioners:

> I would identify as Anglican simply because of my heritage.

> For me there's a strong component of culture and heritage. The fact that my grandparents and my mom are Anglican, I feel that it's kind of been passed down on me.... The culture, the heritage, the fact that it's passed down on to you, you feel part of this church from a very young age. Your grandparents were part of it. My grandparents are buried there. To be honest, I never considered a different one. I don't think I ever had a reason to.

> I was reaching out to Anglican [churches about baptism] because that's how I was raised, that's what my family is, and that's the beliefs that I fit more with. So I was going primarily for Anglican along with the fact that my husband was baptized there, so we just felt we were more comfortable with it.

The power of deep cultural or familial connection to a religious tradition should not be underestimated. Experiences of religion as ascribed rather than chosen are valid, although they may go against the grain of modern individualistic urban culture. Those who identify as Anglican by heritage in Toronto may be among Wilkins-Laflamme's "cultural believers" or have points of connection with Day's "nominal" and Jakelic's "collectivistic" ways of relating to religion in Europe, with the significant difference that the Anglican tradition is not now and has never been the dominant religion in the region.[1]

In contrast to those who are Anglican by heritage, some are Anglican by *choice*, meaning they decided to identify as Anglican at some point in their adult lives despite coming from a different religious or nonreligious background. Of note, choosing to become Anglican does not necessarily correspond with routine religious practice; those who are Anglican by choice are often occasional practitioners. One lifelong Anglican by heritage describes

---

[1] Wilkins-Laflamme, *Religion, Spirituality and Secularity*; Day, *Believing in Belonging*; Jakelic, *Collectivistic Religions*.

how her husband's choice to become Anglican by adult baptism amplifies his sense of connection to the Anglican tradition:

> I: How would you describe your religious identity or answer a survey question?
> R: It would be Anglican most likely. If it just said Christian, I would choose Christian. But I would say Anglican.
> I: Do you have a sense for how your husband would answer?
> R: Anglican. Especially for him, because it's something that he came into later. He's really proud to be a part of the Anglican church. Like he feels a huge connection. I know that's his choice.

A younger woman with a multifaceted religious background articulates how she relates to these religious identities now, with Anglican Christianity emerging as primary:

> I: In terms of how you would name your own identity today, like on a survey question, would you consider yourself Anglican? Or Christian? Or Orthodox?
> R: Christian. Definitely not Orthodox. Definitely not Orthodox.
> I: Would you say Catholic?
> R: I'm baptized Catholic so, I would say Catholic, only because I'm baptized Catholic. Not because I believe in the practice of Catholicism. I would say definitely Christian. Christian Anglican but baptized Catholic.

Other former Catholics practicing in the Anglican tradition describe a similar tension between their religious background and current occasional practice, such as this Italian Catholic mother who baptized her child at a local Anglican church:

> I: How would you describe your religious identity being raised Roman Catholic attending an Anglican Church now?
> R: I think I'm making the transition to be full Anglican. I associate myself with that church, with being Anglican. I think because the practices and the way that the church is structured are a little bit different that it's taking a little bit to get used to the structure of it. The mass is pretty well the same, but I think the structure of how the priests work is a little bit

different, and then again with the belief system. So that's something I'm still exploring.

In this case, more routine participation is part of exploring Anglican identity; in many cases it is not.

Numerous participants claim *Anglican identity without routine practice*. This is one of the more common identity statements among occasional practitioners who initiate Anglican baptisms and funerals:

> I'd say I'm Anglican, and I am. I just don't go to church that often.

> ·I mean for me, like I always considered myself Anglican. Like if someone asked me what religion I was, I would say Anglican. I'm not actively religious and I'm not attending church every Sunday.

> I am not a practicing Anglican. I don't know. I'm an Anglican but I do not attend church whatsoever.

> I'm Anglican so you know, and I don't attend church as frequently as I should.

Especially for those who do not practice routinely, occasional practices such as holidays and life transitions are a key marker of Anglican identity:

> I would just say I'm Anglican. That's what I was baptized as. That's what I was married as. That's what I am confirmed as. An Anglican. I don't see changing any of that.... I'm comfortable being an Anglican.

> I: Yes. Would you identify as Anglican yourself?
> R: Yes. Yeah. I was confirmed into the church. I was baptized in the church. Confirmed in the church. Yeah. I mean there's no reason to change that.

While participants do not consider routine practice to be essential for maintaining an Anglican religious identity, they do find occasional practices to be important for claiming ongoing affiliation.

Christian

Identifying as "Christian" also carries multiple meanings. Clarke and Macdonald's quantitative analysis of why respondents to the Canadian Census select the category "Christian not included elsewhere" when a vast array of more specific options are available, points to three distinct ways this category operates: it is used by a small number of conservative Protestants; it is a default identification for white Canadians; and it is a primary identification for racialized Canadians.[2] These patterns have echoes in this qualitative analysis.

First, Clarke and Macdonald acknowledge that some *conservative Protestants* may select this identification for theological reasons, yet they argue persuasively that this represents only a small proportion of the total.[3] Two participants in Anglican baptisms who could be called evangelical do indeed identify as Christian in this way:

> I would just say a Christian, or a believer in Jesus.
>
> I: You mentioned "Bible believing" a bit earlier. Could you say a bit more about what that means for you?
> R: When I was younger, evangelical meant someone who wanted to live biblically. I never want to say evangelical now because I don't want to be confused with the far, far right because I think it's got all mixed up with white supremacy and just all sorts of terrible issues. So I'm in the middle of the road trying to do the best I can.... So you can probably tell I'm anti-Trump.... So personally, I will not be called evangelical anymore. I'm a committed Christian. That's my new title for myself.
> I: That's helpful. And would you also identify as Methodist, or is that secondary to being a committed Christian?
> R: Christian always comes first. Protestant denomination comes second.

Most of the respondents who identify primarily as Christian appear more aligned with Clarke and Macdonald's other categories.

Second, according to Clarke and Macdonald, Christian appears to function as "*a default or attenuated identification*" for white Canadians; for example, "one might claim one were Christian, rather than Muslim or Jew, without indicating a strong attachment to the Christian religion."[4] This use of Christian is especially common among younger Canadians in big cities.[5] Some participants in baptisms and funerals may identify as Christian as this kind of default:

---

[2] Clarke and Macdonald, *Leaving Christianity*, 173–183.
[3] Clarke and Macdonald, *Leaving Christianity*, 178, 186–187.
[4] Clarke and Macdonald, *Leaving Christianity*, 180.
[5] Clarke and Macdonald, *Leaving Christianity*, 183.

I: How would you describe your own religious identity? If you were to imagine answering a survey question, for example.

R: I don't think I could really describe it.

I: Some of the options that might be there would be things like nonreligious, or spiritual but not religious, Christian, culturally Christian, Catholic, Anglican. Those are kinds of categories. Do any of those seem like they might kind of fit?

R: It would probably be a mix of a few of them because I'm not one or the other.

I: What group of options might you choose? They are not at all exclusive categories. You could choose many.

R: Probably spiritual and Christian.

"Protestant" may function in a similar way, especially in contexts that are dominantly Roman Catholic:

[My husband] always—like the whole family they always said they are Protestants—always they identified as being Protestant. . . . They always saw themselves as part of that religion. . . . But I would say he's less, maybe a little bit less religious.

Some participants also use "Christian" (meaning Protestant) and "Catholic" as their primary categories for distinguishing different expressions of Christianity. For young, white, urban Canadians, claiming Christian identity is a way to point to a European heritage and a specifically non-Catholic Christian background in a highly pluralistic context in which many world religions are present and Roman Catholics are the largest Christian group.

Third, according to Clarke and Macdonald, Christian may serve as "*a category of primary identification*" for racialized Canadians.[6] This pattern is also present among participants in this research, including a woman who immigrated from East Asia to Canada, where she converted to Christianity and was baptized in the Anglican church:

I: So at this point how would you describe your religious identity if you were to answer a survey question?

---

[6] Clarke and Macdonald, *Leaving Christianity*, 180.

> R: Religious identity? I don't understand. What do you mean by religious identity?
> I: For example, would you identify as Christian or Anglican or something else?
> R: Oh, I think Christian. I don't think Anglican church brings any emphasis on the Anglican side nowadays. Whatever—there is only to be a Christian.

Another first-generation Canadian from East Asia, who was raised in the Christian tradition and who baptized her child in the Anglican church, likewise struggled to find language for her religious identity before settling on Christian for herself and her husband, who is a second-generation Canadian from a different country in East Asia:

> I: What would be some of the words that you would use to describe your religious identity today, if you were to imagine a survey question?
> R: Yeah, I don't know. I don't have words to put it.
> I: Examples would be things like Christian, a specific denomination, spiritual, agnostic, these kinds of terms.
> R: Oh, okay, Christian.
> I: And do you have a sense for how your husband would describe his religious identity?
> R: Christian.

A man born in Jamaica, who has spent his adult life in Canada and has had connections to Anglican congregations in two cities, describes himself simply as "spiritual and Christian." As Clarke and Macdonald note, "a member of a visible minority in Canada who is a Christian but not a Roman Catholic is most likely to respond simply as 'Christian' on the census."[7] They observe that this is true even among those from regions with strong ethnic denominational ties, such as Korean Presbyterians and Chinese Baptists. The two patterns Clarke and Macdonald extract from the census data, as well as the tendency for conservative Protestants to identify as Christian, are present in this series of qualitative interviews. "Christian" does not mean the same thing to all who claim this identity.

---

[7] Clarke and Macdonald, *Leaving Christianity*, 190.

Roman Catholic and Other Christian Traditions

The Roman Catholic tradition features prominently in this ethnographic study of Anglican occasional practice. There are many parallels between how participants describe Catholic and Anglican identity, although these patterns are often expressed with greater intensity in relation to Catholicism.

There are a couple of participants who could be considered "*100% Catholic*" in terms of this identity reflecting their religious background, beliefs, and present routine practice. However, in part because this research is based in the Anglican tradition, more participants have a complicated relationship with Catholicism. For example, one younger mother routinely practices in both the Catholic and Anglican traditions and identifies to some extent with each:

> It's easier for me to say I'm Catholic than for me to say I'm Anglican, even though I attend the Anglican Church. But I mean, if anyone asks me, "What's your religion?" I quickly say, "Catholic" before I—but I attend Anglican Church now, so I'll say I'm Anglican now. But when I go to the Catholic Church, it's like I'm at home, like I'm back to my roots.

For this participant, identifying as both Anglican and Catholic is linked to current identity and practice.

Catholic identity is often closely tied to *heritage*, whether Italian, Polish, Irish, Filipino, or another cultural background. The fusion of religion and ethnicity makes it particularly difficult for participants to separate themselves from Catholic identity, as one participant vividly describes in the case of her Irish Catholic husband who is skeptical about religion:

> It is an interesting thing with the Catholic church. On one hand, there is skepticism and distrust. On the other hand, it is part of who you are. And so, it has quite a big hold on its constituents because it's part of their identity. It's like family, you know, you have a sister you may not like, right? You may not get along with them and you may not like them, but it's still blood. And so when you're brought up in the Catholic church, I think it's very similar, right? Like you have this, it's part of who you are as your identity, and you can't really cut it out. But at the same time, there are parts of it that you maybe are less fond of.

This may in part be why many participants identify as *non-practicing Catholics*. A key marker of being "lapsed" is not participating routinely in prescribed practices, even if other values and beliefs remain important:

> I would say lapsed Catholic. I guess is the way you can put it. I hope that like the values—and this isn't just Catholic—I hope I have strong values, like treating people well and helping out if you can. I do have those core beliefs. I just don't go to church. . . . I think I'm a lapsed Catholic. I just don't go to church. I think if I was a devout Catholic, I would have to go to church. . . . I can't be like half a hockey player—if I won't play offense, or if I don't play defense. I do one part of it, but I don't do the other part, which I think is getting more and more common in our society to be honest with you.

> I'm religious, but I wouldn't say I follow like Roman Catholicism, but I have faith and stuff like that, my husband not as much. . . . If someone asks me, I normally say, "I'm raised Catholic, but I don't practice, I'm not a practicing Catholic." If someone says like, "Are you Christian?" I'd probably be like, "I'm more Christian than I am Catholic." Yeah, I mostly say "I'm raised Catholic, but I don't practice it."

> My husband is also Catholic, and I would say we are now probably lapsed Catholics because we haven't been to mass very frequently.

The relationship between Roman Catholicism and occasional practice in the Anglican tradition is explored more extensively in Chapter 7.

Participants mentioned other Christian traditions as well: several Orthodox traditions, which are described as having strong ethnic ties; various other Protestant traditions, such as Lutherans, Presbyterians, and the United Church of Canada; and charismatic and independent churches. Participants use these categories to name their own religious backgrounds and experiences and to describe those they know who identify with these traditions.

Non-Christian Religious Traditions

Those who identify with non-Christian religious traditions may occasionally participate in Anglican practices. Although none of the participants in this research identified with a non-Christian religious tradition at the time of the interview, several were raised in homes with one Christian parent and one parent who was Jewish, Muslim, or Buddhist. Many describe family members and friends who identify with a range of religious traditions attending Anglican baptisms and funerals:

> [My friend] had some neighbors who I think were Muslim and I noticed that they didn't go up [for communion]. They were sitting at the back.

> [My father's] old secretary who worked for him like years ago, [name], who I believe is Muslim, was also there and like we hadn't seen her in years. It was so nice to see her.

> There were well, a couple of people there were Jewish.

> We also have some Jewish family members. So [my husband's uncle] was there, he will be [my daughter's] great uncle and he just loved it.

> I've been with my husband and he's Hindu. [The baptism of my granddaughter] was just an occasion for him. He's not practicing, he doesn't come with me to church or anything, so he's not disrespectful, but I don't think he can make a connection ... because he's Hindu. I've attended lots of Hindu religious functions from his side of the family.

Participants likewise describe attending life transition events in other traditions to support their friends and family and see this as an opportunity for learning, mutual support, and potential spiritual connection:

> Everybody in my family is really Anglican or Catholic. And the ones that are Catholic don't go to church. So you know, it's all—we're not particularly diverse that way. But when we've had these like weddings, baptisms, the funeral, there were a bunch of people that were invited to these events that are not religious or from different religious communities that aren't Christian and that was interesting. But more within my friend group. Like we're a particularly diverse group of people where everybody is kind of from all over the place and of different religious backgrounds. And when it comes time for one of us to get married or there's—I mean, for those of us who do the baptism thing or whatever, like everybody is—or there's funerals or whatever, we all participate in everybody's everything. I've been to a couple Hindu weddings now, they're pretty cool. And I think the way that my group of friends and I kind of look at all of those things, is just a really neat experience to see what people of other backgrounds do to celebrate

those types of things. I think we've all just come from a place of interest and wanting to participate as much as we can and see what it's all about.

The presence of the Holy Spirit. I've experienced it at a friend's shiva, when all the men were downstairs praying and the women were upstairs sitting around the table. It was so foreign to me, foreign to her, foreign to all of us, including her. And we felt very connected. And I felt like it was the Spirit was there with us.... It was a kitchen, but a family kitchen. So, it was [a] big, big, big, big table. And lots of chairs. All of us sitting around. And lots of people walking around. But it just felt really—yeah, the feeling of being able to put your hands around each other. Yeah. And it was teachers. Yeah. So, there were Muslim and Hindu women there too. But it was a heartbreaking kind of death. And so, it was very powerful, that feeling of wanting to hold her up. And that's it. That breaks through.

At times, people who identify with non-Christian religions may be more than supportive observers. In several cases, participants describe those who identify with non-Christian religions as central actors in occasional Anglican practices. One participant describes a Jewish father participating in the Anglican baptism of his child:

My cousin baptized her two children at [name of parish] downtown. Her husband is Jewish and not a practicing Jew but feels very uncomfortable in a church. That was awkward. He stood—because the font was in a different part of the church, it's in a semi-circular room ... it's at the side ... but he was standing outside of the door peeking in.

Another describes a close friend who is Hindu serving as the maid of honor at her Anglican wedding, and as the godmother for her child, although she was not able to attend the baptism itself:

We have two sets of godparents, my good friend, my best friend—I was maid of honor at her wedding, she was maid of honor at mine—her name is Ruby.... Her family is Hindu, so she doesn't really know all that much about baptism. She was living in New York, so I didn't want to impose on her travel back. To be honest, I haven't even been in that many baptisms myself, so it wasn't like this big, big, big, big deal with some families where it would be like unheard of for the godparents not to be there. But for me, I don't like to impose, so it's really nice that the church gives you that certificate with their names and able to give that to them and send them pictures and stuff.

Maid of honor, while not a central role from a liturgical theological standpoint, is significant for participants, including a woman whose nonreligious friend with a Muslim background served in this capacity at her Anglican wedding:

> Like my maid of honor in my wedding, well, she's not really religious at all. Traditionally, she's Muslim. She was my maid of honor, like no one noticed, no one cared.

In a city as culturally and religiously diverse as Toronto, it is unsurprising yet encouraging that people come together across religious traditions to mark important occasions in the lives of their family members and friends. These events also include many participants who do not identify with any religious tradition.

Spiritual (But Not Religious?)

"Spiritual" is a common response when I ask participants about religious identity, both among those who identify with a religious tradition (as in several examples above) and those who do not. As with each of these categories, participants employ the term in a range of different ways.

Some identify as spiritual to emphasize a *sense of spiritual connection* in their lives. For example, I was surprised when one participant identified as "spiritual but not religious" while frequently referencing a robust personal relationship with God and commitment to the teachings of Jesus. She primarily uses the term to express strong personal faith while acknowledging that she does not participate routinely in organized religion:

> I'm probably spiritual but not religious. But if I'm understanding it, I think in terms of religious as being this notion of the ritualistic aspect of religion. Sort of, you're only a good Christian if you're attending church every week. And that's not how I view things. . . . I don't think of God only at times where I'm suffering or struggling or in times where things are great. I think of God routinely. And just sometimes, when things happen, I do ask him— in those prayers, those conversations with God—I'm just like, help me to understand what you're trying to teach me. There's a lot of things that I see

in my life that I know are part of God's plans and his timing—yeah, I firmly believe.

For another younger woman, identifying as "spiritual but not religious" also reflects a lack of routine public practice, although this is not accompanied by a strong personal relationship with traditional Christian understanding of God, but instead a recognition that "there is more to life than meets the eye":

> So [my husband] and I are both spiritual and when it comes to religion, it's an important piece, but it's also not like we all go to church every Sunday. But we do on holidays. I guess some people can think that's positive or negative when you just go on ceremonial events and stuff.

An older woman, who is a lifelong Anglican and currently practices incidentally, describes spirituality found at a distance from established religious tradition, especially in nature:

> I think we are spiritual people. We are convinced there's a higher energy, if you want to call it that way. That we know that there is something more than our physical world. But I wouldn't say that we are really religious to the point of doing Bible study. That would be interesting. But we certainly are not people that would point at something in the Bible and say: this is what you have to do. And we're a little more practical or broad-minded, or I'd say, take the good out of it and leave the bad, right? ... I'm just so close to nature. ... Even here in the backyard, just lay on the ground and look up the sky and look at the stars and just thank God for this beautiful world. That's not a religion, but that is spiritual, that's your spirit being connected to this universe to where we are.... That's not a religion, but that is spiritual.

As in this case, some participants identify as spiritual in order to point to participation in *alternative spiritual practices*:

> I'm a little bit more unsure about where my beliefs kind of lie. It was hard for me to say that I'm religious. I really find myself a little more spiritual, I think. That's the way that I would describe it. My mom and I, we consider ourselves more spiritual in other ways. We do tarot cards and we go and see mediums and things. We have kind of connections that way with our spirituality. And I think it's parallel to religion. Not really the same thing. But

I think that's really where we find our comfort.... I would find myself more in the spiritual side of the spectrum.

Practices that participants identify as spiritual include meditation, yoga, martial arts, gratitude practices, tarot cards, dream interpretation, listening to music, spending time in nature, deer hunting, and even a commute, driving to and from work.

Although some identify as spiritual to indicate that they value spiritual experiences and practices, others identify as "spiritual but not religious" to describe *nonreligious but not anti-religious* identity, especially when it comes to occasional practice:

[My husband] would identify as probably nonreligious, sure. . . . Nonreligious but I wouldn't suggest that he's an atheist. He's not quite, but yeah.... So yes, I guess somewhat spiritual, but nonreligious.

[My cousin] is more I think what she would describe—I think she would describe herself probably as agnostic. I don't think she would describe herself as atheist. Like she definitely has a spiritual side to her, but it's also definitely not a traditionally Christian one, if that makes any sense. Same thing with my uncle, he's not religious at all. There's plenty of people in my family that grew up going to church and don't have the particular religious connection. But I don't think any of them have a problem with being in a church for any of those ceremonies or participating in any of those things.

The way some use the term spiritual to distance themselves or their family members from atheism points to the nuanced ways in which participants dance around atheist and agnostic identity.

Atheist or Agnostic

Atheism, disbelief in the existence of God, and agnosticism, uncertainty about the existence of God or belief that one cannot know about the existence of God, are identities discussed by various participants in this study. One of the challenges of these identity categories is that they speak to matters of belief rather than tradition or practice, which makes it possible for multiple seemingly inconsistent layers to coexist. For example, one participant identifies as agnostic, with a Roman Catholic background, and participates occasionally in Anglican practices. Another identifies as atheist, and has practiced routinely in the United Church, and occasionally in the Anglican tradition. One participant describes her brother as a "lapsed atheist" meaning that "He says he's an atheist, but then he's the first person to want to go to church on Sunday morning, so figure that out!" Categories of belief and practice overlap in complicated ways. The focus here remains on how participants self-identify in relation to religion.

Only one participant openly identifies as *atheist* when prompted. He is a good example of Manning's "philosophically secularist" category of nonreligion:[8]

> I: How would you describe your religious identity? If you were to imagine like a survey question.
> R: None.
> I: So nonreligious.... Would you also identify as atheist?
> R: Yeah. I mean that's the word for me. I believe fully that we are—it's not even belief. From what I can see there is no evidence to suggest that there is a higher power in the world. We are here. We are on our own. And I choose to put my faith in myself and other human beings. That's just the logic of it.

The hesitation around claiming atheist identity, even by those whose "logic" clearly points in this direction, may be the result of awareness of the potential for anti-atheist bias and discrimination, or experiences of it in their social circles.[9] One younger participant describes how this plays out in her Italian Catholic extended family and progressive friendship network:

> [My husband would] probably say he's atheist. But he doesn't really use that word because it makes people upset. Even like me, I'm like "no." He sometimes will be more agnostic—maybe there's something there, but I don't know whether or not you're going to search for it. But I think deep down he would probably say atheist. Probably around me or his mom, who's like "How did you become an atheist?" It's just that the words I think are just so intense. Even if I was going around being like, "I'm Catholic. I practice Catholicism." I'm sure there'd be reaction. People would be like, "Aren't you

---

[8] Manning, *Losing Our Religion*, 41–43.
[9] Thiessen and Wilkins-Laflamme, *None of the Above*, 150–152.

a feminist?" That's why I think maybe spiritual would probably be the word I would use.

Two participants show their personal reluctance to be categorized as atheists, despite other statements that point in this direction. One woman, who participates in religious practices only in association with the life transitions of others, resists all religious labels:

I: How would you describe your religious identity? Nonreligious or atheist or agnostic or something else? Imagine a survey question.
R: I don't like being labeled [laughter].
I: Or if you...
R: I know. You want some kind of data, right? You need data. What is a— agnostic is somebody who...?
I: Doesn't know. You either can't know or don't know about God.
R: Probably more closer leaning to that than atheist. Because I like to think of the concept of God as being quite broad and open. I don't think about the concept of God as being like this guy, right? So, I like to think that the concept of God is—can be just about anything that helps people.... And no, we don't need this authoritarian figure, if I can describe the Anglican God that way. Yeah. I kind of resist that idea. So, I don't need to define—I guess I don't need to define for myself what it is. It's just, trying to be a good person and that kind of thing. I know you don't really—yeah, I don't want to be labeled. Don't want to be labeled.

A man who identified himself as a "nonbeliever" earlier in the interview interjects and reacts defensively when I repeat this term later in the conversation:

I: Yes. As someone who's agnostic or a nonbeliever, how do you—
R: Nonbeliever. I mean, I don't take—I mean nonbeliever is a word in Christian theology, I'm a nonbeliever, but I am—I hope that there is a higher being, but I don't believe in any particular theology surrounding that I guess is where I would put myself.
I: Are there other ways that you would describe your spiritual or religious or nonreligious identity?
R: No, I guess, I don't know. I guess perhaps it's my training as a scientist that makes faith a difficult—it's not a concept with which I am as

> comfortable as belief. And so, I'm fine in my hope that there is something beyond what we can observe or what we currently can observe. But I have trouble with the literal interpretation of most Christian theology in that it is not backed up by our observation of the real world. I guess I do have problems with certain theologies that require literal understanding of teachings that are contrary to our understanding of our scientific understanding of the world. . . . Yeah, so that's—I guess why I don't ascribe to any particular faith. I hope that there is something beyond what we can observe, and it seems like there should be. I guess that is faith, right? Believing that there's something beyond what you can observe. Yeah, so I guess that's where I stand.

With many respondents, there was this consistent reluctance to identify with atheism or disbelief in God.

As these participants suggest, *agnosticism* appears to be a far more comfortable identity to claim than atheism. Another participant, a younger mother with a Roman Catholic background who is a life transition occasional practitioner, also openly identifies as agnostic:

> If anything, I'm probably agnostic. There's something, I don't know what it is. The teachings I grew up with and the church as it is today, the Roman Catholic Church as it is today, a lot of it I don't agree with. And that's just growing up in the world, and learning to think for myself, and certain things don't jive, and I don't understand it, and I don't agree with it. That's not how I want to identify anymore. But I still believe there's something, so you just respect that something.

Although only a few participants primarily identify as agnostic, many speak about God or "something more" in ways that point toward uncertainty and unknowability. Chapter 10 addresses how occasional religious practitioners with a range of religious identities talk about God.

Other Ways of Being Nonreligious

Nonreligion is an internally diverse category. Many of those above who identify as spiritual, agnostic, and atheist would also be considered nonreligious. However, those who identify using these categories are more likely to have spent time reflecting on religion and arriving at a "philosophically secular" position, to use Manning's terminology, or a decision to identify as "spiritual but not religious."[10] Nonreligion also includes people who would not describe themselves as spiritual, agnostic, or atheist, especially those who are more "indifferent" toward religion, those who, as Manning describes, "do not so much reject religion as ignore it."[11] At times, participants describe themselves and their family members as *indifferent* toward religion:

> My brother I don't think cares either way, because he's so nonreligious. He just—like my brother stopped going to church as soon as my parents would let him stop going to church.

> But the boys are not interested. My grandsons are not interested.

> [My mother] was very private about her religion. She never talked about it directly with my brother and I. It wasn't like she was being secretive. She understood that we weren't particularly interested, if that's the right word? I don't know what the right word is. And I mean, I can't really speak for my brother. But for me, she knew that I was not—what's the right word? That it didn't mean a lot for me. And it wasn't something that was significant for me. And I didn't relate to it.

However, participants are eager to make it clear that being nonreligious does not prevent their family members from being good people or participating in religious practices:

> My daughter's godmother is not religious at all. But she's just a really, really good person.

> My husband, even though he's not religious, we go as a family to do communion when we do go to church.

> R: [My godson] knows he was baptized, yeah, he was. He was baptized in—I can't remember what church. I mean that's ... coming up on like 30 to 33 years ago. But yeah, he was, even though his family, they're totally nonreligious. So that's interesting that they're nonreligious yet I think all their kids were baptized.

---

[10] Manning, *Losing Our Religion*, 41.
[11] Manning, *Losing Our Religion*, 44.

I: Do you have a sense for why that was important for them?
R: I've never asked them, and I'm going to now. But yeah, they were all baptized. And when they were little we used to—some of their aunts we would all go to church on Christmas or something. But no, they're very nonreligious. Yeah, very secular. That's a better word.

Indifferent nonreligion is often associated with an easy-going attitude toward religious practices. While those who are indifferent are unlikely to initiate religious practices, they are open to casual participation on certain occasions.

Being "Not Very Religious"

A repeated refrain in interviewers is the claim that participants are not very religious: "we're not overly religious"; "we're not a super religious family"; "religion does play a role, even if it is a minor role"; "you're talking to very not super religious people"; "I'm religious but not to the extent that everything is followed to a 'T'"; "not heavy duty." Participants with very different relationships with religion—people who self-identify with all of the possibilities outlined above—describe themselves as "not very religious."

There are some occasional practitioners who point to *the occasional nature of their practice* as their reason for identifying as not very religious:

We're not overly religious. We do celebrate Christmas. We celebrate Easter. I was baptized. [My husband] was baptized.

Many would likely agree with this self-assessment, including scholars of religion such as Bibby and Thiessen, who consider occasional practice a mark of "low" or "marginal" religion.

However, more routine practitioners also describe themselves as not very religious. At times, they appear to do so to *differentiate themselves from conservative Christianity*:

I try to practice being kind to others. But I'm not like a Southern Christian in the States. It's almost fanatical.... I don't see that as being helpful. Rather than forcing somebody to be Christian, I think you should probably practice Christianity by showing kindness to others and helping others wherever possible. But you don't have to be a Bible thumper. But it doesn't mean to say that you're not religious.

I: I was hearing earlier a bit of hesitation with identifying as being too religious.
R: Well, it's odd. It's odd because when people know how involved we are with the church, they think I know the Bible inside and out. I don't. So how do you describe yourself as religious? To me it's the formal religion of Bible study and quoting the Bible and that is not us. That to me is formal religion. I'm just lucky that I enjoy the church.

Such routine practitioners minimize their connection to religion to separate themselves from a certain type of religion and the beliefs and behaviors of its adherents.

In other cases, it appears to be the *motivations* for religious practice that prompt participants to claim they are not very religious. One man, who at the time of the interview attends routinely and has served in numerous leadership positions in the church, develops an impromptu scale when I ask about his deceased father's religious identity:

Probably on the scale of religious to not religious, with religious as a ten, you know, [my father was] maybe a two or three. It's just not something that I feel was ever really terribly important to him.

He then applies the same scale to himself and, as one of the most routine practitioners in this research, someone whom many would consider close to "100% Anglican," gives himself as a six out of ten:

R: My religious identity, I've kind of said it, right? I'm not about the prayers. I'm kind of about the experience, if you will. I very much like the people and that's really the most important thing to me is the church family. So my dad was a two. I don't know, maybe I'm a six. But I'm not hung up on all the churchy stuff....
I: What makes something churchy?
R: Well, that's a good question. I don't know if I can really answer that. You know, if you read the church newsletter, [the priest] will always have a spiel in there. It'll be very churchy because she'll quote scripture and she'll have a little prayer in there and talk a lot about Jesus and relate that to things. That's very churchy, right? So if I'm writing a letter I'm probably not going to put a prayer in it, I'm not going to talk about how Jesus relates to what I'm trying to say.

For this participant, community is not considered a "churchy" enough motivation for religious practice. Other participants also describe social motivations, such as community belonging or social expectations, as the reason why they consider themselves or others not very religious, as is the case with this woman in her fifties:

> I don't think we were a super religious family. It was more what you did. Do you know what I mean? It wasn't like connected to these deep spiritual reasons or anything. It was just part of life and what people did and part of the—I guess, community, like expectations of what people did of a certain age.... It's sort of like different levels of religiousness. So, like, some people are—they do it, they participate. But they're not really into the whole—I'm searching for a word. It's like they're not going to Bible study and trying to delve into the deep meaning of everything. And it's more like they're there for the people. They're there for the community. They're there for the basic sort of ideas behind the religion and the basic concepts. But they're not going to push anything on anybody else. And they're not—so I would say that's sort of more how my parents were. At least that's my impression. Nothing's too heavy duty, right? Yeah.

For both routine and occasional practitioners, participating in religious practices because of family relationships is associated with participants considering themselves not very religious:

> We're not a super religious family, Anglican family. But [baptism is] just one of the milestone events that a lot of my family either (a) believe in, or (b) insist on having. So just by sheer nature of tradition and myself being baptized, I broached the topic with [my husband], and he's very receptive to those things, even though his family is not very religious and doesn't follow any particular religion.

Participants who have a taken-for-granted religious background at times present this as a reason for considering themselves not very religious:

> I think I do have a bit of religion because I grew up with it, not heavy duty, but it's just, it was there for me.

> I guess like I was never super religious, it was just like part of everyday life.

Some describe themselves as not very religious because they assume practices have certain meanings for others, meanings that they do not share:

> I'm not a very religious person and [the baptism] didn't mean the same thing to me as for somebody else going through that process.

However, as this analysis shows, it is very likely that others involved in the baptism process associate a diversity of meanings with the practice. In each of these examples, participants identify certain motivations for occasional, routine, and even intensive religious practice as inadequate for unequivocally identifying as religious. They perceive certain types of practitioners as more religious than others—and group themselves with the others.

Several dynamics may be at play in this resistance to identifying as religious. One possibility, which is reflected in the previous quotation, is the assumption that everyone else is committed to religion in a different way—that the others present are firm believers in God, who seek deep spiritual meaning in the Bible, attend church every Sunday, place religion at the center of their lives, and try to recruit others. At this point in the analysis, it is clear that this is simply not the case, especially when life transitions are celebrated. A culture of privacy around matters of faith may perpetuate these kinds of inaccurate assumptions, which may also be reinforced by the media.

A second possibility is that the dominant presence of certain forms of religion in the media and popular culture prompts those who practice in more progressive traditions to distance themselves from religion. Specifically, the dominance of the Roman Catholic tradition globally and in Canada, and the vocal nature of conservative American evangelicalism, may make participants in this research who are often socially progressive resist being associated with these expressions of religion and therefore any form of religion.

A third possibility, potentially related to the second, is a general negativity toward religion in Canadian society that makes participants understandably hesitant to associate themselves with it. The 2017 Angus Reid Institute poll shows that Canadians are more likely to view the word "religion" negatively (33 percent) than positively (25 percent) (Figure 3.1).[12] Although there is variation across the Angus Reid Institute spiritual spectrum, even 11 percent of the religiously committed understand the word "religion" to have a

---

[12] Angus Reid Institute, "A Spectrum of Spirituality."

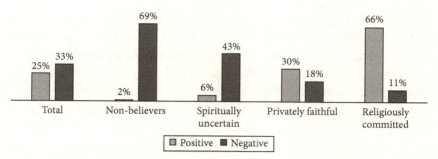

Figure 3.1 Percentage of Canadians who say the word "religion" has a positive or negative meaning.
Reproduced with permission from Angus Reid Institute. (2017). A Spectrum of Spirituality. https://angusreid.org/religion-in-canada-150/.

negative meaning. To claim to be religious in Canada in 2017 is not a good thing. Canadians have moved away from religion as a positive social norm. However, those who identify as "not very religious" are still claiming to be religious. In fact, being "not very religious" is an ordinary way to be religious in Canada today.

Recognizing the Diversity in the Room

Participants who claim each of the religious identities described here—and likely others—are present at Anglican baptisms and funerals, among other occasions for Christian worship. Occasional participants in Anglican practices in Toronto include those who identify as Anglican because of past and present belief and practice, cultural heritage or family background, or personal choice. Many participants claim Anglican identity apart from routine practice. Roman Catholics and those who affiliate with other expressions of Christianity who occasionally participate in Anglican practices understand these identities in a range of ways that parallel those who identify as Anglican. Some occasional practitioners identify simply as Christian, either as a default category among white Canadians, or as a primary category of identification among racialized Canadians. Conservative Protestants may identify as Christian as a theological statement. Some occasional practitioners identify with non-Christian religious traditions. In addition to occasional practitioners who identify as religious, there are those who claim a range of nonreligious identities. Occasional practitioners may identify as spiritual to indicate a sense of spiritual connection in their lives, to point to participation in alternative spiritual practices, or simply to suggest they are nonreligious but not anti-religious. They may also identify as atheist or agnostic or be indifferent to religion.

Attention to occasional religious practice reveals the eclectic mixture of participants who are present at Christian worship in the Anglican tradition in Toronto. There is tremendous diversity in religious identity, belief, and practice represented in the room. In addition, those who claim certain religious or nonreligious identities understand and live into these categories in a wide range of ways. Furthermore, although baptisms and funerals were the starting point for this series of interviews, these conversations reveal that participants with diverse identities are also present occasionally at routine liturgies. Careful attention to who is present for occasional and routine religious practices and an awareness of the diversity of ways that they understand their identities dispel the notion that most participants in Christian worship are formally affiliated, fully believing, actively practicing, and morally compliant with a tradition. This is simply not the case for either occasional or routine practitioners. Instead, occasional Christian practices are gatherings amid difference and opportunities for dialogue through practice and mutual learning in contemporary urban contexts such as Toronto. It is with this recognition of who is in the room that we turn our attention to the range of meanings and motivations associated with occasional practice.

4
Why Practice Occasionally?

Milling around at a conference, I speak with colleagues, many of them clergy, about my research on occasional religious practice. When I mention interviews with occasional practitioners, one priest responds knowingly, "Ah, you want to ask them *why* they choose to baptize their children." Although I usually politely redirect this common reaction with a response like, "Yes, but I am especially interested in *how* they experience Christian worship on the occasions when they *are* there," something about the smugness behind this priest's comment prompts me to respond abruptly, "I never ask 'why.'" I go on to explain how this question is laden with unhelpful assumptions: that occasional practitioners must justify their choices in ways that differ from routine practitioners; that participants can or should be able to offer a rational, perhaps even theological, argument for their practice; and that the occasionality of their practice is irregular and in need of a defense. Participants in interviews hear "Why?" as an accusation rather than an invitation. Instead, I invite participants to "tell me the story" of the baptism or the funeral. And, if it does not come up naturally in the narrative, I may ask *how* they decided to baptize the child or mark the death with a Christian funeral. I never ask "why."

Although unhelpful in conversation with occasional practitioners, the question of why people practice occasionally is central for many routine and intensive practitioners. It is also an important research question for understanding occasional religious practice and occasional practitioners.

Types of Occasional Practitioners

Why do occasional practitioners participate in religious practices? What motivates occasional participation in religious practices? What do occasional practices mean to practitioners? These questions are interrelated. Having considered different types of occasional *practices*—holiday, life transition, crisis, and incidental—it is possible to consider different types

Occasional Religious Practice. Sarah Kathleen Johnson, Oxford University Press.
© Oxford University Press 2025. DOI: 10.1093/9780197806579.003.0005

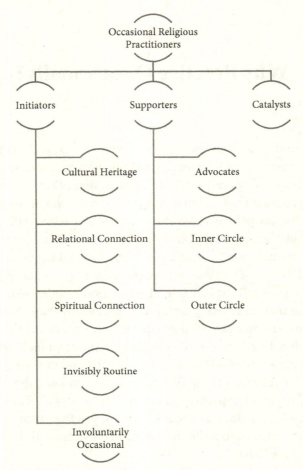

Figure 4.1 Types of occasional practitioners.

of occasional *practitioners*. The types of occasional practitioners in this taxonomy are associated with *situational roles and motivations*, not stable identity categories, although individuals may tend toward certain patterns of behavior (Figure 4.1).

There are two broad categories of occasional practitioners. The first is the *initiators*. These individuals bring about the practice: the mother who reaches out to congregations to arrange for a baptism, the son who plans his father's funeral at a local parish, the grandfather who decides the family is going to church together on Christmas Eve, or the lonely young woman who moves to a new city and stops by a Sunday service. The second category is the *supporters*. These individuals do not initiate the occasional practice but are happy to support it: a parent who stands by their partner in baptizing their child, an old family friend who attends a funeral, or a college student who goes to church with their family on Easter when they are home for the holidays. The line between initiator and supporter is sometimes blurry. There may be multiple initiators connected to a single event. Being a key initiator does not necessarily mean being the primary organizer and planner of the event, although these roles often align. Individuals may be initiators on some occasions and supporters on others.

One limitation of the initiator and supporter framework is that individuals at the center of baptisms and funerals—the infant and the deceased—do not fit tidily in this structure. They are not necessarily supporters, although the deceased may have advocated for and appreciated the approach that is taken, and the baptized child may later come to value their baptism. At the same time, they are not quite initiators; although the event would not take place without them, they cannot make the event take place. Therefore, these individuals can be understood as *catalysts* in that they—through the fact of their birth or death—precipitate the event without being directly involved in how it unfolds.

Initiators feature prominently among interview participants in this research because they are often the main point of contact for conversations about baptisms or funerals. Twenty-four of the forty-one interviews with participants are with initiators of the specific event in question. Those who are supporters in relation to the specific event may describe similar events on other occasions when they have been initiators. Likewise, initiators of these specific baptisms and funerals describe being supporters in other contexts. Drawing on the interviews, I outline five types of initiators and three types of supporters.

Initiators

I identify five types of initiators of occasional religious practice. These types are associated with the reasons why individuals and families participate in religious practices on these occasions, which is connected to what these events are meaning and doing for them. The first two types of occasional practitioners—cultural heritage and relational connection—center on collective motivation and belonging. The final three types of occasional practitioners—desire for spiritual connection, invisibly routine practitioners, and involuntarily occasional practitioners—are oriented toward individual decisions and experiences. Sometimes, practitioners clearly articulate these motivations. At other times, they occur in the background as conditions of possibility. Often these motivations occur in combination. While specific motivations may be more likely to be associated with baptism, marriage, funerals, or specific holidays or moments of crisis, the focus here is on what motivates occasional religious practice broadly.

Cultural Heritage

For some participants, occasional practice is closely tied to cultural heritage. As one would expect, these are many of the same individuals who associate their religious identity with their cultural heritage, as discussed in the previous chapter. There are important variations in how cultural heritage is connected to religious practice in the Anglican tradition, especially between for those with a longer history in Canada and ancestors from the British Isles, and those who immigrated more recently from elsewhere.

Some *white participants with British ancestry* connect occasional practice to cultural heritage in a diffuse manner. This may include an interest in the broader history of the tradition, as one woman describes:

> For me, I think, I'm just like my mother. I was baptized. I wanted [my children] to be baptized in the Anglican Church. I like its connection to England. My last name is [English last name]. We're so freaking English. The history of that is important. I used to be a history major, so we could talk about Reformation, if you'd like, and Henry VIII and his divorce, Edward VI and his Book of Common Prayer. I like the Anglican Church.

Local history may also be significant, as another participant observes in relation to sacred space:

> There's a lot of history in that building. A lot of local history. That church has been around for a very long time and there's plaques in there that mention people that used to live in [city], like quite famous people that attended

that church. I mean, for local history speaking, I guess.... And that's one of the things that I think I appreciate about going to church; is like that connection to something that's older than you and bigger than you.

Another participant describes religious practice in terms of participating in a broader Canadian religious culture received through the English cultural heritage of her family:

R: But I guess [religion] is part of [my husband's Eastern European Catholic] culture and sure I could say it's—I don't think it's Canadian, you know, in terms of Canada as having a culture—but I guess cultural for me too. So sometimes it's not always necessarily religious, that is personal belief, so much as that it's what you do.
I: Could you say more about how it's part of your culture or your family's culture?
R: Well, being raised in a Christian household, you know, we celebrate Christmas, we celebrate Easter. I don't have overly religious parents, but certainly they talked to us when we were kids and they told us the story of Jesus, and Mary, and you did get the outline of it. And again, when we were kids, we went to church, and we were baptized in church. And so you feel that when you grow up you carry it with you. Like, when I have children, I'll probably have them baptized too. But I couldn't make the connection outside of culturally.

In each of these examples of white participants, the cultural heritage of Christianity is more generalized and diffuse. While they mention family connections to the Anglican tradition, they describe them as something that fosters broader connections with culture, not something that sets them apart. Even in a majority minority city like Toronto, white British culture may be operating as an invisible norm.

Participants in this research who are *people of color with heritage in British colonies*, notably Jamaica, also connect cultural heritage and occasional practice. However, they do so in ways that indicate separation from as well as connection to broader Canadian Anglican culture, and they struggle with the history of colonialism. One first-generation Canadian from Jamaica describes how the connection between culture and religion shaped participation in the funeral of a Jamaican Canadian friend:

I think it's very much part of the immigrant experience.... It was very much about our feeling of ourselves as very religious people. Yeah. That we were comfortable in the church, as being part of a Christian context. I don't think that's my imagination. I think that's true. I've been to many English-Canadian funerals. And Italian and Portuguese weddings, funerals. A lot of the people don't know the prayers. They don't take part in the rituals. But at [my friend's] funeral, everybody knew what to say and what to do. We were all part of that orally. We were all part of that. It felt very comfortable and comforting.

A second-generation Canadian also describes a fusion of cultural identities, including Jamaican culture, shaping her participation in occasional Anglican practices, and how this is complicated by colonialism:

R: The connection I feel to my family in particular through that tradition—because all my mom's cousins or siblings, or all the generation before, so my grandmother and all her siblings, and then her mother and all her siblings—are all baptized in the Anglican church. It's just a way of keeping the tradition going. I would say, particularly as people from colonized countries, there isn't a whole lot of tradition that we can really say is ours because we're so diverse. Like within—my family is from Jamaica—within my family, we have . . . very large African roots, we have huge Scottish roots, and on my dad's side, we have Lebanese roots. That's everyone, the whole country is like that. No one is one of anything. It's very hard to say this is traditional because it's like, well, from where? Then when you're colonized, you always pick up the colonizers' traditions. It's the one thing that I know for sure is a tradition that connects to my family. My cousins who are just a little bit older than me, their kids were also baptized. It's just something to be a part of.

I: Framing it in terms of colonization, I wonder how that relates to the Anglican tradition being closely tried to Britain—there's a Union Jack hanging in [the church building]. How do you relate to that aspect of it?

R: I just feel like there's no way to negate it. You can't pretend. I would say the majority of Jamaican culture is British, right? Like you have teatime. People go to church wearing hats, right? They're very, very, very, very British.... Things are definitely not, I would say African, because that is lost. That's lost and then if you don't, I guess, participate in sort of the colonizers' traditions, then you have nothing, right? You'd be like totally lost. But if you choose something, that I would say for the most part has lifted up my family and been a source of like strength, then you have something.

While the ways that Jamaican Canadians experience the Anglican tradition in Canada is distinct, Jamaica and Canada, as two former British colonies, share certain similarities in language and culture.

Participants newer to Canada who are connected to communities who *speak languages other than English* point to the importance of ties between language, culture, religion, and occasional practice. One participant describes the significance of the Korean Presbyterian church in her upbringing:

> I was born in [small city in Ontario] when my parents had to migrate a couple of years before my older brother was born. And I'm careful to say that's it's Korean Presbyterian. I think it's just—that it was a church that was really for the Korean community. And when I was growing up, and we were up in [small city], the church plays a really important role for immigrants. It's a way for immigrants to feel a sense of belonging. Like, I've always felt that. And so, there's a sense of community that you develop within the Korean Presbyterian church. Not only with the church there, but with other Korean Presbyterian churches. It's very community based. There are multiple times a year that a lot of different Korean Presbyterian churches would get together.

She emphasizes that the entire church community expected to be invited to family occasions like weddings and funerals. Another participant describes the importance of language in uniting Spanish-speaking newcomers to Canada in church communities that cross denominational lines but are united by shared language and culture.

In some cases, ties between occasional practice and cultural heritage may be so strong that participants *return to their home country* for occasional practices. One younger mother who is an occasional practitioner in Canada returned to Bavaria, where she was raised, to baptize her child in the Roman Catholic tradition:

> The way I grew up, religion was always part of my everyday life. So I'm from a small town, there's like a thousand people living there now. When I was

growing up was like 600 people. So, everyone—it was just normal to go to the church. So, we always had religion classes in school—like it was always part of everyday life. I was an altar girl, I guess, you would say. And a lot of activities we had . . . during weekends or after school was like something that the church organized. I just loved it. There's like this feeling of community and for me it was important to have my daughter be part of that community as well. I guess I was never super religious, it was just like part of everyday life. And I think once I started moving, when I grew up, and the more I moved around, the less important it kind of became. But now that I have a daughter, I feel like I want to have the same upbringing for her that I had.

Another couple celebrated their wedding in Ireland, and the baptism of their children in Toronto, where one of them grew up, despite now living elsewhere in Canada:

My husband is of Irish descent. His family are Irish first-generation immigrants. So, his parents were born in Ireland and came to Canada in the late twenties. So, all of his family is there, we tried to get married in Ireland.

These examples are of first- and second-generation Canadians.

Even those who *have been in Canada for three or four generations* can maintain strong ties between culture and religion, as is the case for several Italian Catholic participants. One grandmother describes how her grandchild—the fourth generation of her family in Canada—will be the first one not immersed in Italian Catholic culture but who instead has "other grandparents" who do not understand these traditions, including giving gold jewelry on the occasion of baptism:

R: My parents were born in Sicily. My husband's parents were born in Sicily. Their parents did this for their grandchildren. My in-laws did it for my children. I didn't think twice about having to do it for my grandchildren because I've just seen it done over and over and over with all my nieces and nephews, my brother and sisters. It is our tradition. I grew up with it. It's not something I even really thought about. It just happened.

I: For so many generations too. I can see why it would just be what you do on this occasion.

R: Right. You understand. It's lovely to be brought up in a big family where both sides do the same thing. You're proud of being so comfortable. My parents were Sicilian. Then my husband that I married, his parents were Sicilian. We have the same tradition. I didn't have to learn anything new. It just was so comfortable. [My grandson] will understand our tradition of why we gave him the gold to carry the cross close to his heart, how we got it when we were young, so we believe that he should get it. Now his other grandparents didn't even understand why we were giving gold. They didn't give any gold. He's going to learn something new, which, when I was growing up, I didn't learn because everybody was doing it. I just took it for granted that's the way everybody did it.

A younger mother with Italian Catholic background also describes a close connection between cultural heritage and occasional practice in her family:

R: I'd say we are religious, but it's more the cultural and traditions that keep the family together. Like we celebrate Good Friday, we celebrate Easter, as a way to come together.... It's more cultural for us, I guess. We are both Catholics and we're both Italian, so we use religion. Those religious holidays as a family and coming together, pray before we eat and that's about it. I think baptism is kind of similar to a cultural thing in our family....

I: Are there other practices that are part of that cultural Christianity or Catholicism in your family?

R: I would say besides like the major holidays, like Easter, Good Friday we have like a feast of a fish.... Christmas just generally, I guess come together, have a big dinner.... We do baptism.... We do communion and confirmation.

I: Do you have a sense for why those particular moments are still significant or are really important culturally?

R: I think in today's day and age, everyone's so busy and caught up in their own life that—if you take those things away—you got to make time to see each other, just bringing the family together. Over the years, my mom's side, my grandfather passed away, he would always do those things. It's like you keep them going, almost like history and legacy of other people in the family, and just to bring everyone together.... If you lose those traditions, especially when I feel like young people in my world are getting more disconnected from religion, you would just lose it. I can feel we already lost so much from going to church when we were little on these days to not anymore, then you take away this. It'll just end up everyone all by themselves, everyone in their own little corners.

This participant also points to the importance of relationships, in this case her grandfather, for maintaining these practices over time, as well as to the importance of these practices for maintaining family ties.

Each of these examples reinforces the close connection between religion and ethnicity in Canada, in the past and in the future.[1] They also gesture toward the collectivistic understanding of religion outlined by Jakelic, especially in the case of the young mother from Bavaria, yet also for the Italian Catholics in Canada.[2] Parents who initiate the baptism of their children in connection with their cultural heritage may be among the "cultural believer millennials" described by Wilkins-Laflamme.[3] Although Smith and Baker might dismiss this as "culturally religious" nonreligion, that interpretation does not reflect the nuance of these conversations.[4] Cultural heritage is a legitimate motivation for occasional religious practice.

Relational Connection

Occasional practitioners motivated by cultural heritage may overlap with occasional practitioners motivated by relational connections. Several of the examples above point to the *importance of family relationships*, especially with preceding generations, in the choice to participate in religious practices occasionally. While one priest dismisses this as "doing it for grandma," in my observation participants reflect deeply and personally on these decisions, which includes caring for relationships that they value in their families. One older routine evangelical participant describes her decision to baptize her children as infants in the Anglican tradition out of respect for her mother-in-law, despite her own theological understanding of child dedication and the baptism of adults upon confession of faith:

---

[1] Bibby, *Resilient Gods*; Paul Bramadat and David Seljak, eds., *Christianity and Ethnicity in Canada* (Toronto: University of Toronto Press, 2008); Paul Bramadat and David Seljak, eds., *Religion and Ethnicity in Canada* (Toronto: University of Toronto Press, 2009).
[2] Jakelic, *Collectivistic Religions*.
[3] Wilkins-Laflamme, *Religion, Spirituality, and Secularity*, 110–114.
[4] Baker and Smith, *American Secularism*.

> Both my children were baptized at [name of Anglican parish]. It wasn't my church of—I made a choice, a different choice. It's not that I didn't like [name of parish]; I went to another church. It's out of respect for my mother-in-law.... She wanted them baptized there, so I agreed to it, and that was fine. Both of our children were baptized there.... I believe in baby dedication. But I also understood, when I think back, that the baptism of our children was an outward sign to those present that we would raise these children in a Christian environment. That's how I looked at baptism. I don't look at that child baptism as, oh, they're going to go to heaven now.... So I did it out of respect for my mother-in-law.... My mother-in-law had asked if I would consider it and I said, "Of course."

A younger mother describes navigating family relationships surrounding the baptism of her child in ways that attend to these relationships, as well as to her own commitments and life circumstances:

> We're actually, me and my husband, we're Roman Catholic but we're not super religious. We weren't even sure if we wanted to baptize [our daughter]. It was really important to our parents and our grandparents. And we also weren't opposed to it because we were baptized. We just weren't like, "This is something we have to do."... And I knew my parents and his parents would be super disappointed and like really, it's not like I'm so against it.... It just came through a process, a final answer: I'm going to do this, we're going to do this, and you're happy about it, but we're doing it our way. No one's allowed to choose where we do it. It's going to be in the city. We pick everything and you guys come. And they're like, "That's fine." Because we had our own kind of agency about it, it became like a nice thing that we were deciding to do.

In these examples, personal relationships are central for initiators. Family relationships are often even more central for supporters, as discussed later in this chapter.

In some cases, the relationship motivating the practice is not with family members but is instead with a certain *congregation or clergy person*. As one younger woman who practices occasionally describes, feeling a personal connection to clergy in a specific congregation matters:

> I like the tradition, I like the ceremony, I like all of that, but that's not really the reason why I'm there. The reason why I am there is really specifically

because of the people that happen to be at that church. Like if it wasn't [name of priest] up there giving a homily, it wasn't—[name of other priest] is wonderful too. If it wasn't either of them up there giving a homily or somebody that I could really identify with and understand and have that connection with when they speak, I don't think I would bother to go, you know?

Similarly, a son arranged for an Anglican funeral for his father, who was an occasional practitioner, after initially considering a celebration in a hall, as was the case for his grandmother. Relationship with the specific congregation and clergy was an important factor:

The one thing is at our church, like we have a fantastic relationship with [name of priest] and she's fantastic. And I was just very comfortable with that, right? So if I'm not as comfortable with the priest, maybe I don't do that, but I knew that [name of priest] would be open to having something a little less formal and she would do a great job with it, which she did. So that level of comfort allowed us to suggest it and go ahead.

Occasional participation in religious practices that is motivated by relational connections and cultural heritage is legitimate and substantial. Collective rather than individual understandings of religious practice are a crucial corrective to measures of sincerity associated with modern Protestant individualism. At the same time, for some occasional practitioners, personal motivations are significant.

Desire for Spiritual Connection
Certain occasional practitioners who do not engage in religious practices routinely in their everyday lives desire spiritual connection on significant occasions. Religious rituals are one way to convey the spiritual importance of an event. Significant events may also prompt a desire for spiritual engagement. For some, the birth of a child invites reflection on priorities and commitments, as this younger mother, whose faith was rekindled by the birth of her child, describes:

We all start with a foundation, and we all find our path, but I think there's people that support us. So I think finding that again, and reconvening as a family, and seeing how important it is—I think it takes a baby for us to see that. So at least for me, having a new life and seeing this little being really makes you think, again, about what's really important in your life, and why this all means something to us. So sometimes it just takes that extra step to be like, "Oh my gosh, this is it. This is what's so important. This means everything."

Another mother speaks about the importance of celebrating the birth of a child with occasional religious practice as a way to make a spiritual connection and care for the spiritual well-being of her children:

Just recognizing that spirituality and that there is more to life than meets the eye. . . . Jokingly, I don't know, it's just like they are on a good foot. They're in. They get to go to heaven. They're good. They've already signed the dotted line. I know that I'm being flippant and silly, but I don't know. It's just like their little souls have been taken care of and their parents feel good that you've made that first step for them and then they can do whatever they want as they get older.

Likewise, participants describe the importance of a spiritual connection at the end of life:

I don't think my sisters would have been happy to just all come back and bury [my mother's] cremated remains in the cemetery. That's not enough of a recognition of our mother's life, I think. I think that's why the church service is more important than the funeral home. Again, we wanted that gathering of family and friends. Well, all this, saying "in the sight of God, and the presence of God." [We wanted] to have that traditional root stability in our community for us to gather and be thankful for our mom's life. There you go. You're still thanking God for her life.

One participant offers a vivid example of what it was like for her to lose friends and mark their passing without religious practices for support or spiritual connection:

If we didn't have these religious beliefs and traditions, what would something as major as a funeral look like? And I have a hard time imagining, like would we dig a hole in the backyard and bury our loved one? It would— religion has such a huge part in helping us transition from childhood to adulthood, from adulthood to old age, and then into death. It has so many traditions that I hope make those moves. I can't imagine life without it.

I lost several friends to AIDS when the scourge first began. Some were very close friends and they were very nonreligious people. And their ceremonies were more about, in certain cases, going to a crematorium and a bunch of people gathering together and deciding which bar to go to and have a drink. And it was cold, and it was lonely, and it was unsatisfying, if that's the right word, I don't know. But yeah, I haven't thought about—that was a long time ago, I'm in my 50s now and that was back when I was in my teens. And several gay friends who died and we were young and they were separated from their families, because this was the time when homosexuality was still quite unaccepted by families. So when they died, we were a bunch of kids trying to figure out, what do we do? And we didn't have religion to lead us through that and it was awful, it was really awful. So I guess I do know, yeah. If we had a pastor, somebody to walk us through what had happened, it would have been a very different experience.

Spiritual connection is desired not only at the time of life transitions but also in connection with holiday occasional practice, as two participants describe, one in relation to herself, and the other in relation to the occasional practice of her children and extended family:

I think it's good for kids to learn about religion and tie that to all the holidays. Otherwise, Christmas is just consumerism.

Everywhere Christmas and Easter time people just flock to the church, you know, whether it's a Roman Catholic or it doesn't really matter. But there's something that touches them around that time of the year, and they all seem to go. I know for me, it's a special time because that's when Jesus was born and, if you believe in that, then that is a very special time for you. And Easter is when he died for your sins, so that's a special time for you. But for the other people, I think in the back of their mind they have this spiritual feeling, they just don't have the time. They already don't give it the time during the rest of the year, but when it comes to Easter and Christmas it really comes home, you know.

In these cases, certain occasions are the only times when participants express a desire for spiritual connection that takes the form of participation in religious practices, either publicly or privately.

Invisibly Routine Practitioners

In contrast, some participants in this research are invisibly routine in their religious practice: while they only participate in public worship on certain occasions, religious practices are a routine part of their domestic lives. These participants could be among Manning's "unchurched believers" or those whom the Angus Reid Institute poll describes as "privately faithful": they describe belief in God or a higher power and private prayer, although they only rarely attend religious services.[5] Nevertheless, on certain occasions, those who are routine in their private practice initiate participation in public worship. There are a handful of participants in baptisms and funerals who make vague statements toward being invisibly routine:

> We're on and off in terms of going to church but we try to at least read the Bible and pray.

> I will say that we're not regular churchgoers ... but we do raise our children in a Christian household. So Bible stories, things like that. The belief system, those things are part of our life.

> We do believe in God and all that. Unfortunately, our schedules don't really allow us to attend church as we'd like to, but we have our own way of worshiping.

Other participants, however, describe specific and concrete ways that private religious practices are part of their everyday lives. For young families, these practices often involve children. Two younger mothers who are occasional practitioners share how they incorporate prayer into bedtime routines with their children:

> I try as much as I can at night—especially we want to end the day, whatever we've gone through that day, whether it's bad, it's good—that we are able to pray and thank God that we survived that day. And that no matter how annoying your partner would be, or your children, you're still thankful that they're there with you. So, during nighttime it's the routine that we pray and we bless the children and now [my older daughter] says, "Bless this daddy, bless this mommy, and bless this [name of baby brother]." So, she's also incorporating that.

---

[5] Manning, *Losing Our Religion*; Angus Reid Institute, "A Spectrum of Spirituality."

R: I had been doing with my son—and now my daughter since she was born—we do this thing every night and it's called "Thank You God." And we go through everything that we're thankful for.... So, I'd already been doing that with my son and now my daughter since they were, quite frankly, in my belly. My son actually says to me now before I put him to bed, he wants to do "Thank You God." I guess—I mean right now, it's a game for him. He doesn't have a good understanding as to what it is. But it's a start.

I: Yes.

R: So, we start on his hair, we go all the way down to his toes. And we have tickles in between. And then we say thank you God for mommy and for daddy and for food and for where we live. And we know that he doesn't understand it, but it's the routine, it's the practice that's important. So, he always asks me for "Thank You God" and he asks me for "Our Father." So, he goes through the words of the prayer again. He has no idea what it means. He thinks the words are hilarious. But he likes to repeat them after. And he just wants to keep saying amen, amen. And that's what he waits for. And he's two and a half so—I can't....

I: He engages at his level, right?

R: Exactly. Exactly. So, he asks for it, I give it to him. It's a routine. I think it's a comfort for him as well because it's a routine before we go to bed. And literally that's all they want. Later on in life, we can go through why it's important, why he should care and what it truly means. But if he's getting into the routine now, we can go through the deeper meaning of it later on.

Another invisibly routine occasionally religious woman describes how prayer and reliance on God flow through her daily life on a consistent basis, as well as in response to times of need:

> I have my daily prayers. It's not, like, every morning or every night per se. But there are times where—on a daily basis—I'll have a conversation with God. I have just sort of started waiting for him. And I am in a state of career transition as well. So, I always look to him for some guidance and advice.

One Italian Catholic participant describes her family's ongoing private religious practice, although they no longer attend religious services routinely:

R: My family still believes in God and they're still faithful but not as religious in terms of going to church or having that strictness. Does that make sense?

I: They have personal beliefs, but it wouldn't necessarily mean participating regularly in the church?

R: Correct. That's exactly what it is. So they will still wear a cross. They still will say prayers. And will still thank God before we eat. But they won't go to church every Sunday.... Not to say that it still isn't meaningful for them and that they still don't have their personal religion.

Finally, there are those who practice privately because of bad experiences with the church. One woman describes how a priest extorting money from family members made her wary of organized religion, while remaining very devout in her private life:

> I'm going to be brutally honest. Going to church is something I've struggled with, and that's because we've had previous bad experiences. And I don't want to get into detail regarding what those experiences were. But that isn't to say I do not practice. Like, I read the Bible every day, I study it, I talk with people about it.

Whether or not those who read the Bible or pray daily can truly be considered occasionally religious is a question, since they are routinely religious in their private lives. Nevertheless, it is significant that their routine practice is invisible; to outside observers, including clergy, routine practitioners, and researchers who rely on participant observation, they appear to be occasionally religious.

Involuntary Occasional Practitioners

Finally, it is crucial to recognize that there are involuntary occasional practitioners—those who would practice routinely, but who, for reasons beyond their control, are unable to do so. This group includes older occasional practitioners who depend on others for transportation:

> I used to drive myself, but my daughters and my children don't want me to do too much driving, especially in the wintertime, because I'm 92 years old and they claim that I'm not as sharp as I used to be. So, my daughter drives

me on Sunday mornings but sometimes she's away or whatever. . . . I go whenever I can.

[My friend] was quite elderly and she was kind of out of circulation. She hadn't been able to go to church very often because, of course, she couldn't drive anymore, and it wasn't always convenient for [her son] to get her there. I know she was a stay-at-home person.

However, disability limiting religious participation is not always associated with age:

I don't attend church as frequently as I should because, as I said, my husband is disabled, and I just can't get coverage for him in the mornings when I need to go to church. . . . We moved here in 1988, it was a long time ago. And shortly after we moved, eight months after we moved, my husband became paralyzed. And so everything changed. I couldn't attend church on a regular basis at all.

At times, church communities may reach out to those who are involuntarily occasional through home visits, gifts, and the celebration of communion:

[My mom] couldn't make it to church. Somebody would come and give her communion here. And like every couple of weeks, they'd send flowers from their altar. So, that was—I mean they do that for all the shut-ins.

Those who are involuntarily occasional may also practice their faith privately at home:

I used to go on, but I don't go now because I have no one to take me, they've gone to work. I find it a little bit difficult and sometimes a downright distressing part of the situation that we're in. I can still pray, I can still read my Bible, and I can still sing some hymns. I have a hymn book here. You know, I don't really have to be there every single Sunday to keep my faith.

This is an example of how some who are involuntarily occasional practitioners may also be invisibly routine. While the involuntarily occasional can be considered initiators of religious practice, their initiation is frequently unsuccessful, potentially in relation to both routine and occasional practices.

The motivations driving these five types of initiators often overlap. For example, cultural heritage may be part of what shapes a desire for spiritual connection, or invisible routine practice may foster relational connections that lead to occasional public practice. These five types of religious practitioners are not stable identities but are instead motivations connected to specific situations. The same person may be a different type of occasional practitioner with respect to different events. Initiators may also become supporters, and supporters may share some of these motivations for occasional religious practice.

Supporters

In addition to occasional practitioners who initiate participation in religious practices, there are also occasional practitioners who support the religious practice of others. These individuals do not take responsibility for facilitating participation in a particular practice, but they do join in. There are three categories of supporters: advocates, inner-circle supporters, and the outer-circle supporters. These categories may overlap in various ways with each other, and with the five types of initiators above.

Advocates

Advocates encourage occasional practice without being in the position to initiate it. Advocates are often connected to occasional practitioners motivated by relational connections. Advocates may be routine or occasional practitioners themselves, yet they have a strong desire to see others participate in religious practices on certain occasions. One Italian Catholic grandmother, who practices occasionally in relation to life transitions, describes how relieved she is that her daughter decided to baptize her grandson, and she reinforces this point at the end of the interview:

> I hope that I have helped you to understand that it's really important for people who grow up with a faith to have their children accept their faith, and then it's a pleasure when their children who have accepted their faith try to teach their kids to have the faith, because you feel like you've done the right thing. It makes you feel like you're investing all this time in your

children's faith that it was all worth it. I hope everybody has this opportunity and understands that they will just feel good from it.

Another grandmother was also an advocate for the baptism of her grandchildren, who are now adults with children of their own and who practice only occasionally, such as at the funeral of their grandfather:

> I had all the grandchildren christened at [name of parish], but then I have no more influence. That's as far as my influence went. They were all christened.... So that's where it ends. I mean, it's up to them what they do. The example is there for them to follow.
>
> And especially they know that when the grandfather died, they see how much the church has helped. It's not just you know, I go to church every Sunday, I pay my dues. It's like a community and [the priest] she reaches out to all the people....
>
> But I wish they would go to church more often, but again they're adults now, they choose. When they're young it's the parents' duty, I think, to bring up the children the way they think the child should go. But when they go, they say don't depart from it, but they do. They do depart from it, so that's where we are.[6]

Advocates may be involved in occasional practices other than baptism, as in the case of one unsuccessful advocate who remains disappointed that her daughter was not married in the church:

> Because my daughter, she didn't get married in a church, and she hasn't baptized or christened her children. They don't have the religion in her family and it's just something that she doesn't want to partake in.... And I think it was, I don't know, maybe ten years ago I said to [my daughter] my only regret is that my one and only daughter did not get married in a church. You decided to get married outside.

---

[6] This is a commentary on Proverbs 22:6: "Train up a child in the way he should go: and when he is old, he will not depart from it" (King James Version).

Advocates may take more or less overt approaches to advocacy, and these yield various results.

One gray area is whether and how the *deceased* may function as an advocate, in addition to a catalyst, in relation to their own funeral. Although they are unable to initiate the event, they may be a strong supporter of a certain approach. In some cases when the deceased takes a very active role—from choosing hymns, to selecting flower arrangements, to organizing photographs for a slideshow—it may be possible to consider them an advocate, as in the case of this lifelong Anglican occasional practitioner, as her daughter describes:

> It's a bit of an odd situation in that my mother and I were very close to the point where over hopefully the last ten years of her life, any time we attended another funeral, she was quite specific to me, saying, I like that, but I don't like that. Make sure I only have red roses, a big spray on the casket. Or she'd say, for goodness' sake, don't let them sing a certain song. So, it was almost five years in the planning, but very specific to her likes and dislikes.

Advocates are distinct in that they are often strongly attached to the practice but not central participants; if they had the capacity to be central actors, they would likely be initiators. The motivations behind this advocacy often parallel those of initiators, including cultural heritage, relational connections, and desire for spiritual connection.

Inner Circle
In contrast to advocates, supporters in the inner circle may have central roles yet little personal investment in the practice. These are the partners and the godparents at baptisms, the children and grandchildren who offer readings and eulogies at funerals, and the close friends of those who initiate the practice. They are often involved in decision-making alongside the initiator, at least in a supportive capacity. At times, supporters in the inner circle may even become primary planners and organizers, although they are not initiators.

Partners, in the case of both weddings and baptisms, are key supporters in the inner circle since they are often making public faith commitments alongside initiators. A common pattern is for a husband to support a wife who is the initiator of the occasional practice:

[My husband] actually, in all honesty truth, did the baptism because he knew it was really important for me. So he was supporting my beliefs and what I wanted for us.

R: It felt like the baptism was much more important for my parents than my brother per se. I know it meant a lot for [my sister-in-law]. It didn't mean a lot for [my brother], but I don't think he would have—he wouldn't have had a difference of opinion if the children had been baptized or not. It was, I think, maybe more for my parents.
I: So, he's sort of happy to support it.
R: Yeah. Exactly. I mean if he had to like plan it and really be involved, I think it would have been a very different story.

Partners may also join in other occasional practices, such as holidays, to support their spouse, as is the case with this occasional Anglican practitioner who also attends mass as a Catholic schoolteacher:

I: Why is it important for you to be there for Christmas and Easter? What is it about those events?
R: Because my wife wants to go. If it was up to me, I wouldn't go. I'm not trying to be mean. I like going and I'm actually welcome there.... We don't go during the other months, during the rest of the year. Then like, well this is Christmas, okay, so we go on Christmas. When it's Easter, why, because it's Easter. I usually go because my wife wants me to go.
I: Yeah, it's a family event.
R: If it was up to me, I wouldn't go. Period. It's not saying, I don't have faith and I don't believe. We have mass at school all the time and I'm a regular participant in mass in school and everything.

Some partners even provide concrete support to facilitate more routine practice without joining in themselves, as this wife describes:

We do attend. It's usually just myself. My husband does not go to church. My husband will happily chauffeur me to church and say, "When would you like me to come and collect you?" If I asked him to go to church, he would come with me.

At times, supportive partners may shift roles and become initiators or advocates, as in the case of a family where the mother initiated the baptism of her first two children, and the agnostic father initiated the baptism of the third:

> [My wife] just said that it was important to her and she wanted to have a baptism. And yeah, I'm not against it. I was fine with whatever she wants to do. I just supported her in what she wanted to do, I guess for the first one.... She's really the driving force behind that side of our family life, I would say. My perspective is that it was much more important [laughter]—probably as with most families—with the first born, she was very eager to go through this process of baptism and such. I think that desire maybe has fallen away over time. It seems less important as things get busier and busier. Perhaps with this one, I was the driving force behind baptism, but more from an equity point of view. I feel like if we did it for one of our children, then they should all kind of have the same experience and have the same introduction into the church.

One especially common pattern, which is the case in all the examples above, is a female partner acting as the initiator and her male partner taking on a supporting role. This reflects a well-documented broader pattern of women being more involved with religion than men and may also reflect a broader pattern of women being more involved in initiating and organizing family events.[7]

Godparents are often important inner-circle supporters at baptisms. Both parents and godparents tend not to view being a godparent as a religious role but see it instead as a way to recognize and strengthen close family and friendship networks. Nevertheless, godparents have a religious role in the context of baptism, especially in making faith commitments on behalf of the child. Godparents often find ways to be supportive while also acknowledging dissonance. One occasional Anglican practitioner describes asking her nonreligious sister-in-law to be the godmother to her daughter:

> R: This whole other wonderful closer relationship with her came out of that moment of asking her to be [my daughter's] godmother. And so that was really nice. Like I said, religious stuff is definitely not her thing.

---

[7] Clarke and Macdonald, *Leaving Christianity*, 39–41, 134; Pew Research Center, "The Gender Gap in Religion Around the World," March 22, 2016, accessed December 11, 2023, https://www.pewresearch.org/religion/2016/03/22/the-gender-gap-in-religion-around-the-world.

I: So how did she and her partner feel about like having to stand up there and make those commitments?
R: Well, she kind of talked to me before and she's like, "Okay, here's the deal." She's like, "If you want me to be the spiritual guide for your daughter, I am definitely not the person to ask. If you want me to be the person that is going to help her be a better person, then okay." And she's really doing all of the godmotherly things without the label of religion attached to it. And I was like, alright. That's cool. Because fundamentally, what she believes in, her values, and the things that are important to her about becoming a good person and all of that are no different than what a traditional godparent would have expected of them, except for the religious aspect.

Another mother similarly describes how she prepared her nonreligious friend, a supportive occasional practitioner in her inner circle, to serve as the godmother to her daughter:

R: She knew what to expect. She knew all of it. I do remember her being a little uncomfortable when we were going through the proclamations.
I: Do you have a sense for what she was thinking or how she was kind of navigating that for herself, knowing she wants to be there for you as a godmother, but also, kind of...
R: She loves my daughter like she was her own. She's never going to have kids, so, this is her daughter as far as I'm concerned. What I described to her was, take out the word God from this, do you agree to do all these things? Do you agree to help me raise my daughter just to be a good person? Because that's what these—right? That's what these things are, is—like do you renounce all sins? Do you renounce evil powers? Do you want to help the child grow into their full stature? That's what this is. Take out any God references, and you scale it back. That's what you're proclaiming. It's just to help me raise my child as a good, compassionate human. And she was okay with that. She was able to wrap her head around that.

There are also times when godparents are more aligned with the tradition in which the practice takes place. Chapter 5 explores the religious and nonreligious aspects of godparenting in greater depth.

Outer Circle

Finally, an outer circle of extended family, friends, and community members are also supportive occasional practitioners. This group tends not to have leadership responsibilities. It is straightforward for them to opt in or out of participating in various aspects of the practice. This is also the group that exhibits the greatest diversity in religious identity and practice, although in some cases this is also true of the inner circle.

Nonreligious participants clearly describe their participation as centered on the initiators and their inner circle. One nonreligious participant, who only practices in association with the life transitions of others, describes this in terms of supporting the choices of those who initiate the practice:

> The service itself, the words, like, what does it mean to me? When it relates to someone else, when it's a funeral or a baptism or whatever, a wedding, it's about the people—it's about how that all relates to them. That's the important thing. So, you respect that relationship because it's not your business what they think. How they feel about things. And that's wonderful. It's good to see people engaged in that world where they want to be. Or they're comfortable. Or they draw inspiration from or whatever. And you're just there to witness whatever. . . . It's like you're making an appearance to support those people in whatever it is they choose to do, right?

This atheist participant is generous in his interpretation of the value of occasional religious practice for others, and for himself:

> When you're at a funeral, it's not necessarily for the deceased. It's for everybody that's there. And I understand and recognize that there are lots of people that still have that belief and that faith. So I sit and I listen. I mean, I take it in, because these are the words that give people comfort, that help other people navigate through grief. And at one time they would have helped me. . . . When it comes to a funeral, if somebody needs that at a funeral, by all means. I mean we're in a church. The departed was a religious person. Most of these people share those beliefs. It makes sense for us to be there. I am kind of the odd man out. And so I will—I grit my teeth and bear it. It's just okay, here comes this to help these folks. And I mostly just—as I said, I take it in. It helps me understand people better. If that's what helps people, then that's what helps people. And if down the road that needs to be a part of my—if that knowledge will help me down the road, then that's that.

In increasingly nonreligious social contexts, it is reasonable to expect a significant number of nonreligious participants to attend occasional practices marking life transitions, and even holidays.

Participants who identify with and practice *other Christian and non-Christian religious traditions* are also often part of the outer circle (and at times the inner circle, as previously discussed in relation to religious identity). It may be possible to observe visually those who practice other religious traditions attending Anglican services if they wear Muslim headscarves or Sikh turbans. Embodied practices may also suggest formation in a different religious tradition, such as participants in Anglican funerals making Roman Catholic ritual gestures when entering the space, like genuflecting and making the sign of the cross (although these are common in certain Anglican liturgical contexts, they are relatively rare in the settings that I observed). Multiple religious participation is common in the outer circle, especially in families that bring together different traditions and practice occasionally or routinely in each of them.[8]

These types of occasional practitioners—including five types of initiators, three types of supporters, and catalysts—are situational roles, not stable identity categories. An individual may inhabit various roles in a relatively short time frame. For example, over the course of a few months, an individual may initiate the baptism of a child in the Anglican tradition due to a desire for spiritual connection, be an inner-circle supporter to a spouse by facilitating attendance at Roman Catholic midnight mass on Christmas Eve with family members, and attend the Jewish funeral of a colleague as an outer-circle supporter. In addition to engaging in multiple expressions of occasional religious practice simultaneously or in quick succession, it is also possible to consider changing patterns of occasional religious practice over time.

Changes in Occasional Practice over Time

How participants relate to religion through occasional practice is often not stable over time. Individuals and groups may participate in different

---

[8] Peniel Jesudason, Rufus Rajkumar, and Joseph Prabhakar Dayam, eds., *Many Yet One? Multiple Religious Belonging* (Geneva: WCC Publications, 2016).

practices for different reasons over the course of the year, throughout a lifetime, and in response to pivotal events.

Annual Cycles

Annual rhythms shape religious practice for some participants. Religious calendars, especially holidays like Christmas and Easter, are one factor influencing these patterns. One occasional practitioner who attended religious services more often with her father when he was alive outlines this pattern:

> In the summer, not quite as much, because we'd be up at the cottage and stuff over the weekends. And probably a little bit more often surrounding Christmas and then again surrounding Easter, because that's when [my father] decided that it was more important to go more often.

This statement also points to other annual cycles that shape religious participation. For Anglicans in Ontario, spending weekends at the cottage during the summer reduces routine practice, as these two participants describe:

> Oh, [we attend church] every Sunday pretty much. Yeah. And [my wife] sings in the choir, and so she's there every Sunday. Now, we hardly ever go during the summer, but in the—from September till May, June, we're there just about every Sunday. Yeah, except when we're—we go away in the winter for a month or whatever. But when we're home, we go every Sunday.

> Well, we used to go every single Sunday. I think it's awful we got out of the habit of it because I'm going to the cottage more in the summer. Especially after my parents passed because we had to take care of it obviously. And then a few years ago we joined a ski club and quite often we ski on Sundays. So unfortunately, we don't go as often as we like. But I don't just go just at holiday time. I like to go during—I always find it's good for your spirit. It's rejuvenating. It's kind of a nice pick-me-up.

While there are Anglican churches in Ontario cottage country, for most participants being at the cottage means not attending religious services, even if they attend somewhat more routinely the rest of the year, at least during certain periods of their lives.

Life-Course Factors

Changing patterns in religious participation over the life course are well established in the literature, and sufficiently recognizable in everyday life that participants name them in interviews.[9] One younger mother, who is an occasional Anglican practitioner, describes seeing these patterns unfold in her own life, which was largely spent in the United States:

> I think it's pretty typical of most people's lives for culture or faith. So, I think that as people develop, when you're a child, you're taught practices, whether it's your faith or your culture, whether it's certain things that are part of your life and explanations that are part of your life.
>
> And then everyone goes away. Well, not everyone, but most people in their twenties start to explore the world, right? And explore, whether it's through college, or travel, or just getting a job, to kind of separate yourself from your family. And you start to figure out who you are as an individual. And I think that the things that you learn as a child, that your parents instill in you, are your grounding or your baseline, but you try to figure out where you fit into the world.
>
> And then when you figure that out—it's kind of like seasons, right?—then you have a season where you may want to find someone to settle down with and then start a family.
>
> One of my good Indian friends told me that in her faith . . . they teach that there are seasons in life and a time for everything. The first is just growing up as a child and yourself. Second is exploring the world. Third is family and dedicating to the family. And the last is religious cooperation as an older person. . . .
>
> I think that progression was natural for me. So, the faith has always been there, my relationship with God has always been there. It's just . . . how much it's permeated in my life, and which aspects, right? As a twenty-year-old, very selfish, running around, doing things for myself, dating, my career, all these things, God is there, but it's not as burning center. And I think that when you have children, then you have to reassess. How am I going to bring this little child into the world, and what principles do I want them to believe in and uphold?

---

[9] Michele Dillon and Paul Wink, *In the Course of a Lifetime: Tracing Religious Belief, Practice, and Change* (Berkeley: University of California Press, 2007).

While this participant is distinct in drawing on Eastern religious thought to interpret these patterns, the patterns she describes are present in many conversations.

Many occasional practitioners have *childhood* memories of attending religious services, either routinely or occasionally. Some also point to childhood religious formation in Catholic schools:

> I: It seems like your relationship with the Catholic tradition has changed over time. Can you say more about how that shifted for you?
> R: I think it's like with anything, you're young and you learn what you learn because everyone else is learning it and you do these things. You don't really have a choice. It's not like my parents ever said, "Do you want to be confirmed? Or do you want to take communion?" You would just do it. It's part of Catholic school. It's part of the curriculum.
> I: So your whole class is going though it at the same time.
> R: Yeah, the whole class. If you're not going to do that, why are you sending your kid to a Catholic church? It's kind of weird I'd never had anyone opt out of those things. Or maybe they did and we weren't aware, but pretty much the whole class did them.

Religious practices in childhood generally reflect the practices of parents or other adults. One of the intriguing things about the generations that are the focus of this research is that, while many of the baby boomers whom I interview have childhood memories of routine religious participation, they have only occasional experiences as adults. Their adult children, then, are drawing on occasional childhood experience as they baptize their children. This pattern may reinforce an idea present among participants that religion is primarily for children, not adults. It also points to a relationship between occasional religious practice and generational religious change.

Participants who were raised in a routinely religious family frequently describe how they stopped participating routinely in their *adolescence*. Occasional practices associated with life transitions may even mark these shifts, as these two participants describe in relation to confirmation:

Well, I mean, as a child I went to church, maybe not every Sunday, but almost all Sundays. As I got a little older, my mother didn't make me come. But we used to go a lot when I was a kid. Then I got confirmed and once

I got confirmed I hardly ever went. I went once in a while, but the attitude seemed to be well, now that you're confirmed, it's kind of your choice. And well, if it's my choice, I'm not going.

When I was young, like I went to youth group, and I was confirmed when I was fourteen. I was going along with the program and trying very hard to understand and believe and get it, right? But it just didn't resonate for me. And at a certain point, I was like, you know this thing is not really for me. I just don't get it. Like, I don't—it doesn't make sense to me. . . . And then I just drifted off and didn't go to church anymore.

Moving away from a family home for university is another important transition point:

Yeah, when I was young, you just kind of go through it. Everyone's doing, your friends are doing it. And then I guess when I went away for school, university, you don't do those things. I guess you meet so many different people. And my parents don't really go to church anymore.

So when I became—as a teenager, like everyone goes through a phase I guess, and when I was—I dropped out of being an altar boy. I think it was just like, okay, I need to go out on weekends and party and drink. I can't go to church every Sunday morning. So yeah, I just I dropped out of that. And then when I turned eighteen, I moved to [another city]. . . . Then it was like, I dropped most all of the ties with like any of those organizations.

One exception to these patterns is a younger mother with no religious upbringing who joined a youth group and was baptized during high school. However, she also describes moving away from religion during her university years, and of returning primarily to mark occasions such as her marriage and the birth of her children.

Parenthood, especially the birth of children, has a complicated relationship with religious participation. On the one hand, there are participants who feel drawn to reconnect with religion when their children are born, whether in terms of practice, belief, or affiliation, as these three mothers describe:

We started going to church together, [my son] and I, probably around when he was only two months old, and I was starting to get out of the house more and wanting to go to church on Sundays. I think that just comes from my pregnancy experience and just being so thankful. I hadn't gone to church as much prior to, but just finding more of my faith even after that whole process.

[Faith] came to the forefront when we started having children because I thought in terms of I need a foundation. I need something that I can rest on that is beyond myself, that I can totally rely on, that is unchanging. . . . That's when I recall it being very important to me that, hey, this is what I want for my family going forward.

We were busy with working and my first baby didn't come along till almost nine years of marriage. We were looking for a church during those nine years, but once I was pregnant, we looked for a family doctor that hopefully would be our family doctor forever, just like my husband and I still had this same family doctor that birthed us until our thirties. So, we shopped for a family doctor here to give our children also that wonderful experience, and we shopped for a church.

These movements toward religion may be associated with routine or occasional practice, which may also vary over time.

In contrast, the birth of children can make participation in religious practices more challenging. One mother, whose partner does not attend church services with her, describes how the logistics of being the only parent managing four children are a barrier to frequent participation:

It's just really, really hard. I think now that [the twins] are getting bigger and my husband's getting more confident with them, I can start taking the other two children. I don't think I'll take the twins. It's just a matter of me figuring out my own logistics. How do I handle four children? I know that they have a lovely little nursing room and a playroom, but will my kids go? We'll see, we'll see.

Another mother describes the possibility of taking her two young children to church when they are a bit older:

We haven't been going to church even for Christmas and stuff. I think again just being overwhelmed, like it's just a lot when you have babies to go to church. It's just a bit of an excuse, but to be honest, it's a little practical as well. But when they get a bit older and their attention spans are a bit longer, it's definitely something that we will continue to do and expose them to.

However, the priorities and schedules of older children may also be a barrier to participation, as this mother describes:

> To be honest with you, the routine of family life on the weekends sometimes makes it hard to get there on a Sunday. Our son played hockey and, you know, the kids are busy with their own thing.

There are very few families with younger children included this research who attend routinely; however, partly because of the selection criteria, they do attend occasionally.

Aging similarly has divergent impacts on religious practice. On the one hand, grown children and retirement may create more space for religious participation, as this daughter describes:

> But as my dad got older, he started to go to church more and more often. And especially once he retired, he got super involved. He really liked [the priest]. I used to go with him sometimes, it was like our daddy-daughter outing that we would do.

At the same time, at a certain point, older adults, even those who attended routinely throughout their lives, may become involuntarily occasionally religious, as previously discussed, for reasons of health or transportation. While occasional religious practice may be associated with each of these life stages in different ways for different families, life transitions are often associated with shifts in practice.

Turning-Point Events

Turning-point events may also prompt changes in religious practice. While the *life transitions* above are important turning points for many, other events may be tipping points into a different relationship with religion. Some of these events may be *encounters with religion*. One former Anglican and former routine practitioner, who now identifies as nonreligious and attends occasionally to support the life transition practices of others, describes two events that solidified his departure from church. The first is an encounter his son had at a conservative Christian summer camp:

> What really put the nail in the coffin as it were—forgive the expression—my son was at a Bible camp run by the Salvation Army.... And they were doing the story of Genesis. And so they said earth was created in six days. He was eight years old at the time I believe. And he puts up his hand. "Well, if the earth was created in six days and mankind came along immediately afterwards what about all the dinosaurs and stuff and they're billions of years old." And to the instructor's credit they had an interesting solution to that question. They said well, what is a day to man is different to a day to God. And that was interesting. And then they said mankind came up with the idea of a twenty-four-hour day and stuff. And Joseph immediately counters with, "No. That's just the earth rotating all the way around." So okay. So they actually called me about this and said this is what happened. And we're not trying to explain it. I said, "Don't worry. He won't come back." So that was—I mean, if an eight-year-old can put that kind of logic to work, why can't I? So, I thought okay, I think I'm done. And so, it was actually my son that did it at eight years old. That kind of just inspired or kicked off the whole withdrawal from religion and everything like that.

Notably, this was not an encounter within his own tradition of practice at the time, the United Church of Canada, which would not take this approach to the interpretation of Genesis, but it still shifted his overall relationship with religion. The second event is the funeral for his grandmother, who was herself occasionally religious, which he felt was not reflected in how the pastor presented her faith and life:

> My grandmother's funeral actually kind of angered me because we sat in—it was the same church and the service was very I don't want to say it was extravagant but it was much more religious than I feel was necessary. A lot of the stuff that was said by the minister about my grandmother didn't seem entirely true to her character or her personality because there was a lot of—it almost seemed like the church was trying to take credit for my grandmother saying, she was a very religious woman and also that God came first.... But it just seemed like, I don't know if contrived is the word, I don't think it is. But it didn't fit. And that kind of put me off religion in general. I've been a nonbeliever for years. I bought out of the belief in God years

ago, but I continued going to church because it was part of routine. It was a community. It did good in the community. You give back and they help out with various things, and it seemed like it was a good thing to do. But after my grandmother's funeral I lost my taste for the whole organization.

This funeral is an example of how occasional practice itself can be a turning point, either away from or toward connecting with the church on these occasions. One woman describes a positive experience of a Christmas Eve service as the initial point of connection with a community where she now practices occasionally:

Another Christmas Eve, I was pregnant, and we went to [name of parish] for the first time. And we went to the 11 o'clock mass and it was lovely. I mean there's something magical about Christmas Eve when all the lights are on, and the poinsettias are there, and it's really pretty, and the church is full.... So, my husband and I started going there. We felt at home there.

Occasional practices may be significant in shaping how participants relate to religion more broadly. Their experiences on these occasions can prompt participants to turn toward or away from religious participation.

Turning-point events may relate to *changes in life circumstances* rather than experiences of religion. One example is the loss of a key advocate for a particular occasional practice. One woman describes how her extended family stopped attending religious services as part of holiday celebrations when her grandfather died:

We used to always do midnight mass on Christmas Eve. And I guess people have babies and kids and people go home early and we just stop going. Or I guess also when my grandfather on my mom's side died, that was a big driver. He was very religious—church every Sunday.... In a way, I think when he died, like we did it for a bit, and then there was no real almost like governing person to be like, "Come on, we should go."

Geographic moves are also often connected to changes in religious practice. Immigration to a new country, moving to a new city, or even moving out of the neighborhood of a specific congregation can change how individuals and groups participate in religious practices. A geographic move may be an opportunity to reconnect with the church:

> I moved down to Toronto with my son and my wife at the time. And we started going to church again just to get out into the community and whatnot. It was the same church my mom went to when she was a little girl.
>
> I left that neighborhood because I moved. And in my new neighborhood I also saw the Anglican Church and I joined it. I joined it, yeah. I joined the choir. So I think I—what I try to find is that kind of belonging, a feeling, and I think I've found it.
>
> Certainly, when I moved to [Europe] and I didn't know anybody . . . we happened to find a flat on a street where, at the end of the street, was a [church]. I was like, "Oh, maybe I'll just go on Sunday," and I met all kinds of lovely people. Most of them are sixty-five and older. So I met a lovely little group of elderly ladies and we had tea once or twice a week.

Alternatively, moving may be a time for leaving the church:

> As a young family, our family did attend a Presbyterian Church. We were in [a small city in Ontario] at the time, and then we moved when I was about six to [a suburb of a larger city in Ontario]. And after that it got pretty busy, you know, we were four kids actually. And so we never really got into—we went to church a couple of times there, but never really got going again. So it just kind of wasn't convenient.

Some even return to locations where they have not lived for years for certain types of occasional practices:

> We know we're probably, we are not going to stay in [Western Canada] forever, so the [church] in Toronto had more meaning to us because of [my husband's] family growing up there and going to school there. He has a longer history there than here. [Western Canada], we'll be here for a total of five years in our life. And [my husband], he was in Toronto for close to twenty years. And so I think that's why we decided to do it there and why we had no problem with having such a brief relationship with the [church in Toronto for the baptism].

In a transient urban culture, many participants who grew up with a connection to a congregation no longer relate to that community in a sustained way.

These examples, among many others, show how the types of occasional practices in which individuals engage, and their roles and motivations in relation to these practices, change over time. Most individuals do not fit tidily into the same category throughout their lives but instead move through different ways of relating to religion as circumstances evolve and significant events take place. While this largely reflects patterns in the literature, a focus on occasional practice highlights that occasional practice may characterize each life stage in distinct ways: young children practice occasionally because they are difficult to manage in corporate worship; young adults practice occasionally when they visit family during holidays; young families practice occasionally out of a desire to introduce children to religion while struggling to balance schedules; older adults practice occasionally because of health concerns. Invisibly routine practice and involuntary occasional practice may also characterize these life stages. These are only tendencies; there are routine practitioners and those who never practice at each of these life stages as well. A key conclusion is not to assume that a particular way of relating to religion through practice is a stable identity and enduring pattern across the life cycle. How individuals and groups relate to religious practices changes over time. Occasional practice may be an important feature of those shifts and stages.

The Experience of Occasional Practice

How do occasional practitioners experience the occasionality of their religious practice? This is a distinct question from how participants experience the content of occasional practices, which is the focus of the following two parts of the book. The issue here is instead how they experience the fact that their practice is occasional: Do they find this way of relating to religion positive or problematic? My overwhelming impression of the interviews is that most occasional practitioners are content with their current form of religious practice.

Some *see occasional religious practice as the norm*—"Really good Anglicans—they go Easter and Christmas." This group tends to see their occasional practice as meeting or exceeding their own expectations for religious participation. They understand it to be adequate and comfortable for them to participate in religious practices in relation to holidays, life transitions, crises, and when circumstances arise.

For others, *routine religious practice is seen as the norm*—"attending every Sunday" is the standard. A small number of occasional practitioners experience some level of *guilt* about not living in to this standard. For some, this guilt may be connected to the idea that Christians should attend religious services frequently:

> I: Could you say a bit more about the guilt? If it's guilt about not attending...
> R: The guilt is because I did not attend church for about ten years.
> I: And you sort of feel like you should have...
> R: Yes. And the reason being is because when talking to people, they said how I just should have gone to church, why didn't I go? That it makes you a bad person, a bad Christian. I had an aunt who said I was going to go to hell because of it. And it just ate away at me. It just ate away and I found, if these people who I am quite close with were coming and saying that, what would a stranger say to me? And so I guess, I then started to feel—so that's more fear. But then the guilt started to come in the fact that I had been away for so long and I can't go back. And I'm not a good Christian because I didn't go back and how can I just walk in there and think I should be accepted if I hadn't gone in ten years? And that's where I start to feel guilty. Like, why didn't I just go back? Like, why did I take that hiatus for so long?

For others, guilt is associated with having positive experiences of connection with the community on the occasions when they are there, and feeling a desire to reciprocate these relationships:

> R: Like we just don't go. I don't know. Again, I don't know. That's a good question. I don't know what to tell you. I guess I should want to bring [my daughter] to church more often but we don't.
> I: Why do you think that you should?
> R: I don't know. That's actually—I don't know why I should. I don't know. Maybe it's that guilt because I don't know. Because they are so good to us, they're so good. I felt so welcome there, maybe I should go there more often.

It may also be related to feeling that routine participation is necessary when expecting the church to provide occasional practices:

I've been a very bad churchgoer since having these twins or being pregnant with these twins. I really haven't gone probably since—last September was the last time I've really been. So I'm shameful. And then I expect them to baptize my child when I haven't been.

Again, these experiences of guilt are present but not widespread among participants. Participants generally reported that being occasionally religious is a positive or a neutral experience. Those who report neutral experiences include those with mixed feelings who are open to the possibility of more frequent participation, and may even vaguely desire it, but who easily accept occasional practice as their present reality.

Most who see routine religious practice as a norm *feel no obligation to meet this standard*. They are okay with being occasional. As one participant put it:

I do support [the church], but there's a quote from Winston Churchill that says, "I'm like a flying buttress. I support the church from the outside." That's sort of how I am, I'm not a regular churchgoer, but I am supportive of them.

Most occasional practitioners feel no obligation or desire to attend religious services more often than they currently do. This aligns with their preference for identifying as "not very religious."

Understanding Occasional Religious Practice

Describing and understanding occasional religious practice—a way of relating to religion that is defined by occasional participation in religious practices, usually in association with specific occasions—is crucial for adequately describing and understanding the contemporary religious landscape in the Global North. Rather than omitting participation in weddings and funerals from studies of religion, we must attend to these practices as a primary way that people relate to religion today. Rather than being "low," "marginal," or "soft," occasional religious practice is an ordinary, central, and serious way of being religious in Canada and beyond.

Occasional religious practice occurs on a range of occasions, especially holidays, life transitions, and crises, as well as in connection with incidental circumstances. Occasional practitioners claim a diversity of religious identities, and understand these identities in disparate ways. Occasional practitioners occupy various roles, from being at the center of the event to casually observing from the edges. Many different motivations drive occasional practitioners, whether they are initiating religious participation or supporting others.

This chapter has outlined a typology of eight types of occasional practitioners. This typology includes five types of initiators: (1) cultural heritage, (2) relational connection, (3) desire for spiritual connection, (4) invisibly routine, and (5) involuntarily occasional. It also includes three types of supporters: (1) advocates, (2) inner circle, and (3) outer circle. These motivations are personal and social, spiritual and cultural, although these dimensions of human experience are often difficult to differentiate. How participants relate to occasional practice changes situationally and over the course of their lives. Each of these types of occasional practitioners deserves respect and attention from scholars and religious leaders. This analysis makes several claims that are important going forward.

First, occasional religious practice is shaped by *complex motivations and circumstances*. There is no single type of occasional practitioner. There is no single motivation that drives occasional practice. There is no simple explanation for occasional practice. Occasional practitioners are not all invisibly routine or looking for spiritual connection. Neither are they all connected by culture or relationship. Occasional rather than routine practice is not necessarily voluntary. For many occasional practitioners, there is ongoing tension between personal choice and established cultural practices. A diffusive Christianity does not structure these occasions. Participation in a practice cannot be assumed; it must be chosen. At the same time, there may be strong advocates and deep cultural connections that span generations. Individuals and communities negotiate these tensions in a variety of ways. Occasional practitioners are internally diverse in their motivations and circumstances.

Second, occasional religious practitioners occupy *various roles*. While at times they may be quietly supportive from the back pew, in other instances they are asked to make public faith statements or offer liturgical leadership. Sometimes those at the center of practices associated with birth and death navigate ambiguous relationships with religion. Sometimes a key advocate for the practice does not have a formal role.

Third, *each type of occasional practice is valid*—sound, reasonable, and cogent. None of these types of occasional practice can be easily dismissed as merely "cultural nonreligion," to use Baker and Smith's category.[10] In a range of different ways, on various levels, these practices are significant for participants—they are meaningful and purposeful. It is inaccurate and unhelpful to assume that legitimate religious practice consists primarily of cognitive assent and routine or intensive participation. Occasional practice, in its diversity, is a significant and ordinary way of relating to religion.

Fourth, occasional practitioners offer a crucial *critique of establishment prescriptions and interpretations* of religious practices. Through their words and actions, they participate in cultures that prescribe practices that are often in conflict with the prescriptions of religious authorities and institutions: "Good Anglicans—they go Easter and Christmas," for example, instead of "Good Anglicans, they go every Sunday." Occasional practitioners thoughtfully negotiate dissonances between official prescriptions and subjective dispositions. Their actions and voices reveal how "power, authority, continuity, voice, inclusion, exclusion, alienation, critique, transgression, and dissent work in religions in the real world."[11] This critical potential is developed further in Parts II and III of the book.

Imagine looking around at a community gathered for Christian worship—for a baptism or funeral, on Christmas Eve, or even on an ordinary Sunday. In the Anglican tradition in Toronto, the diversity in the room may be similar to the religious and nonreligious diversity described here. It is impossible to assume that participants are routinely practicing, formally affiliated, theologically aligned, or morally compliant with the tradition. Acknowledging who is really present is a crucial starting point for reflection on what is actually happening. This reflection must attend to the stories of those who relate to religion in different ways, including scholars and clergy, but also occasional practitioners of all types. The religious and nonreligious diversity associated with occasional religious practice has tremendous implications for how we understand religious ritual and how we do liturgical theology, to which we turn in the next two parts of the book.

---

[10] Baker and Smith, *American Secularism*.
[11] Smith, *Religion*, 15.

PART II
OCCASIONAL RELIGIOUS PRACTICE AS SELECTIVE PARTICIPATION IN RITUAL SYSTEMS

5
Ritual Systems

The small flame of the Paschal candle leads us into the cavernous darkness of the cathedral nave. Each carrying our own small flame, we process into the familiar space made unfamiliar by candlelight. There is a mysterious and compelling beauty to the single, central candle, and to each one of us held in our own glow—anonymous, equal—yet drawn by the same light, "The Light of Christ," as the chant declares. This fire of new life, of death and resurrection, of Paschal mystery, shines through the Easter season, and at every funeral and baptism. From this flame, a candle is lit for each person newly baptized, with the gentle command to "Receive the Light of Christ."[1]

Receiving the candle often stands out to participants as a significant moment in the baptism service. In some cases, it is the challenge of juggling an infant, an order of service, and a live flame, which demands a different type of attention and responsibility:

> The candle, I remember our daughter tried to grab it when it was lit, and we were just like, oh my God, all we need now is the church on fire! That would be so horrible.

More often participants recall the candle as something to hold on to—literally and metaphorically—in a largely unfamiliar liturgical landscape. It is concrete: seen and smelled, its wax touched, its warmth felt. It is elemental: transcending the boundaries of tradition and time.[2] It is accessible, even to other children, including older siblings:

> It was nice to see [my younger son's baptism] through [my older daughter's] lens. She remembered that she was gifted a little lamb. And now [my son] has his own lamb and has his own candle. And so, there are these connections. And I think it was nice to sort of see it through her lens as

---

[1] General Synod of the Anglican Church of Canada, *Book of Alternative Services*, 160.
[2] Romano Guardini, *The Sacred Signs* (St. Louis: Pio Decimo Press, 1956).

well. And reminding her, "You went through this too, it's not just for your brother."... She saw that [the priest] handed us [the lamb] and then handed us a candle and that we lit the candle and then we get to keep it. So, she was like, "Do I have my candle?" I said, "Well, you do." And I showed her [it later] and she's like, "Oh, I remember that this comes from church."

As these participants describe, the baptism candle is something to bring home. The candle may be used to remember the baptism and to teach the child about baptism as they grow older:

It's one of those moments that you don't really forget. So, for example, like the candle, like it's something that you just keep. And even though I can't remember my own baptism, I feel like I still can because of all the pictures and all the memorabilia that we have. And I kind of, yeah, I just want to create that for [my daughter].

One day when she's older, she can look back at a photo. She has her... they give you that baptismal candle, she has that. She'll never remember it, but she can look back and it shows that we did that for her.

We have the baptismal candle lit, which is a tradition. Then every year you can light the candle if you want to, to commemorate the baptism. But it's typically something that you pass on to your child when they're older, and then they have it when their child has their baptism. It's like that kind of thing.

The candle is one of the aspects of the baptism service that is mentioned most frequently and positively by participants as they reflect on the event weeks or months later: "The lighting of the candle was really beautiful."

The ritual of receiving a baptism candle is part of a Christian ritual system. Through the framing words and connection to the Paschal candle, "The Giving of the Light" at baptism connects various Christian rituals.[3] It connects the rituals that mark birth and death as moments in the Christian life and the human life cycle. It connects cycles of time, linking baptism to the seasons and days of the Christian year, particularly its culmination in the Easter Vigil and Easter season. It connects ritualized layers of theological meaning, including baptism as participation in Christ's death and

---

[3] General Synod of the Anglican Church of Canada, *Book of Alternative Services*, 160.

resurrection, and baptism as a sign of the Reign of God in the world.[4] It also resonates with popular and culturally prescribed religious practices, as two participants describe, drawing on experiences in Roman Catholic and Eastern Orthodox traditions:

> The cathedral had candles, which have been banned in a lot of places. Real candles with real fire—I haven't seen that in a long time. It just brought me back to when I was a kid. When my mom had a problem, she would take us to the church. It was always open and we put money in the section where the candles were. Then we would light a candle and there would be fire—a real candle. We would say a prayer and then we'd go home.
>
> I: You mentioned still having the candles. Do those candles have significance for you? Or what significance do they have?
> R: God's light. So, without a doubt they do. We renovated last summer. And just three weeks ago I was going through all the extra boxes and I found them in there. So, I packed them up in tissue paper and put them away. They'll be given to my kids. They'll be brought out probably every Easter and anything that's special. To me it's God's light and it's out there welcoming us to his home.
>
> There's a thing in the Orthodox church that when you pass—so, one of the worst things that could happen is if you pass without a light. I know, it's funny. But—so if you know you're going to pass or if you have a family member that's going to pass, like the number one thing that you have to have at the bedside is a light—a candlelight. Because it takes you to the light of God. That's what the thought behind it is.
>
> And certainly, I don't want my kids to have this candle until they pass. But there's a real significance to me about what the light means. . . . And to me, light always means good and light means God. A re-centering. And that's why it's important to me that they keep them, that I want them to bring it out on special occasions.
>
> But even if they're just having—as they grow up, a bad day, something's not working for them, I want them to feel comfortable lighting that. It's how they're going to get re-centered, how they're going to get reconnected.

---

[4] World Council of Churches, *Baptism, Eucharist and Ministry*, 1–2; General Synod of the Anglican Church of Canada, *Book of Alternative Services*, 146.

Through the material object of the lit candle, the baptism candle connects other aspects of the Christian ritual system that may be present in the space at the celebration of the baptism and beyond: altar candles, torches, prayer candles, Advent candles, and more.

Many families who participate in baptism receive the baptism candle, and the baptism itself, apart from connections to the broader Christian ritual system. They are unaware of the echoes between the rituals of Christian baptism and Christian burial. They are not present at Easter Vigil or on Sundays with sufficient frequency to track the patterns that mark the seasons and days of the Christian year. They cannot articulate the official theological layers of meaning illumined by the candle.

At the same time, families introduce new connections. The baptism candle might have a place in everyday life alongside the other candles that set time and space apart: birthday candles, formal dining practices, community vigils, and yoga class or meditation, among many other possibilities. Through the presence of occasional practitioners who are embedded in multiple ritual systems, additional ritual systems overlap with the ritual system associated with Christian baptism. These overlaps add layers of meaning. Although always present, these overlapping layers are particularly pronounced among occasional practitioners in increasingly nonreligious and religiously diverse settings.

The focus on ritual systems in Part II of this book provides a bridge between the sociological reality of widespread occasional religious practice described in Part I and Christian theological understandings of occasional religious practice discussed in Part III. In this chapter, I draw on the work of Catherine Bell and Kimberly Belcher to outline and develop a theory of ritual systems, with a specific focus on overlaps between ritual systems that emerge in relation to occasional religious practice. In Chapter 6, I examine occasional religious practice as selective participation in a ritual system that some practice routinely, and explore the implications of this for the meanings and functions of Christian ritual in contemporary contexts. In Chapter 7, I apply this theory in a case study of how occasional practitioners understand and astutely navigate the overlaps between the Roman Catholic and Anglican ritual systems. Ritual systems provide an intuitive framework that explains why occasional practitioners continue to select certain Christian rituals, what these rituals mean and do for occasional practitioners, how occasional practice both does and does not change the rituals themselves, and how people who relate to religion in different ways can learn from one another. Building on this discussion of the baptism candle, the practice of Christian baptism continues to be an example throughout Part II.

What Are Ritual Systems?

The concept of ritual systems is intuitive yet powerful: *ritual practices relate to other ritual practices in systems; relationships within and among systems interpret and reinterpret ritual practices, informing the meanings and functions of rituals for participants.* Despite, and perhaps because of, the commonsense nature of the concept, Catherine Bell observes, "How rites relate to each other within a ritual system and how such systems differ from each other may be one of the most undeveloped areas in the study of ritual."[5] With the exception of two articles by Kimberly Belcher,[6] this remains the case more than two decades after Bell made this observation in 1997. I therefore begin by offering a comprehensive treatment of ritual systems, with particular emphasis on the value of this theoretical framework for understanding religious ritual in increasingly nonreligious and religiously diverse contexts, including occasional religious practice.

Ritual systems exist at many levels. At the macro level, there are ritual systems that span time, geography, and tradition, such as the Christian ritual system or the democratic ritual system. At the micro level, there are systemic relationships within practices, such as the mutual interpretation of elements within the performance of a song: notes, rhythms, lyrics, verses and refrains, emphases, improvisations, and more. At the mezzo level, ritual systems are associated with particular ritual practices, such as baptism or Christian burial, and groups of practices, such as the liturgical life of the Anglican Church of Canada or the traditions associated with a professional sports team. The mezzo level is usually the primary arena for ritual systems analysis and is my focus here.

While my primary interlocutors in this discussion are ritual theorists anchored in religious studies, anthropology, and liturgical studies, there are significant parallels in sociology of religion. Specifically, the definition of

---

[5] Catherine Bell, *Ritual: Perspectives and Dimensions* (New York: Oxford University Press, 1997), 173.
[6] Kimberly Hope Belcher, "Ritual Systems, Ritualized Bodies, and the Laws of Liturgical Development," *Studia Liturgica* 49, no. 1 (2019): 89–110; Kimberly Hope Belcher, "Ritual Systems: Prostration, Self, and Community in the Rule of Benedict," *Ecclesia Orans* 27, no. 2 (2020): 321–356.

religion as practice, borrowed from Martin Riesebrodt and Christian Smith to develop the concept of occasional religious practice in Chapter 1 and to inform an interdisciplinary methodological approach in Appendix A, contains a sense of ritual systems. Smith defines religion as "a complex of culturally prescribed practices."[7] In other words, *religions are ritual systems*:

> Religions are formed of networks of practices grouped together into complexes. A single practice does not make a religion. One does not simply burn some incense or read the passage of a text and thereby have a religion. Religions are composed of *conglomerations of interrelated practices*, sometimes so many that it takes a lifetime to learn to perform them well. Each of the practices has its own meaning, and each usually *adds extra meaning* to the others in the larger complex of practices to which they belong.... The combined meaning is more than the sum of its parts. Complexes of religious practices, which are part of even the simplest of religions, thus generate synergies and experiences that individual practices alone do not.[8]

Smith's approach to complexes of practices closely corresponds to Bell's and Belcher's approaches to ritual systems discussed in this chapter. Martin Riesebrodt, on whose theory Smith's is based, even uses the language of systems:

> Religion, as a complex of practices, is marked by a certain *interpretive systematicity*. It need not be a theologically "pure" system. Its systemic character emerges from the context of meaning that has been institutionalized and is bound to various practices.[9]

Therefore, according to Riesebrodt, the study of observable ritual systems, including syncretic systems, is a crucial dimension of the study of religion:

> In order to understand a religion and explain it, neither constructions of worldviews nor the selective analysis of a randomly chosen ritual—on the basis of which the whole society is explained in symbolico-theoretical,

---

[7] Smith, *Religion*, 22.
[8] Smith, *Religion*, 26. Emphasis added.
[9] Riesebrodt, *The Promise of Salvation*, 77. Emphasis added.

structuralist, or functionalist terms—are adequate methods. Instead, *systems of practices and their own structures of meaning must be investigated in mutual relationship.*[10]

This sociological framework for understanding religion as a complex of practices can be clarified and deepened through the integration of ritual systems theory emerging from the discipline of religious studies.

In the discussion that follows, I unpack four key questions associated with defining and theorizing ritual systems, especially in relation to occasional religious practice: *Who* demarcates ritual systems? What kinds of relationships exist *within* ritual systems? What kinds of relationships exist *among* ritual systems? What do ritual systems *do* in terms of the meaning and function of ritual practices? I draw on the example of occasional practitioners participating in Christian baptism to explore these questions.

Who Demarcates Ritual Systems?

Who determines what rituals are part of a given ritual system and what relationships exist among these rites? This question arises when there are conflicting interpretations of a practice. For example, many occasional practitioners understand baptism as *giving their children the choice* to engage with the Christian tradition *in the future*:

> I feel because I was baptized, I had lots of choices. I got to go to Catholic school, I got to get married in a Catholic Church, I baptized my children—I had choices. My biggest thing is to give [my grandson] the choice when he's old enough to make choices. Let's say he was old enough and he meets a Catholic girl and things get complicated because he was never baptized or had communion or his confirmation. I would hate for him to say to his parents, "Well, why didn't you give me that choice?" That's my biggest thing. I want my kids to have every opportunity and my grandchildren to have every opportunity, every choice. I think by him being baptized, he has a choice.

---

[10] Riesebrodt, *The Promise of Salvation*, 94. Emphasis added.

This approach contrasts with the interpretation of many Anglican priests, who understand baptism as *parents making a choice* to raise children in the Christian tradition *in the present*:

> I think there does have to be like a hoop to jump through, like not a hoop, but sort of you do have to want to raise your kid as a Christian. Yeah. See, to my mind, baptism and pedagogy—the education of your child, it's almost like that whole process of forming a child in the gospel is sort of already there in baptism, prefigured. Like this is what baptism is supposed to result in, and if it doesn't, that's kind of somehow a perversion of the sacrament. . . . Baptism is to pass on something. There's a deposit of faith that's being passed on. There's an inheritance. There's a tradition.

Conflicting interpretations of choice and agency coexist in the ritual system surrounding Christian baptism. Theorizing who demarcates ritual systems provides a framework for understanding these dynamics.

Ritual systems, to some extent, define themselves: "the content or structure of the rites themselves create links that group them into a coherent set."[11] At times, scholars may identify these coherent sets from an *etic* perspective, as Bell does in developing analytical genres of ritual action, such as rites of passage and calendrical rites.[12] However, a ritual systems approach is primarily *emic*, relying on "distinctions and connections among rites that are *made by the ritual performers themselves* by virtue of replicated symbols, gestures, and terminology."[13] Attention to the emic interpretations of practitioners is aligned with ethnographic methods that aim to observe and listen for these interpretations. Furthermore, attention to the systemic relationships expressed by performers positioned differently within ritual systems, including occasional practitioners, results in different understandings of the ritual systems.

Relying on connections made by ritual practitioners is complicated because practitioners occupy different positions within ritual systems, and their distinct positions inform how they describe and understand these ritual systems. Clergy may perceive a ritual system differently than occasional

---

[11] Bell, *Ritual: Perspectives and Dimensions*, 174.
[12] Bell, *Ritual: Perspectives and Dimensions*, 94–102.
[13] Bell, *Ritual: Perspectives and Dimensions*, 174. Emphasis added.

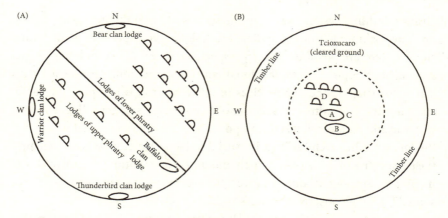

Figure 5.1 Two groups diagram the same community in different ways. (A) Plan of a Winnebago village according to informants of the upper phratry (after P. Radin, *The Winnebago Tribe*, Fig. 33). (B) Plan of a Winnebago village according to informants of the lower phratry (after Radin, *The Winnebago Tribe*, Fig. 34).

Reproduced with permission from Claude Lévi-Strauss, *Structural Anthropology* (New York: Basic Books, 1963).

practitioners, for example. Drawing on the work of Claude Lévi-Strauss,[14] Jonathan Z. Smith describes how two groups within the same tribe diagram their community in different ways: one group depicts two distinct symmetrical sections, and the other group depicts a center and periphery (Figure 5.1).[15] Following Lévi-Strauss:

> the question is not necessarily one of alternatives. These forms, as described, do not necessarily relate to two different organizations. They may also correspond to two different ways of describing one organization too complex to be formalized in a single model, so that the members of each moiety would tend to conceptualize it in one way rather than the other, depending upon their position in the social structure.[16]

---

[14] Claude Lévi-Strauss, *Structural Anthropology* (New York: Basic Books, 1963).
[15] Lévi-Strauss, *Structural Anthropology*, 134–135.
[16] Claude Lévi-Strauss, in Jonathan Z. Smith, *To Take Place: Toward Theory in Ritual* (Chicago: University of Chicago Press, 1987), 43.

Groups within a system may map the same system in different ways based on their positions within the system. Multiple valid perspectives on the same ritual system are possible. These perspectives reveal the complexity of the system, not a failure in mapping. Jonathan Z. Smith identifies power as a crucial factor shaping the perspectives of different groups mapping the same community: "It is from a perspective of power that A sees the village as symmetrical and reciprocal; it is from a position of subordination that B pictures the village as hierarchical."[17] It is crucial to be aware of how power shapes the perspective of individual participants and groups within systems: Whose maps are considered authoritative? Whose maps are not being seen or shared? What perspectives are missing?

To extend this social and spatial analysis to ritual systems, within the Christian ritual system at the center of this research, clergy and theologians occupy positions of power. This shapes their perception of the nature of the systems and relationships within it. People in the pew, especially those present only on certain occasions, tend to have less power. The power differences associated with different relationships with religion are often amplified by power differences associated with gender, race, age, class, education, and more. For example, many of the family members connected to baptisms who participated in this study are younger, female, and newer to Canada. Many of the clergy who were interviewed about baptism are older, male, and long established in Canada. Although those interviewed are not intended to be representative, these trends likely indicate broader patterns. The position and power of individuals within ritual systems impact the ways in which they perceive and interpret distinctions and connections among rites. Occasional practitioners and intensive or routine practitioners may define the same ritual system in different ways. Echoing Lévi-Strauss, the question is not necessarily one of alternatives. Practitioners positioned differently within a ritual system offer distinct, valid, potentially conflicting ways of describing a system that is "too complex to be formalized in a single model."

Baptism, Choice, and Agency

One example of how different positioning contributes to different interpretations of the Christian ritual system is how parents and clergy understand the relationship between infant baptism and choice. Parents and

---

[17] Smith, *To Take Place*, 44.

grandparents, who are often occasional practitioners positioned at the margin of the Christian ritual system, tend to describe baptism as *giving their child a choice in the future*:

> We figured as long as [our children] have step one, they have more options open to them. It makes it a little easier down the road if they want to continue following the religion and be more active in it. . . . If you don't introduce children to religion, then basically they don't have a choice. Their only choice is to ignore it or be ignorant to it. At least if you do introduce them, they can choose, learn what they want to understand. . . . Because if they didn't get baptized and then they don't feel they have a connection, would never go to church, would never go even for once a year for service for Christmas or Easter or something. Then they'll just be ignorant, and they'll only hear half of the argument and not really know that much. So, I think it's more powerful to them individually to be able to learn more and make their own decisions.

> Parents can feel good that you've made that first step for them and then they can do whatever they want as they get older.

> I: Do you hope that [your children] would choose to be confirmed, or how do you feel about that?
> R: I'm completely neutral on that, to be quite honest with you. If that's something they're interested in, then that's fine. If it's not, that's fine. Yeah, for me it's not an important part of the way I understand things, and so it's not something I would necessarily—but I'm not against it. Yeah, either way is fine with me. I would support them in whatever they want to do.

> For me there is more curiosity about why you believe what you believe. And I'd like to pass that on to [my children]. That if they decide to be a Christian, they have to do their own decision. That has to be a decision that they made conscientiously because they've explored all avenues, not just because they're mirroring my faith.

At the time of baptism, these parents and grandparents understand themselves to be making a choice to give their child a choice about how to relate to religion in the future. In other words, they demonstrate what Christian Smith describes as "default religious laxity" in terms of making a modest religious investment in the present to maintain the possibility of future opportunities for their children to increase their religiousness.

In contrast, clergy, positioned at the center of the Christian ritual system, tend to depict baptism as *making a choice for the child in the present*, specifically in terms of parents and godparents making a commitment to raise the child in the Christian tradition:

> We're trying to capture weddings, funerals, baptisms, those moments, under the umbrella of discipleship, and connecting people with faith and community.... We've pushed pretty hard for a kind of baptismal discipline that I think is welcoming, but also raises the bar for expectations.

> We're trying to help [families] see that baptism is not an isolated event. It's not an inoculation, like you go to the doctor to get your child their MMR shots every so often. Baptism does not work like that. That usually comes as a surprise. Most people think baptism is a standalone event, and we're trying to say it's a community event, because you're part of a community, and it's this great adventure—this is where it formally begins.

One of the ways that clergy enact an emphasis on parents and godparents making a choice on behalf of the child is by focusing the preparation process for baptism on the baptismal promises made in the liturgy, as is the case in this example, which has many parallels:

> I usually have a meeting with [the baptism family], and then we go through the actual baptism service. The vows are quite in-depth and extensive. I have an electronic copy of the presentation and examination and all of the promises that I send to them ahead of time so that they can look at it. And then we walk through each one of them, and just talk about what it means, to "renounce Satan and the all the spiritual forces of wickedness that rebel against God," let's unpack that, right? So that's typically what we do with all of them. "Do you turn to Jesus Christ and accept him as your savior?" What does that mean, to turn to Jesus? So in part I do that with them because I want them to be comfortable, not in the laissez faire sense of comfort, but to know what it is they are saying "I do" to and to know what it means.

Although there are exceptions among both groups, these patterns are pronounced: clergy emphasize the agency of parents in making a choice to place their child at the center of the Christian ritual system; parents who are occasional practitioners emphasize giving their child the choice to exercise their own agency by maintaining a point of connection to the Christian ritual system.

These are both reasonable interpretations of the rite of infant baptism. As a practice of initiation into the Christian ritual system, baptism is a ritual practice at the margin or boundary of the system. In some Anglican church buildings, baptism literally occurs at the entrance: it is a threshold rite. Those who participate in baptism may have little experience of the fullness of the Christian ritual system, or a sense of the points of connection between baptism and other rites, when the baptism occurs. At the same time, baptism is a ritual practice at the center of the Christian ritual system that identifies the individual and the community with the person of Christ, who died and is risen. In some Anglican liturgical settings, the baptism takes place at the front and center of the space, or the community physically gathers around those being baptized, locating them in the center of the church as a people. For those immersed in the Christian ritual system, baptism has resonances that echo through many rites. Baptism is *both* at the boundary and in the center.

Although parents recognize their role in raising children, they also acknowledge the agency of their children and that, at some point in the future, their children will make their own choices about how to relate to religion. As people marginalized by the Christian ritual system who tend to see themselves as "not very religious," this is an intuitive and accurate mapping of the system. In contrast, clergy emphasize the current role of parents in shaping the religious faith and practice of their children, which clergy often understand as best accomplished through placing the child in the center of the religious community and placing religion in the center of family life. As people who exercise significant religious authority from their position in the center of the Christian ritual system, this is an intuitive and accurate mapping of the system. These perspectives are complementary, not contradictory: *both* children and parents have agency; choices are made in *both* the present and the future; baptism *both* gives the child a choice and makes a choice on behalf of the child.

These dimensions of the practice exist in tension with one another. Practitioners positioned differently within a ritual system—in this case, occasional practitioners and clergy who together practice the ritual of baptism—offer distinct, valid, and conflicting ways of describing the ritual system which reveal the internal complexity of the system, not a failure in mapping.

What Kinds of Relationships Exist Within Ritual Systems?

The relationships between ritual practices within a ritual system are complex. It is impossible to outline all potential types of relationships that can exist within ritual systems in general, or all of the relationships within a particular ritual system. The description of the baptism candle at the outset of this chapter illustrates many of these types of relationships within the Christian ritual system. Here, I identify three broad categories of relationship through which rituals can be systemically interpreted *within* a ritual system: (1) repetition, (2) opposition, and (3) centrality.

Repetition of Rituals

The *repetition* or *replication* of symbols and gestures is the primary feature of ritual systems examined by Bell and Belcher.[18] At the most basic level, this involves examining repeated instances of a symbol or gesture within a system, such as the repetition associated with the candle described at the beginning of this chapter. Belcher models this approach through a detailed analysis of the five instances of prostration in the Rule of Benedict to demonstrate how "participants in a ritual system naturally use the other instances of a gesture to interpret the gesture in each particular instance."[19] A similar process could be applied to various aspects of the rite of baptism.

Bell, however, sets ritualization in the sweeping context of tradition to imply three specific types of repetition. First, *historical repetition* focuses on the repetition of the ritual over time, including the sense that ritual practices are "thought to have been handed down from previous generations."[20] In the case of baptism, the baptism of a child may be anchored in the baptism of the parent, grandparent, and great-grandparent. As discussed in Chapters 3 and 4, this type of repetition may be especially significant for occasional practitioners who understand their religious identity in terms of cultural heritage or family background, and for those who initiate participation in occasional practices in connection with their cultural heritage.

---

[18] Bell, *Ritual: Perspectives and Dimensions*, 173–174; Belcher, "Ritual Systems."
[19] Belcher, "Ritual Systems," 336. Participants also interpret the gesture in relation to adjacent and canonical texts.
[20] Catherine Bell, *Ritual Theory, Ritual Practice* (New York: Oxford University Press, 1992), 118.

Historical repetition could also refer to the repetition of the ritual within the Christian ritual system across the centuries.

Second, *temporal* and *regional repetition* centers on the repetition of rituals in local contexts. In the case of baptism, the practice may be repeated four times each year in a particular parish in connection with specific feast days, or a parish may be open to repeating the baptism ritual for anyone who identifies with the tradition who lives within the parish boundaries.

Third, *organization and standardization by ritual experts* inform repetition within ritual systems. Although the role of experts and degree of standardization vary, one example is the creation of liturgical books, such as the *Book of Alternative Services,* that lead to near uniform repetition of liturgical texts for baptism across parishes in the Anglican Church of Canada, regardless of the religious identities or commitments of specific participants. Such attempts at liturgical standardization emerge at points of change in a ritual system and are inevitably political.[21]

Identifying repeated symbols and gestures may be the most significant, straightforward, and well-developed approach to ritual systems analysis, but it is only one tool among many for analyzing relationships within ritual systems.[22]

Opposition of Rituals

Ritual practices exist in relationships of opposition within ritual systems. Opposition refers to instances in which *difference rather than repetition* defines the interpretive relationship between practices. Bell outlines a range of possible oppositions:

> The internal organization of such a ritual system is usually a complex orchestration of standard binary oppositions that generate flexible sets of relationships both differentiating and integrating activities, gods, sacred places, and communities vis-à-vis each other. Domestic rites contrast with communal rites, male rites with female rites, preliminary rites with culminating ones. Three interrelated sets of oppositions in particular reveal the more systematic dimensions of ritualization: (1) the vertical opposition

---

[21] Belcher, "Ritual Systems, Ritualized Bodies," 108–109.
[22] Bell, *Ritual: Perspectives and Dimensions*, 173.

of superior and inferior, which generates hierarchical structures; (2) the horizontal opposition of here and there, or us and them, which generates lateral or relatively egalitarian relationships; and (3) the opposition of central and local, which frequently incorporates and dominates the preceding oppositions.[23]

Any number of other distinctions may also be identified, including those Bell names among her tools for analyzing ritual systems: periodic and occasional rites, individual and collective rites, and high and low ritual practices.[24] In each case, difference rather than repetition is the interpretive principle.

One example of opposition applied to Christian baptism is Gordon Lathrop's liturgical theological focus on juxtaposition. Lathrop claims that "meaning occurs through structure, by one thing set next to another ... the use of the old to say the new by means of juxtaposition."[25] In baptism, people are brought into the community "by being led through a great chain of linked and mutually reinterpretive events, a chain of juxtapositions."[26] The most foundational juxtaposition associated with baptism, according to Lathrop, is: "we teach and then we wash," or "we wash and then we teach,"[27] and even the juxtaposition between these two approaches. This juxtaposition is evident in the range of approaches Anglican clergy take when responding to requests for baptism from occasional practitioners, with some requiring a substantial process of preparation or teaching before baptism, and others seeing baptism as a beginning that may precede teaching. However, opposition may be as simple as a lit candle in a dark nave, differences in dress between clergy and laity, or the contrast of silence and sound.

Centrality of Rituals

A third type of relationship between ritual practices within a ritual system is the relative *importance* of rituals within the system, which Belcher describes in terms of practices that are *central* or marginal. "A ritual system," according to Belcher, "includes *central rituals* (those established within a social group

---

[23] Bell, *Ritual Theory, Ritual Practice*, 125.
[24] Bell, *Ritual: Perspectives and Dimensions*, 173–176.
[25] Gordon Lathrop, *Holy Things: A Liturgical Theology* (Minneapolis, MN: Fortress Press, 1993), 33.
[26] Lathrop, *Holy Things*, 59.
[27] Lathrop, *Holy Things*, 59–60.

as having cosmogonic significance), and all behaviors within the cultural community that are linked to those central rituals."[28] She describes two kinds of central rituals:

> *infrequent*, solemn/ludic rites and *frequent* rites that define daily existence. Each of these kinds of rites can be identified as central by the way that their strictures for embodied posture and gesture, the divisions of space and time, linguistic patterns and symbols are *replicated throughout the cultural system*, even being echoed in behaviors established by non-ritual experts performing improvisation or bricolage.[29]

Central rites have more points of connection within the ritual system. In contrast, marginal rites have fewer connections within the system and therefore "can be fluid and ambiguous in their meaning."[30] Centrality is about *interconnectedness*, not opposition; centrality and marginality are not experienced in opposition by those inhabiting the ritual system.

I extend the concept of central and marginal rites and examine ritual systems as *centered sets*, categories created by defining a center and the relationship of things to that center, rather than *bounded sets*, categories created by listing essential characteristics of objects in the set. Ritual systems are best understood as *centered sets*. A central ritual practice (or group of practices) is dynamically related, more or less closely, to a range of other practices in a ritual system. Instead of having clearly defined and static boundaries, and while retaining a sense of direction and coherence, ritual systems are characterized by variation and fluidity. Understanding ritual systems as centered sets means that the focus is not on determining whether a particular ritual practice is or is not part of a system; instead, a wide range of practices can be viewed as more or less closely connected to a center.

I borrow this mathematical metaphor from theological literature on Christian identity and mission.[31] In a 1978 article, Paul Hiebert outlined the characteristics of bounded and centered sets (summarized in Table 5.1)

---

[28] Belcher, "Ritual Systems," 325. Emphasis added.
[29] Belcher, "Ritual Systems," 351. Emphasis added.
[30] Belcher, "Ritual Systems," 350.
[31] Because of the context of origin of this concept, I reiterate here that this research is not oriented toward mission and does not aim to change how people relate to religion in terms of increasing frequency of religious participation. Instead, I use this concept to analyze relationships among practices within ritual systems. In addition, because this mathematical concept is received through theological literature, this discussion is not intended to satisfy mathematicians.

Table 5.1 Ritual Systems as Centered Sets

Centered Set	Bounded Set
The category is created by defining a center, and the relationship of things to that center.	The category is created by listing the essential characteristics that an object must have to be within the set.
While the centered set does not place the primary focus on the boundary, there is a division between things moving in and those moving out.	The category is defined by a clear boundary.
Centered sets reflect variation within a category.	Objects within a bounded set are uniform in their essential characteristics.
Centered sets are dynamic.	Bounded sets are static sets.

and argued that it is beneficial to consider Christian identity as a centered set rather than a bounded set, particularly in the context of mission.[32] Not only does this language resonate with Belcher's concept of centrality, it also connects with Ronald Grimes's approach to defining ritual in terms of a family of characteristics that keep us "from thinking of activities as if they either are or are not ritual," yet allows us to specify "in what respects and to what extent an action is ritualized."[33] Furthermore, this metaphor is somewhat emic to the study in that several clergy describe the relationship between participants and the church in these terms in interviews; one priest even drew a diagram with arrows in different positions, oriented in various directions. However, I want to be very clear that I am using the language of centered and bounded sets to refer to *practices* within ritual systems, *not* to people as in the mission literature, or to stand-alone practices as in Grimes.

For example, the seminal ecumenical statement on baptism from the World Council of Churches, *Baptism, Eucharist and Ministry*, places baptism with water in the name of the triune God at the center of the baptism ritual system, which is reflected in the Anglican *Book of Alternative Services*, where it is surrounded by a system of closely related and interconnected practices.[34] In the Anglican tradition, baptism is often celebrated in the context of a eucharistic liturgy, through which a range of practices are linked to

---

[32] Paul G. Hiebert, "Conversion, Culture and Cognitive Categories," *Gospel in Context* 1, no. 4 (1978): 24–29.

[33] Ronald Grimes, *Ritual Criticism* (Columbia: University of South Carolina Press, 1990), 9–10.

[34] World Council of Churches, *Baptism, Eucharist and Ministry*; General Synod of the Anglican Church of Canada, *Book of Alternative Services*, 151–166.

the baptism ritual system. A family gathering for a meal and the giving of gifts may follow, extending the baptism ritual system beyond the liturgical structure and space.

It is crucial to note that the relative centrality or importance of a ritual within a system based on the density of the network of relationships that surround it, both in terms of number and proximity, does not necessarily correspond to the importance of the practice for all, or even most, participants. Rites that are marginal in terms of density within a system may be central to the experience of practitioners, and rites that are supposedly central may be experienced as largely irrelevant. For example, invoking the triune name of God is at the heart of a dense network of relationships surrounding baptism in the Christian ritual system—it has many points of connection within the rite of baptism, the liturgy that surrounds it, and broader Christian liturgical life. However, very few occasional practitioners reference the Trinity directly or indirectly, or refer to this invocation as an important aspect of their experience. In contrast, gifts given to a child by family members on the occasion of baptism are not densely networked in the Christian ritual system, yet may be very important to occasional practitioners, possibly due to their centrality in other ritual systems. In some cases, a ritual may be densely networked in multiple systems. For example, white clothing worn by the child being baptized may be densely networked in both the Christian ritual system—in symbolizing putting on Christ, the priesthood of all believers, and new beginnings—and in the family ritual system—in linking this baptism to past family baptisms, or being a gift or an heirloom (for more on clothing, see Chapter 9). The position of participants within the system, and within overlapping systems, shapes their understanding of what is central and what is marginal in relation to baptism. This raises the question of the relationships *among*, as well as *within*, ritual systems.

What Kinds of Relationships Exist Among Ritual Systems?

Individual ritual practices not only relate to each other within systems; entire ritual systems also relate to other ritual systems. It is crucial to recognize the relationships that exist *among* distinct ritual systems, especially in the case of occasional religious practice in increasingly nonreligious and religiously diverse social contexts. Relationships among ritual systems include *nesting* and *overlapping* ritual systems.

Examples of these relationships include the nesting of the baptism ritual system within the larger Christian ritual system, as well the overlap between the Christian ritual system and family ritual system that is present in many baptisms that involve occasional practitioners. As this occasional practitioner describes, *godparents* who participate in baptisms often connect through the family ritual system more than the religious ritual system:

> I had godparents when I was young. They were an elderly couple, and things were a lot different back then. We would go to see them every weekend, but not so much because they were my godparents, but because they were my mother's close friends. . . . They worked a lot with a church and they were friends with some of the nuns. Every weekend, we go to see them. They'd have this big Sunday dinner and there'd be one or two [religious] sisters there, but they never made it, they didn't go there to discuss religion and stuff. It was more of a family community thing and they're all close together. So even though they were my godparents, and you saw them all the time, apart from saying grace, even though they were very active in church, they never really discussed religion with me or teachings, principles, any of that.
>
> It was more like they were part of the family. I think that's what it carried on of what godparents are, rather than the official definition which is to be the person to give and pass on teaching, so that religion, to be the primary source of information and guidance on that. However, the experience I had was that they're just someone close to you that treats you like family. That's the kind of role that we are looking to pass on as godparents. So yes, they're connected through the church as well, but I think regardless for anyone it's a lot to ask them unless they are a preacher. It's hard to fill that role, so I think the default role most godparents end up filling is just being the additional caregiver who cares for that child.

While this participant's godparents were routinely religious and likely identified as Catholic, family members who claim a diversity of religious and nonreligious identities are often invited to serve as godparents who make faith commitments in the context of the baptism liturgy. The roles of godparents draw attention to the way that the baptism ritual system is nested within the Christian ritual system, while also being an overlap between the family ritual system and the Christian ritual system. Theorizing the different types of relationships that exist among ritual systems can illuminate the dynamics surrounding the religious and nonreligious aspects of godparenting that emerge in association with occasional practice.

Nesting Systems

Entire ritual systems relate to other ritual systems, which includes the possibility of smaller systems nesting within larger systems. In several instances, Bell points to the possibility of ritual *subsystems*:

> Some cultures . . . appear to have had a relatively neat ritual system that explicitly integrated, however loosely, multiple and sometimes competing *subsystems* by means of a loose hierarchization.[35]

These subsystems are relatively contained within larger ritual systems. For example, the Anglican baptism ritual system and the Cathedral Church of St. James ritual system can be interpreted as subsystems nesting within the larger Anglican ritual system. Routine participants within these systems would recognize these subsystems as distinct from, yet held within, the larger ritual systems that encompass them.

Some ritual systems could also be described as *supersystems*. Supersystems are so expansive that no one person, or group of people together, could ever participate in the fullness of the ritual supersystem, yet the supersystem still has a coherence that holds it together. For example, Christianity, spanning centuries, cultures, and traditions, is a ritual supersystem. Primarily the academic construct of scholars who theorize relationships within the supersystem, it would be impossible for any individual or cohesive group even to begin to engage the whole. Nevertheless, there is enough coherence that practitioners can find their way through various parts of the supersystem, although certain aspects may be considered very foreign, and some parts may be unrecognizable to some ordinary practitioners. Any ritual system associated with a major religious tradition, as well as nonreligious ritual systems, such as democracy and capitalism, are supersystems.

The lines between ritual supersystems, systems, and subsystems are blurry and contextual. For the purposes of this analysis of occasional participation in Christian baptism, three nesting layers within the Christian ritual

---

[35] Bell, *Ritual: Perspectives and Dimensions*, 174.

system to consider are: (1) the Christian ritual supersystem; (2) the Anglican Church of Canada ritual system and the baptism ritual system, which both nest in the Christian ritual supersystem; and (3) the various subsystems within the Anglican and baptism ritual systems, such as the ritual subsystems associated with the congregations where the rite is celebrated, the process of baptismal preparation, and the baptism rite itself. However, there may be times when the relationships between these ritual systems and other systems are best described as overlapping rather than nesting.

Overlapping Systems

In addition to nesting ritual systems, it is important to attend to overlapping ritual systems— instances when certain rituals are shared between two or more systems while other rituals remain unique to each system. Particularly striking are the overlaps between religious and family ritual systems that are present in relation to godparenting. As this godmother describes, she does not see a significant difference between her role as an aunt and her role as a godparent:

I: How do you understand your role as a godparent? What does that mean?
R: Yeah. I have to say I don't think I necessarily think of it any different than I do as sort of my role as her aunt. . . . I know I've had friends and sort of, they talk about just needing to buy extra presents for their godchildren and things like that. And it's just, those were in the cases where they're not like a blood relative. And so, I don't know if I necessarily distinguish my role any differently. But it's to support these children as they grow. To help them learn. Yeah. And I think I see it now a little bit more with [my niece]. She's inquisitive in certain things. And sort of just by answering questions and sort of—not to take away anything from what her parents are doing. But she'll sometimes listen to us in different ways than she'll listen to her parents. And I think it's just—yeah. Just encouraging her to be—it sounds a little superficial to say, but just encouraging her to just—her and [her brother]—to just be good people. . . . And to sort of just raise these children well. Yeah. And [my sister-in-law] will tell me sometimes when they've gone to church. And it's just kind of nice to be able to encourage that as well.

I: Yeah. Is there a religious or spiritual aspect to godparenting for you?

R: I mean, I'm constantly lifting them up in my prayers. It doesn't feel—I don't think that this is different because I'm a godparent. It's because they are my family as well.

In contrast, an Anglican priest emphasizes that the religious commitments made by godparents are very different from being a relative committed to caring for the child:

> I make it clear to the couple when we're having the interview that I don't want Uncle Tom and Aunt Mary to be the godparents just because, if something happens to you, you want the child to be raised in their home. They might be nice people, but are they Christian? They need to take their vows very seriously.

Theorizing overlapping ritual systems helps make sense of the tensions that can emerge at overlaps between the Christian ritual system and family ritual system when occasional practitioners desire baptism.

Bell offers several tantalizing insights into overlapping ritual systems without fully developing the implications of the theory. Bell herself states, "There has been too little analysis of the historical and sociocultural dimensions of ritual systems to give much sense of the basic principles at work."[36] While Belcher has developed principles regarding the role of ritual systems in the historical development of ritual practices,[37] I am primarily interested in how the sociocultural dimensions of ritual systems overlap in the present, which is particularly significant in relation to occasional religious practice. First, to synthesize Bell's insights into overlapping ritual systems:

(1) Overlapping systems are *common*. According to Bell, "the more common state of affairs" is "the simultaneous presence of competing, complementary, or overlapping social and ritual systems."[38] It is normal for a society to have multiple ritual systems and for individuals and groups to participate in multiple ritual systems.

---

[36] Bell, *Ritual: Perspectives and Dimensions*, 209.
[37] Belcher, "Ritual Systems, Ritualized Bodies."
[38] Bell, *Ritual: Perspectives and Dimensions*, 185.

(2) Overlapping systems *sometimes conflict and sometimes correspond*: "Religious cultures are complex, often including more than one ritual style or system, sometimes in tension, sometimes coexisting in complementary harmony."[39] Different types of relationships between overlapping systems are possible.

(3) In many cases, ritual *practitioners exist relatively comfortably in overlapping systems*, even in instances of perceived conflict. Bell offers the example of the colonial expansion of the Christian tradition:

> At times, the Christians of China and Africa have felt caught between two ritual systems deemed incompatible—traditional rites to the ancestors on one hand, and Christian rites that explicitly forbid the "idolatry" of worshiping other gods, on the other hand. Some groups ... burned their ancestral tablets so as to comply with the demands of the Christian system. Other groups tried to work out a compromise, frequently arguing that ancestral practices are not rituals of worship addressed to gods but simply customs signaling great respect. *Most often, people tried to participate in both ritual systems without worrying too much about how they fit together.*[40]

Belcher unpacks several examples of the complex colonial contexts toward which Bell gestures, emphasizing the importance of power and liturgical recording technologies in conflicts that occur between ritual systems.[41] However, conflict among systems is often the preoccupation of ritual experts and scholars, not ordinary practitioners, unless limitations on certain practices are imposed.

(4) Overlaps with other systems can *change a ritual system*. As Bell observes:

> If a society passes through social and historical changes affecting its worldview, organization, economic activities, and exposure to competing ideas, for example, it will probably witness concomitant changes in its ritual system—even though ritual systems can be particularly resistant to change.[42]

---

[39] Bell, *Ritual: Perspectives and Dimensions*, 190.
[40] Bell, *Ritual: Perspectives and Dimensions*, 174.
[41] Belcher, "Ritual Systems, Ritualized Bodies," 105–108.
[42] Bell, *Ritual: Perspectives and Dimensions*, 190.

Belcher more fully develops how systemic relations shape the development of ritual practices over time, as discussed in greater depth below.[43]

(5) A ritual system can *change other overlapping systems*. Although Bell is hesitant to make strong claims in this regard, she points to potentially wide-reaching implications of a ritual system within a larger overlapping network of systems:

> A ritual must be understood within the context of its larger system, whether this system is elaborate or minimal and the connections overt or latent. *What is less clear is how the internal organization of multiple and overlapping ritual systems relates to the sociocultural roles and meanings of the rites.* Some evidence suggests that the very practices that generate and maintain the systematization of ritual— processes of hierarchization, centralization, replication, marginalization, and the like—can be powerful forces in politics, regional identity and interregional relations, economics, social stratification, philosophical speculation, and theological abstraction. As such, *the systematization of ritual practice would not simply relate to other social and cultural phenomenon as much as it would help constitute them.*[44]

The relationships within one ritual system may be part of establishing relationships in other overlapping ritual systems.

In light of (4) and (5), we can presume that influence among ritual systems is often, if not always, mutual, while likely also asymmetrical.

Attention to overlapping ritual systems is crucial in contemporary cosmopolitan settings where an abundance of ritual systems overlap. As Bell observed in 1997, "it is not hard today to find a great variety of communities, worldviews, and styles of ritualizing living in close proximity to one another"[45]—a reality that is even more prevalent decades later. The close proximity of diverse ritual systems and the overlaps among them are especially significant when considering occasional religious practice in contemporary contexts. As discussed in Part I, multiple intersecting systems are visible in

---

[43] Belcher, "Ritual Systems, Ritualized Bodies."
[44] Bell, *Ritual: Perspectives and Dimensions*, 177.
[45] Bell, *Ritual: Perspectives and Dimensions*, 252.

the diverse religious identities that participants in Anglican ritual practices claim. In addition, overlapping systems are evident in the motivations that drive participants who are both initiators and supporters. Several overlapping systems that are prominent in this analysis in relation to baptism include extended family ritual systems, ethnic subcultural ritual systems, ritual systems associated with infancy and childhood, and the secular urban ritual supersystem.

Religious and Nonreligious Godparenting

Different understandings of the role of godparents or sponsors is one illustration of how overlapping ritual systems interact in baptisms that involve occasional practitioners. As discussed in Chapters 3 and 4, the godparents connected to this study claim diverse religious and nonreligious identities and are inner-circle supporters who typically do not initiate the practice but nonetheless have a key role in enacting the ritual. Godparents frequently occupy a ritual space at the intersection of the religion and family ritual systems (Figure 5.2).

In the Anglican Christian *religious ritual system*, being a godparent—or a sponsor, to use the formal language of the rite—is a religious role. As previously discussed in relation to questions of choice and agency, when children are baptized, sponsors, along with parents, make public faith commitments

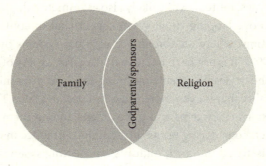

Figure 5.2 Overlapping ritual systems and religious and nonreligious godparenting.

on their behalf. In addition, they make specific commitments regarding the religious upbringing of the child:

> *The celebrant asks the parents and sponsors,*
>   Will you be responsible for seeing that the child you present is nurtured in the faith and life of the Christian community?
> *Parents and sponsors,*
>   I will, with God's help.
> *Celebrant*
>   Will you by your prayers and witness help this child to grow into the full stature of Christ?
> *Parents and sponsors,*
>   I will, with God's help.[46]

Anglican clergy frequently emphasize the religious role of godparents and the importance of choosing godparents who can fulfill this religious function:

> My expectation around godparents, they are not necessarily connected to my parish, but I do expect them that they have a Christian faith that they can articulate, and that they have been baptized, in part because I understand the role of godparents—or as we call them in our order of service, sponsors—that they've been chosen because of their fitness to help raise a child in the life of faith. So, if they can't articulate a Christian faith, then they can't very well serve in that capacity.

> I would say, "Who are the godparents going to be?" Very often there are people who don't live in the parish for a period of time and they want the godparents to be people back in Africa or the West Indies. And we have to say, "Well, are they going to be very useful godparents?" Because we are still in the Anglican tradition, godparents are still the ones who promise to bring the child to church, not the parent.... Sometimes people will get very upset about that, and they'll say, "Well, but this person is my best friend, or is my sister's best friend, or my mother's whatever." And you have to say to them..., "They are going to be close to the child and that can't be taken

---

[46] General Synod of the Anglican Church of Canada, *Book of Alternative Services*, 153.

away. But the point of the godparents is to bring [the child] to the church if the parents can't, and to make sure that [the child is] brought up in the faith and learn it." Now some of them kind of immediately get that and there are some who remain kind of resistant.

These clergy are interpreting the rite and the role of godparents within the Christian ritual system and interpret the Christian ritual system as bounded in ways that exclude certain potential godparents. However, the resistance from parents is understandable because being a godparent is frequently a role that overlaps with the family ritual system, where it is interpreted primarily in relational terms.

In the *family ritual system*, being a godparent is not primarily understood as a religious role. Godparents are generally chosen because of close family or friendship relationships, with religious significance being secondary, if present at all. Parents tend to see godparents as making a commitment to the child rather than a commitment to the church. As described in two examples in Chapter 3, parents may choose nonreligious godparents for their children.

Some parents understand godparents as those whom they hope will care for their children if anything happens to them (although these legal arrangements would need to be made apart from the religious rite):

For me, I guess, for the legal side of things, if anything happens to us, we would leave our children to you. And then I think [the godparents] and even my husband have been like, "Okay, I think that has to be done legally." It's more of like a ceremonious-like gesture. It's just an honor to be asked and it's implied, I guess, that you will look after the children. I don't know. I don't think it's legally binding in any way, but it's just this moment where you're like very selective with whom you would actually trust to parent your children should something happen to both of you. So I did take that decision very seriously.

I: What does being a godparent involve?
R: For me being a godparent is—and I let her know this too—if something should happen to me and my husband, you step in as that parental figure. Now, you're still a parental figure.... Like if you [referring to her daughter] feel as if you're getting in—and mommy and daddy just don't understand where you're coming from, I want you to feel comfortable enough to go to her and be like, "I need to tell you something, I need to ask you something, if I need anything I can go to you."

I: Another supportive adult to confide in or to guide her.
R: Exactly.
I: Is there a spiritual or religious aspect to being a godparent in your family?
R: No, I don't think so.

As in the example above, godparents are primarily seen as an extension of the family system that can be an additional caring adult presence in the life of the children. This is the most common understanding expressed by parents, as in this example (and in previous quotations):

> It's that extra person that just has that little bit extra connection with the child. She's already obviously auntie, but now she's just that "plus-one" auntie. So yes, it's just that extra connection. I'm godmother to one of my nephews and it's the same thing. It's like, "Yeah, I'm your auntie, but I've got this extra little piece." It's almost like an extra level of looking out for them and making sure. It's just somebody that I know loves my kids and thinks the world of them and it's just going to be that extra little thing for them to have this place of importance, especially as they get a little bit older.
>
> I remember my godfather is my uncle. Growing up, he was my uncle but you're my godfather too. It was almost that little bit [of] extra respect I had for him. That little bit [of] extra reverence that I had for him. My relationship with my uncle that's my godfather is [a] closer relationship than [with] any of my other aunts and uncles on either side of the family. And it's just that reason.

As this example and others demonstrate, parents are frequently interpreting the ritual role of the godparents of their own children through their own experience of having godparents—through the repetition of the ritual in the family ritual system.

Godparents themselves describe their role in nonreligious terms, instead emphasizing being an additional caregiver and confidant. This is the case for two occasionally religious godmothers who self-identify as Christian and spiritual:

> My first godchild, he just had his first child three years ago. So I've watched him grow up and become a man and a father and a husband, which has been wonderful. And again, I was just like the aunt he could come to and

say or do anything. I know that I was always going to be there for him. And then the other two little guys are younger, so just waiting to see who they're going to become....

So I don't think I have ever approached this as a religious duty at all. I've never had to talk about God with any of them. When I'm ready to talk about that I can tell them my thoughts and listen to theirs. But I guess traditionally it was supposed to be the role of the godparent to make sure that they were on the spiritual right track. I see it more as just being that extra parent, who is there to catch them when the parents are too busy or need a little extra hand or whatever.

I: Could you say a bit more about what being a godmother to your nieces means to you?

R: Oh, being there to certainly love and support them and they're young and they're learning and so being there to teach them things and when the time comes. And I want to say focused on that. You know, they're kids, they're curious about the world and they have lots of questions. They're inquisitive. Like, I want to say good guidance, but by the same token, we all grow up, we make our own decisions, right? We make mistakes and [my job is to] be there I guess when they make their mistakes, help them out.

I: Be another supportive adult in their lives.

R: Oh, for sure. Yeah, for sure be there. And I guess also my sister needs help, she has five children. That's a big responsibility. But no, it's nice. It's lovely seeing them grow up and watching, you know, it's interesting to see what kind of adults they'll be turned into. And of course, you want them to be successful. Well also not just successful but, that's a very, how do I say, there's different definitions of successful, that they are happy.

I: Are there any more specifically religious aspects to being a godparent for you?

R: Well, I guess if they have any questions on faith or if they—I don't know how to answer that to be honest. I don't know how to answer that.

I: That's a good answer too.

R: Yeah, I don't know. It's something I've just honestly never thought of. Like I have my own beliefs that certainly that I'm not necessarily going to push on to my nieces, but should they have questions or should they like need to go to church with them or should they get, you know, take on a bigger role in the church, I'd support them.

Like these two godmothers, most participants in this research interpret the practice of godparenting in relationship with other ritual practices in the family ritual system, such as family gatherings, gift giving, and offering guidance, rather than practices within the Christian ritual system.

Of the many participants in this research who have chosen godparents, who themselves are godparents, or both, there are only two who understand godparenting as having a religious dimension—one who is routinely religious and the other who is an invisibly routine occasional practitioner:

> I: Could you say more about what it means for you to be a godparent?
> R: For me, I have a lot of close friends that are not necessarily family. And so, for me, it sort of extends our family a little bit with people that are close to us in a kind of way; it sort of connects us. People that we grew up with or that we've been friends with forever and ever, it just sort of connects us in a deeper way. Our children are each other's godchildren. And then for me, it's just an opportunity to like, I have a reason to sort of teach these kids what I know about religion, even though it's not—we generally have different religions, but same types of beliefs. . . . It's funny because I could talk to a godchild about prayer and stuff before my own because we're all going through the day-to-day stuff with our own kids. And then, yeah, the godparents I think are important for that reason and yeah.
> I: So there is a religious or spiritual aspect to being a godparent for you?
> R: Yes, yes.

There was someone [my husband] wanted as a godparent, and she refused because she is atheist. And that brought in some contention for me as well because choosing a godparent, for me, it's important that they hold the faith to teach her [my daughter], to guide her along the path of Christianity. So, I won't lie, that did bring up some arguments. But at the same time, it helped [my husband] and I grow because with that person, because like I said it was not a judgment on their behalf. And I spoke to [my husband]—it made him and I really come to realize what we wanted for her, and the importance of religion in our relationship and our family right now. And so the person we originally—he, I should say, originally wanted, we just gently—we just simply didn't bring it up until we knew for sure. And [my husband] didn't feel so bad, but he did have an honest discussion with her [telling her that] he was going to choose her and why we didn't go forward with it.

This is the only example where a parent experiences a significant conflict or dissonance at the intersection between religious and family ritual systems in relation to godparents. Far more often, as Bell anticipates, practitioners exist relatively comfortably in overlapping ritual systems. As the examples above and in Chapters 3 and 4 demonstrate, they find ways to inhabit two systems simultaneously, even when those systems appear to conflict. Furthermore, the overlap with the family ritual system may lead to a reinterpretation of the meaning of the baptismal rite, as the mothers in Chapter 4 describe and as the godparents imply in the examples above, to understand it as a commitment to support the children in their journeys to be good people, rather than specifically good Christians. At the same time, the rite also changes the dynamics in the family system by setting apart certain individuals as godparents. Parents, godparents, and clergy continually negotiate this overlap between ritual systems.

Ritual practices exist within a thick fabric of ritual life, as is demonstrated in this discussion of the relationships among ritual systems and in the previous discussion of the relationships within ritual systems. Bell observes:

> A ritual never exists alone. It is usually one ceremony among many in the larger ritual life of a person or community, one gesture among a multitude of gestures both sacred and profane, one embodiment among others of traditions or behavior down from one generation to another. In other words, for each and every ritual, there is a thick context of social customs, historical practices, and day-to-day routines that, in addition to the unique factors at work in any given moment in time and space, influence whether and how the ritual action is performed. The warp and weft of handed-down customs and real-life situations form the fabric from which specific rites are constructed and found meaningful.[47]

Relationships *within* ritual systems include (1) repetition, (2) opposition, and (3) centrality, and relationships *among* ritual systems include (4) nesting, and (5) overlapping (Figure 5.3). Exploring the relationships within and among ritual systems is important for understanding the meaning and function of ritual in contemporary contexts, including occasional religious practice.

---

[47] Bell, *Ritual: Perspectives and Dimensions*, 171.

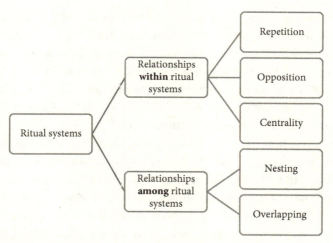

Figure 5.3 Relationships within and among ritual systems.

What Do Ritual Systems Do?

Ritual systems determine the meanings of ritual practices, the functions of practices, and how practices change. Meaning and function are closely intertwined and, in everyday experience, often inseparable. To make an analytical distinction for the purpose of this discussion, *meaning* will primarily describe how practitioners interpret a practice, and *function* will primarily describe observable outcomes of a practice that practitioners may or may not be able to name.

Participants in this research identify a diversity of meanings and functions in relation to infant baptism, including protection, salvation, blessing, gratitude, belonging in the church, belonging in a family, laying a foundation, beginning a journey, and, as previously discussed, making a commitment or giving the child a choice. These sometimes contradictory meanings and functions emerge through intuitive interpretation of the ritual systems surrounding baptism.

Interpret the Meaning of Practices

Practitioners interpret the meanings of ritual practices through the systemic relationships between practices characterized by repetition and opposition, as well as the importance or centrality of practices as established by the proximity and density of links. Interpretations of practices are further shaped by nesting and overlapping ritual systems that may be either in tension or in harmony. Practitioners are always doing this interpretive work, which is often intuitive and implicit. While conversation may elicit more explicit reflection, much remains obscure. In Belcher's words, "a systemic approach foregrounds the allusive intertextuality of rites."[48]

Recognizing how systemic relationships shape the emic insider interpretation of practices demands that scholars looking at practices "from the outside" attend to this network as well. Belcher outlines a method for studying ritual systemically that allows "scholars of religion to recognize the connections of religious and ostensibly non-religious behavior, and to assign the proper weight to cultural context, even while acknowledging that both ritual and ritual practitioners can be subversive."[49]

The method (1) "identifies embodied actions, verbal formulas, and symbolic tropes embedded in different ways within a system," and then (2) "analyzes the links between these instantiations" made by interpersonal, embodied, linguistic, calendrical, spatial, and corrective dimensions of the ritual, "paying particular attention to performances that have a larger number of enacted links and to the possibility of performative ambiguity." It next (3) "evaluates the impact of especially frequent rites or those emically identified as very important," and (4) describes the continual reinterpretation of the practice in relation to canonical texts[50] that "regulates a community's acceptable range of interpretations of the ritual."[51] Within this framework, the intentions of practitioners are significant but do not exhaust the meaning of the ritual.

Ritual systems create abundant and dynamic layers of meaning. The metaphor of layers is not intended to imply a hierarchy in which some layers are more foundational or rank higher in importance. Instead, layers are intended to suggest an array of adjacent and interconnected meanings, and the likelihood that certain meanings will surface for participants or interpreters in particular cases, especially in relation to connections within a ritual system or overlaps between different ritual systems. For example, some of

---

[48] Belcher, "Ritual Systems," 325.
[49] Belcher, "Ritual Systems," 352.
[50] Belcher, "Ritual Systems," 343–346.
[51] Belcher, "Ritual Systems," 352.

the previously mentioned layers of meaning of infant baptism may surface in certain cases, such as protection becoming a focus at an overlap with a health crisis. Different layers may even surface at certain points in time as a single baptism unfolds, such as belonging to the church being more prominent during the liturgy in the church building, and belonging in the family being more prominent during a meal that follows. Many layers of meaning coexist in the baptism ritual system.

Determine the Function of Practices

Ritual does things to practitioners, both through and apart from their interpretations of the meanings of practices. Ritual practices shape personal and group identity, community belonging and solidarity, moral order, aesthetic expressions, social control, and legitimacy.[52] Although practitioners may point toward some of these functions when asked, they are often not their primary focus when practicing. Bell outlines how certain observable effects are associated with ritual systems:

> Intrinsic to this systematization of the ritual ... was the way in which rites echoed other rites, implying them, assuming them, extending them. The effects were many: first, in their differences and similarities, ritual activities simultaneously differentiated and integrated the social world; second, replicated and resonating in this way, the logic of these ritual activities would appear to be the very logic organizing the social body and the rhythms of nature; and third, ritual activities and relationships that did not conform to the basic principles echoed throughout the system would immediately stand out as problematic.[53]

A ritual system, through repetition and opposition, reveals and creates social realities.

In the context of overlapping ritual systems, the capacity of a ritual system to engender social solidarity and differentiation is especially significant. According to Bell, rituals have both functions: "Just as strategic differences

---

[52] Smith, *Religion*, 78–80. Smith identifies these "Secondary Products, Features, and Powers" of religion.
[53] Bell, *Ritual Theory, Ritual Practice*, 129.

in ritual traditions can differentiate particular communities, ritualization can also work to integrate communities. Indeed, ritualization appears to be a type of social strategy that can simultaneously do both."[54] How the ritual system functions for particular practitioners depends, in part, on their position in the system and in overlapping systems. For example, for clergy and routine practitioners, baptism may primarily serve to integrate the child into the church. For family members who are occasional practitioners, including many godparents, baptism may primarily integrate the child into the extended family or a specific cultural tradition.

Change Ritual Practices

Finally, ritual systems affect how ritual practices change over time, whether considering change over a lifetime, changes wrought by sudden cultural shifts or intercultural encounters, or the glacial change of ritual systems over millennia. As Belcher describes, "a ritual system makes particular meanings seem natural, permitting some new liturgical developments, impeding others."[55]

Ritual systems are better able to accommodate changes that echo existing patterns in the system and therefore feel "natural" for participants.[56] For example, a commitment regarding creation care was added to the *Book of Alternative Services* baptismal covenant in 2013: "Will you strive to safeguard the integrity of God's creation, and respect, sustain and renew the life of the Earth?"[57] This development was easily accommodated because it seems "natural" in that it echoes patterns within the Christian ritual system in structure and language, as well as patterns in the wider cultural ritual system regarding awareness of the need for environmental action.

Embodied ritual practice is remembered well by the ritualized bodies that inhabit it and is thus resistant to change.[58] Therefore, "it is the entrance of unritualized bodies into a ritual system that provides the greatest

---

[54] Bell, *Ritual Theory, Ritual Practice*, 125.
[55] Belcher, "Ritual Systems, Ritualized Bodies," 90.
[56] Belcher, "Ritual Systems, Ritualized Bodies," 96.
[57] General Synod of the Anglican Church of Canada, *Book of Alternative Services*, 159.
[58] Belcher, "Ritual Systems, Ritualized Bodies," 102.

potential for changes in the system."[59] These bodies do not remember existing practices but are also not truly unritualized: they are instead differently ritualized.[60] Belcher recognizes that "assemblies from the beginning have been composed of differently-ritualized persons."[61] One of the contributions of the study of occasional religious practice is more accurately describing the presence of differently ritualized bodies at Christian ritual events in increasingly nonreligious and religiously diverse contexts.

Facilitating the Participation of Differently Ritualized Practitioners

Clergy are aware of the challenges of events like baptisms when many differently ritualized bodies enter into a Christian ritual practice. One priest describes how he frames this with humor in an effort to put participants at ease:

> On the day of [the baptism], after I've welcomed everyone, I'll say, "So we've printed everything out." This is my spiel: "So, you'll find the whole order of service in your bulletin. You don't have to fumble with books. And being an Anglican or being in an Anglican church is really easy. We stand for the hymns, unless, of course, they're communion hymns, in which case you're sitting. We sit to hear the readings, unless, of course, it's the gospel, in which case, you're standing. And we normally kneel for prayers, but you can stand, sit, or kneel, whatever you want. And whatever you do, don't follow me, because I'm doing the opposite, and don't watch the choir, because they're always lost." ... Because, I mean, my [evangelical] mother always said to me, "I just found the page you were on and then you went somewhere else." Anglicans, I mean, we love our book, but we bounce around in it. So, anyone who isn't familiar with the bounce is going to be totally lost. So, I print the whole order of service in the bulletin so that they don't have to fumble, including hymns, so they don't have to fumble with books. Get that one out of the way. And then, because posture can always be

---

[59] Belcher, "Ritual Systems, Ritualized Bodies," 104.
[60] Belcher, "Ritual Systems, Ritualized Bodies," 102.
[61] Belcher, "Ritual Systems, Ritualized Bodies," 104.

awkward, I just make that silly joke up at the front to say, you know what? Just be. Just simply be.

Other clergy and congregations also provide a complete printed order of service, project information onto a screen, or offer additional verbal instruction, either at all liturgies, or when a larger number of occasional practitioners are expected. Occasional practitioners affirm the challenges of navigating liturgical books and unfamiliar gestures and express appreciation for these efforts to facilitate the, at least temporary, re-ritualization of their bodies.

The reprinting or projection of material, as a "novel technological aid" (to borrow Belcher's terminology), exemplifies how the presence of differently ritualized bodies facilitates ritual change. When worship materials are printed for each occasion, it is easier to shift to gender-inclusive language, introduce a new expression of music, or borrow from the prayer books of the wider Anglican communion. This subtle centering of differently ritualized bodies on certain occasions facilitates changes to Anglican ritual practice. However, while it acknowledges the presence of differently ritualized bodies and adjusts to accommodate them in terms of facilitating their compliance with the Anglican ritual system, it does not necessarily acknowledge the gifts their different ritualization may have to offer.

In conclusion, ritual systems theory describes and explains how relationships within ritual systems—including repetition, opposition, and centrality—and relationships among ritual systems—including nesting and overlapping—inform the meanings and functions of specific rituals, as well as how rituals change over time. As Belcher describes:

> Systemic study recognizes that for regular (*and in a different way irregular*) participants, a system of ritual behaviors (from more to less formal and official) binds elements of culture (symbols, gestures, metaphors, and narratives) together into an ambiguous but endlessly meaningful network.[62]

Ritual systems theory is a valuable resource for considering how ritual works in the context of contemporary religious change, especially in relation to "irregular" or occasional participants. It provides a framework

---

[62] Belcher, "Ritual Systems," 325. Emphasis added.

for understanding how people who are differently ritualized, and who are positioned differently within ritual systems, may offer different yet nonetheless valid interpretations of the meaning of a ritual and experience the function of the same ritual in different ways. The next chapter examines how occasional practitioners select certain ritual practices from within ritual systems that some practice routinely. Ritual systems theory illuminates how a ritual as simple as lighting a baptism candle can be both ambiguous and endlessly meaningful as it is interpreted and received through overlapping ritual systems.

6
Selective Participation in Ritual Systems

I interview Zack on the phone, although we met briefly at his home a few weeks earlier when he scooped up his toddling daughter so I could speak with his wife in their toy-strewn kitchen. The Anglican funeral for Zack's father-in-law is the starting point for our wide-ranging conversation. Zack is happy to participate in Anglican liturgies with his family to mark life transitions, including the baptism of his daughter, the death of his father-in-law, and his own marriage. He also attends the Anglican church with his family on Christmas and Easter, although he is very clear that "the only reason I go there is because my wife belongs there." Nevertheless, he feels "super welcomed." The priests know his name and are happy to see him and his family: "they're super, super nice, super supportive."

When I ask about his religious identity, Zack responds, "I'm Catholic, I just don't go to church." Zack was raised in the Roman Catholic tradition. He describes himself as having strong Catholic values, "like treating people well and helping out if you can," and provides concrete examples of supporting his community, especially students in need who are connected to the Catholic school where he teaches shop. He attends mass at the school as well; his class is responsible for setting up the chairs.

Zack offers informed, thoughtful, and passionate comparative insights into his experience of Anglican and Catholic practices, yet he reaches the limits of language when I ask about other spiritual practices and he provides a rapturous description of deer hunting:

> Nine out of ten I don't get anything. But sitting alone in the woods is really, it's powerful, it really is. When you're like all by yourself and it's quiet. It really is like, it is crazy. I never would've anticipated that. But when you're sitting all alone, all quiet, . . . it's crazy how powerful it is.

He identifies hunting as a spiritual practice:

I don't know if that's like a spiritual thing, but it really is for me. There's just that quietness, it really is, it's very powerful. . . . You go sit there when it's dark. You kind of walk out to your spot when it's still dark and you're in the middle—there's one spot we go to. It's still dark. I'm sitting there and then the sun comes up and you're just like, I don't know. It's like this crazy feeling that comes over you.

Zack's describes deer hunting as a contemplative spiritual practice that elicits in him a powerful affect that contrasts with his experience of Christian worship, although he also values the Anglican practice of his family, and the Catholic practice of his school community. Zack exemplifies selective participation in multiple overlapping ritual systems—Anglican, Roman Catholic, family, school, and deer hunting—as part of his religious and spiritual practice.

Participation in ritual systems is always selective. In this regard, intensive, routine, and occasional practitioners are no different from one another; each select a subset of practices. As Belcher describes: "a ritual system offers a superabundant set of ritual behaviors and ritual interpretations, from which selections must be made."[1] However, some practitioners are more selective than others. Another way to define occasional religious practice is *selective participation in a ritual system that some practice routinely*. Routine practice, whether institutionally prescribed or culturally expressed in a specific community, sets the standard for occasional practice, making occasional practice possible.[2] In the discussion that follows, I examine which practices occasional practitioners select, and how they select practices in ways that are situational and strategic. In doing so, I integrate theory from sociology of culture with ritual studies. I also consider how selective practice affects rituals and ritual systems. Chapter 8 examines the overlaps between the Anglican and Catholic ritual systems as an in-depth example of the theoretical framework detailed in Chapter 7.

---

[1] Belcher, "Ritual Systems," 326.
[2] Note that here the term "occasional practice" is used in a different sense than Bell uses it in her discussion of ritual systems. Bell contrasts "periodic rites, such as those for life-crises and calendrical holidays" with "occasional rites that respond to specific situations." Her focus is on whether *the practice itself* is periodic or occasional. In contrast, I focus on whether *the practitioner* is routine or occasional. For example, baptism may be a periodic practice in a parish where it is celebrated four times a year and therefore routine for those who are present most Sundays. In contrast, occasional practitioners practice baptism only occasionally, on the occasion of the births of their own children, and these may be the only baptisms they ever attend. Bell, *Ritual: Perspectives and Dimensions*, 175.

Which Practices Do Occasional Practitioners Select?

Belcher describes how "the ambiguity found in ritual systems allows for flexible personal appropriation," including the selection of a set of behaviors and interpretations from a ritual system. Unavoidably, "the process of selection is political: i.e., authority, tradition, accident, and individual preference all play roles."[3] Selective participation may take various forms. These forms parallel the types of occasional religious practice discussed in Chapter 2, including patterns associated with (1) holidays, (2) life transitions, (3) personal or communal crises, or (4) incidental circumstances. Even within these types of occasional religious practice there are variations in the selected practices.

One possibility is *selecting a single practice*. For example, a Muslim woman may choose to attend the Anglican funeral of a Christian co-worker's mother as a supporter in the outer circle. This may be the only practice she selects from the Anglican ritual system and the only time she selects it. In contrast, a family may initiate attending a Lessons and Carols service at the Anglican Cathedral each Christmas as a holiday tradition. This is the only practice they select, but they select it repeatedly.

Another variation is *selecting a subsystem* of practices, or perhaps even creating a ritual subsystem through selective practice. For example, as discussed in Chapter 4, some individuals consistently initiate practices in a congregation with a connection to their cultural heritage at transitional moments in their lives, such as the birth of a child, beginning of a marriage, or loss of a loved one; they select the life-transition subsystem. Another family may attend a local congregation on Christmas Eve, Easter Sunday, and Mother's Day; they select the holiday subsystem from the larger ritual system in the parish and Anglican tradition. Practitioners may select practices with varying degrees of consistency and intentionality.

How Do Occasional Practitioners Select Practices?

Bell describes ritualization as "a strategic way of acting in specific social situations."[4] Both routine and occasional practitioners select practices from

---

[3] Belcher, "Ritual Systems," 326.
[4] Bell, *Ritual Theory, Ritual Practice*, 67.

ritual systems for strategic reasons in specific situations: "Since practice is situational and strategic, people engage in ritualization as a practical way of dealing with some specific circumstances. Ritual is never simply or solely a matter of routine, habit, or 'the dead weight of tradition.'"[5] Even the most routine practitioners ritualize in situational and strategic ways. In many cases, routine and occasional practitioners may be responding to similar situations and may be employing related strategies. In all cases, ritual is a practical response to particular circumstances.

Situational Selection

The situational nature of all ritualization, including occasional practice, makes it impossible to assess rituals apart from the larger context in which they occur. As Bell describes, "Human activity is situational, which is to say that much of what is important to it cannot be grasped outside of the specific context in which it occurs. When abstracted from its immediate context, an activity is not quite the same activity."[6] Something about the situation of occasional practitioners prompts a ritual response. The types of occasional practitioners outlined in Chapter 4, including both initiators and supporters with a range of motivations for participation in religious practices, point to some patterns in the situational factors that motivate occasional practice. These may be *sustained* characteristics of a situation, such as a cultural heritage in the Anglican tradition, a marriage to a Roman Catholic, or the physical location of the cathedral relative to home. They may instead be *temporary* characteristics of a situation, such as the desire for a wedding venue close to a restaurant, or the need to respond to an act of gun violence in the neighborhood. In either case, there is something about the situation of the practitioner, or about their immediate context, that prompts the ritualization. Studying ritual ethnographically (rather than on the basis of liturgical texts, for example) allows practices to be considered situationally in relation to particular events, individuals, and groups, rather than abstracted from any immediate context.

---

[5] Bell, *Ritual Theory, Ritual Practice*, 93.
[6] Bell, *Ritual Theory, Ritual Practice*, 81.

Strategic Selection

Occasional practitioners are strategic in that they select practices that are intended to respond to certain situations. Here it is helpful to turn to the sociology of culture to understand how occasional religious practice is both motivated by deep internal schemas and manifest in the strategic selection of specific external practices.

Since the 1970s, sociology as a discipline has made a slow, steady, and now decisive "cultural turn." However, developments in the sociology of culture have been largely unrecognized in liturgical and ritual studies.[7] The cultural turn in sociology has traversed several approaches to culture, including classical understandings articulated by Max Weber, Talcott Parsons, and Clifford Geertz,[8] repertoire or toolkit theories of culture such as those associated with Ann Swidler,[9] and dual-process cognitive models of culture represented by the work of Stephen Vaisey.[10] Over the course of this trajectory, the focus has shifted from defining and describing culture to explaining culture in action: How do people use culture? How does culture influence action?

In *classical models of culture*, values are the link between culture and action because people are understood to be motivated by values. Culture is the repository of these values, which are transmitted through socialization.[11] Max Weber vividly describes this, using the image of a railroad switchman: material and ideal interests are the engine behind human action that drive it forward, but ideas or values supplied by culture, and specifically religion, "like switchmen," shape the destinations that humans strive to reach and the tracks that are the means of getting there.[12] Geertz describes the influence of culture on action in terms of an indirect and all-encompassing ethos and worldview:

---

[7] This discussion is an initial gesture toward potential connections between the disciplines that could be pursued in greater depth in future research.

[8] Max Weber, "The Social Psychology of the World Religions," in *From Max Weber: Essays in Sociology*, ed. H. H. Gerth and C. Wright Mills (Abingdon: Routledge, 1991), 267–301; Clifford Geertz, *The Interpretation of Cultures* (New York: Basic, 1973); Talcott Parsons, *The Social System* (Glencoe: Free Press, 1951).

[9] Ann Swidler, "Culture in Action: Symbols and Strategies," *American Sociological Review* 51, no. 2 (1986): 273–286; Ann Swidler, *Talk of Love: How Culture Matters* (Chicago: University of Chicago Press, 2001).

[10] Vaisey, "Motivation and Justification: A Dual-Process Model of Culture in Action," *American Journal of Sociology* 114, no. 6 (2009): 1675–1715.

[11] Vaisey, "Motivation and Justification."

[12] Weber, "Social Psychology," 280; Talcott Parsons adopts Weber's model yet substitutes values for ideas: see Swidler, *Talk of Love*, 79; Swidler, "Culture in Action."

A people's ethos is the tone, character, and quality of their life, its moral and aesthetic style and mood; it is the underlying attitude toward themselves and the world that life reflects. Their worldview is their picture of the way things in sheer actuality are, their concept of nature, of self, of society.[13]

Religious rituals synthesize and maintain ethos and worldview, providing models of and models for reality.[14] Weber's and Geertz's formulations of how culture matters apply best when culture is envisioned as a unified whole. Classical models of culture assume a unified cultural system; in contrast, contemporary theorists take cultural disjuncture and contradiction as their starting point.[15]

Repertoire or toolkit theories of culture present an alternative to classical models. Ann Swidler's seminal 1986 article, "Culture in Action: Symbols and Strategies," and her 2001 book, *Talk of Love: How Culture Matters*, crystallize the view that culture influences action not by providing the ultimate values toward which action is oriented, but by shaping a repertoire or "toolkit" of "symbols, stories, rituals, and worldviews, which people may use in varying configurations to solve different kinds of problems."[16] People have cultured capacities; their basic repertoires are constructed, maintained, and refashioned by culture. From these repertoires, people construct "strategies of action," "persistent ways of ordering action through time."[17] These strategies of action are chains of actions based on preexisting links, and the styles of these strategies of action are often more persistent than the ends people initially seek to attain. Swidler argues that culture functions differently in settled times, when culture is intimately integrated with action in providing the underlying assumptions of a way of life, and unsettled times, when people are learning new ways of organizing individual and collective action, and different cultural models make explicit demands in a contested cultural arena. Although Swidler's theory of culture in action is centered on how people use the cultural tools in the repertoires of practical styles and skills available to them to justify and make sense of action, she acknowledges that people are used by culture as much as they use culture.[18]

---

[13] Geertz, *Interpretation of Cultures*, 127.
[14] Geertz, *Interpretation of Cultures*, 93.
[15] Swidler, *Talk of Love*, 12.
[16] Swidler, *Talk of Love*; Swidler, "Culture in Action," 273.
[17] Swidler, "Culture in Action," 273.
[18] Swidler, *Talk of Love*, 24.

Dual-process models of culture in action, such as the model Stephen Vaisey presents in his influential 2009 article, "Motivation and Justification: A Dual-Process Model of Culture in Action," integrate justificatory and motivational theories of culture.[19] Dual-process models of culture and cognition rely on findings from cognitive science that "human cognition is based on two basic processes—one fast, automatic, and largely unconscious [Type 1], and one slow, deliberate, and largely conscious [Type II]."[20] A metaphor for this divided consciousness is a rider on the back of an elephant:

> The rider, who represents our conscious processes, is the part of ourselves we know best—she can talk, reason, and explain things to our heart's content. Yet, for the most part, she is not in charge. The elephant, which stands for our automatic processes, is larger and stronger than the rider and is totally unencumbered by the need, or the ability, to justify itself. Driven by the simple mechanism of attraction and repulsion, the elephant goes where it wants. As the metaphor implies, the rider is no match for the elephant in a direct struggle. While the rider usually only pretends to be in control, she can slowly train the elephant over time or perhaps trick it into going a different way. But in any given moment, the elephant—practical consciousness—is usually in charge. For the most part, this is quite advantageous.[21]

Dual-process models understand culture as acting at both the level of the elephant and the rider: "actors are driven primarily by deeply internalized schematic processes ('the elephant'/practical consciousness), yet they are also capable of deliberation and justification ('the rider'/discursive consciousness) when required by the demands of social interaction."[22] Culture shapes emotions, intuitions, and unconscious judgments as well as stated beliefs and values.[23] Culture is also active in the interaction between the two levels in processes of cultural acquisition, transmission, and externalization,[24] and learning, encoding, remembering, and acting.[25] Although dual-process theory is beginning to encompass repertoire theory in the discipline of

---

[19] Vaisey, "Motivation and Justification"; Omar Lizardo et al., "What Are Dual Process Models? Implications for Cultural Analysis in Sociology," *Sociological Theory* 34, no. 4 (2016): 287–310.
[20] Vaisey, "Motivation and Justification," 1683.
[21] Vaisey, "Motivation and Justification," 1683.
[22] Vaisey, "Motivation and Justification."
[23] Vaisey, "Motivation and Justification," 1684–1685.
[24] Omar Lizardo and Michael Strand, "Skills, Toolkits, Contexts and Institutions: Clarifying the Relationship Between Different Approaches to Cognition in Cultural Sociology," *Poetics* 38, no. 2 (2010): 205–228.
[25] Lizardo et al., "What Are Dual Process Models?"

sociology, multiple approaches to culture can be compatible,[26] and together they help to explain occasional religious practice as situational and strategic selective participation in ritual systems.

Because occasional religious practice associated with baptisms and funerals is almost always intergenerational, it is helpful to consider dual-process theories of culture and cognition through Christian Smith, Bridget Ritz, and Michael Rotolo's research on *cultural models* and religious parenting since the empirical case as well as the theoretical model resonates with this research.[27] Cultural models, according to Smith, Ritz, and Rotolo, are "the mostly tacit, cognitive assumptions and beliefs that people in groups more or less intersubjectively share and use to make sense of their experiences and to understand how to act in the world."[28] Beliefs in this case refer to "the premises or propositions that people consciously or tacitly regard to be true,"[29] *not* beliefs as religious "propositional ideas that people actively consider, adopt, reflect on, and readily express when questioned."[30] Drawing on interviews with religiously affiliated American parents, Smith, Ritz, and Rotolo describe how strikingly similar cultural models are shared by parents across differences in religious tradition, region, race, and class.[31] Many of the cultural models they identify among religious parents are also present in my interviews with occasional practitioners,[32] including, among others, the following:

> The purpose of living is to lead a happy and good life, in the dual sense of both having life go well (enjoying success and happiness) and living life rightly (doing what is morally right).[33]

> Religion is a normal, valuable, meaningful and worthy part of life, at least in its general principles ... its central teachings are good, valuable, and

---

[26] Lizardo and Strand, "Skills, Toolkits, Contexts."
[27] Christian Smith, Bridget Ritz, and Michael Rotolo, *Religious Parenting: Transmitting Faith and Values in Contemporary America* (Princeton, NJ: Princeton University Press, 2020).
[28] Smith, Ritz, and Rotolo, *Religious Parenting*, 213.
[29] Smith, Ritz, and Rotolo, *Religious Parenting*, 220.
[30] Smith, Ritz, and Rotolo, *Religious Parenting*, 220.
[31] Smith, Ritz, and Rotolo, *Religious Parenting*.
[32] Many of the participants in this research appear to share these cultural models, although, because I was asking different research questions and had a different interview guide, I cannot address how religiously affiliated parents in the United States are similar to or different from occasional practitioners in Toronto.
[33] Smith, Ritz, and Rotolo, *Religious Parenting*, 15, 16. For a discussion of how occasional practitioners speak of being a "good person," see Chapter 11.

practical for most people—in ways almost exclusively having to do with this life now.[34]

Religion is a good, too, because it can provide cohesion and solidarity in family relationships.[35]

All or most religions are after the truth.... Two religious truths are paramount for children to learn, one vaguely theological and existential; the second, instrumental and functional. First, children should learn to "believe in something" along the lines that "there is a greater picture" out there, "something bigger" going on, such as a God who is with us and answers prayers or the force of karma. Second, religion can help people live good lives in this world.... Beyond these two paramount truths, however, *one can take from one's own religious tradition the parts that make sense and work best, and leave the parts that don't*, according to "whatever seems right" to you; *nobody needs to accept or be subject to the whole package of a religious tradition*.[36]

Many occasional practitioners in this research who claim a range of religious identities consistently reference these same cultural models. The final model is specifically related to occasional participation in religious rituals in that occasional practice "seems right" apart from "the whole package."

An additional feature of both Smith, Ritz, and Rotolo's empirical data and my own is a lack of emphasis on the particularities of specific religious traditions. It is not just that these analytical models summarize perspectives across a diversity of religious traditions in general terms; it is that parents and participants themselves often speak in *generalities rather than specifics* and even deny the importance of particular religious traditions (they care about their children believing in "something more" rather than the "Triune God," for instance, as will be discussed in Chapter 10). For many, in theory, within the context of their own internal schemas, *almost any religion would do* as a way to embody these deeply held and broadly shared internal cultural models. In practice this is clearly not the case. Although Smith, Ritz, and Rotolo vividly depict the deeply held motivating cultural models behind routine religious practice, and likely much occasional practice as well, they do not address why certain aspects of religion "seem right" and are selected on certain occasions while others are not.

---

[34] Smith, Ritz, and Rotolo, *Religious Parenting*, 50–51.
[35] Smith, Ritz, and Rotolo, *Religious Parenting*, 51, 65.
[36] Smith, Ritz, and Rotolo, *Religious Parenting*, 76; emphasis added.

Therefore, when considering the specific external ritual practices that occasional practitioners select from ritual systems, it is helpful to turn to Ann Swidler's *toolkit theory* of culture in action, especially because of its resonance with Bell's ritual theory. Swidler describes how culture influences action by shaping a repertoire or "toolkit" of "symbols, stories, rituals, and worldviews, which people may use in varying configurations to solve different kinds of problems."[37] Various ritual practices are among the cultural tools available. Various ritual systems are among the cultural repertoires available. Various occasions, such as life transitions, holidays, and crises, are among the "problems" to be solved. From these repertoires, people construct "strategies of action"—"persistent ways of ordering action through time."[38] To apply Bell's terminology, they rely on historic or temporal repetitions within ritual systems. This is usually what participants mean by "tradition" in this research, as will be discussed in Chapter 10. It is also evident in how parents in Smith, Ritz, and Rotolo's research speak of modeling their religious parenting on their own experience of being parented. Swidler's theory of culture in action explains why parents who were themselves baptized are likely to identify the birth of a child as a religious problem to be solved and then follow an existing strategy of action and choose the familiar ritual tool of baptism from their repertoire to address the problem. People develop habitual ways of acting and organizing action over time: "Individual actions do not make sense by themselves, but only as parts of larger patterns,"[39] or, as Bell would say, as parts of larger ritual systems.

In addition, and crucially in the case of occasional practice, Swidler's theory explains how participants respond in situations when a strategy they attempt to employ is impeded. People know far more culture than they draw on in any instance and show great flexibility in how they mobilize parts of their cultural repertoires in complex ways for practical use, moving fluidly between different cultural resources.[40] This is especially true in unsettled times that make the implicit explicit, times which may include crises associated with occasional religious practice such as a birth, marriage, or death, especially if established strategies of action are disrupted. Swidler articulates two models of culture, one that applies in settled times and the other in unsettled times. *Settled culture* is associated with common sense. It has weak direct

---

[37] Swidler, "Culture in Action," 273.
[38] Swidler, "Culture in Action," 273.
[39] Swidler, *Talk of Love*, 82.
[40] Swidler, *Talk of Love*, 40.

control over action and instead refines and reinforces existing skills, habits, and modes of experience creating continuity. In contrast, *unsettled culture* is associated with explicit and newly formed ideology that is in competition with other cultural views. It has strong control over action and teaches new modes of action. In unsettled times, culture creates new strategies of action, which may or may not survive long term.[41] In unsettled times, ritual is particularly significant:

> Ritual acquires such significance in unsettled lives because ritual changes reorganize taken-for-granted habits and modes of experience. People developing new strategies of action depend on cultural models to learn styles of self, relationship, cooperation, authority, and so forth. Commitment to such an ideology, originating perhaps in conversion, is more conscious than is the embeddedness of individuals in settled cultures, representing a break with some alternative way of life.[42]

Unsettled times, which may include crises associated with occasional practice, are instances when ritual may take on an active role and establish new strategies of action. For example, in the case study that follows in Chapter 7, several families strategically transition from Roman Catholic to Anglican baptism when their established strategy of action, Roman Catholic baptism, becomes unavailable. An unsettled time results in the selection of a distinct yet related ritual/cultural tool, from a distinct yet related ritual system/cultural repertoire, that may become an established strategy of action at the birth of future children.

I am drawing on Swidler here to theorize the situational and strategic selection of specific external cultural tools—particular rituals from within specific ritual systems—that occasional practitioners employ in what are often unsettled times. My use of Swidler is not intended to imply that participation in occasional ritual practices is shallow, incoherent, instrumental, or discursively rationalized after the fact. In fact, Swidler holds together the situational and strategic nature of specific ritual actions for occasional practitioners with the recognition that these rituals are part of larger patterns of practice that are meaningfully and functionally anchored in repetition over time and

---

[41] Swidler, "Culture in Action," 281.
[42] Swidler, "Culture in Action," 279.

across contexts (strategies of action). In this way, Swidler's approach to culture in action is especially compatible with Bell's theory of ritual systems.

To summarize, in the case of occasional religious practice, culture is operating in two distinct ways. First, there are deeply held internal cultural models that motivate occasional religious practice as a coherent, reasonable, and purposive expression of foundational beliefs. Smith, Ritz, and Rotolo provide a way of theorizing how occasional participation in religious practices is motivated by foundational cultural models associated with the purpose and nature of life and religion. Second, there are external cultural tools and existing strategies of action that shape how the occasional religious practice is strategically embodied in specific situations and settings and how occasional practitioners adapt when established strategies of action become unavailable, especially in unsettled times of crisis. Both ways of theorizing culture are necessary to understand occasional religious practice as deeply motivated, coherent, and teleological while also being highly strategic, flexible, and situational. These dynamics are illustrated in relation to baptism in the examples in Chapter 7.

How Does Selective Practice Affect the Meaning and Function of Practices?

There is a tension between (1) how ritual systems determine the meanings and functions of ritual practice, and (2) how ritual practice is situational and strategic. This is especially true when some participants routinely practice a larger subset of a ritual system, and others occasionally practice a smaller subset. Nevertheless, ritual systems theory illuminates how occasional and routine practice can coexist, and potentially even be mutually enriching, as occasional practitioners make connections between rites and ritual systems in new and different ways.

Separation of a Practice from the Ritual System

Occasional practitioners, in selecting certain practices, experience those practices apart from the larger ritual system. In the case of Christian baptism, this usually involves attending a service of Christian worship for the baptism without participating routinely in the Christian ritual system.

One consequence is that occasional practitioners *no longer intuitively interpret* practices through relationships of repetition, opposition, or centrality within the Christian ritual system. For example, in certain parishes, baptism is celebrated in connection with specific feasts days such as Baptism of Jesus, All Saints, or Trinity Sunday. When occasional practitioners note this, they often view it as an incidental and either an enhancing or detrimental feature of the liturgy, because of special music or added length, for example. In contrast, as routine practitioners, many clergy emphasize the suitable and meaningful nature of these celebrations in the Christian year in relation to baptism and the priority of ensuring that baptisms coincide with these dates because of their centrality in the Christian ritual system and the many points of connection this activates in conjunction with baptism.

Another potential outcome of the separation of practices from a ritual system is that they *no longer feel natural* to participants: "Ritual behaviors come to feel 'natural' (indigenized) for participants when they echo systemically with postural, gestural, musical, verbal, artistic elements repeated throughout the ritual system and its surrounding culture."[43] The unnaturalness of the practice may impede its *function*. For example, corporate singing is a common practice in Christian worship and has the potential to create social solidarity. However, when this practice is experienced as "unnatural" by occasional practitioners, since they rarely experience it in corporate worship or elsewhere, its function in fostering solidarity may be compromised.

At the same time, it is crucial to note that ritual systems remain intact even if some practitioners only engage in certain subsets of practices.[44] A relatively small number of practitioners is required to maintain a ritual system. For example, attendance at Easter Vigil is rarely selected by occasional practitioners who request the baptism of a children in the Anglican tradition in Toronto. Nevertheless, Easter Vigil and baptism remain connected for the priest who presides and the intensive practitioners who attend both the Vigil and the baptism, whether or not the occasional practitioner requesting the baptism attends the Vigil or makes this connection. As discussed in Chapter 2, the idea that everyone should be intensively or at least routinely religious is a recent concept. Prior to the reforms of the sixteenth century, there was a sense

---

[43] Belcher, "Ritual Systems, Ritualized Bodies," 96.

[44] Some express anxiety that the modern age is one of fragmentation, but selective practice does not necessarily lead to fragmentation. Alasdair MacIntyre, *After Virtue: A Study in Moral Theology* (Notre Dame, IN: University of Notre Dame Press, 1981); Robert Bellah et al., *Habits of the Heart: Individualism and Commitment in American Life* (Berkeley: University of California Press, 1985).

of a religious minority practicing on behalf of the whole.[45] This "multi-speed system,"[46] to use Charles Taylor's term for pre-modern religion, has certain parallels to Grace Davie's contemporary concept of vicarious religion, "the notion of religion performed by an active minority but on behalf of a much larger number, who (implicitly at least) not only understand, but, quite clearly approve of what the minority is doing."[47] Occasional practice does not necessarily threaten the unity of ritual systems, although it does separate certain practices in the experience of some practitioners.

Overlaps with Other Ritual Systems

While certain meanings and functions may be lost for some participants when practices are separated from ritual systems, other layers of meaning may be added, particularly through overlaps with other ritual systems.

Occasional practitioners select practices in ways that are deeply motivated, coherent, and teleological while also being highly strategic, flexible, and situational and often following existing strategies of action. If cultural models and strategies of action associated with a ritual system that the practice has been separated from are not motivating and facilitating the selection of the practice, practitioners are likely motivated by cultural models and following strategies of action associated with *other ritual systems*. These other ritual systems likely overlap in substantial ways with the system from which the practice is separated. For example, if the Christian worship ritual system is largely separated from baptism for occasional practitioners, it may be the overlaps with ritual systems associated with family, culture, or media that provide cultural models and strategies of action that lead to the practice of baptism when a child is born. It is therefore relationships of repetition, opposition, and centrality in these systems that primarily govern the meaning and function of the practice for occasional practitioners. This is illustrated in Chapter 5 in relation to how clergy and parents understand the selection and function of godparents.

As Belcher describes, "ritual actions resist having only a single, stable meaning: in fact, the complex overlap of schemes promotes, rather, a

---

[45] Taylor, *A Secular Age*, 66.
[46] Taylor, *A Secular Age*, 81.
[47] Davie, "Vicarious Religion," 22.

network of possible meanings and heuristics that tend to privilege some meanings over others."[48] Often, routine and intensive practitioners assume that the meanings and functions associated with their primary ritual system are the single, stable interpretations and should be privileged. However, unsettling this assumption and asking instead what meanings and functions are associated with the overlapping ritual systems of occasional practitioners can potentially add layers of meaning and function for all participants. The case study in Chapter 7 and the liturgical theological discussion in Part III of the book explore this possibility in greater depth.

As Bell describes, when ritual systems overlap, they are sometimes in tension with one another and sometimes in harmony.[49] Even dissonant notes—and there are always dissonant notes—can add to the texture of the practice. Negotiating relationships and interpretations within and among ritual systems is an ongoing process:

> The orchestration of rituals in time, some reproducing local communities, others later integrating them or parts of them into larger communities, enables each unity in the system to experience both its own autonomy and its dependent place within a network of relationships with other groups. This orchestration is not a perfect holistic order imposed on minds and bodies but a delicate and continual renegotiation of provisional distinctions and integrations so as to avoid encountering in practice the discrepancies and conflicts that would become so apparent if the "whole" was obvious.[50]

Ongoing negotiation most likely does not result in resolution. For example, occasional and routine practitioners may never map the system in the same way or agree on the meaning or function of a ritual. However, ongoing negotiation may facilitate coexistence and even mutual enrichment within and among ritual systems and practitioners with different types of relationships to these systems.

Transformation of Ritual Systems

Selective practice and the associated separation and overlaps have the potential to change the ritual systems involved. As Belcher describes, "it is the

---

[48] Belcher, "Ritual Systems, Ritualized Bodies," 101.
[49] Bell, *Ritual: Perspectives and Dimensions*, 174.
[50] Bell, *Ritual Theory, Ritual Practice*, 125.

entrance of unritualized bodies into a ritual system that provides the greatest potential for changes in the system."[51] However, when practitioners turn to certain rituals to address problems strategically in specific situations, they are often unable to see the unintended and often unavoidable consequences of their practice:

> What does ritualization see? It is a way of acting that sees itself as responding to a place, event, force, problem, or tradition. It tends to see itself as the natural or appropriate thing to do in the circumstances. *Ritualization does not see how it actively creates place, force, event, and tradition, how it redefines or generates the circumstances to which it is responding....* Ritualization sees its end, the rectification of a problematic. It does not see what it does in the process of realizing this end, its transformation of the problematic itself.[52]

Ritual systems are constantly being transformed. In many contemporary North American and European contexts, selective practice associated with occasional religious practice may be a significant factor in that transformation. Through their presence in the ritual system, occasional practitioners transform the system—they renew strategies of action, and perhaps establish new ones, both for themselves and for others. In the context of the Anglican tradition in Toronto, we are at a moment in history when we can no longer assume that the majority of ritual participants have been formed in the Christian system. Instead, we "must grapple with bodies formed outside the Christian ritual system,"[53] or perhaps bodies that are somewhere in between systems.

Occasional Religious Practice as Selective Participation in Ritual Systems

This chapter has applied the theory of ritual systems initiated by Catherine Bell and developed by Kimberly Belcher to occasional religious practice to examine how occasional religious practice can be understood as selective participation in a ritual system that some practice routinely. I have expanded on Bell and Belcher's theory of ritual systems by introducing sociological

---

[51] Belcher, "Ritual Systems, Ritualized Bodies," 104.
[52] Bell, *Ritual Theory, Ritual Practice*, 109.
[53] Belcher, "Ritual Systems, Ritualized Bodies," 102.

theories of culture to explain how occasional practitioners select certain practices. Deeply held internal cultural models motivate occasional religious practice as a coherent, reasonable, and purposive expression of foundational beliefs. At the same time, occasional practitioners employ rituals as cultural tools in highly flexible and strategic ways in response to specific situations. Multiple ways of theorizing culture are necessary to understand occasional religious practice as deeply motivated, coherent, and teleological while also being highly strategic, flexible, and situational.

While all ritual practice is situational and strategic, occasional practitioners strategically select practices in ways that separate them from some systems and integrate them with other systems, thereby transforming themselves and the ritual systems, as rituals are always being transformed. At the same time, relatively few practitioners are required to maintain the unity of a ritual system. More than Bell or Belcher, I am concerned with how overlaps between ritual systems can help us understand the meaning and function of Christian ritual practices in increasingly nonreligious and religiously diverse contexts in which multiple ritual systems overlap, as well as how ritual systems change over time in these settings.

We see these dynamics in Zack's intentional selection of the spiritual practice of deer hunting for its personal contemplative affective dimensions, alongside his occasional religious practice in the Anglican ritual system due to the overlap with the ritual system associated with his immediate family, and with his ongoing identity and ethical and eucharistic practice in the Roman Catholic ritual system as it overlaps with his work as a teacher at a Roman Catholic school. Zack selects religious practices from a complex of overlapping ritual systems in ways that are situational and strategic, as well as reasonable and purposeful, in the context of his life. In the next chapter, I focus specifically on the overlaps between the Roman Catholic and Anglican ritual systems, toward which Zack's story gestures, through an examination of baptisms that occur at this intersection. In so doing, I apply the theory introduced here to demonstrate the value of an understanding of ritual systems informed by sociological theories of culture for examining how occasional religious practice affects how ritual works in contemporary contexts.

7
Harmony and Dissonance Among Ritual Systems

Zack, the young father with a Roman Catholic background who teaches at a Catholic school, and who was married and baptized his children in the Anglican tradition, vividly contrasts his experience of the communion meal in the two traditions:

> If the Catholic church was more like the Anglican church it would be a little bit better. I went to, it was a wedding, it was maybe a few months ago, it was my cousin's wedding. . . . The priest in this Catholic church was adamant that no, you do not go for communion unless you're Catholic and unless you go to confession. Then I go to [the Anglican church] for whatever, certain random events, and it says right on the program, and they say right before they give communion, all are welcome to have communion, please come up. It's the different attitudes, like, "All are welcome, please come up," versus "No, don't come, unless you're Catholic and you've been to confession." It's just like, what's going on here? Don't you want to, like, be welcoming and caring? You're supposed to be a church. [Name of Anglican church] really does that. They're really welcoming. I always feel welcome there and want to belong there. You know what I mean?

In response to my follow-up question about the significance of receiving communion on these occasions, Zack offers the most thorough and thoughtful eucharistic theology articulated by an occasional practitioner in this research:

> I: How does being able to receive communion change your experience of a wedding or a funeral or whatever else you might be there for?
>
> R: That's a good question. That's a really good question. Well okay, like, going back to JC, the things he did, we see he led by example, like he had dinner with his disciples in the last meal. I guess breaking bread,

Occasional Religious Practice. Sarah Kathleen Johnson, Oxford University Press.
© Oxford University Press 2025. DOI: 10.1093/9780197806579.003.0008

like in a celebration, is an important part of connecting with people. I think it's actually great, like we do it at school, where I work. It's really important.

If you think of every big holiday, you have some important [event] for your family—a birthday, something for your husband, your wife— you go for a nice dinner, you have a nice meal. It's a big thing. It's that connection and having that little bit of, to me, it's like having that, breaking that bread with everyone, so you can have a little bit of everything, so we can all share that. We can all share something together. And that's where communion comes from.

We're representing Jesus's last supper. His last commitment to his friends before he was crucified. That's why we still celebrate it, right? Then there's the whole thing about like, you know, that funny word for the change of the Eucharist into the actual body of Christ, there's a word for it, I forgot what it was. Anyway. I think it's important. I think it's cool. It makes you feel more part of the ceremony. Like, now, now it's a wedding. Right? You think I'm crazy? Don't you?

I: No, that's a really helpful description. At your cousin's wedding, did you receive communion?

R: Yeah. I did. My wife couldn't take it. She's not Catholic. Can you believe that?

I: How does that shape your experience of the wedding then, when it is this family meal and celebration?

R: Yeah like, not everyone can share it—isn't that bullshit? Like you think you'd be more welcoming. What the heck? You ... say only the Catholics can have communion? It's 2020, let's just get over this here. Like, what do you think this is? Really, I'm serious.

In this conversation, Zack interprets the Christian practice of celebrating communion through Christian scripture and tradition, as well as through overlaps between the Roman Catholic and Anglican ritual systems, and especially through overlaps with the ritual systems associated with family gatherings, holiday celebrations, and a school community, particularly gatherings that incorporate meals. He experiences dissonance between the Catholic ritual system and overlapping systems when people are drawn into Catholic ritual through these overlaps yet are unable to enter fully into the communion meal. He interprets this experience in the Catholic ritual system through repetition and opposition with his experience of the Anglican ritual system, where those from overlapping systems are invited to participate in a very similar ritual meal. This is one of numerous examples of how occasional practitioners experience both important repetitions and oppositions in how Roman Catholic and Anglican rituals are enacted and how that informs the meanings and functions of these practices for them.

For an ethnographic study based in the Anglican tradition, I was initially surprised by how often I heard about Roman Catholicism from participants. In retrospect, perhaps this could be expected: Roman Catholicism is the largest Christian tradition in Toronto and worldwide, a tradition that is present in civic life in Ontario due to the publicly funded Catholic school system, and it is an expression of Christianity that receives significant ongoing media attention. However, more than any of these factors, it is the overlap between the Anglican and Roman Catholic ritual systems that likely accounts for the prevalence of the Roman Catholic tradition in interviews with practitioners in the Anglican tradition. This includes nine interviews with participants who have a Roman Catholic background and at least five interviews with participants whose partners have a Roman Catholic background.

In this case study, I first explore how participants understand and experience the overlap between the Anglican and Roman Catholic ritual systems. I then examine how five families negotiate these overlaps in relation to baptism in deeply intuitive yet also strategic and self-reflective ways. This case study demonstrates (1) an application of ritual systems theory to occasional religious practice in a religiously diverse context, with a focus on overlapping ritual systems; and (2) the intuitive and thoughtful approach occasional practitioners take to engaging in ritual practices and negotiating ritual systems.

It is crucial to keep in mind that this analysis centers on how participants perceive and experience the Anglican and Roman Catholic ritual systems, *not* how these traditions describe themselves, either officially or unofficially. Furthermore, the participants in this research were selected because they engage in ritual practices in the Anglican system and were open to speaking about those experiences. Those who practice in the Roman Catholic system may have very different perceptions of the two ritual systems. At the same time, the impressions of participants primarily reflect concrete personal experiences of the Roman Catholic tradition, not stereotypes or preconceived ideas.

Harmony and Dissonance in the Anglican and Roman Catholic Ritual Systems

Participants frequently make comparisons between the Anglican and Roman Catholic ritual systems and, when doing so, consistently communicate two things: Anglicans and Catholics are pretty much the same, and Anglicans and Catholics are very different. To borrow Catherine Bell's terminology, there is both harmony and dissonance between the Anglican and Roman Catholic ritual systems.

Harmony

The consistency with which participants describe the harmony between the Anglican and Roman Catholic ritual systems is striking, especially because most participants in this research consider themselves "not very religious" and often struggle to find words to speak of religious matters. Nevertheless, many of them name a deep ritual resonance between Anglican and Roman Catholic practices, which they perceive through the ritualization of their bodies more than through cognitive analysis. Participants with Catholic, Anglican, and other Christian backgrounds all draw these parallels. Sometimes they describe this harmony in *general terms*:

> It's an Anglican church and the mass is very similar to a Catholic church.

> I think like the Anglican church is pretty traditional. Like the way that they run their services, we're quite traditional, I guess, like a Catholic church.

> [Name of parish] is an Anglican service with all the usual accouterments of an Anglican service. It comes across as toned-down Catholicism.

> Praying in home situations [in Jamaica] is more along the lines of Baptist than Anglican, which is not very different from Roman Catholic. Anglican and Roman Catholic services look pretty much the same. It's the tone.

Participants point to broad similarities in tone or feel, and at times associate this tone with ideas like "tradition" or "ritual."

In other cases, participants draw parallels between the Anglican and Roman Catholic ritual systems through *concrete examples* of repetition, related either to specific liturgical elements or to their ability to participate across traditions:

> The [Anglican] mass was more or less how I remember it in our church—the Roman Catholic Church. I didn't even need the booklet. I remembered all the words. I couldn't believe it. I was so happy that it was so similar to what I was used to because this way I was involved.... The Anglican Church was very similar to our church. I didn't see much difference.

> It's actually kind of funny because my [Bavarian Catholic] wife, she has a much closer connection to the church in her community. When we left [the Anglican service in Canada], she said that she recognized a lot of the prayers in English, but in German. So, even though she was in a different country, different language, she still knew what was going on in the church that day.

> They're both the same kind of services, right? The actual service itself is they read the gospel, then they have the homily, and the prayers of the faithful, and there's communion. The service itself is pretty similar, pretty typical for both of them. The Anglican just has a little more singing than the Catholic church.

> Anglican to me feels almost Catholic. It depends on the church, I guess. The downtown church, [name of church] was—they had the censer bearers and the kneeling and up and down and up and down—so, to me that felt almost Catholic.

While several participants point to common texts, they also highlight the broader structures and embodied aspects of the ritual systems.

In certain cases, the similarities between the Anglican and Roman Catholic ritual systems may establish *common ground* in families that include both Protestants and Catholics:

> I think the real reason we decided to go back Anglican for the baptism is because it's kind of a common ground to call up for the purpose.... [My husband] was [a] choir boy, so he's very used to the structure of the Catholic service. I think the Anglican service is a little bit similar. So both families were very comfortable with the service. The Catholic side was very comfortable with the Anglican service because it's very structured. You know, you have readings that you read back and forth, scripture, you know, it just has a very structured format. And then for us [my family], we were fairly

familiar [with it] because my brother and I had gone to Anglican services growing up.

I met my husband. We dated in Chicago and he went to church every Sunday and I was like, "Okay, this is interesting, like this is great," because definitely parts of me are very religious or spiritual. And he went to a Catholic church. I thought that was interesting coming from more of a Christian [evangelical] background and he more so was into it for the ritualistic nature of Catholicism and the routine and the going every Sunday.... Then he moved from Chicago to Toronto where I was living. And we were like, "Okay, let's find a church to go to in Toronto." So, it was funny, my husband actually shopped around for a church in Toronto and went to quite a few Sunday services and all different faiths—Anglican, Catholic, United, Christian—he went to all of them. And to be honest, the Anglican tradition was the only one [where] we really felt at home.

The capacity of occasional practitioners to identify the similarities between the Anglican and Roman Catholic ritual systems, often in ways that are more visceral and sensory than theological or analytical, reveals how the bodies of occasional practitioners are indeed ritualized into these (and other) ritual systems in ways that enable them to negotiate these practices occasionally.

Dissonance

While recognizing the many similarities, participants in this research are also very clear that there are major differences between the Anglican and Roman Catholic ritual systems and that these oppositions matter to them. In this sense, for some participants connected with Anglican practices, the Roman Catholic tradition is a proximate "other," in opposition to which they define themselves and the Anglican tradition. Comments on dissonance between the Anglican and Catholic ritual systems relate to observable ritual practices, impressions of different teachings, and contrasting moods.

Perceptions of difference are sometimes rooted in clearly *observable ritual practices*—such as whether and how those in attendance are invited to receive communion, as Zack describes at the beginning of this chapter. The distribution of communion is often a ritual moment through which opposition between the Roman Catholic and Anglican ritual systems becomes apparent to occasional practitioners. Numerous participants describe attending Roman

Catholic weddings or funerals at which priests have made it very clear that only Roman Catholics in good standing are invited to receive communion. Whether or not this boundary maintenance is directed toward them or their friends or family, participants tend to express anger and sadness, and describe this as a barrier to communal and spiritual engagement in the event. They also contrast this experience in the Roman Catholic ritual system with the sense of welcome they receive in the Anglican system.

The role of women in liturgical leadership in the Anglican tradition is another observable opposition between the Anglican and Roman Catholic ritual systems that is significant for many occasional practitioners, which may in part reflect the number of younger women in this study. Participants consistently identify women in leadership as a defining feature of the Anglican tradition and their experience of it:

One of the things that I love about [name of parish] is that [name] is the priest and [name] is a woman. And I love that because that's not a thing in the Catholic Church, that's not allowed. And that's kind of always sort of bothered me, that there's not that gender equality there. And so I love that [name] is like badass and doing it her way and it's great.

R: There was a female, there was a female—I don't know what the word is—there was a female, can you say she was a priest in the Anglican . . . ?
I: Yes, you can say she is a priest.
R: Priest. Which I thought was really great. That's one of the reasons why I'm not super into Roman Catholicism. I feel like it's a little bit exclusive of women.

My mom's sisters, my aunts really liked it. I think some people were surprised we had a woman minister. [Name] was the one who officiated.

R: I get asked by people like, who are even Christian, "Oh, what is your faith?" When I say "Anglican" they have no idea what I'm talking about. . . .
I: How do you explain it?
R: It's kind of complicated, like wow. . . . Then they'll say to me, "What's the main difference then?" And I'll say, "There are many, but one of the main ones is we can have reverends who are women." They're like, "What do you mean?" I'm like, "You can have a reverend, or a bishop, be a woman." They're like, "Run a church?" I'm like, "Yeah." They're like, "Oh, that is very different." That is one of the main differences that I highlight, that's just concrete for people.

One younger mother, who is an occasional practitioner in the Anglican tradition, describes her Italian Catholic family-in-law's response to women in liturgical leadership at her wedding and at the baptism of her son. Her nonreligious sister-in-law who served as the godmother, who is a "hardcore feminist," loved that there was a woman at the head of the church. However, while her Italian Catholic grandparents were appreciative of the liturgy, they seemed more skeptical of women in leadership:

> They said it was lovely and I don't think—[my husband] jokes about it all the time that like, they're going to think we're not really married. "No, no, we call Father Mike. We fix it, we fix it." Like, where is the real priest, right? This is what we joke. I don't think they actually believe that for a second. It was just we had such a tough time explaining to them what Anglican is, like that kind of became the running joke, and it was the same sort of thing for the baptism. And there are things that are slightly different, like the wine with communion or whatever.... And [the grandparents] have all said to me that they really thought that both our wedding ceremony and the baptism were lovely, and they thought, oh, the church is very beautiful. But none of them have ever made a comment about [the priest], which is interesting. I think they're just kind of thrown off by her. It's not really what they're used to.

The gender of liturgical leaders is, in most cases, immediately obvious to occasional practitioners, including both initiators and supporters, and is understood as a significant difference between the Anglican and Roman Catholic ritual systems, although in fact this is a relatively recent change. While there are expressions of surprise, and even subtle suspicion on the part of older family members, the presence of women in leadership is generally seen as a positive dimension of Anglican ritualization.

In other cases, rather than being rooted in ritual experience, the perception of difference between the Anglican and Roman Catholic ritual systems is anchored in *popular understandings of different teachings*. There is a sense among occasional practitioners that the Anglican and Roman Catholic traditions have contrasting teachings on topics that matter to them, whether or not these perceptions accurately reflect how these traditions would articulate themselves. At times, participants point to differences between Catholic and Anglican teachings with a focus on contentious social issues, especially those related to gender and sexuality:

> [My husband] is against beliefs of the Catholic Church against stem cell research, and procreation, and abuses against women and children.
>
> I dislike some of the harsher sort of implications of the Catholic faith in terms of women and their rights and that sort of thing. The abortion thing. Birth control. All those kinds of things.
>
> [My husband] is not sure about like where he stands because there were some awful aspects of the Catholic church. His experience wasn't as good. He actually remembers growing up and going to like anti-abortion rallies. And as an adult, and as a physician especially, I think his views on that have changed significantly.
>
> If I take issue with any religious organization, it's largely the Catholic church for that stoicism and that stubbornness to move along. But as I said, the current pope seems to embrace evolution along with other things. So it's progress.
>
> In the sermon at the [Anglican] baptism, [the priest] said that we have our rainbow flag out and people are coming out.... Whereas, we do know that the Catholic church in our community is very conservative to the extent that they would be confronting young children about LGBTQ attitudes.

This contrasting of a progressive expression of Anglicanism with the conservative aspects of Catholicism is common in interviews and is, to an extent, a reflection of the specific Anglican congregations engaged in this research.

Instead of social issues, certain participants focus on theological differences in their experience of the Catholic and Anglican traditions, including common Protestant suspicions of Catholicism related to the pope, Mary, and the symbol of the crucifix:

> We do not believe that there is one man on this earth that's any closer to God than any of the rest of us [the pope]. We just cannot accept the authority of that person being between us and God, we're sorry, that's just not us. When I want to talk to God, I'll talk to God.
>
> My [Catholic] husband always hoped I would find my way to Catholicism, but no way. I can't do it. There's too much emphasis on Mary. There's too much emphasis on Mary and not enough emphasis on Jesus. That's why I won't convert to Catholicism.

> The Catholics have a crucifix and they believe in putting Jesus on that crucifix. Anglicans don't believe in that. For Anglicans it's just to be the plain cross and yes, we admire Jesus and his teachings, but we really don't feel it necessary to have him hanging there.

Some occasional practitioners also describe different teachings about church authority structures:

> The Catholic Church is still like a big institution where there's like specific rules to follow and it's just like a very strict organization.

> The style of the Anglican church, the fact that it isn't so focused on kind of—in the same way that the Catholic church has this heavy governance on top of it.

Again, participants reference concrete similarities and differences in their perceptions of Roman Catholic and Anglican teachings.

Most often, however, the differences that participants identify between the Roman Catholic and Anglican ritual systems are associated with the *mood or attitude* they experience within and beyond the ritual activity itself. Rather than being anchored in specific observable differences in practice or teaching, this reflects a subtler, more emotional, evocative dimension of ritual experience. Especially in relation to this ephemeral subject matter, the consistency with which participants emphasize this difference and its importance to them is striking. They use words like "cold," "strict," "rigid," and "formal" to describe Catholic ritual, and "warm," "welcoming," "personal," and "informal," to describe Anglican ritual, while at the same time acknowledging that the practices are almost identical.

In some cases, these impressions are rooted in specific, passing, *informal encounters*, especially with clergy:

> I found everybody was very warm, like the priest, the female priest, she came up to me and my husband and she was like, "Congratulations, mama." Like in [the] Catholic church, it's big, I don't mean to like bash Catholicism, but it's very formal. Like nobody would ever come up to you and be like, "Congratulations, mama." Me and my husband, and even my husband who's not super religious, we were so happy with the day because there were all these little touches that just felt just more special than when we attended Catholic baptisms. There was more, like, emphasis on the person and us

and [my daughter]. And just eye contact.... And even when [my daughter], the holy water was being poured on her, she was like touching [the male priest's] face and he was like so sweet to her. It just felt different.

It all depends on whoever's running the service. I think that makes a huge part for me. That's probably why I feel less connected to the Catholic church and I feel more connected to the Anglican church. I just perhaps, I had a few experiences with priests, I didn't really feel they were committed or didn't feel they genuinely cared, and then I lost interest. That's why I feel more connected at [the Anglican church]. Everyone in [the local congregation] is super caring, super nice, super committed, and that's why I feel more accepted. The actual service is the same. There's not much difference in the service. They do the same kind of thing. It's just the priests I run into in Catholic churches are like super, super, "You must follow these rules or you're not Catholic." Whereas in Anglican [churches they say], "We keep everyone, we love everyone, we wish everyone got along," and that very kind of thing.

[My husband and I] are pushing [my daughter's] stroller and [the priest] is like, "Oh my wife and I are looking for a stroller." Whereas in Catholicism they cannot be married. But they still have the basic beliefs of like Christianity and Jesus—that's all still there. It didn't feel like we were in this foreign place. It still felt like you're at church. It just didn't feel as, like I said, like you're at school, strict, like you're going to get in trouble. Even all the things that you would do like take communion, and the breaking the bread, the Lord's Prayer, we know all that.

These brief interpersonal interactions appear to set the tone for many occasional practitioners. It is important to note, however, that in each of these cases the participants are not rushing to judgment after an initial encounter, but instead are pointing to examples of patterns they have experienced over time.

In other instances, it is something about *the embodiment of the liturgy* itself that carries the mood of being warm or cold. The tone may defy the expectations of those in attendance, whether they come from an evangelical or Roman Catholic context, as in these two examples:

I think the integration of [the Anglican funeral] service, as a traditional service but with the warmth of making it personal, really stood out in my mind because I wouldn't have conceived or perceived that the, especially the Anglican church, I would think the same even in the Roman Catholic church. And I'm just using those two out of several denominations that I feel have very strong traditional values as far as prayer books and hymns and so on that lend itself to more tradition than something personal and meaningful.... Every time you read a prayer after you've learned the prayer by memory, which comes very quickly because you say it every single service that you go to, the prayer loses its meaning because you're just reciting words, so it's just memory. But when it came to this service, I felt that things stood out that much more because the element of a personal part of the service was included. So, it's almost like all those prayers that were said jumped out and you could really listen to the words because it wasn't just the traditional, it was the combination of the two.

It's nice to have something where you know that you go through the [Catholic] mass and you have certain points where you will participate and others where you're quiet. There's a time to pray, there's a time to sing, it's all laid out for you. It's nice and clean and packaged. I guess when I said earlier that both my husband and I are a bit lax in our attendance. I guess, to be quite honest, it's because we kind of feel it's not enough. There's this feeling that you're going and you sit down, you do your thing, and you leave. It does not feel like there's a whole lot of community there. So it's a beautiful religion, truly is. I know it's going through some difficult times now, some very controversial times, and the church I'm sure will adapt to those. It is a tremendously beautiful tradition, but it can be cold.

The differences in perceived mood, often described through metaphors of warm and cold temperature, are shaped by participants' sense of high-level structures, right down to the smallest interactions with clergy in specific contexts. Impressions of mood and attitude are key to participants' experience. The aphorism rings true: people will not remember what you said or did, but they will remember how you made them feel.

At this point, it is helpful to reinforce that this is a discussion of the impressions and experiences of differences between the Roman Catholic and Anglican ritual systems described by certain occasional practitioners who have engaged in Anglican practices in Toronto. This does not reflect all Catholics or all Anglicans in this or any context. Nor does this necessarily reflect how Catholics and Anglicans understand themselves. However, this emic mapping of the harmonious and dissonant overlaps—the ritual similarities and differences in practice, teaching, and mood between the Anglican and Roman Catholic ritual systems—is crucial for understanding how occasional practitioners negotiate these overlapping systems.

Clergy Impressions of Fluidity Between the Anglican and Roman Catholic Ritual Systems

Anglican clergy are very aware of the overlaps between the Anglican and Catholic ritual systems. In interviews, clergy speak to these similarities and differences and the fluidity that this generates in their ministry contexts. While certain Anglican clergy claim the term "catholic" for the Anglican tradition, whether in reference to the "universal" Christian tradition or specifically "Anglo-Catholicism," clergy across a spectrum of church styles describe the prevalence of participants with Roman Catholic backgrounds in their congregations, especially on occasions such as holidays and life transitions.

Clergy, as ritual experts, are very aware of the similarities and differences between Anglican and Roman Catholic liturgy that research participants have articulated. They are also aware of the ways these patterns shape participants' ritual practice, including moving from the Roman Catholic tradition into the Anglican tradition, either routinely or occasionally:

> We do get a fair number of people who have more of a Catholic background because they can find here a liturgical expression which is familiar but with some significant differences around ordination of women, the place of gay, lesbian, queer people, even just the piety, the institutional structure. So, we will tend to attract those kinds of people.

> I probably would say 15 to 20 percent of this congregation are ex–Roman Catholics. Some have come over because I would do yes, a wedding, where their church wouldn't, because one was divorced, okay? They're certainly looking for liturgy. They're used to that stuff from their upbringing.

> I've had requests [for baptism] from, actually lots of different combinations, requests from parents, one might be a long-time Anglican and the other is Roman Catholic but has sort of fallen out of love with the Roman Catholic Church and they've decided that they want to make the Anglican Church their home.

We do the First Communion too. Because the majority of the immigrants who come to my parish, they are coming from the Roman Catholic tradition. So, they like to do in the Anglican Church, the baptism, the First Communion, the confirmation, the weddings, last rites, funerals, so I'm involved in all of those sacrament expressions.

Some Anglican clergy are intentional about performing rituals for Roman Catholics who are unable or uncomfortable accessing these practices in their own tradition. Some even see this as a form of compassionate care and Christian witness that they can offer, including these three priests who serve very different congregations—one Anglo-Catholic, one that emphasizes family ministry, and one with many participants who are newer to Canada:

I think if you polled our people there's a decent number who were raised Roman Catholic who land here for one reason or another.... I think it has historically happened a fair amount where Anglicans [clergy] are asked to marry Roman Catholics because one or both of them are divorced. Yeah. We're in a whole other area out here because we're now authorized to marry same-sex couples. I mean it hasn't happened but I can see, I could see that there might be a gay Roman Catholic couple who want to remain faithful to their tradition but who sought that and I would be open to that.

I: The role of the Catholic church is something that I'm hearing about, especially in terms of families seeking an option that is more flexible or a bit more open. Is that fairly common in your experience?
R: Oh, quite often. Where there's something that the Roman Catholic Church has done or said and this left them feeling disconnected or hurt, or sometimes it's just inconvenient.
I: Do you have a sense for why the Anglican Church may be the next place they go?
R: Because they often say it feels, the worship feels, the liturgy, it feels the same. I love that if they've not been to an Anglican church before and say, "It was just like our church"—it is really funny, like they've discovered this whole new thing.... If there's a Roman Catholic in the crowd [at an interfaith wedding or funeral], it's always fun because at the rehearsal, every single time some will say, "Man, my church would never let this happen. This is so great to be a part of. Why am I not coming to this church?" I go, "Why indeed? What's wrong with you? Why aren't you coming to this church?" I tend to joke about it with them, but you

know, you have that eye-opening moment when they go, "Ha, I'm welcome to be here, but my church wouldn't welcome you. What's wrong with this picture?" We'll say, "Well, what do you believe about God's grace in love? What [does] that look like for you? Here's what it looks like for me."

Many families, they come to baptize the kids, you know why? Because they are rejected in their church. Why are they rejected in their church? Especially, in the Roman Catholic Church—I am not nervous to say that—because, in their church, they say if you are not married, you cannot baptize a kid. Secondly, if your godparents belong to another church denomination or another religion, you cannot baptize your child. Period. If you are a single mother, you cannot baptize your children. I'm thinking of the practice of those priests, and I'm thinking of the practice of the historical Jesus Christ. How far apart are the two guys? And, I love the liberation theology, I love the Protestant theology, and, I love my vocation being a simple instrument of the historical Jesus Christ. When they come to my parish, they say, they ask me, "Will you baptize my child, if I am a single mother?" I ask them, "Why are you asking me that? Who am I? Absolutely, you have more rights than me! Because you are the mother. You took this child into your womb for nine months. And you have the authority." Not all of them have that mindset.

Clearly, clergy as well as occasional practitioners are negotiating the overlap between the Roman Catholic and Anglican ritual systems in thoughtful ways.

These reflections from occasional practitioners and clergy demonstrate an emic awareness of the complex relationship between the Anglican and Roman Catholic ritual systems. Neither occasional practitioners nor clergy are deceiving or misleading the other: there is a clear-eyed transparency to how they negotiate these overlaps. In many cases, these dynamics are at the center of the occasional practice of Anglican ritual in Toronto today.

Negotiating Overlapping Ritual Systems: The Stories of Five Baptisms

With this context of overlapping Roman Catholic and Anglican ritualization in mind, I turn to five specific baptisms in the Anglican tradition. I observed four of these five baptisms and interviewed multiple family members connected to three of the five baptisms. In all five cases, the mother of a child being baptized has a Roman Catholic background and was at the center of initiating a ritual practice in the Anglican tradition. These younger mothers were also surrounded by advocates and inner-circle supporters who facilitated the baptism. Each of these five cases has points of connection to other examples described in interviews with participants and clergy. I consider these five cases in the context of three intersecting themes associated with how occasional practitioners negotiate the overlaps between the Roman Catholic and Anglican ritual systems: ritual familiarity and progressive theology; ritual rigidity and practical flexibility; and multiple ritual practice.

Ritual Familiarity and Progressive Theology

Andrea was raised in the Roman Catholic tradition. As a young adult she drifted away, frustrated by inadequate answers to questions of human suffering and the conservative stance of the Catholic church on social issues. When she became pregnant, she began praying the rosary and attending liturgies at a local Anglican parish. She appreciates the openness of the parish to the LGBTQ+ community, as well as the familiarity of the words and music. Her husband has a Protestant background but was raised largely nonreligious; he is willing to support her renewed engagement with religion but would not pursue it himself. When their son is born, Andrea decides to reach out to the Anglican congregation she has been attending about baptism. Baptism seems like a way to acknowledge her gratitude for her son and lay a foundation for him in a church community. It is also important to her family, including her mother, who only occasionally attends Roman Catholic liturgies but has a strong sense of Catholic heritage. Her mother is absolutely delighted—and perhaps a bit relieved—when her grandson is baptized, and she showers him with traditional gifts. She experiences the Anglican liturgy as deeply resonant with her Catholic upbringing and as exceptionally beautiful. Andrea's sister, who was raised Roman Catholic but is currently not practicing, and Andrea's nonreligious brother-in-law, serve as godparents. The baptism draws the entire family into a new Anglican ritual context. It also includes small family gatherings before and after the liturgy to celebrate, as well as a larger family gathering at a separate time in Andrea's hometown. In this case, the birth and baptism of Andrea's son also becomes a moment of transition between traditions for Andrea, and a moment marking a shift from occasional to more routine practice.

Andrea is an example of an occasional practitioner with a Roman Catholic background who initiates a life transition ritual in the Anglican tradition in part because of the combination of ritual familiarity and progressive theology. Although she has recently become a more routine practitioner, the others involved are occasional practitioners, including her husband and the godparents, who are inner-circle supporters, and her mother, who is an advocate for Anglican baptism despite identifying as Roman Catholic and practicing only occasionally in the Roman Catholic tradition.

In addition to Andrea following familiar strategies of action associated with her religious, ethnic, and family background in selecting Christian baptism and in doing so through the local congregation she attends, her final decision to pursue baptism is shaped by observation of a repetition of the practice, apart from the Anglican system, in popular culture: "was actually watching, I think it was *The Handmaid's Tale*, to be honest. There's a scene where they baptize their child. It really spoke to me about how important it was for me to go through that process." In other words, Andrea describes how viewing this scene evokes her deep cultural model that baptism was something important to do for her child, especially as an expression of gratitude and to establish a foundation, which echo the cultural models that Smith, Ritz, and Rotolo examine in relation to religious parenting.[1] An overlap with the pop culture ritual system therefore plays a role in bringing about a religious practice and in its interpretation.

The overlap between the Roman Catholic and Anglican ritual systems facilitates the ritual event itself, with the similarities allowing Anglican baptism to substitute for Roman Catholic baptism for Andrea and her mother, and the differences making space for Andrea to feel alignment with the tradition. However, because the practice is experienced largely apart from the Anglican ritual system by the participants (except Andrea), they interpret it through relationships of repetition, centrality, and opposition connected to overlaps with the Roman Catholic, ethnic heritage, family, and popular culture ritual systems. Repetitions include historic repetition expressed in drawing parallels between the baptism of the child and the baptisms of Andrea and her sister (multiple participants note that Andrea and her son were baptized on the same calendar date) and the giving of the same

---

[1] Smith, Ritz, and Rotolo, *Religious Parenting*.

traditional gifts. One of these gifts—a cross necklace to wear daily—is densely networked as a frequent rather than ludic central rite. Wearing the cross is repeated daily by Andrea, her sister, and her mother, named multiple times as a key marker of religious identity and practice, and is a ritual they hope the newly baptized member of their family will also repeat, as Andrea describes:

> [Wearing the cross] represents both my religion and my background being Italian and having family and having that protection and luck. So that all starts, I think, in baptism. I still carry that with me. So, I wear the same cross what I was given when I was baptized. So that's what we hope for [my son] when he grows up.

Oppositions include the recognition that the non-Catholic parents of Andrea's husband do not understand the ethnic traditions associated with baptism, including the gift of a gold cross necklace sized for an adult, which they call "bling." The "other grandparents" are part of a different ritual system that does not include this gift, and therefore they understand this aspect of the Italian Catholic baptism ritual system in a different way, a way that Andrea and her family perceive as incorrect. Multiple overlapping systems interact in this ritual event.

Beth has a Roman Catholic background but is now deeply skeptical of the tradition; she identifies as a non-practicing Catholic who is spiritual and a feminist. Her husband was likewise raised Roman Catholic and now identifies as an atheist. Beth and her husband deliberately chose not to be married in the Catholic Church. When their daughter is born, it becomes clear that baptism is very important to the grandmothers of the child, although they are occasional practitioners. Upon reflection, Beth realizes that baptism is important to her as well, but she is committed to pursuing it in a way that reflects her values and lifestyle. She initially reaches out to the Roman Catholic Church, calling multiple parishes and encountering many roadblocks: required attendance, proof of living within the parish bounds, meetings with priests, and more. She then calls the Anglican parish around the corner from her home and is welcomed warmly. Beth is impressed by having women in leadership and by the warmth and personal connection offered by clergy. Her Roman Catholic sister and brother-in-law, who have become more religious since their Catholic wedding, serve as godparents, which includes dressing the baby from head to toe in brand new, gleaming white baptismal attire. Fifty family members attend the baptism service and an extravagant celebration afterward. They are impressed with the Anglican ritual, calling it a "royal baptism"—a reference to the baptisms of children in the British royal family, which are often widely publicized in Canada—and saying, "It feels like I'm in Italy. It feels like I'm at the Vatican."

Beth is another example of an occasional practitioner with a Roman Catholic background who turns to Anglican ritual to baptize her child. Unlike Andrea, Beth never attended another Anglican liturgy, either before or after the baptism. Although she initially chose baptism due to deep cultural models that bind together family, cultural heritage, and religious ritual, and although she chose the Anglican tradition strategically due to roadblocks encountered in pursuing the Catholic ritual, Beth becomes appreciative of the progressive Anglican theology and practice, which becomes central to her experience. The overlap introduces oppositions that satisfy Beth's strong feminist identity and her hopes for her daughter. She is pleased to be able to share an experience of women in leadership with her extended Roman Catholic family. Although the Anglican baptism is separated from the larger Anglican ritual system in the experience of Beth and her family, the overlaps with other ritual systems provide ways to interpret the practice. This includes interpretations based on repetitions in the Roman Catholic system, it feels like "the Vatican," and popular culture, like a "royal baptism," as well as repetitions in their family ritual system, such as the specific roles for godparents and the traditional celebratory lunch. In addition to exemplifying the pattern of ritual familiarity echoing the Catholic tradition and progressive theology distinguishing the Anglican tradition, Beth's experience of baptism in the Anglican tradition also introduces the theme of ritual rigidity in the Catholic system, compared to a practical flexibility in Anglican settings.

Ritual Rigidity and Practical Flexibility

Catherine has a Roman Catholic and Orthodox background and now identifies as agnostic. *Cameron* has a Roman Catholic and Anglican background and was raised in the Anglican tradition. When Catherine and Cameron's first child is born, they initially pursue Roman Catholic baptism. However, the Roman Catholic parishes which Catherine contacts require godparents to participate in baptismal preparation in person, which was not possible for Catherine's brother, who lives in China. Catherine next inquires about baptism at a local Anglican parish and discovers they only baptize older children,[2] which is not an acceptable option for Catherine's Orthodox extended family, who are anxious for the child to be baptized as soon as possible "just in case." Catherine and Cameron persist and reach out to a large historic Anglican parish at a distance from their home, where Cameron's cousins had their children baptized and where his family has a cemetery plot. They receive a generous welcome and the flexibility they require. The baptism of their first child in this parish establishes a pattern for their next two children. Although they attend only on the occasion of the baptism of their children, Catherine and Cameron appreciate the warm welcome from the clergy and the lack of pressure to attend routinely. They also express appreciation for what they experience as a more positive mood in the Anglican tradition relative to the Catholic tradition—more celebration and less admonition. Cameron especially values the music, which resonates with childhood memories. Cameron's mother, who has practiced routinely in both the Roman Catholic and Anglican ritual systems at different times in her life, notes the many similarities between the Anglican and Roman Catholic liturgies, and is mostly just relieved that her grandchildren are baptized, pointing to the implicit opposition that the baptism might not take place at all.

Catherine and Cameron are an example of life transition occasional practitioners who separate baptisms and funerals from the Christian ritual system. The extended family ritual system is the primary location of these rituals—a family system that brings together Orthodox, Roman Catholic, and Anglican ritual expectations—and they pursue various strategies until they identify a ritual option that has the practical flexibility necessary for their situation. Deep cultural models motivate Catherine and Cameron's persistent pursuit of baptism, yet the specifics—including the specific Christian tradition and geographic location—are adaptable, and they test out various "tools" in their repertoire before finding one that can solve their "problem." The baptism of their first child in this parish then establishes a strategy of action which they follow for subsequent children. Although they express appreciation for what they perceive as a warmer mood of the Anglican ritual system, the practical flexibility that a specific parish affords

---

[2] This is surprising to me since this would not be an official teaching in the Anglican theological tradition and since I have not encountered this departure in interviews with diverse Anglican clergy. Even if this is an outlier or misunderstanding, it nevertheless shaped Catherine and Cameron's choices around baptism.

in comparison to the rigidity they experience in the Roman Catholic ritual system is the primary reason they engage it. The ability to separate the baptism smoothly from the Christian ritual system and integrate it with the specific life circumstances and expectations in their family ritual system is what is most important to them. Other repetitions and oppositions across ritual systems are less significant.

In contrast, *Dora* grew up in a small town in Bavaria that is deeply Roman Catholic and, when her son was born in Toronto, she knew immediately that she wanted to return to her hometown and baptize him in her home parish. The specific repetitions within this ritual system are essential for her—the same priest that baptized her would baptize her child, in the same church building, in the same Roman Catholic Christian tradition, giving her son a connection to family, culture, and homeland. At the same time, Dora desires to connect her Canadian family-in-law to the event, including her husband, who identifies as Anglican by heritage although he has never practiced routinely, and her sister-in-law Danielle, whom they choose to be their son's godmother. However, the Catholic priest in Dora's home parish requires godparents to be baptized, which Danielle is not.

Danielle identifies as spiritual and recognizes the Christian heritage of her family, yet has never practiced routinely. Before Danielle was born, her parents had a negative experience in marriage preparation, which pushed them away from the church. Danielle's mother decided to baptize Danielle herself at home with water "in the name of the Father, the Son, and the Holy Ghost": there is, of course, no formal record of this baptism. In order to serve as the godmother of her nephew at his Roman Catholic baptism, Danielle decides to pursue a second baptism as an adult in her local Anglican parish. Danielle's mother, who had very occasional connections to the parish over the years, nervously reaches out about the possibility of the baptism. The whole family meets with the priest and is overwhelmed with the compassionate and understanding response. They are also delighted by the progressive theology of the parish, especially its affirmation of the LGBTQ+ community. Even Dora expresses that it is more resonant with her values than her Roman Catholic tradition of origin. Yet this adult baptism was never about theological conviction or routine practice. When Danielle is baptized during a Sunday liturgy, the priest introduces her to the community and explains, "she is doing it for love."

Dora and Danielle, along with their family, are very occasional practitioners. For Dora, Roman Catholicism seems to be collectivistic in the sense that it is ascribed more than chosen and communal rather than individual. It is a deeply rooted cultural model. Even if the Anglican ritual system is better aligned with her values, her cultural model and the strategies of action surrounding baptism are so firmly established that for her, her child's baptism must not only be Roman Catholic but also take place in her home parish in Bavaria. However, the rigidity of the Roman Catholic system in requiring proof of baptism for godparents poses a problem when this collectivistic system intersects with a family ritual system from a different social, ethnic, and religious context. Therefore, Danielle follows her very different established yet instrumental strategy of action and is baptized at an Anglican parish in Toronto, which is sufficiently aligned with her progressive values and family heritage for her to feel comfortable doing so. Dora and Danielle have already ensured that this baptism will be recognized by the Roman Catholic priest, who formally acknowledges the overlap of these ritual systems. In this case, numerous occasional practitioners—Dora and her husband, Danielle and her mother—astutely negotiate the overlaps between the Roman Catholic and Anglican ritual systems. They exercise agency in systems controlled by others, noting existing maps and boundaries but also making their own way. In the Anglican ritual system, they find the practical flexibility necessary to meet the rigid requirements they encounter in the Roman Catholic ritual system.

Multiple Religious Practice

In the final example, *Eden* is a routine practitioner in both the Anglican and Roman Catholic traditions. She identifies as Roman Catholic and her husband as Anglican. When their young family immigrated to Canada from Jamaica a couple of years ago, her husband chose a local Anglican church for their family to attend weekly. Their children attend a local Catholic school. Christian practices are also a significant part of their family life at home. When their son is born, the priest, family, and parishioners at their Anglican parish simply assume he will be baptized; after all, they are routine practitioners in this community. However, as I wrap up my interview with Eden about her son's Anglican baptism, she casually mentions another baptism. A couple of months after the baptism in the Anglican church, her son was also baptized in a local Catholic parish. Eden explains how, when she and her husband married, they made a commitment to baptize their children in the Roman Catholic church, and Eden is determined to keep this promise. Eden did her research: she is aware that baptism is not supposed to be repeated and that Roman Catholics recognize Anglican baptism. She emphasizes that she personally believes in the validity of Anglican baptism. Nevertheless, Eden and her husband pursue baptism in both traditions. The Catholic church did not ask whether her son was already baptized; as Eden says, "Nobody thinks that you'll baptize your child twice."

In Eden's case, the family participates routinely in two distinct yet overlapping ritual systems. Eden recognizes the deep similarities between these systems, as well as the ways they formally recognize one another. Yet, at the same time, one does not substitute for the other in the same way as with other practitioners. Eden's commitment to baptize her children in the Roman Catholic ritual system stands firm; this promise is deeply motivating. At the same time, it does not prevent the Anglican baptism in the community where her family attends routinely. This striking repetition of the baptism in each ritual system reflects the family's routine practice in two distinct yet overlapping ritual systems. Eden is responding to her situation in strategic ways that require ongoing negotiation.

Ongoing Negotiation

These five stories, among the many narratives of families negotiating overlaps between the Roman Catholic and Anglican ritual systems in relation to baptism that appear in this research, are a way to begin unraveling the nuances of the strategic ways in which occasional practitioners respond to specific situations through ritualization. One mother makes a transition from the Roman Catholic system into the Anglican system, with baptism as a turning point, due to the progressive theology and ritual familiarity she encounters. Another mother chooses baptism for her child in the Anglican tradition due to its progressive theology and ritual flexibility, yet does so apart from ongoing involvement in the Anglican tradition. A family turns to the flexibility of the Anglican ritual system in contrast to the rigidity of the Catholic system to practice baptism in ways that align with the specifics of their family situation. A godmother meets the rigid requirements of the Catholic system by choosing adult baptism in the Anglican tradition thanks to its flexibility and progressive theology. Finally, a family practices fully in both traditions, including baptizing their child twice. Apart from Eden, each of these cases involves occasional practice on the part of at least some of the family members, and often the initiators and inner circle of supporters. Therefore, this case study and these specific narratives offer insights into overlapping ritual systems as well as occasional religious practitioners, clergy responses to occasional practice, and the Anglican tradition in the context of a changing Canadian religious landscape.

The case of Anglican baptisms in Toronto demonstrates the complex relationship between the Anglican and Roman Catholic *ritual systems* in this setting, as well as the intricate ways in which these and other ritual systems overlap, including ritual systems associated with family, ethnicity, popular culture, and other Christian traditions. Repetitions and oppositions in multiple ritual systems interpret the ritual of Christian baptism. The Christian ritual system is not necessarily the primary interpretive system for many occasional practitioners.

At the same time, baptism matters intensely to *occasional practitioners*. Deep cultural models motivate baptism. The occasional practitioners in these narratives, especially the initiators, advocates, and inner-circle supporters, are very invested in the practice and are willing to go to great lengths to facilitate it. This includes both following well-established strategies of action and charting creative and adaptive new courses. Occasional practitioners reflect deeply on how to baptize their children and intuitively negotiate ritual systems and practices they often would not have the theological language to describe.

Clergy are an important part of this story and respond to requests for baptism in a diversity of ways. Small interactions with clergy contribute to strongly felt impressions of the Anglican and Roman Catholic ritual systems, as well as Christianity and religion more broadly. How clergy respond matters to occasional practitioners, especially in these moments of crisis—and crisis is a helpful framework for understanding the practices associated with life transitions, including baptism. Practitioners feel deeply and value highly a compassionate response in these moments of ritual need. These are significant ministry opportunities.

Finally, these narratives at the intersection of the Roman Catholic and Anglican ritual systems reveal patterns associated with the *changing religious landscape* in Toronto. One is simply that a surprisingly large number of Anglican baptisms may not be for families with a background or future in the Anglican tradition. This should give us pause when interpreting data on the number of baptisms in the Anglican diocese or specific parishes. Another is the emergence of a grassroots ecumenism that would have been inconceivable a century or two ago, in which Anglican rituals may be substituted for Catholic ones, at least in certain cases. The ways in which the progressive theological leanings of the Anglican tradition shape these decisions reinforces the idea that progressive–conservative polarities are becoming more significant than denominational divisions. Finally, this case study highlights that understanding occasional practice as a way of relating to religion is important for understanding a contemporary religious landscape in which participants engage in ongoing negotiation of multiple overlapping ritual systems.

Ritual Systems and Dialogue with Occasional Practitioners

In conclusion, in Part II of the book, I have drawn on ritual studies, specifically the work of Catherine Bell and Kimberly Belcher, to explore how the systemic nature of ritual influences occasional practice, and how occasional practice shapes ritual systems. Theorizing not only the relationships *within* ritual systems, but the overlaps *among* different ritual systems, is especially valuable when considering the ongoing roles of Christian ritual in a contemporary religious landscape characterized by multiple overlapping ritual systems.

There are four specific contributions that ritual systems theory makes to understanding occasional religious practice.

First, rituals systems provide a way to theorize *why occasional practitioners continue to select certain Christian rituals* from the Christian ritual system. This ritualization is a strategic response to specific situations that, if not motivated by cultural models or following strategies of action associated with the Christian ritual system, is likely associated with cultural models or strategies of action related to an overlapping system, such as the ethnic heritage or family ritual system.

Second, ritual systems provide a way to theorize *what rituals mean and do for occasional practitioners*. The systemic nature of ritual means that practitioners within ritual systems interpret these systems through relationships of repetition, opposition, and centrality. These interpretations do not depend on formal theological training or routine practice. Instead, they may point to patterns both within ritual systems and also across multiple overlapping ritual systems. Those who practice only occasionally are likely to rely more on interpretive relationships with other overlapping ritual systems.

Third, ritual systems provide a way to theorize *how occasional practice both does and does not change rituals themselves*. Relatively few practitioners are required to sustain a ritual system. The selection of a subset of practices does not necessarily change the network of connections between those practices and the rest of the system for routine and intensive practitioners. At the same time, the entrance of differently ritualized bodies into a ritual system creates tremendous potential for change, and the presence of occasional practitioners is a significant factor to consider when examining how ritual practices are changing in increasingly nonreligious and religiously diverse contexts.

Fourth, ritual systems theory establishes a framework for how people positioned differently within ritual systems, and in different overlapping ritual systems, can *learn from one another*. It provides a way of understanding why routine and occasional practitioners may understand the same ritual system in different yet valid ways. It explores how those who relate to the system in different ways may make different connections, both within and beyond the system, that can potentially enrich the meaning and function of the ritual for participants. In Part III of the book, I build on this theoretical insight to consider why and how routine practitioners can do liturgical theology together with occasional practitioners.

PART III
DOING THEOLOGY WITH OCCASIONAL PRACTITIONERS

8
The Necessity of Doing Theology with Occasional Practitioners

I am sitting at a small table in a bustling downtown coffee shop, where I just concluded an interview with a young mother about the baptism of her daughter. As I settle in to write fieldnotes and transfer audio files, the casually fashionable mother comes rushing back through the door, "I forgot to show you the pictures," she exclaims. She holds out her phone and, standing by the table, we look through photographs of the event: a crib with a white dress, shoes, tights, and diaper laid out as the godparents prepare to dress the child; portraits on the lawn in front of the church building with many different configurations of extended family members; images of the cake and food at the lunch reception; and a photo of the family by the font during the baptism celebration.

I begin this chapter with an extended example of photography to center the experience of participants in this research and to begin to explore the ways in which they do liturgical theology—how they know and communicate what is *significant* about Christian worship—which may be distinct from how clergy and academic theologians do liturgical theology. I use the term "significant" in a twofold sense to refer both to what occasional practitioners consider *important*, as well as to what they experience as *meaningful*, in terms of signifying or communicating meaning. Many participants speak of photography during interviews. In addition to the mother in the coffee shop, other participants show me photographs related to baptism, including a mother who had professional portraits taken the day after the baptism that feature her children in their baptismal gowns carefully positioned on a white couch, and a grandmother who, during a conversation about the baptism of her grandchildren, leads me to another part of her home to show me photos of the baptisms of her sons that hang on the wall.

Conversations about funerals also prompt participants to share photographs. One woman begins an interview focused on her mother's

Occasional Religious Practice. Sarah Kathleen Johnson, Oxford University Press.
© Oxford University Press 2025. DOI: 10.1093/9780197806579.003.0009

funeral by pulling out a large scrapbook that she made about the event. The book includes the order of worship, her eulogy, the text of the hymns, and many photographs, including an image of the casket topped with the family tartan and a spray of white roses, and one of the chancel of the church, where a large portrait of her mother in her prime is flanked by flower arrangements. The same portrait hangs in the living room where we meet, among many other family photographs that adorn the walls. Near the end of another interview about a funeral, the middle-aged man with whom I am speaking takes out a tablet computer and narrates a slideshow of photographs of his mother's life that he created for the funeral: "It was actually very cathartic. Just looking back over the years and stuff. . . . I'll show you."

Participants not only show me photographs related to these events, but also speak about the role of photography in their experience of baptisms and funerals. Even a brief outline of the day of the baptism or funeral often includes mention of a time to take or view photos. For them, photography is part of the event, not a distraction from it.

At funerals, photographs are described as an important part of *sharing the life story of the deceased*, including capturing different time periods of their life:

> Not everybody in the room knows the person at every age, so it's nice to have a lot of images around, so everybody gets a sense of who it is they're there for.

> My sister had arranged my mom's photo albums. My daughter created a slideshow. I believe she worked on the slideshow for almost two years with her grandmother, with my mom, because my mother was determined she was going to have a slideshow and what each one of the pictures had meant. Again, as I say, she had been ill, but she was definitely still sound of mind and was quite determined [about] what she wanted to see happening. But it was—she made the slide show and stuff and everybody was laughing. . . . Some of us didn't even realize different things about my mother, my father, in their earlier years and stuff, right?

> There's one where [my mother] is on a motorcycle, obviously about 1950, and she's only like eighteen years old. So, one of the granddaughters, she says, "What's grandma doing on a motorcycle?" And I said, "Well, that was your grandfather's motorcycle." "You're kidding! She wouldn't let us be on any motorcycle." So yeah, it was a great chance to just all connect.

Photographs facilitate a relational connection, often across generations. They prompt the sharing of stories and the accompanying laughter and tears.

At baptisms, photographs and videos may be a way *to include those who cannot be physically present*, such as grandparents who are ill, godparents who live at a distance, or a large extended family:

> [My mother-in-law] is in Alberta so she wasn't able to make it, but we took video and she sent us a baptism gift and a card so he would have it on the day. So, she's also very, very supportive but just couldn't be here for the day.

> [My husband's] grandfather wasn't able to make it. He is experiencing some health issues. He turned 97 last week. So, it's a really big deal but [he] wasn't actually able to come all the way downtown so he also saw the video, and was also very supportive.

> [The godfather] is my husband's best friend who lives in New Zealand. So, when we actually did the baptism, we filmed the whole thing. And it's very—we shouldn't have been allowed to do it, but [the priest] again, given how kind and understanding she is, she allowed it. Typically, they don't allow filming, but she allowed us to film it, and then we sent it back home to [the godfather]. It was five in the morning his time.

> We kept [the baptism] a little bit smaller.... We're going to a family reunion this Sunday, so we shared pictures, and we shared some video, and [my family is] just so happy.

Beyond including additional family members in the celebration, photographs are also used to *celebrate and solidify family relationships* in connection with these events, as one participant describes:

> We took a group shot with everyone that came for [my daughter's] baptism where the altar is. And we did the same thing for my son. I really remember that that was very special. Like all the family support was really great and having that shot again was nice.... Also it was like another way for my husband's family to be included because we are not very close with them. My husband has had a lot of issues with, I guess, his family understanding him.... They were all there as well. We got to take a picture with them, which was very nice.

Photographs at baptism are often relational. Taking photos is a creative act that usually involves two or more people; such photos depict people in relationship with one another; and they are typically shared widely with family and friends.

For some participants, photographs are central to how they *remember* and connect with their own baptisms. By extension, photography is how they imagine sharing the experience of baptism with their children as they get older:

> Even though I can't remember my own baptism, I feel like I still can because of all the pictures and all the memorabilia that we have. And I kind of just want to create that for her.
>
> I: Could you say more about your own baptism? Where and when did it happen and what does it mean to you today?
> R: So, I only can speak from pictures. Both of my parents are deceased, so I did not have that conversation with them when my children were born. But I see the pictures—that I was baptized, that it was a big thing that was with family and friends. It was at an Anglican church in New York City.... And yeah, it was in 19—maybe 1980.
>
> I know [my granddaughter] is really small. I took a lot of pictures. There are some gorgeous pictures of her looking up at the stained-glass windows and the people in the congregation and she is a very calm and happy girl. So, I look at that and I hope that maybe we can look at those pictures in a few years and she can look at all of those symbols of the church and ask about them and then want to maybe pursue it a little more and it'll add to her faith journey.

Photographs are important not only at the time of the baptism but also in the years that follow, as participants continue to reflect on the event and invite their children into the experience as they mature.

In addition, photography may be a way that participants *define what they consider to be part of the baptism ritual system*. It may begin with preparations for the baptism, include the liturgy at the church, and continue through events that follow, such as the giving of gifts and a family gathering:

> I got her some gifts. I got her first necklace and that's a pretty nice sterling silver necklace in commemoration [of the event], and I took a picture of her wearing it, which was nice.

> We had everyone over if they wanted to. The kids all changed their clothes and ran out in the backyard, and we had soccer, we had a whole bunch of stuff. There was lots of food. Then [my daughter] just went from person to

person and [got] lots of attention and her godparents wanted to take more pictures with her.

Taking pictures is a practice that bridges and connects different parts of the baptism ritual, extending beyond the church to the family gathering.

Finally, photography is, at times, used *to identify significant moments* during the celebration of baptism, moments that are often considered important and meaningful because they are associated with strong emotions:

> When the priest took [my grandson] from his dad and brought him over to the water and he was holding him, I had tears in my eyes. I was thanking God for having the opportunity to be in this place at this time and that I actually was blessed with a grandson.... And when [the priest] gave him back to his dad, I couldn't keep the camera steady because [I had] tears to my eyes. I was so happy. I was happy that he had blessed them and that he had had his baptism. I was really emotional. I was happy to have witnessed it.

> I took pictures where I was sitting when that guy in front of me wasn't obstructing my view. I did get a couple of good ones with the water being put on her head.

> I: So thinking a bit more about the baptism service itself on Sunday morning, are there moments that stood out to you as especially significant?
>
> R: There are, but I'm not sure that it means anything to you. I desperately hope my friend got a picture because I know [the priest] is really anti pictures at the font. My friend came up with a camera and I was like, "[whispering noise]" and she was like, "[whispering noise]." And that was the moment when [my older daughter] went up and she helped [the priest] lift the water and pour the water. To me, I think that will be my Polaroid in my head more so than the rest.
>
> I don't know why, but it was just because I've been so guilt-ridden about [my daughter] not being included and becoming the middle child and being left out. She's really had to take a backseat as soon as the baby came into our households and her role in the family. I just thought that was just so, so sweet that she had that little moment. It probably meant nothing to anybody else, but it meant something to me that she was in—I'm going to start crying.
>
> Also, there was a picture of when my sister, who's five years younger than I am, when my sister was baptized, there's a picture of me holding,

helping with the font. So, it was kind of like cyclical or generational or whatever you want to say. I hope that [my friend] got that picture, I really hope she did, but I don't know if she did. And then [the priest] poo-pooed her, she was like, "no pictures."

As in this example, photography may create or strengthen repetitions associated with the baptism ritual system, among siblings or across generations.

Given the centrality of photography to the relationships and remembrance of baptism for occasional practitioners, it is significant that priests employ various *rules related to photography* at baptisms and funerals. One priest is very clear that photos are not to be taken during the baptism ceremony itself, which is noteworthy to many parents. While some appreciate this rule, others would rather have a photographic record of the event:

> In this social media age, we're taking pictures, posting everything. It was really special that [the priest] informed us to be in that moment, stop taking pictures, be in that moment. Like we're not allowing you to take pictures, not because we're trying to be mean, it's a sacred moment. We were informed during the baptism rehearsal and everyone was informed. And I took pains to inform my guests, because they're very much into social media as most of us are, not to take pictures. This is the moment we are in. Just soak in the moment. Just be with us in the present. And that was very important. Mind you, sometimes we're looking at him and we're like, oh, we don't have a picture of him being baptized. But the most important thing was we were there in the moment experiencing it.

> R: Another difference [from my daughters' baptisms in a different parish] is we were allowed to be taking pictures during the baptism. Here it is not allowed, there it was allowed.... You don't get to see the pictures of the child actually being baptized. I mean the memories you just try to remember for yourself.
> I: Did you take pictures afterwards?
> R: Afterwards, yes, with the priest. I mean it could have been any other day. The only thing is I was putting on white, so you just say that was his baptism. But there was no actual picture of that part of the baptism, which usually we have for the girls, we have pictures of them being baptized. The actual process, that was allowed. Maybe during the service you wouldn't be taking pictures, but for the baptism part, yes, you are allowed to take pictures of that part of the celebration.

As the previous quotation suggests, it is not only taking pictures (or not) that matters, but also what is photographed.

As is evident in these examples, participants not only understand taking and sharing photographs to be an important aspect of baptisms and funerals, they also use photographs to interpret these events: to identify rituals that are central or repeated; to confirm and strengthen relationships with those who are both present and absent; to capture emotion in particular moments; to depict material objects—water, clothing, flowers, space; and to narrate the meaning and function of the baptism or the story of the deceased's life for themselves and for others, both at the time and in the years that follow.

In contrast, while participants are eager to volunteer photographs, occasional practitioners often struggle to find language to speak of their liturgical experience. Many of them do not know technical terms that ritual experts would readily apply to aspects of the experience: preaching is referred to as "her speech," "when she was talking," and "the eulogy"; the font is called "the bowl," "the fountain," and "the water"; and Anglican services of worship are named "sermons" and, very commonly, "masses." Participants often pause or equivocate as they try to recall religious language to name aspects of worship, objects in the space, or leadership roles. Their vocabulary for theological concepts is even more limited. During interviews, I do not fill these gaps or correct their terminology unless I need to clarify the meaning of what is said. I am less concerned about the words that occasional practitioners use than about the stories they tell about their liturgical experiences. The occasional practitioners whom I interview reflect deeply on their experiences of Christian worship. They have intentionally chosen Christian baptism or burial or attendance at a holiday service. They tell powerful stories about how these practices function in their lives. They vividly describe fleeting moments of meaning, often with tears in their eyes. Occasional religious practitioners are doing theology, although perhaps not with the words used in the academy or by church leaders.

The extended example of photography begins this theological discussion to center the experiences and voices of occasional practitioners. It highlights how ordinary participants, including occasional practitioners, often rely on different ways of knowing and communicating what is significant about Christian worship than do clergy and academic liturgical theologians as ritual experts and intensive practitioners. Doing theology with occasional practitioners challenges ritual experts and liturgical theologians not only to rethink the content of liturgical theology, but also to shift how theology is done—to reconsider what sources count, what language is used, and even what is considered liturgy. In this chapter, I explore how people who relate to religion in different ways can do theology together, and why we would want to.

Why and How to Do Theology with Occasional Practitioners

Attending to the experience and insights of occasional practitioners is possible and necessary for doing liturgical theology today. Occasional practitioners help us all set aside the false, yet persistent, assumption that liturgical participants are fully believing, actively practicing, morally compliant, and formally affiliated with the Christian tradition. Very often, they are not. Many participants are not aligned with some of these assumptions, at least some of the time. In increasingly nonreligious and religiously diverse contexts, many participants, including occasional, routine, and even intensive practitioners, are not aligned with these assumptions much of the time. An accurate understanding of who is participating in the liturgy, in their diversity, is a crucial starting point for doing liturgical theology. By letting go of these assumptions, in part by being in conversation with those who never shared them, we can together discover additional dimensions of what Christian worship is meaning and doing. We can attend to the liturgical and theological margins as privileged places of theological insight. We can adopt an attitude of openness to learning with and from occasional practitioners in ways that are always local and particular, yet also have the potential to cast broader light.

My approach to doing theology with occasional practitioners is anchored in a turn toward *ethnography as theology*.[1] It takes as a methodological starting point the understanding that the situation of occasional practitioners has "embodied within its life substantive contributions to theology."[2] The experiences and reflections of occasional practitioners are in

---

[1] The methodological approach is discussed in detail in Appendix A.
[2] Christian Scharen and Aana Marie Vigen, eds., *Ethnography as Christian Theology and Ethics* (New York: Continuum, 2011), xxii. Dunlop explores various approaches to using photography to do qualitative theological research that could be valuable for studying occasional religious practice. Sarah Dunlop, *Doing Theology with Photographs* (London: T&T Clark, 2024).

and of themselves theological. Recognizing theology embedded in everyday life does not preclude engagement with other theological and theoretical materials, but it does not automatically privilege them. Instead, it aims to facilitate dialogue between the everyday theology of occasional practitioners and the academic theology of ritual experts. As a step toward addressing the historic and ongoing imbalance of power between occasional practitioners and ritual experts, I privilege the voices of occasional practitioners here and aim to approach this dialogue on their terms. For example, my method of requesting a single interview in which I invite participants to share the story of a specific event that is important to them reflects their occasional relationship with religion, in contrast to ethnographic approaches that involve multiple meetings[3] or conversations focused on the concerns of academic theologians.[4]

More than the preceding chapters, this discussion centering the perspectives of occasional practitioners is written with an audience of ritual experts in mind, including liturgical theologians and religious professionals, and I identify myself with this audience here. Occasional practice has been noticed in the discipline of liturgical studies since at least the 1970s.[5] Since the 1990s, there have been various studies based in Europe that employ social scientific methods to engage theological and pastoral questions surrounding occasional practice. These include research on Christmas attendance and infant baptism in England and Wales,[6] and studies of baptism, First Communion, and funerals in the Netherlands.[7] Intriguingly, much of this

---

[3] Nelson Robert Cowan, "Liturgical Biography as Liturgical Theology: Co-Constructing Theology at Hillsong Church, New York City" (PhD diss., Boston University School of Theology, 2019).

[4] Natalie Wigg-Stevenson, *Ethnographic Theology* (New York: Palgrave Macmillan, 2014).

[5] David Power and Luis Maldonado, eds., *Liturgy and Human Passage* (New York: Seabury Press, 1979).

[6] Leslie Francis, Keith Littler, and T. Hugh Thomas, "Fenced Fonts or Open Doors? An Empirical Survey of Baptismal Policy Among Clergy in the Church in Wales," *Implicit Religion* 3 (2000): 73–86; Leslie Francis and David Lankshear, "Asking About Baptism: Straw Polls and Fenced Fonts," *The Modern Churchman* 34 (1993): 88–92; David Walker, "You Don't Have to Go to Church to Be a Good Christian: The Implicit Religion of the Cathedral Carol Service Congregation," *Mental Health, Religion and Culture* 16 (2013): 903–908.

[7] Gerard Lukken, "Infant Baptism in the Netherlands and Flanders: A Christian Ritual in the Dynamic of the Anthropological/Theological and Cultural Context," in *Christian Feast and Festival: The Dynamics of Western Liturgy and Culture*, ed. P. Post, G. Rouwhorst, L. van Tongeren, and A. Scheer (Leuven: Peeters, 2001), 551–580. Paul Post and Louis van Tongeren, "The Celebration of the First Communion: Seeking the Identity of the Christian Ritual," in *Christian Feast and Festival: The Dynamics of Western Liturgy and Culture*, ed. P. Post, G. Rouwhorst, L. van Tongeren, and A. Scheer (Leuven: Peeters, 2001), 581–598; Thomas Quartier, "Liturgy Participant's Perspective: Exploring the Attitudes of Participants at Roman Catholic Funerals with Empirical Methods," *Liturgy* 21, no. 3 (2006): 21–29.

research has been based on surveys rather than on interviews or participant observation. The only monograph with a focus on occasional practice is Thomas Quartier's quantitative exploration of Roman Catholic funeral practices in the Netherlands.[8] However, French Roman Catholic sacramental theologian Louis-Marie Chauvet concludes his influential small volume, *The Sacraments,* with a pastorally oriented reflection on occasional participation in baptism—"managing the request for rites of passage"—thus suggesting that occasional practice is among the pressing sacramental theological questions of our time.[9] My research on occasional religious practice shifts the geographic focus from Europe to North America, employs a ethnographic approach, and aims to be ecumenical rather than Roman Catholic. My overarching objective is to consider occasional religious practice in ways that are expansive and encompassing, and equally sociological and liturgical theological. Most significantly for this discussion, my approach represents *a theological shift in orientation from seeing occasional practice as a problem to be solved to recognizing it as an opportunity to be embraced.*

In the preceding chapters, I demonstrated, from a social scientific perspective, why it is crucial to consider occasional religious practice when describing the contemporary religious landscape and assessing the meaning and function of rituals today. In the following chapter, I consider specific liturgical theological themes offered by occasional practitioners in this case study, including Christian worship as material more than linguistic, emotional more than conceptual, and relational more than personal. I then examine how occasional practitioners speak into themes of interest to liturgical theologians, including God, tradition, and ethics. But first, in this chapter, I go beyond social scientific reasoning and make a theological argument for why it is necessary to attend to the experience and perspectives of occasional practitioners. I provide three distinct yet interrelated ways to explore this possibility. The first is engagement with scripture in the company of Tomáš Halík and Todd Whitmore. The second is a return to the familiar figure of Mrs. Murphy in dialogue with Aidan Kavanaugh, David Fagerberg, and Anna Petrin. The third draws inspiration from liberation theology through the liturgical theological work of Cláudio Carvalhaes.

---

[8] Thomas Quartier, *Bridging the Gaps: An Empirical Study of Catholic Funeral Rites* (Münster: LIT Verlag, 2007).
[9] Louis-Marie Chauvet, *The Sacraments: The Word of God at the Mercy of the Body* (Collegeville, MN: Liturgical Press, 2001), 173–200.

Scripture: Zacchaeus and the Woman at the Well

Christian scripture—specifically two encounters between Jesus and people who were marginalized in his context—is one starting point for exploring why and how routine and extreme practitioners may do theology with occasional practitioners.

Zacchaeus

Czech Roman Catholic priest and theologian Tomáš Halík, who has served as an advisor to the Pontifical Council for Dialogue with Non-Believers, invites readers into the story of Zacchaeus in a volume titled *Patience with God: The Story of Zacchaeus Continuing in Us*.[10] The story of Zacchaeus, the wealthy tax collector who climbs a tree to get a look at Jesus, is found in the Gospel according to Luke:

> [Jesus] entered Jericho and was passing through it. A man was there named Zacchaeus; he was a chief tax collector and was rich. He was trying to see who Jesus was, but on account of the crowd he could not, because he was short in stature. So he ran ahead and climbed a sycamore tree to see him, because he was going to pass that way. When Jesus came to the place, he looked up and said to him, "Zacchaeus, hurry and come down, for I must stay at your house today." So he hurried down and was happy to welcome him. All who saw it began to grumble and said, "He has gone to be the guest of one who is a sinner." Zacchaeus stood there and said to the Lord, "Look, half of my possessions, Lord, I will give to the poor, and if I have defrauded anyone of anything, I will pay back four times as much." Then Jesus said to him, "Today salvation has come to this house, because he, too, is a son of Abraham. For the Son of Man came to seek out and to save the lost."[11]

Halík uses the story of Zacchaeus to consider Jesus's attention to those on "the fringes of faith," those who are "curious seekers" but at the same time want "to maintain a certain distance."[12] Halík then invites those who

---

[10] Tomáš Halík, *Patience with God. The Story of Zacchaeus Continuing in Us* (New York: Doubleday, 2009).
[11] Luke 19:1–10 (NRSVUE).
[12] Halík, *Patience with God*, 3.

consider themselves disciples of Jesus to join Zacchaeus, "to make ourselves seekers with those who seek and questioners with those who question."[13] It is an invitation not only to acknowledge those on the fringes, but to identify with them.

A significant contribution of Halík's account is how he names Jesus's attention to forms of marginalization that are not economic, including religious marginalization. Zacchaeus was wealthy and powerful, yet on the fringes of society and the fringes of faith. Halík emphasizes the need to imitate Jesus's interest in those on the religious margins, who likely include many occasional practitioners:

> As I meditated on Jesus's encounter with Zacchaeus and the many other examples of his "prior interest in people on the fringes" it struck me that perhaps something extra was needed today in order to fully follow in Christ's footsteps: an interest, or better still *a prior interest*, in people *on the fringes of faith*, in those who remain in the anteroom of the church, should they actually come that close to it. It is an interest in people in the "gray zone" between religious certainty and atheism, an interest in the doubters and seekers.... However, my interest in these people on the fridges is not of the narrowly missionary variety. My chief interest is not to "convert" them, not to bring "certainty" to the uncertain.[14]

"Those who remain in the anteroom of the church" include many occasional religious practitioners. Halík aims to honor the way these Zacchaeuses relate to religion rather than trying to change them:

> I feel concern for the Zacchaeuses, for the church, and for the society that the church and the Zacchaeuses inhabit—in equal measure. I feel a responsibility to ensure that "individual seekers" of the Zacchaeus type are not manipulated by anyone to conform to the present notion of "standard believers," that they are not driven out of the ambit of the church—that they are, quite simply, *accorded freedom to determine how close they want to be to the visible forms of today's church-based Christianity*.... We have to learn to create space for the Zacchaeuses, including those who will never become

---

[13] Halík, *Patience with God*, 8.
[14] Halík, *Patience with God*, 16. Emphasis added.

"standard parishioners," or at least respect the space that they create around themselves.[15]

Halík is not interested in converting occasional practitioners into routine "standard believers." In fact, he goes a step further to suggest that dialogue with those on the fringes of faith is an opportunity for mutual learning:

> Our closeness to the seekers ought also to teach us openness; we don't have to solely think about having to teach and edify them—we can also learn a great deal from them. And we can try to show those people in the church who are self-assured and "satiated" about their religion that it is necessary, at least sometimes, to reach out to people on the fringe of the churches—and not just to "convert" and assimilate them. Being able to take a look at how God appears from the standpoint of people who are searching, doubting, and questioning—isn't this a new, exciting, necessary, and useful religious experience?[16]

In the story of Zacchaeus, Halík finds a model for how people who relate to religion in different ways can relate to one another. Halík offers one theological approach to why liturgical theological dialogue with occasional practitioners is desirable, particularly in his openness to hearing from those who are not "standard parishioners"—those who are not formally affiliated, fully believing, actively practicing, and morally compliant with the church—but whose religious experience is nonetheless valuable.

However, there are barriers to borrowing from Halík. First, not all occasional practitioners are seekers—doubters for whom God is a question. As discussed in Chapter 3, some identify as committed Christians, others are firmly nonreligious, and most of those with whom I speak are quite content with their current relationship with religion. Second, Halík's account is narrowly centered on matters of belief, particularly atheism and the question of God, while I am more interested in religion as practice.

When considering religion as practice, it is helpful to supplement Halík's reading of Zacchaeus with Catholic ethicist and ethnographer Todd Whitmore's interpretation of the same biblical text. Like Halík, Whitmore draws our attention to Jesus's care for the marginalized beyond the poor: his

---

[15] Halík, *Patience with God*, 77.
[16] Halík, *Patience with God*, 18.

mission is to both the poor and the wicked.[17] Although I would certainly not equate the occasionally religious with the wicked, this still points to Jesus's care for the marginalized, broadly understood. However, it is another part of Whitmore's reading of Zacchaeus that is helpful when considering religion as practice. As Whitmore describes, Zacchaeus reminds us that Jesus's call is not the same to everyone. For example, in another gospel narrative, the rich young man is asked to give up all his wealth and follow Jesus.[18] Zacchaeus gives up only half his wealth and remains home, extending hospitality instead of joining the disciples on the road. There is a "two-tiered ethic": "one tier shaped for those who follow quite literally in his itinerancy and one oriented to those who remain in settled lives but who offer material support for the itinerants."[19] Whitmore's reading of the story of Zacchaeus is a reminder that Jesus's call is not the same for all. Not all of his disciples give up everything and join him on the journey. Some give up something and invite him into their homes. This can create space for different ways of relating to religion today, including intensive and occasional practice.

Although both Halík and Whitmore lay a foundation for a relationship of respect and collaboration with those who relate to religion in different ways, neither of them directly addresses questions of worship practice or liturgical theological dialogue.

The Woman at the Well

In the Gospel according to John, there is another story of Jesus reaching out across difference.[20] A woman encounters Jesus in the course of her everyday life while undertaking the ordinary task of drawing water from the community well:

> A Samaritan woman came to draw water, and Jesus said to her, "Give me a drink." (His disciples had gone to the city to buy food.) The Samaritan woman said to him, "How is it that you, a Jew, ask a drink of me, a woman of Samaria?" (Jews do not share things in common with Samaritans.) Jesus

---

[17] Todd Whitmore, *Imitating Christ in Magwi: An Anthropological Theology* (London: T&T Clark, 2019), 16.
[18] Mark 10:17–31, Matt. 19:16–30, Luke 18:18–30.
[19] Whitmore, *Imitating Christ*, 18.
[20] John 4:1–42.

answered her, "If you knew the gift of God and who it is that is saying to you, 'Give me a drink,' you would have asked him, and he would have given you living water." The woman said to him, "Sir, you have no bucket, and the well is deep. Where do you get that living water? Are you greater than our ancestor Jacob, who gave us the well and with his sons and his flocks drank from it?" Jesus said to her, "Everyone who drinks of this water will be thirsty again, but those who drink of the water that I will give them will never be thirsty. The water that I will give will become in them a spring of water gushing up to eternal life." The woman said to him, "Sir, give me this water, so that I may never be thirsty or have to keep coming here to draw water."

Jesus said to her, "Go, call your husband, and come back." The woman answered him, "I have no husband." Jesus said to her, "You are right in saying, 'I have no husband,' for you have had five husbands, and the one you have now is not your husband. What you have said is true!" The woman said to him, "Sir, I see that you are a prophet. Our ancestors worshiped on this mountain, but you say that the place where people must worship is in Jerusalem." Jesus said to her, "Woman, believe me, the hour is coming when you will worship the Father neither on this mountain nor in Jerusalem. You worship what you do not know; we worship what we know, for salvation is from the Jews. But the hour is coming and is now here when the true worshipers will worship the Father in spirit and truth, for the Father seeks such as these to worship him. God is spirit, and those who worship him must worship in spirit and truth." The woman said to him, "I know that Messiah is coming" (who is called Christ). "When he comes, he will proclaim all things to us." Jesus said to her, "I am he, the one who is speaking to you."[21]

Despite and across many barriers—gender, nationality, race, morality, and religion—the woman and Jesus have a substantial conversation.[22] In fact, it is the longest conversation Jesus has in the gospels.[23] In this conversation, Jesus and the woman become vulnerable to one another. They see each other for

---

[21] John 4:7–26 (NRSVUE).

[22] Joy Jones-Carmack, "Relational Demography in John 4: Crossing Cultural Boundaries as Praxis for Christian Leadership," *Feminist Theology* 25, no. 1 (2016): 41–52; Bernadeta Jojko, "At the Well: An Encounter Beyond the Boundaries (Jn 4:1–42)," *Gregorianum* 99, no. 1 (2018): 5–27.

[23] Barbara Brown Taylor, "Identity Confirmation: John 4:5–42," *Christian Century*, February 12, 2008.

who they are. Jesus knows the woman's history and speaks with her anyway. The woman is the first person to guess Jesus's identity and the first person to whom he reveals himself in the gospel of John.[24] The woman and Jesus challenge one another, asking questions and making demands. They discuss matters of ultimate concern—life and death and living water. The woman and Jesus discuss proper worship, not on a mountain or in the temple, but in spirit and in truth. When the disciples return, they are dismayed and wonder why Jesus is talking with this outsider—this woman who is not formally affiliated, morally compliant, fully believing, or actively practicing their religious tradition.[25] But Jesus listens to her, and shares with her, and when she returns to her family and friends, Jesus goes with her to stay with her community for a couple of days.[26]

The woman at the well is another starting point for reflection on liturgical theological dialogue with occasional practitioners. Occasional practitioners may encounter Jesus at the well, in everyday places that are sources of life and death. These may be places that are associated with their heritage, the wells of their ancestors. In icons, Jesus and the woman are often depicted in conversation alongside a baptismal font. Occasional practitioners may have the capacity for conversations and actions that disciples do not expect, including sharing hard truths and asking tough questions. They may worship, not in the temple or on the mountain, but in speaking the truth and sensing the Spirit. Routine practitioners such as clergy and academic theologians may be the disciples who are astonished and dismayed that Jesus would listen to this woman on the fringes of faith. Yet, they may also choose to follow Jesus, and sit down at the well for a conversation with vulnerability and challenge, and together search for living water and worship in spirit and truth.

Liturgical Theology: Mrs. Murphy's Great-Granddaughter

The mythical liturgical theological figure of Mrs. Murphy, who has loomed large in the discipline of liturgical studies for forty years,[27] is another

---

[24] Taylor, "Identity Confirmation."
[25] John 4:27–31.
[26] John 4:39–42.
[27] Michael Aune, "Liturgy and Theology, Part I," *Worship* 81, no. 1 (2007): 46–68.

starting point for considering why it is necessary to do liturgical theology with occasional practitioners. In parallel to the discussion of Zacchaeus and the woman at the well above, in her 2020 article, liturgical historian and theologian Anna Petrin re-examines the "Murphy project" with an emphasis on the need to "attend to marginalized voices in the Christian tradition" and "listen to their accounts of liturgical and theological experience at the margins of the church."[23] Her discussion begins with "the birth of Mrs. Murphy."[29]

Mrs. Murphy

Benedictine liturgical theologian Aidan Kavanagh brought Mrs. Murphy into being in 1981 to speak about a distinction between primary liturgical theology—the liturgical assembly's direct liturgical experience—and secondary liturgical theology—reflection upon that experience, usually in a clerical or scholarly mode.[30] Middle ground emerges between primary and secondary liturgical theology when ordinary worshipers reflect on and speak about their experience of worship,[31] as in the interviews in this study. However, for Kavanagh, Mrs. Murphy is not simply an opinionated parishioner, but the *theoretical embodiment of tradition in practice*. As Kavanagh writes:

> The language of the primary theologian ... more often consists in symbolic, metaphoric, sacramental words and actions which throw flashes of light upon chasms of rich ambiguity. As such, Mrs. Murphy's language illuminates the chaotic landscape through which I must pick my professional way with the laser-like beam of precise words and concepts—which is why what she does is primary and what I do is secondary; which is why, also, what she does is so much harder to do than what I do.[32]

---

[28] Anna Petrin, "Insights from Mrs. Murphy: Caryll Houselander as Liturgical Theologian," *Worship* 94 (2020): 206–227. Petrin helpfully summarizes feminist critiques of Mrs. Murphy; I do not repeat those arguments here.
[29] Petrin, "Insights from Mrs. Murphy," 208.
[30] Aidan Kavanagh, *On Liturgical Theology* (Collegeville, MN: Liturgical Press, 1981).
[31] Cowan explores this "interstitial" space. Cowan, "Liturgical Biography."
[32] Kavanagh; in David Fagerberg, *Theologia Prima: What Is Liturgical Theology?* (Chicago: Liturgy Training Publications, 2004), 133.

Liturgical theologian David Fagerberg, whose work represents the "mature Mrs. Murphy" according to Petrin,[33] summarizes in this way: "I think Kavanagh uses Mrs. Murphy to name someone who has been *capacitated by liturgical rite* in the language of primary theology."[34] The language Mrs. Murphy uses is a "natural language" of theology, rather than a formalized one, according to Fagerberg, but it is still "the tradition of the church as it is learned by *constant and regular exposure* to the proletarian, quotidian, and communitarian theologia prima."[35] Mrs. Murphy is the archetypal fully believing, actively practicing, morally compliant, and formally affiliated worshiper.

Likely because she is the theoretical embodiment of tradition, secondary liturgical theologians usually tell Mrs. Murphy what she experiences and how she feels and thinks about that experience. Although primary liturgical theology would suggest the use of ethnographic methods and expansive textual sources, in practice the focus has often been analysis of prescribed rites and hypothetical assumptions about what participants experience. Petrin demonstrates the potential for hearing from "*real* Mrs. Murphys" through historical and literary sources.[36] Rarely, however, have actual living and breathing Mrs. Murphys been intentionally observed and listened to as partners in liturgical theological dialogue. As liturgical ethnographer Nelson Cowan argues, "Liturgical theology needs more than a hypothetical thin description of Mrs. Murphy; it needs real bodies and thick description."[37] Although some recent scholarship has taken this approach,[38] it is too late for Mrs. Murphy.

Mrs. Murphy is dead. Imagine that Mrs. Murphy was 65 in 1981—she would be 104 at the time of this research (born 1916). Mrs. Murphy is no longer with us. Mrs. Murphy's daughter is now 79 (born in 1941) and her granddaughter is 54 (born in 1966). When I speak with adult children about their parents' funerals, I am usually speaking with Mrs. Murphy's granddaughter. When I speak with thirty-year-old parents (born in 1990) about the baptism of their children, I am speaking with Mrs. Murphy's great-granddaughter.[39] We have missed the opportunity to hear directly from

---

[33] Petrin, "Insights from Mrs. Murphy," 210.
[34] Fagerberg, *Theologia Prima*, 133.
[35] Fagerberg, *Theologia Prima*, 135.
[36] Petrin, "Insights from Mrs. Murphy," 206.
[37] Cowan, "Liturgical Biography," 24.
[38] See Appendix A for more on ethnographic methods in liturgical studies.
[39] The majority of participants in this research were women; see Appendix B.

Mrs. Murphy, but we may still be able to hear from her great-granddaughter, and her granddaughter, and maybe even her daughter, although she is aging as well.[40]

Mrs. Murphy's Great-Granddaughter

Mrs. Murphy's great-granddaughter was raised in and inhabits a profoundly different religious landscape than that of her great-grandmother. Her primary liturgical theology is formed by different liturgical experiences. Specifically, Mrs. Murphy's great-granddaughter *is almost certainly occasionally religious*. As discussed in Chapter 3, religious change in Canada and comparable contexts is generational.[41] Each generation is successively less religious than the generation before in measures of affiliation, belief, and practice. The quantitative data suggest that Mrs. Murphy's granddaughter is most likely occasionally religious as well, making Mrs. Murphy's great-granddaughter a second-generation occasional practitioner.[42] Of course, these are only trends and there are exceptions, including intensively religious thirty-year-old Anglicans in Toronto. Nevertheless, we must account for the changing experience of ordinary primary theologians in this changing religious landscape. Furthermore, it is actually possible to account for this experience because Mrs. Murphy's great-granddaughter is a real person—or millions of real people—whose liturgical practice we can observe and with whom we can speak about their lived liturgical theology.

Because she is occasionally religious, Mrs. Murphy's great-granddaughter has not learned the so-called "natural language" of primary liturgical theology by "constant and regular exposure." She has not been "capacitated by

---

[40] Summerson uses a literary source, a short story by Flannery O'Connor, to consider *theologia prima* in relation to the increasing number of people who identify as nonreligious, including "Mackenzie Murphy," his version of Mrs. Murphy's granddaughter. Summerson describes Mackenzie as a "none" who is "unaffiliated, unchurched, and uninterested in the faith of her grandmother" yet also suggests that she is an occasional practitioner: "Mrs. Murphy will pass away and her funeral may provide some consolation, but the rate of Christian burial means little more to the granddaughter than obscure cosplaying, as she lacks the implicit grammar necessary to receive and understand the message." While Summerson recognizes generational religious change and occasional religious practice, he approaches it as a problem rather than an opportunity, and his concern is conversion rather than dialogue. Andrew Summerson, "The Church on Parker's Back: A Primer in *Theologia Prima* for the 'Nones,'" *Worship* 96 (2022): 323.

[41] Voas and Chaves, "Is the United States a Counterexample?"; Cornelissen, "Religiosity in Canada."

[42] Clarke and MacDonald, *Leaving Christianity*.

liturgical rite" in the way Kavanaugh and Fagerberg suggest. Mrs. Murphy's great-granddaughter is likely not fully believing, actively practicing, morally compliant, or formally affiliated with the tradition, even if her great-grandmother was (although we never got to ask). However, as discussed in Chapter 5, Mrs. Murphy's great-granddaughter's body and language are not unritualized, but differently ritualized.[43] She brings a different set of experiences to her intuitive interpretation of the liturgy. With Mrs. Murphy's great-granddaughter, we may have a different conversation, but she is still a primary liturgical theologian. Her words and actions still "throw flashes of light upon chasms of rich ambiguity." Mrs. Murphy's great-granddaughter is the archetype of a very different type of worshiper, one to whom we need to attend when we consider what Christian worship is meaning and doing today.

Liberation Theology: On the Liturgical Margins

Liberation theologies inspire the third approach to why and how to do theology with occasional practitioners. Petrin concludes her discussion of Mrs. Murphy by pointing toward the potential for "more extensive engagement with liberation theology, which privileges the voices of marginalized Christians."[44] Although she is primarily referencing those marginalized due to poverty or gender, this can be extended to those on the theological margins. Halík explicitly cites liberation theology as a model for his approach to engagement with "seekers":

> Liberation theology issued a very important challenge: to read the Gospel with the eyes of the poor. Its proponents called for scripture and witness of the tradition to be read *from the standpoint of the poor*, as a message for the poor, which can be understood authentically only by those who are themselves poor or who demonstrate active solidarity with the poor. And in that spirit they proposed a fresh examination and reinterpretation of theology as a whole. Yet we can now offer another, different hermeneutical rule, another key to a fresh understanding of scripture and the Christian message: it

---

[43] Belcher, "Ritual Systems, Ritualized Bodies," 102.
[44] Petrin, "Insights from Mrs. Murphy," 226.

is necessary to read scripture and live the faith also *from the standpoint of our profound solidarity with people who are religiously seeking, and, if need be, with those who experience God's hiddenness and transcendence "from the other side."* We must hear Jesus' call "with the ears of Zacchaeus"! We must look at him from the viewpoint of Zacchaeus's hiding place and distance—which is also, however, a place of observation and expectation.[45]

Halík claims this is a theology of "inner liberation," likely due to his focus on belief and context of dialogue with atheism. In contrast, I emphasize that liberative solidarity with those on the theological margins must include those on the liturgical margins, such as occasional practitioners, and address concrete outward embodied ritual practices alongside inner belief. I now turn to the work of Brazilian Presbyterian eco-liturgical liberation theologian Cláudio Carvalhaes, who writes at the intersection of liberation theology and liturgical theology, as a third way into the question of why and how to do theology with occasional practitioners.[46]

Attention to the Margins

Liberation theologies are committed to attending to people who are marginalized in a diversity of ways. While Carvalhaes's central concern is for the earth and nonhuman beings,[47] as well as the poor who are economically and socially marginalized,[48] he also acknowledges the need to attend to margins associated with race, class, gender, and sexuality, as well as religious differences, including other religious traditions[49] and unbelief.[50]

---

[45] Halík, *Patience with God*, 18. Emphasis in original.

[46] In 2019, Carvalhaes experienced a "conversion" that shifted the focus of his work primarily to climate change. Cláudio Carvalhaes, *How Do We Become Green People and Earth Communities? Inventory, Metamorphoses, and Emergenc(i)es* (York: Barber's Son, 2022), 72–73. The discussion here draws on his theological work from both before and after this turning point.

[47] Cláudio Carvalhaes, *Ritual at World's End: Essays on Eco-Liturgical Liberation Theology* (York: Barber's Son, 2021); Carvalhaes, *How Do We Become Green People and Earth Communities?*

[48] Cláudio Carvalhaes, *Praying with Every Heart: Orienting Our Lives to the Wholeness of the World* (Eugene, OR: Cascade, 2021); Cláudio Carvalhaes, *Liturgies from Below: Praying with People at the Ends of the World* (Nashville, TN: Abingdon Press, 2020).

[49] Cláudio Carvalhaes, *Eucharist and Globalization: Redrawing the Borders of Eucharistic Hospitality* (Eugene, OR: Pickwick Publications, 2013), 203–241; Carvalhaes, *Ritual at World's End*, 185–218.

[50] Carvalhaes, *Eucharist and Globalization*, 129.

Furthermore, he emphasizes the intersections of these many dimensions of difference:

> We must work on intersectionality of the body, class, gender, race, ableism, immigration-refugees, earth, nuclear weapons, militarism, extractivism, erotics, aesthetics, economics, and so on to create transnational, pluriverses, natural-cultural, and interreligious work. We must activate a network of corporeal gestures that turns our habits into a life of reciprocities, solidarities, and mutual care between all beings.[51]

I argue that different ways of relating to religion, including occasional religious practice, can be added to this list of intersections, and be attended to as a potential site of marginalization.

Occasional practitioners are a marginalized group in the *theological academy and in the church*. Occasional practitioners, in their diversity, share a sense of being on the theological and liturgical margins. They are rarely acknowledged in discussions of the contemporary religious landscape, which tend to focus on strong religion and nonreligion. When occasional practitioners are recognized, they are named with terms that trivialize this way of relating to religion as "soft," "marginal," "fuzzy," "fringe," "cultural," and "nominal," as discussed in Chapter 2. Furthermore, occasional religious practitioners are rarely seriously engaged in liturgical theology. When they are mentioned, they are usually dismissed as irrelevant, disparaged as lesser Christians, or fetishized as a target for evangelistic or catechetical efforts. This is also true in some congregations and among certain clergy, where they may be the butt of jokes or nicknames, such as "Chreasters" (a fusion of Christmas and Easter). Christian comics often poke fun at occasional practitioners:[52]

> "It's good to see you, Mr. McWit, but do you realize that today is neither Christmas or Easter?"

> "Our super busy Sundays are Christmas, Easter, and hurricane season."

> "This Sunday: Eastmas—the festival for once-a-year churchgoers. Attend Christmas and get Easter thrown in free or attend Easter and get Christmas thrown in free (depending which way you look at it)."

---

[51] Carvalhaes, *Ritual at World's End*, 76.
[52] These quotations from comics were found using a Google image search.

"Pastor, 'confirmed' means we only have to attend church on Christmas and Easter, right?"

"Easter coming so soon after Christmas has almost turned Anthony into a regular churchgoer."

"Examples of 'Twice a Year' Churchgoers: (1) We only go at Christmas and Easter—for the kids mainly; (2) We go when it is a parade service—Mother's Day and Remembrance Day usually; (3) We tend to go on the third Sunday of Epiphany and the sixteenth Sunday after Trinity—I don't know why really—it's just a habit we've got into."

These kinds of jokes, which are intended to resonate with clergy and intensive or routine practitioners who are in positions of power, reinforce the sense that occasional practice is widespread; however, they also reflect the smug or dismissive attitudes of some routine practitioners and church leaders. These attitudes are evident in some interviews with clergy and often arise in informal conversations about my research with clergy and academic theologians. At times, occasional practitioners encounter these attitudes directly in connection with their occasional practice. They may approach the church in a time of crisis and ritual need and be turned away or met with a response they experience as lacking in compassion. Stories like this from participants have been shared throughout this study.[53] The marginalization of occasional practitioners is not an abstract academic concept; individuals and families in this research have been marginalized by the church in connection with their occasional practice.

In addition, it is important to remember that some people are *involuntary occasional practitioners* who would practice routinely but cannot do so because of certain barriers beyond their control, as discussed in Chapter 4. Involuntary occasional practice is often associated with other forms of marginalization, such as disability, advanced age, geographic isolation, or family conflict. Dismissive attitudes toward occasional practitioners are particularly harmful for those who have not chosen this way of relating to religion.

Followers of Jesus concerned with those on the social and theological margins of the church and society must take seriously the marginalization of

---

[53] Although many of these stories are found at the overlap of the Roman Catholic and Anglican ritual systems, as discussed in Chapter 7, it is likely that occasional practitioners experience similar marginalization in other traditions, including the Anglican Church, yet because of how participants were selected for this research, these stories are less present in the data.

occasional practitioners simply because they relate to religion in a different way than intensive and routine practitioners.

Starting Where It Hurts

In addition to attending to the margins, Carvalhaes describes how liturgy and liberation theology start where it hurts:[54]

> A liberation theology of worship starts where it hurts, where people are wounded, where life is threatened, where hearts have fallen to the ground, where hope is lost, where there is little singing. It is at these places of destitution that the glory of God can restore humanity![55]

A liberation theology of worship starts where it hurts because this is where liberation is required. When speaking with occasional practitioners about both funerals and baptisms, I hear a lot about hurt. Sources of grief are more obvious in the case of death, but birth brings its own losses. As discussed in Chapter 2, occasional practice connected with life transitions is often also associated with crisis. Stories of hurt have already been present throughout this analysis, so I share only two more here as examples of starting where it hurts when doing theology with occasional practitioners.

First, when speaking about her husband Frank's funeral, Florence, who is a lifelong occasional practitioner, describes the experience of arranging for the funerals of her husband's father and their infant son, who died in close succession:

> Frank's father had died. His father died the night before our son was born.... The priest was very inflexible about the arrangements, and Frank had to be with me because I'd had the baby and he couldn't go with his mom. I'd be fine but I had a little bit of complication, and the baby was premature, so he was in the neonatal unit for a little bit. Frank couldn't be with his mom when she had to go to the church and arrange the funeral. He was very upset by the way she was treated....

---

[54] "Black liberation theologian James Cone reminds us that theology starts where it hurts, and this has impacted me deeply. I add that liturgy also starts where it hurts." Carvalhaes, *Ritual at World's End*, 25.

[55] Cláudio Carvalhaes, *What's Worship Got to Do with It? Interpreting Life Liturgically* (Eugene, OR: Cascade, 2018), 237.

> When we had to have [our infant son's] funeral, we called the Anglican church. The child had been baptized just a few weeks before that and the reception was, "We're very sorry to hear this. You tell us what you want." And the priest at the time was a stand-in priest because the church was between priests. And he said, "You tell me what you want and I will rearrange my schedule to accommodate you." Coincidentally, Frank's father had died about three months before [our son] and they are Catholics. The reception that his mother got was ... the polar opposite. "This is the way we do it. This is the time it's going to be, this is how it's got to be done." She had a terrible time with them.

The crisis which Frank, Florence, and their family were facing would not necessarily have been evident to a Catholic priest performing an ordinary funeral for Frank's elderly father. However, the priest's response in the midst of Frank's hurt—losing his father, his wife and son in crisis in the hospital, feeling unable to support his mother, and then the death of his months-old son—is what ended up defining the experience of the funeral for Frank. The wounds felt fresh when Florence spoke about the experience decades later. These wounds were also passed on to the next generation, as her son shared the same stories in his reflections on his father's funeral.

Second, another participant, Gretta, who at the time of the interview was occasionally religious and invisibly routine, describes looking for a church where she and her husband could celebrate their marriage with a Christian ceremony:

> We did things a little bit backwards. So, we actually got married for visa purposes in our backyard. And throughout the process of us meeting and getting married the first time and then getting married at [the Anglican church], we had lost four children along the way. Four miscarriages. And then we were pregnant with my fifth. So, our first son that made it through.
>
> And I'm Catholic, my husband is Anglican. Even though we were already married, we couldn't get married in the Catholic church. They wouldn't take us because I was pregnant. My family is very Orthodox. We're Greek. They're very Greek Orthodox and then the Greek Orthodox church wouldn't marry us either because I was pregnant. So, again, even though we were married legally, it was very important to me to get married in a church.

And we contacted [the Anglican church]. They were—I can't even describe just how welcoming they were, just how open they were to all different facets of life. All different types of people. All different family circumstances. The way that they project themselves and God. It's very liberal, which is exactly sort of who I am. So, I just felt so ready to get married. So anyway, we ended up getting married. And then we had our son. And then 15 months later we had our daughter. And then both were baptized. Yeah, so it's a very cool story....

It's interesting because my husband is spiritual but not religious. And I'm more of the religious one of the two of us. So, he didn't disagree with [the baptism]. He just—he was okay with it given how important it was to me. But yeah, because we got married there, it was very important for us that we baptize there. And I wanted them to be baptized in the Anglican church because of how, again, just because of how they were welcoming to [my husband] and I and our situation.

And—I'm starting to get emotional. When we met [the priest], I was very pregnant so, it was very obvious that I was expecting. The natural question is, oh the baby and sort of your situation. And I spoke to her about the four that we had lost, and it was almost like she was on a journey with us. And she was so empathetic and so kind. And she gave us a prayer blanket which was completely unexpected. So, incredibly appreciated. So, she has certain members of the congregation who make these blankets and whenever she feels that someone is in need of a little extra prayer, she gives them to them. And that's our first baby blanket. So—sorry [crying]. So, yeah.

The priest exceeds Gretta's hopes and is not only willing to perform the wedding and baptism, but also to surround her and her child in the prayer and support of the church community.

Both Frank's and Gretta's stories reveal how what on the surface may appear to be an ordinary occasional practice—the funeral for an older man whose death was expected and the wedding of a young couple—are events enmeshed in webs of hurt. The widow met alone with the priest to discuss her late husband's funeral since her son was at the hospital with his wife and struggling newborn. Gretta and her husband had been rejected by two church traditions in the process of seeking a place to celebrate their marriage and had lost four children before finding a church where they could baptize the child they were expecting. At the same time, these stories reveal the potential for occasional practice to embody compassion and liberation, to be part of healing these hurts. How the church handled the funeral for his father prompted Frank and Florence to turn to a different Christian tradition for the baptism and funeral of their son, a tradition where they discover caring flexibility in a time of tremendous grief. Gretta likewise encounters empathy and kindness there, as well as a concrete symbol of support.

The stories that occasional practitioners bring are diverse and complex. Occasional practice is often a moment of vulnerability, of ritual need, on the part of participants. It is a place to begin a liberative liturgical theology, because it is a place where it hurts.

Thinking at the Border

In addition to attention to the margins and starting where it hurts, Cláudio Carvalhaes describes liturgical liberation theology as "thinking at the border." Carvalhaes borrows from Catholic liturgical theologian Nathan Mitchell to describe how Christian liturgy must hold together the liturgy of the world, the liturgy of the church, and the liturgy of the neighbor. The *liturgy of the world* is "the whole network of connections between countries and the globalized conditions of human life." The *liturgy of the church* is "the sources and histories of many traditions." The *liturgy of the neighbor* is "the ways in which the existential and confessional forms of living of [our] neighbors are respected and cherished, which includes the multiplicities of religions."[56] Occasional practitioners are enmeshed in these three interconnected liturgies. They are part of modern and globalized, secular and religious networks. They are participating in the traditions of the church. They are neighbors, in their diverse ways of relating to religion. To use the language of Chapter 5, they negotiate the overlaps between these ritual systems. Carvalhaes describes these overlaps as a key site for theological reflection:

> The connectivity of these three liturgies is the way of *thinking at the border*. These liturgies and this form of border thinking are fundamental components to the formation of different liturgical assemblages, connecting local sources, diverse groups and ethnicities, and forms of life, feelings, and subjectivities that formet different forms of marginal thinking. . . . These

---

[56] Carvalhaes, *What's Worship Got to Do with It?*, 10; Nathan Mitchell, *Meeting Mystery: Liturgy, Worship, Sacraments* (Maryknoll, NY: Orbis Books, 2006), xiii.

intersectionalities and connections imply a multiplicity of sources, symbols and perspectives coming from below, from local contexts in constant relation to global forces.[57]

Occasional practitioners hold together the local and the global, and have sources, symbols, and perspectives to offer "from below" that differ from the sources, symbols, and perspectives "from above," from clergy and academic theologians.

Carvalhaes calls for attention to *juxtaposition* not only within the liturgy but between the liturgy of the church and the liturgy of the world. In other words, he emphasizes overlapping ritual systems, as well as opposition within ritual systems. We do well to pay particular attention to what is spoken and what is silenced at this intersection: "These amplified forms of juxtaposition call us to engage the places between the altar/table and the world, asking for what has been silenced, denied or simply not spoken."[58] More than routine and intensive practitioners, occasional practitioners explicitly occupy places between the altar and the world. However, their liturgical experiences in these places are often "silenced, denied, or simply not spoken," despite, and perhaps because of, the ways they are thinking at the borders.

Carvalhaes is clear that borders are unavoidable; it is not his intent to "naively destroy liturgical borders," but rather to challenge beloved and established borders to "see how we can improve, develop, and adjust them."[59] To this end, Carvalhaes develops the concept of *borderless borders*:

> These two words together, *borderless borders*, create the necessary tension between the borders that we need to live and then to challenge in order to expand them toward the other, thus offering hospitality in ways perhaps never considered and foreseen before.[60]

These borderless borders help communities explore within and beyond known borders in an ongoing negotiation.[61]

The ongoing process of negotiating borders necessarily involves *power*,[62] whether they are the borders around a ritual practice or religious community,

---

[57] Carvalhaes, *What's Worship Got to Do with It?*, 11. Emphasis added.
[58] Carvalhaes, *What's Worship Got to Do with It?*, 12.
[59] Carvalhaes, *Eucharist and Globalization*, 286.
[60] Carvalhaes, *Eucharist and Globalization*, 297. Emphasis in original.
[61] Carvalhaes, *Eucharist and Globalization*, 12.
[62] Carvalhaes, *Eucharist and Globalization*, 21, 281.

or between the liturgies of world, church, and neighbor. Very often, it is ritual experts and clergy who wield the power to draw the borders; occasional practitioners have little power to define these boundaries. In part this may be why occasional practitioners find themselves beyond and within borders in sometimes surprising ways, such as when they are denied access to a practice in a Christian tradition they consider their own, or are invited into a practice in a tradition they consider foreign. A liberative liturgical theology invites the sharing of power in the ongoing negotiation of borderless borders; it calls for doing liturgical theology *with* occasional practitioners.

Dialogue Through Praxis

Carvalhaes argues that interreligious dialogue through praxis is a crucial component of the work of liberation. He sees the challenges of his specific context in Brazil as indicating a broader need for dialogue anchored in common practices in contemporary globalized societies:

> The issues at stake in Brazil's reality and the format of praxis proposed here can perhaps illustrate the growing need for churches everywhere to engage with strangers through new forms of theological dialogue and liturgical practices that can in some ways provide dialogue, justice, peace, and hospitality. Moreover, our globalized world continues to spread many forms of religions everywhere and Christians need to learn how to relate, dialogue, and live together with different forms of people's beliefs, practices, and worldviews.[63]

While Carvalhaes is primarily speaking of dialogue among different religious traditions, we might extend this to include dialogue among those who relate to religion in different ways.[64] Occasional practitioners have diverse beliefs, practices, and worldviews. They may or may not identify as Christian. If they do identify as Christian, or even Anglican in this case, they may engage in religious practices in very different ways. In addition to dialogue among

---

[63] Carvalhaes, *Eucharist and Globalization*, 204.

[64] Carvalhaes gestures in this direction in a narrative describing two men who "did not believe a thing about the Christian faith but loved the fellowship" yet could affirm that "[y]our neighbor is important to you. You are responsible for everyone who is here and we are connected to everybody around the world," and were therefore invited and able to participate in the Eucharist. Carvalhaes, *Eucharist and Globalization*, 129.

different religious groups, there is a need for dialogue among people who relate to religion in different ways, including occasional and routine or intensive practitioners. Furthermore, dialogue with those who relate to a religious tradition or community in different ways does not involve complex relationship building and interreligious learning beyond the community, but simply listening deeply and openly, and practicing deeply and openly, with those who are already choosing to be present.

Doing theology with occasional practitioners involves exploring a range of ways to theologize. Dialogue with occasional practitioners cannot rely on terms set and language employed by ritual experts, as the opening discussion on photography and language in this chapter suggests. Instead, ritual practice itself, understood through a diverse array of interdisciplinary tools, can be at the center of this dialogue:

> The organic liturgical theologian must learn how to best engage this dialogue through religious and non-religious practices. Thus, ritual theories, liturgical reasoning, performance studies, everyday life theories, affect theories, constructive inter-religious theologies, and so on can and must engage dance, songs, bodily movements in order to help frame this interreligious dialogue.[65]

A specific ritual may be at the center of this dialogue, for example, a baptism or funeral which occasional practitioners and clergy negotiate together, in relationship with one another and other human and nonhuman beings:

> Rituals and worship spaces can also become sites where these learnings will help us perform these relations, connections, limits, and life together. Rituals and worship are fantastic places for us to learn how to *go through things*. Theology alone will not do it—we need *theology in motion*, lived in our bodies, made in gestures, pauses, breaths, songs, stories, relation. Worship puts us together with somebody, something else, other territories, and we have to figure out how to honor each other, how to live and how to an honor an always plural/common/diverse ground.[66]

---

[65] Carvalhaes, *Eucharist and Globalization*, 220.
[66] Carvalhaes, *How Do We Become Green People and Earth Communities?*, 140. Emphasis in original.

While this chapter is more explicitly theological in its argumentation and interlocutors, when ritual itself is understood as a means of theological dialogue, then the ethnographic description and engagement with social theory and ritual theory in the preceding chapters can also be understood as ways of doing theology with occasional practitioners.

The Limitations of Liberation Theology in Relation to Occasional Practice

Through attention to the margins, starting where it hurts, thinking at the border, and dialogue through practice, Carvalhaes's liturgical liberation theology offers a third way to approach why and how to do theology with occasional practitioners. However, there are important questions to ask when drawing inspiration from liberation theologies in relation to occasional practice, especially Anglican occasional practice in Toronto, both in relation to who occasional practitioners are and what the objective of liberation is.

First, it is crucial to recognize that there are both similarities and differences between the earth and the poor who are at the center of Carvalhaes's liturgical theology, and those who participate in Anglican practices in Toronto. Carvalhaes writes:

> What is at stake among liberation theologies is the search for difference, alterity, i.e., other ways of speaking, listening, understanding, believing, and experiencing life. Differences that were denied, avoided, and erased in the construction of Western theological thought. In this process, the task of hearing the voice of the voiceless has been a major and complicated one. Among many questions, we should ask: can we hear and move beyond the pleasurable tone of our own voices to hear the voice of the other?[67]

I am confident framing occasional practice in these terms. Can ritual experts and routine practitioners hear beyond the pleasurable tone of their own voices to hear the voices of the occasionally religious? But Carvalhaes continues:

> If so, how can we hear the voices of those who have been silenced for so long, the poor and the oppressed, whose voices have been smashed down

---

[67] Carvalhaes, *What's Worship Got to Do with It?*, 130.

and whose mouths have been brutally shut up? How can we hear if they don't speak? Why don't they speak?[68]

Now, I am no longer sure.

Occasional practitioners are diverse. There are some who are able to practice only occasionally because they are economically or socially marginalized: a new Canadian Uber driver struggling to support his family; a man who is paralyzed and his caregiver, who are unable to leave their home; a grandmother who depends on her children for a lift to church; and a young mother struggling with her nonreligious husband about religion. However, many of the participants with whom I speak are economically and socially elite. The Anglican tradition has historically been the tradition of the upper class in Toronto. Some practice occasionally because of their social and economic status: they spend their weekends at the cottage; they join a ski club; and they treasure quiet family breakfasts in the midst of successful professional careers. Although they may be theologically and liturgically marginalized, and although they may be hurting, they are not the poor and oppressed that Carvalhaes describes, the ones for whom he adamantly advocates. These dynamics are further complicated by the complicity of the Anglican tradition in British colonialism, which both clergy and participants in this research acknowledge and desire to address.

However, we must not fall into the trap of pitting marginalized groups against one another in a contest of hardships: those Carvalhaes has in mind would clearly triumph.[69] As Carvalhaes writes:

> Liberation theologies call for our attention to the extreme conditions of someone's living. When liberation theologies call for the love of God for the "least of these" it is a way of saying: *everyone will be attended to, but the worst cases first*. Pope Francis has said the church is like "'a field

---

[68] Carvalhaes, *What's Worship Got to Do with It?*, 130.

[69] "Theology should start from where it hurts, among those who are despised in our society, those who make up the official garbage list of society: Black and Indigenous people, the poor, the unemployed, battered women, prisoners, queer people and those who cannot consume. From those places, from the refugee camp, private and public prisons, public squares with spikes everywhere so the poor cannot lay their heads, from the outskirts of society where none of us live and are scared to drive by, yes ... it is from these places that we have to figure out how to pray and worship God, how to interpret the Bible, decide what songs to sing, discern what to ask for forgiveness, choose what to eat and at whose table, learn how to use the water for Baptism, and how to be sent forth into the world. From these places we can create many public liturgical theologies." Carvalhaes, *Ritual at World's End*, 149.

hospital' that must care for the sick." Liberation theologies are like triage in a hospital.[70]

While occasional practitioners may not always be first in line, we must recognize that we are all in need of liberation and that our liberation is bound up with one another. "Everyone will be attended to" and, to this point, occasional practitioners have received very little theological and liturgical attention. Furthermore, if we are to address the ecological and systemic injustices that Carvalhaes names, then occasional practitioners, as a significant proportion of the population in the Global North, must be engaged in this process. In addition to being freed from theological and liturgical marginalization, occasional practitioners may join in freeing others from economic and social oppression, and in deepening relationships of reciprocity and care with all beings. As Sallie McFague says of North Americans in her ecological liberation theology, *"we are the oppressors and must, if we are Christians, liberate others from our domination."*[71] The ethical vision of Jesus compels many of the occasional practitioners in this research (as discussed in Chapter 10), and they are also painfully aware of Christianity's complicity in oppression. It is, in fact, precisely this kind of thinking at the border that is needed to unsettle those too comfortable with the pleasurable tone of authoritative Christian voices.

Second, it is critical to distinguish the objective of liberation in the case of liturgical and theological marginalization from the objective of liberation theologies centered on the poor. Economic liberation has the goal of ending poverty, of changing the identity status and material conditions of the poor to relieve suffering and premature death, as well as the systems that create these conditions.[72] Liberation on the liturgical and theological margins does *not* aim to change the identity status of occasional practitioners or the way in which people relate to religion. To return to the words of Halík, the goal is not that occasional practitioners would "conform to the present notion of 'standard believers.'" Therefore, the approach articulated here is more akin

---

[70] Carvalhaes, *How Do We Become Green People and Earth Communities?*, 86. Emphasis added.

[71] Sallie McFague, *Life Abundant: Rethinking Theology and Economy for a Planet in Peril* (Minneapolis, MN: Fortress Press, 2001), 34.

[72] Carvalhaes draws on Eduardo Viveiros de Castro to complicate the approach to who must change without denying that changing the material conditions of the poor is crucial: "De Castro asserts that looking at the poor as an outsider keeps our gaze towards the transformation of the poor, who we believe are the ones who need to be changed. Those on the positive side never consider interior transformations and change to their own lives necessary to pursue." Carvalhaes, *Ritual at World's End*, 32.

to liberation theologies associated with gender, race, or ability that are concerned with *changing the systems* that make these differences problematic, not with the differences themselves.

Carvalhaes's engagement with feminist liturgies is a helpful illustration. The goal in this case is certainly not to transform women into men, or even for women to fit themselves into liturgical spaces designed for and dominated by men. The intention is instead to create a liturgical place "in which women's experiences can be shared, memory and imagination freed, and movements open to perform what could show the truth of their lives, instead of following a preset rule that failed to give adequate consideration to women's lives as important to be mentioned or *liturgized*."[73] Likewise, the goal of theological engagement with occasional practitioners is not to transform occasional religious practitioners into routine practitioners. The goal is instead to create a liturgical place in which their experiences can be shared and liturgized. Changing *how differences are perceived* is part of creating this liturgical place, especially perceptions of difference that result in marginalization. The first step, therefore, is to *change attitudes* so that the liturgical and theological margins are viewed as privileged places of liturgical theological insight and so that a dialogue through practice among all liturgical participants becomes possible.

Although there are limitations to borrowing from liturgical liberation theology when reflecting on occasional practice, and although such inspiration must be sought with care, Carvalhaes's theology remains a valuable approach to considering why and how to do theology with occasional practitioners.

The Necessity and Challenge of Doing Liturgical Theology with Occasional Practitioners

I have presented three theological ways of understanding why it is necessary to do liturgical theology with occasional practitioners. The first is rooted in Jesus's attention to those on the margins, not only economically and socially, but also theologically and liturgically. This includes those who wish to remain at a distance or who are separated by various forms of difference. The second is anchored in the desire to understand liturgy from the perspective of ordinary participants. This includes learning from those who are

---

[73] Carvalhaes, *Eucharist and Globalization*, 146. Emphasis in original.

capacitated by the liturgy through occasional rather than routine practice, who may be differently ritualized, but are nevertheless primary liturgical theologians. The third is inspired by liberation theology and the call to attend to theology from below and at the borders. This includes doing theology with occasional practitioners who are marginalized in the church and the theological academy. These three ways of thinking about why it is necessary to do theology with occasional practitioners are interconnected and share an emphasis on meeting occasional practitioners where they are, as they are, and the mutual learning that can occur in this place of encounter between those who relate to religion in different ways. This approach does not aim to change how occasional practitioners relate to religion, but rather to engage occasional practice as a legitimate and valuable vantage point for understanding Christian faith and practice.

Once we determine that doing theology with occasional practitioners is desirable, the next step is to consider what this involves in practice. Doing theology with occasional practitioners requires *openness to changing how we do theology*. It raises questions about what sources count and what language we employ. As the vignettes at the outset of this chapter suggest, doing theology with occasional practitioners cannot rely on academic theological language or the language of routine practice. Even an ethnographic approach focused on observing practice and hearing stories cannot ask occasional practitioners for more than occasional engagement. Collaborative forms of ethnography that involve multiple interviews, reviewing drafts of findings, and more are not true to how occasional practitioners relate to religion. We need to consider how to build on traditions of theology embedded in stories, relationships, art, photography, and material objects. We need to listen for and learn new language for speaking of God, Christian community, and religious practice. It is for this reason that occasional ritual practices, and the negotiations that surround them, are a crucial focal point, although what is considered part of these practices is also a question.

Doing liturgical theology with occasional practitioners requires openness to *redefining what is considered liturgy*. The question of what counts as liturgy has preoccupied liturgical scholars in the past, particularly in terms of differentiating the proper and official liturgy of the church from so-called popular piety, although this distinction is beginning to fall away.[74]

---

[74] Nathan Mitchell, *The Mystery of the Rosary: Marian Devotion and the Reinvention of Catholicism* (New York: New York University Press, 2009); Layla Karst, "Reimagining Pilgrimage" (PhD diss., Emory University, 2019).

Occasional practice further stretches these boundaries since occasional practitioners map the ritual systems associated with certain practices in different ways and interpret them through various overlapping ritual systems. For example, the experiences of occasional practitioners may prompt ritual experts to reconsider what is included in baptism. Is it only the official rite, or also the informal moments? Is it only what happens in the church building, or does it include the celebration afterward? Is faith essential to baptism and, if so, whose faith? Must baptism occur in the context of a community and, if so, which community? Who gets to decide what counts as liturgy, and do we need to decide at all? Defining liturgy may not be important for occasional practitioners, although it has been a key question for academic liturgical theologians. Doing theology with occasional practitioners invites all participants to reconsider what is necessary in relation to Christian practices.

This proposal may be uncomfortable and threatening for ritual experts and routine practitioners. That would be understandable: it challenges presumed authorities, it unsettles long-held assumptions, and it pushes past a casual tolerance of occasional practice toward embracing this way of relating to religion. As Carvalhaes describes, it establishes a different horizon of possibility:

> Recognition or even the idea of tolerance for that matter is not what we need, since recognition and tolerance are concepts organized around those who control the fences and decide what or how to recognize or tolerate the other. Instead of that, we should work from another horizon of possibilities. We must engage with the fluidity of definitions/practices of the *cognito*, of knowledge, of understandings, of ways of beings, of languages etc. This means that we will never know who is at the table, who we clearly are, and who God might be. We will need to share power, governance and authority. The task to know is a communal one, always unfinished, always dreadful, but *always leaning on each other to know a little more*.[75]

Doing theology with occasional practitioners means that routine practitioners and ritual experts need to share power and to welcome other ways of knowing and being in relation to shared practices. Giving occasional practitioners a voice does not silence ritual experts or routine practitioners, but rather invites those who relate to religion in different ways to lean on

---

[75] Carvalhaes, *Eucharist and Globalization*, 263–264. Emphasis added.

each other and to learn from one another. Mutual respect—rather than tolerance, a desire to change the other, or worse, to manipulate the other or take advantage of their hurt and need—is necessary for this mutuality and learning. My hope is that the nuanced depiction of the diversity and depth of occasional practice presented in this research can contribute to movement toward mutual respect and to "knowing a little more" about practices that are held in common by those who relate to religion in different ways.

In the context of interreligious dialogue, encounter with a different tradition often leads to deeper awareness of one's own tradition. Likewise, encountering occasional practice as a way of being religious can provide routine practitioners with new clarity about their own assumptions, understandings, and practices. Doing theology with occasional practitioners not only has the potential to be liberating for occasional practitioners in the places where it hurts and on margins made problematic by the attitudes and structures that surround them; it also has the potential to be liberating for routine practitioners and ritual experts.

Together, it is possible to discover new dimensions of what Christian worship is meaning and doing today. This may include exploring enriching intersections between the lived liturgical theology of occasional practitioners and ritual experts, as well as areas of productive conflict. Although this is a mutual relationship, my primary focus here is on the liturgical experiences and theologies of occasional practitioners because it is their voices that have been largely absent from the conversation to this point. We must begin, therefore, by listening closely to the experiences of occasional practitioners. What is being whispered at the well? What has been "silenced, denied or simply not spoken"? How can the words and actions of occasional practitioners "throw flashes of light upon chasms of rich ambiguity"?

9
Lived Liturgical Theologies of Occasional Practitioners

After more than a year without in-person worship gatherings due to the COVID-19 pandemic, Kim attends Easter Vigil. Afterward, she posts a photo for her friends and family on social media (Figure 9.1). The picture is taken from the balcony in a modern medium-sized church building with wide wooden beams spanning the ceiling. The focus is the people. The congregation fills about three-quarters of the pews. They stand facing the altar, their backs to the camera. Each person holds a lit candle and the candlelight gently illuminates the space. She captions the photo with two words: "I cried."

This social media post would be a good example of the focus on materiality, emotion, and relationship that characterizes the lived liturgical theology of the occasional religious practitioners who participated in this research. However, this post was shared by Dr. Kimberly Belcher, a Roman Catholic sacramental theologian and professor of theology at the University of Notre Dame. She could have interpreted this moment through the vast array of connections that make Easter Vigil a central ritual in the Roman Catholic ritual system, the layers of history behind this liturgy, or the theological interpretations of contemporary theologians—and she may well have done so. However, she mentioned this social media post to me several weeks later when we were discussing this research to highlight the parallels between her own experience and the patterns present in the experiences and lived liturgical theologies of occasional practitioners.

Theology embedded in ordinary experiences, such as material objects, emotions, and relationships, is not unique to occasional practitioners. Instead, occasional practitioners reveal ways of doing theology in which others, including routine and intensive practitioners, also engage. These ways of doing theology are simply more visible among occasional practitioners who, in part because they cannot rely on historical or systematic theological knowledge and technical liturgical language, rely instead on other ways of knowing and communicating the theological significance of their liturgical

LIVED LITURGICAL THEOLOGIES   255

Figure 9.1 Easter Vigil social media post.
Reproduced courtesy of Kimberly Belcher, USA.

experience. This invites routine and intensive practitioners, including many academic theologians, to greater awareness of how these ways of doing liturgical theology also shape their work, implicitly or explicitly.

In the next two chapters, I explore the lived liturgical theologies of occasional practitioners. I draw on ethnographic research to illustrate what doing theology with occasional practitioners might look like. I do not claim that the perspectives presented here are broadly representative of occasional practitioners, only of those who connect with the Anglican tradition in Toronto and specifically with the congregations at the center of this research. Although my primary focus is hearing from occasional practitioners whose voices to this point have been largely absent from liturgical theology, at times I gesture toward contemporary liturgical theology to illustrate mutually enriching points of connection and tension. In this chapter, occasional practitioners set the agenda as I explore three key themes that emerge from the qualitative data: the material, emotional, and relational dimensions of liturgical experience. In the next chapter, I turn to themes that are important for clergy and theologians and examine how occasional practitioners speak to questions of God, tradition, and ethics.

These chapters are both social science and theology, both lived religion and lived theology.[1] For social scientists, this analysis is undeniably lived religion; it is about "how religion happens in everyday life."[2] It can be approached from the perspective of sociology of religion as a description of the human phenomenon of religion. Theologians may also approach it as lived theology.[3] Charles Marsh differentiates the two approaches in this way: "Lived religion examines practices, beliefs, and objects to understand more clearly the human phenomenon of religion, while lived theology examines practices, objects, and beliefs in order to understand God's presence in human experience."[4] Marsh is clear that not all ethnography is theology; rather, "theology, drawing on the wisdom of confessional, evangelical, and liberal expressions, focuses the perceptions needed to *see experience against the horizon of the Triune God*."[5] Because this ethnography centers on practices of Christian worship—the preeminent site of encounter with the Triune God in the Christian tradition for liturgical theologians—it necessarily occurs against the horizon of the Triune God. This does not mean that occasional practitioners name the Triune God explicitly. However, in reflecting on their experience of occasional practice, they offer "stories that can be observed, reflected upon, and rendered into multilayered theological

---

[1] For further discussion of the relationship between liturgical studies and sociology of religion, see Appendix A.

[2] Nancy Ammerman, *Studying Lived Religion: Contexts and Practices* (New York: New York University Press, 2021).

[3] Lived theology has certain parallels with Jeff Astley's concept of "ordinary theology," which he defines as "the theology and theologizing of Christians who have received little or no theological education of a scholarly, academic or systematic kind." While I strongly affirm Astley's plea to take seriously "ordinary theology," Astley's approach is primarily focused on beliefs and reflective God-talk, whereas I am especially interested in participation in religious practices. Jeff Astley, *Ordinary Theology: Looking, Listening and Learning in Theology* (London: Routledge, 2002), 56; Jeff Astley and Leslie Francis, eds., *Exploring Ordinary Theology: Everyday Christian Believing and the Church* (London: Routledge, 2013).

[4] Charles Marsh, "Introduction: Lived Theology—Method, Style, and Pedagogy," in *Lived Theology: New Perspectives on Method, Style, and Pedagogy*, ed. Charles Marsh, Peter Slade, and Sarah Azaransky (Oxford: Oxford University Press, 2016), 7.

[5] Marsh, "Introduction," 7. Emphasis added.

narratives."[6] Furthermore, they invite awareness of divine encounter in worship beyond the sites anticipated by liturgical theologians and intensive practitioners, such as the proclamation of scripture or the eucharistic epiclesis, and instead direct attention to other aspects of worship: the delight of a child at wearing a bow tie, a shimmering moment marked by tears, or the sacredness of showing up to support a friend. As both lived religion and lived theology, this chapter encourages a more complete understanding of liturgical experience.

To center the experience of liturgical participants, I first consider three key themes that arise from interviews: liturgical practice as material more than linguistic, emotional more than conceptual, and relational more than personal. While these themes can be anchored in specific narratives and quotations, they also reflect broader impressions and patterns that emerged as I coded and analyzed the qualitative data. I present these themes as comparisons since they reflect both what is present and what is largely absent in the data, with the latter being more difficult to capture. Although I introduce the themes sequentially, these three aspects of liturgical experience— the material, emotional, and relational—are interconnected for many participants.

Liturgical Practice as Material More than Linguistic

Liturgical participants speak more frequently and more passionately about the material dimensions of their liturgical experience than they do about the linguistic aspects of Christian worship. I explore three specific examples: architectural space, clothing, and material objects.

Space

Architectural space is important to occasional practitioners. This focus is aligned with one of very few prior studies that considers the worship experience of occasional practitioners.[7] Canadian sociologist Joel Thiessen's

---

[6] Marsh, "Introduction," 12.
[7] Thiessen, *The Meaning of Sunday*, 79–81; Joel Thiessen and Bill McAlpine, "Sacred Space: Function and Mission from a Sociological and Theological Perspective," *International Journal for the Study of the Christian Church* 13 (2013): 133–146.

interview research suggests that "marginal affiliates" (to use his terminology) are motivated to attend on certain occasions "because they connect to a higher power in a more profound way in a sacred place."[8] According to Thiessen and Bill McAlpine, for "yearly attenders,"[9]

> the primary function of sacred space is to help centre them with some semblance of meaning and direction, transition and transformation in life—a function fulfilled when we think about sacred space as (a) a meeting place between Heaven and Earth, God and humanity, and (b) an earthly representation of beauty.[10]

My qualitative data confirm Thiessen and McAlpine's findings that sacred space is important for occasional practitioners in terms of *connecting with God and anchoring individual identity*, especially through a "constant" place set apart as sacred and linked to memories of meaningful life events.[11] Some participants in this research express similar ideas to Thiessen's respondents, such as speaking of a church building in relation to "memories" that make it feel like "home" or having a special sense of "connection" to God in liturgical space:

> I don't get down and say prayers every day. No, not in my everyday life. Just when I choose that it's time to go connect. That's just where I feel that I can do that is physically going into a church to do it.

> I think it's just—the church is a beautiful church. It's an old church. Very similar to what we had in Jamaica. The church that we grew up in.

> When we went to Montreal and Quebec City, I always made [my husband] go to all the churches because it's just something that feels familiar to me, and I just like the feeling of being inside.

> Sitting there was very comforting and nice. That's terrible—"nice." And just sitting in those pews that have been there forever, right? Like just, here I am sitting in these pews again. So, that sense of continuity is important, I guess. Yeah. Continuity. And maybe it's comforting that some

---

[8] Thiessen, *The Meaning of Sunday*, 79.
[9] Thiessen and McAlpine, "Sacred Space," 134.
[10] Thiessen and McAlpine, "Sacred Space," 136.
[11] Thiessen and McAlpine, "Sacred Space," 136–139.

things don't change. Maybe there's comfort there too, like stability in a certain way. Stability. Like a touch point. Just something that's still there.

The church [building] holds a lot of memories for me. My parents are buried there. I know other people that are buried there. When I go in there—I was married there. My cousin was married there. My kids have been baptized. There's a lot of it. There's a lot of connections for me and it's more, the church [building].

R: When a funeral happens, some people will just use the funeral home chapel for the funeral. But I knew that wasn't going to be the same for me because I guess—I don't know, it's hard to explain, but I think there's something about having it at your church. It's almost like—it's kind of like you're at home. Whereas, when you're having a funeral home, it's like this doesn't feel like home. I don't know. I'm trying to express it, but I can't. I don't know. It doesn't feel right for me.

I: What does it feel like for you to be in the church building? How do you experience that space?

R: It's very intimate. Like it's—it's like I feel the presence of God. Whereas I guess, I don't always feel that somewhere else. Like I said, if we had had the funeral at a funeral home chapel, I [wouldn't have felt] that strong connection. But when I'm in [name of church], I feel that the moment I walk into the church. It's like I can feel a presence there. And I don't know, it's—sometimes because of the other parishioners too, it's not just the building. I don't know. It's because we all believe, we all embrace it.

I: Yeah. So, it's who is there as well.

R: Yeah.

I: Or some combination? Even if some of those people were at a funeral home chapel...

R: It just doesn't feel the same and I don't know why. I'm still respectful about everything, don't get me wrong. It's just, it's not for me. I don't feel that close to God there.

I: Are there other spaces where you feel close to God?

R: Yes. When I pray. When I'm alone. When I'm quiet and reflective. Sometimes even in the car. Like I said, through music sometimes. Yeah, just when I'm sort of introspective. But even just sometimes when I hear of miracles happening, yeah, I feel close.

However, as the final four examples above suggest, the interviews that I conducted reveal how these personal and spiritual connections are closely intertwined with human relationships, both real and imagined. In contrast to Thiessen and McAlpine's emphasis on individual identity, how occasional practitioners speak of sacred space in this research highlights a corporate and relational understanding of religion.

For some participants in interviews, liturgical space is connected to *specific personal relationships*. One occasional practitioner describes how she attended church services with her deceased father and the poignancy of returning to the church building, and specifically their pew, following his death:

> I have to admit I haven't been to church nearly as often now that he's gone. And then some of that is to do with the fact that I have a toddler whose nap time and lunch time happens to fall over 11 o'clock service. But I mean, part of it is also that I kind of feel lost there without him. So like I went at Christmas. I'm going to get emotional about this now. I went at Christmas and I went with [my husband].... After my dad passed away, there were a couple of people that he was kind of close with at the church and they said to me "You know, when you come back you can sit with us." And I thought that was really nice, but then I was like, they sit on the other side of the church. That's not where I sit. I have to sit in our spot. But we saw them at Christmas—it was so nice—I hadn't seen them in so long and it was like I never left. So, I like the community of people that's there too, like they're good people. A lot of them are older, a lot of them remind me of my grandparents.... It was like I hadn't gone in so many months and then I came back. And it was like I was never gone. I sat in my spot.

Speaking of the space, and specifically this pew, was the only time this participant cried during a two-hour interview about her father's funeral. An older woman, an occasional practitioner who identifies as spiritual, also describes experiencing a connection to a deceased family member in the church building. Several decades prior, shortly after her brother was killed in a car accident, her father invited her to attend church with him. During the service she heard a bird singing loudly in the rafters of the nave, yet her father and others did not hear the bird. She interprets the bird as a sign from her brother: "I think that was him just letting to me it's okay." When I ask whether it is significant that this took place in the church building, she is unsure, but does have a sense that it is a place open to this type of spiritual and relational connection, similar to a cemetery. For both participants, the worship space is associated with specific personal relationships and memories.

For others, liturgical space communicates a sense of *present-day community*, even if it is not a community with which they connect routinely. The space is about the people who gather there:

> A lot of it is the stained-glass windows and just the lovely front of the church, the pulpit, and everything is so pretty. . . . It was very nice to have that grandeur. And again, because the parishioners are so open and there were so many of them, like the church was never empty, it was always full. Just to have that nice community sense when you're in the church. And everybody walking in, as soon as they see the baby dressed for the baptism, it was, "Oh, so cute" and "Welcome." It didn't matter if it was one of the ushers at the church or one of the regular parishioners walking around. It was always so open and so nice and we really just enjoyed the openness and the grandeur of the space and just the loveliness of the space.

> That sense of the Holy Spirit, like, when we're all in it together, it's like then you're kind of like a church. The building becomes like this cocoon, but it's not the building, but you know, we're all in this together.

> Not that I'm overly religious, but I like it for the community, I like it for reflection and the music, and just being with the stained-glass windows. It's pretty and it's something nice to do on a Sunday and then go out for breakfast afterwards. It's kind of a togetherness thing, not so much that I need to speak to God or I need to pray.

> It's not a big church, but it's a beautiful, it's a beautiful old church, has got lovely stained-glass windows. It's not those huge, cavernous churches which can hold hundreds and hundreds of people, it's quite an intimate size. And as I mentioned a bit with the hymn singing, just seeing familiar faces, you know, seeing familiar faces.

Whether or not the faces are familiar or new, the concept of a particular church community and a particular church building—even a very specific part of it—are closely linked for many occasional and routine practitioners.

Finally, numerous participants speak of how liturgical space connects them to a *historic community*. The building links people who have cared for and worshiped in the space across time. All three congregations where this study was based worship in spaces that communicate this type of history: Gothic arches, stained glass, intricately carved wood, stone walls, and pews. This sense of history is important for motivating and interpreting occasional practice, as these two occasional practitioners describe:

> Why [do people marry] in the church? You're right. I'm sure God would be out in that pasture or on the beach, right? He's everywhere. He's everywhere. But I don't know. I think it's just the tradition. It's very traditional. It's very solid. It's just strong, strong, and yet peaceful. It gives everybody a good feeling. I know when their families, when they come for the rehearsals, many of them were just so impressed. Oh my goodness. Not only how beautiful, but how old it is. So I think that gives some strength to it. Yeah, there's hundreds of couples that have been married here for the past 150 years and it's still here and the people are still here, but it's good. A hundred years: it has good, strong, stable roots.

> The old architecture and like the wood and the stained glass—it was an aesthetic that my dad was particularly drawn to and I'm very much like him in that way. Like, we just appreciated the beauty of the space and you feel like—it just feels like an old traditional church to me. And that's one of the things that I think I appreciate about going to church; is like that connection to something that's older than you and bigger than you. And I don't know, something about that building just makes you feel that, I guess.

Even occasional practitioners who identify as nonreligious value the historic connection provided by church buildings:

> To be back in the church, it's a very positive thing for me because I've always loved physical—that church, physically, is beautiful. And I've always found that just to be wonderful. It's such a nice room, right? That's such an understatement. But there's history, there's local history. The windows are so—like the handwork, the craft. It's quite distracting really! So, it's very nostalgic for me, but in a really nice way because the hours I spent just looking around that place, right?

> The church itself is very different from most others that I've been in because it's extremely old and it's not very bright. There's no paint in the church. It's all stained wood and it's very Gothic in its design. So it's extremely dark and

it—you could spend hours just looking at the intricacy of the woodwork within the church itself. And that's fascinating regardless of your beliefs.

In Toronto none of these liturgical spaces would be more than two hundred years old. However, some participants describe encountering spaces that have a deeper history when traveling. After reflecting on the moving grandeur of cathedrals, one occasional practitioner offers a vivid description of a spiritual experience in a simple chapel in a cave in Italy where Francis of Assisi prayed:

> I could go in there and just weep. It was like I had just stepped into a vortex and gone somewhere. It was the most powerful place I've ever been to.... Literally a hole in the side of a mountain about this big that you creep into and then [it] opens up a little bit. And there's candles that the monks keep lit at all times. Tiny little altar and the seat is all worn out from bottoms over the centuries [so] that [it's] all nice and smooth and carved. And you sit down, I remember the first time I sat down there our dog was quite sick, and I thought: let's go and see Saint Francis of Assisi because he's the patron saint of animals and I'll say a prayer for her. And then I sat down. and I got this feeling that she's fine, don't worry, she's fine. And I literally looked over my shoulders, it just felt like somebody was there and was just reassuring me.... I guess I was at first saying that the building makes a big difference, but then it can also be a cave. I guess it's the spirit that's put into the building by the people that makes it powerful or not.

Ritual space is a way in which occasional practitioners connect to past worshipers, to something "bigger than" themselves.

One of the only times an occasional practitioner expressed disappointment in liturgical space (apart from complaints about a lack of air conditioning, which is a downside of historic buildings) was when visiting a space that did not adequately convey this type of history. She describes the contrast between taking her granddaughter to a newly built church in her hometown in British Columbia and attending a wedding in an older worship space in Ontario:

> I chose to take [my granddaughter] to a brand spanking new church here in town and it's a Catholic church. And when we walked into the church it was, to me, it wasn't church. It was just drywalled walls and

chairs. It wasn't pews. It wasn't—it didn't give me that feeling of being in a church. . . . When we went to Ontario to a wedding at [an older] church, . . . [my granddaughter] said, "Oh Grandma, I just love it!" I think it's just everything that's so old and ancient looking. I'm not sure about that particular church but to me that's a church. And then when I took her to this church here, it was just kind of like, meh, I don't think this is a church.

For this occasional practitioner, and potentially her granddaughter, the sense of history communicated by the building is what defines it as a church.

In addition to human community, for some the space communicates *mysterious beauty*. A nonreligious occasional practitioner describes her nonreligious sister-in-law's reaction to the church building at a funeral:

My sister-in-law . . . she said, "Oh, I saw the church and the churchyard. I totally get it now." And I think what she meant was, "I totally get why your mother would go to that church." Because she would have problems understanding why somebody would go to church, right? In that old-fashioned way. She said, "Oh, it's so beautiful. It's so beautiful." So, that was kind of interesting.

One formerly nonreligious participant who is now a routine Anglican practitioner likewise describes her first encounter with the worship space:

I just went into the nave of the church, the back hall, the nave, yeah, because, you know, there's a mysterious atmosphere there that's quite comforting. I need that kind of connection with some mysterious power, so I sat there trying to absorb everything around it.

There is transcendence alongside immanence.

There are parallels between how occasional practitioners speak of their intermittent engagement with liturgical space and Anglican liturgical theologian Lizette Larson-Miller's reflections on the potential for liturgical space to be part of a renewed contemporary sacramentality:

We welcome both the human stranger and the divine stranger in liturgy and in the building in which we meet, and we are in turn welcomed and drawn in by both human community and divine presence, immanent and transcendent.[12]

She suggests that sacramental theology is a way of holding together hospitality and mystery in relation to sacred space, instead of pitting them against one another.[13] Although occasional practitioners would not use this language, they inhabit this tension. One of the primary functions of church buildings for the occasional practitioners in this research is to make a connection to something larger than themselves. This may include spiritual connection or a sense of mystery, yet for many it is more connected to human relationships and community, past and present. The space is a significant aspect of why participants practice religion occasionally, and relationships are key to the interpretation of the space where that practice takes place.[14] Space is central to the material experience of occasional practitioners, as are other embodied aspects of Christian worship.

Clothing

Participants dress differently to attend religious services on Christmas Eve. When I look around during these crowded liturgies, I see festive sweaters, holiday jewelry, glittery scarves, children in plaid, and lots of red and green—along with a few teenagers wearing hoodies featuring high school sports teams. Plenty of people wear winter coats. Although the attire is festive, it is not especially formal. As on an ordinary Sunday in the three congregations at the center of this research, there is a broad range of dress on Christmas Eve, with a few people wearing suits, a few wearing jeans, and most dressing somewhere in between. The parents and godparents involved in a baptism, or the family at the center of a funeral, may choose somewhat more formal attire, although a wide spectrum is still socially acceptable. Despite the broad

---

[12] Lizette Larson-Miller, *Sacramentality Renewed: Contemporary Conversations in Sacramental Theology* (Collegeville, MN: Liturgical Press, 2016), 163.
[13] Larson-Miller, *Sacramentality Renewed*, 167.
[14] Occasional practitioners may contribute to the larger conversation about ritual and liturgical space in contemporary contexts. Paul Post and Arie Molendijk, eds., *Holy Ground: Re-inventing Ritual Space in Modern Western Culture* (Leuven: Peeters, 2010); Jeanne Halgren Kilde, *Sacred Power, Sacred Space: An Introduction to Christian Architecture and Worship* (New York: Oxford University Press, 2008); Richard Kieckhefer, *Theology in Stone: Church Architecture from Byzantium to Berkeley* (New York; Oxford: Oxford University Press, 2008).

range of appropriate options, occasional practitioners frequently speak of clothing in connection with religious participation. They describe "dressing up" for church in either positive or negative terms, give particular attention to the clothing of the child or the deceased who is the catalyst for the event, and notice the clothing worn by clergy.

Dressing up for church has positive significance for some participants. One occasional practitioner describes dressing up as an important feature of her mother's funeral:

> On the day of the funeral. We had—I'm just trying to think. Everybody got up. Everybody got ready. We were all dressed up, which was nice because some people don't dress for church anymore. Most people go very relaxed, so it was nice to be able to have an occasion.

Another occasional practitioner describes how dressing up is an important part of attending church with her daughters:

> R: I would take the two older girls on Sunday, we would get up and we would, not overly churchy dress, like not the way I used to when I was a kid, like you'd have to wear patent leather shoes and tights and stuff, but something a little more formal to get dressed up. And that's only just to feel special. It's only just, not because you need to be dressed up to go to church, but just not jeans either.
> I: It sets the time apart.
> R: It does. But my guess, again, it's my mother coming out in me, because you had to get dressed up to go to church, but you don't need to be dressed up to pray. Maybe it's in my head. But yes, I make my girls dress up a little bit and we would go to church.

Other participants also associate getting dressed up with childhood memories of church, especially on certain occasions, as these older and younger occasional practitioners describe:

> It's the whole ambience of being in the church. And those are things that you just miss from your childhood. I just recently saw a post on Facebook about ... do you remember this, like and share if you remember your white shoes and your Easter hats, Easter bonnets and stuff, right? And it's just

something that you remember, that Easter time was the time that you got your white shoes, you got your white socks. You got your little hats. And then you went to Sunday school. You went to church. That's where you went and wore your good clothes. And I think that part is what's missing sometimes.

I think it's just the tradition. Like I grew up going at Easter and I have a lot of memories. Like I'd always wear like a very nice dress. I'd always have like a bow in my hair. You would feel very special.

Parents today describe how their children associate getting dressed up with attending religious services and value this aspect of their experience:

[My daughter] likes going to church. She will often—now for her, I think a lot of it is getting dressed up, so she likes—and I guess that's part of the ritual, right? She gets dressed up and she goes and she feels grown up.

I: Moving back to the day of the baptism. I know there was a lot going on that Sunday. What do you remember about the service itself that day? Are there moments that stand out?
R: Yeah, I remember my son being very happy. He got to wear like dressy clothes and like a bow tie.
I: He likes that?
R: Yeah. He got to wear a bow tie like dad, they both wore bow ties. He was really excited about it. And it was nice to see him watch it happen because obviously you don't remember your own, well, usually, right? He has no recollection of it, but he got to see his sister's.

Dressing up for church is something that stands out to occasional practitioners as a positive part of their experience and part of what makes these events significant, especially through connection to childhood memories or connections across generations.

However, for some occasional practitioners, *dressing up for church is negative*. There are some who simply do not like getting dressed up:

[My husband] has said that he did not like going to church and he doesn't like that you have to get dressed up to go. So, unless it was a baptism, I probably wouldn't have got him there.

Others describe the challenge of preparing children for church:

> It's not something we can wake up on Sunday and be like, do you want to go? Do you feel like going? The day before we definitely have to plan. My daughter's clothes are laid out. My son's clothes are laid out. We have to load things in the car already, the stroller, everything's ready, like it's a big activity.

> It's stressful getting to church for 10 o'clock with five children and yourself and getting up and trying to have a shower, and get tights on two kids, and dresses, and buying dresses, and buying shoes, and figuring out what I'm going to wear—something that I can wear that I can nurse in.

With these challenges in mind, it is understandable that some parents express appreciation for no longer feeling like they need to get dressed up to attend religious services:

> I just feel like we could go there once a year or ten times a year and everyone sort of treats you like they just saw you last week. And it's just a group of the nicest people. We never feel judged for not attending regularly. The kids do make noise and we don't judge. Yeah, I mean, down to what people are wearing is not even a thing. I mean, you're often, when we're growing up you learn that you got to get dressed to the nines to go to church. And we've been just—meaning that people just can relax, you know, it sounds silly, but it makes things a lot easier to attend not being worried about what's clean.

Whether dressing up is viewed positively or negatively, considerations about what to wear are frequently mentioned in conversations about religious services with occasional practitioners. Clothing is a theme that they introduce when speaking about their occasional participation in Christian worship.

The *clothing worn by the individual who is the catalyst* for the event may be particularly significant. If there is an open casket at a funeral, the clothing worn by the deceased is often mentioned. In one case, the primary request made by the deceased regarding his funeral was that he be buried in the jersey of his favorite hockey team:

> He said this to the kids at one time, he said, "Anything happens to me, I want to be laid out in my Leafs sweater. I'm telling you guys, because your mother will make me wear a suit. I don't want to wear a suit. I want to wear my Leafs sweater." When he died, I said to the kids, "Well, you better go on

and find your dad's Leafs sweater because you know what the instructions are." We did that. He wore his shirt and tie, but he had his Leafs sweater on instead of a suit jacket.

The clothing worn by children being baptized also receives significant attention. As mentioned in the discussion of ritual systems in Chapter 5, this clothing is robustly networked in religious ritual systems as well as family ritual systems. Most occasional practitioners focus on the family connections to baptismal attire:

> We wanted her to wear my christening dress, which was my mom's christening dress, but it was small. So we had a very narrow window of opportunity in which she would fit [into it]. So we're like, okay, let's go.

> I'll show you a picture. . . . This was worn, this was their great-great-grandfather's, grandmother's. It was all silk.

> Yes, the long dress. My mom made it. If you want, I can get it. I swear, she must have probably spent sixty or seventy hours making this dress.

> Always white. The babies always wear white. It's like white like a wedding day. It's just what would you do since white is clean slate. So starting your new life in whatever ceremony it is. So as a baby you're baptized and you wear white. That's what we've always done and that's what it is. It used to be more like a dress. I think the styles have changed a little bit, I think, but I happened to find this white suit. This is perfect. This is what I'm looking for. There's always the price too because it can be expensive but we did okay. My sister actually paid for it. So I found it but my sister was like, "I want to pay for this gift because it means so much as a godparent." She was like, "I want to give this to him as a gift for him to wear." That's also a thing. You shower the babies with gifts.

> Buying the clothes of the child, buying the white clothes, that's part of the preparation. I mean, you won't just wear any regular clothes, you have to buy the baptism clothes.

Even adults who are being baptized speak of choosing what to wear as part of their preparation for the event:

> I was a little nervous going in for whatever reason. I just wanted to be dressed well and kind of put forward a good appearance.

I bought a new sweater for the ceremony. [Laughs] Yeah, I guess that's it.

Clothing is part of planning and preparing for the event in ways that shape the significance of the event.

Especially for those who are not routinely involved or contributing to liturgical leadership, clothing is one aspect of religious practice that participants have the opportunity to influence. They can choose how to embody the practice through their choice of what to wear, setting this event apart, personalizing the experience, and passing traditions across generations. Clothing may be a source of anxiety or positive value for occasional practitioners, but even in brief descriptions of occasional participation it is often mentioned. As one participant observed in relation to her own comments: "The conversation went from religion to fashion quite quickly." I responded, hopefully reassuringly, "It's all connected."

The *clothing worn by clergy* is also significant for occasional practitioners. It is noteworthy that clergy themselves reference their own clothing in relation to occasional practice. One priest even opened the closet in his office during an interview to show me the vestments he wears for funerals (black cassock, white surplice, black tippet) in contrast to the business casual attire he usually wears on Sunday morning in his evangelical Anglican congregation. Clergy, as ritual experts, know that the clothing they wear can both create barriers and open doors, especially in relation to occasional practitioners:

> I don't always wear a clergy shirt. I'm pretty reformed about stuff and I find the collar, it can create a barrier in many circumstances in life, but on the other hand it can be a real bridge builder and like it opens doors for me if I'm in the hospital, or in the funeral situation.

> There's a lot of prejudice against the Christian church. Culturally, particularly against the Catholic Church at this moment. A lot of caricature, a lot of stereotyping of clergy.... So, people, many people have a tremendous wariness of the institutional church.... You're the object of projection. At least I am. I wear this collar, the object of projection. Not only negative projection, sometimes positive projection. Sometimes positive projection. And that positive projection sometimes opens doors in ways that I could never anticipate. I can think of lots of times walking through hospitals or nursing homes, or even on the street, people will just stop you and say, "Father, this is happening, and I don't, would you pray with me, or would you give me a

blessing, or would you pray for my sister who's undergoing chemotherapy right now?" They'll pour out their hearts to you. You've never met this person.... The work is done apart from the personality of the individual, the gifts or liabilities of the individual. The sign signifies, the sign does its work, the sign opens doors, the sign opens people to the Holy Spirit, or the action of God. It's nothing that you did or said. You're just wearing this costume, right?

This priest's understanding of how clerical attire is perceived is reflected in comments from occasional practitioners. One participant with an evangelical background describes how vestments shaped her experience of the baptism of her grandchild:

I'm not into the pomp and circumstance of the bishops or the high priests with all the big hats on and all that stuff. I could care less. You go back to early United States Puritans. The reason ministers wear black was to keep all the emphasis off of them and on the message that they were talking about. Sometimes I get distracted by these guys and the—I don't want to use the word get ups—ornate clothing. The clothes are pretty ornate, and it takes my eye sometimes—often—off the message and all to them. Like I said, I'm like, "Oh, okay. The Puritans had a couple of things going for them." I understand the black clothes things and how it helped to keep focused.

Especially for those who do not come from an Anglican background, business attire instead of formal vestments feels "warm" and "approachable." However, for those with an Anglican or Roman Catholic background, vestments seem to be a largely taken-for-granted background to religious practices.

Whether worn by participants, the baptized or deceased, or clergy, clothing is a material manifestation of the embodiment of the liturgy.[15] What people wear is a site of repetition and opposition within ritual systems and between ritual systems. Clothing is part of how participants prepare their bodies for the event, perceive the bodies of others present at the event, and how they interpret their liturgical experience through embodied practices.

---

[15] Anna-Karina Hermkens, "Clothing as Embodied Experience of Belief," in *Religion and Material Culture: The Matter of Belief*, ed. David Morgan (New York: Routledge, 2010), 231–246; Dick Hines, *Dressing for Worship: A Fresh Look at What Christians Wear in Church* (Cambridge: Grove Books, 1996).

Clothing is one way that occasional practitioners do liturgical theology. Although religious traditions, including Christianity, have long histories of policing dress, these Anglican congregations in Toronto do not establish specific expectations regarding dress for participants, beyond those of everyday life. Therefore, their own clothing, and at times the clothing of catalysts, is an area in which occasional practitioners exercise significant autonomy and agency in shaping their liturgical experience and interpreting the significance of these events. They choose their clothing, while they do not directly choose other material objects present in the liturgy.

Objects

Material objects, as well as space and clothing, feature prominently in occasional practitioners' reflections on their liturgical experience. In connection with *baptism*, these objects include the water, oil, the baptism candle, the baptism garment, gifts, and more. Perhaps unsurprisingly, the water is often seen as particularly central to the baptism:

> The minister—priest—the one who actually took [my granddaughter] and placed her head down so that he could put the Holy Water on her, that was obviously really significant because that is the act of baptism itself. That's what's moving. I was able to move around enough to get to see that part. That definitely was a highlight for me.

> Where he's baptized with the water, being reborn, on his head, just sort of—he was a little fussy, so, sort of anxiety of is he going to scream—but just knowing the significance of the water with the baptism ceremony.... And I think it [is] something really precious to see.

> Letting him go and have his own moment, to have his baptism, and to have the water on him, and that whole process—I started tearing up. I was like, "Oh, this is the moment for him." This is what's happening, he will be baptized and now he's in this community and he has that foundation to start his life in the Lord's footsteps. So that was really, really awesome. That's when really that hit me. So yes, that was really special.

> Well, obviously the physical, like the water going on, a very, very—like that was really important to me. It's something I've dreamed about as a little girl, like wanting my own family and that was a significant moment.

Although these participants have different associations with the water, for each of them the moment the water is poured on the head of the child is the center of the baptism.

In connection with *funerals*, important objects include the casket or urn, flowers, photographs, memorabilia, and gravestones. The specific objects selected often carry meaning, such as a pall made of the family tartan, or tropical flowers chosen for a woman with Jamaican heritage. The challenge of navigating a range of decisions associated with the materiality of death, often on short notice and with little experience in such matters, is central to many participants' descriptions of a funeral, especially for those who are initiators or inner-circle supporters.

In the case of both baptisms and funerals, as well as other occasional practices, *food* features prominently in descriptions of the events. Months later, numerous participants describe the menu for the meal or the details of the cake in greater detail than the baptism or funeral liturgy. Food is especially important for bringing people together and connecting with cultural heritage:

> I'm West Indian, so food at the end [of the funeral] is always a good thing. It's something to gather around and have a cup of coffee. Yeah, I think that's with most traditions.

> We're Italian, it's more of a production almost like obligation event. Like you have to serve—food's almost the religion of our family more than anything. Sometimes at these events the secondary element is religion, the primary is like family food, hosting, gifts.

> I think the day went off really well.... I felt good about it. I felt even better after it was done. I did invite—I would say a little lunch, early dinner. And, of course, I cooked everything, almost everything, and for a lot of friends who had never had my cooking. And for that to work out well and everybody to be happy and full and taking home leftovers to their places, it made me feel like, not only baptizing my child, but everything that I did, all the work that I put into this one day, it was just perfect.

Intriguingly, the bread and wine of communion are rarely discussed, either as food or liturgical object, unless there are barriers to reception. Many participants struggle to remember whether communion was celebrated as part of a funeral, for example, regardless of whether they receive the elements.

This is a brief discussion of material objects, in part because material objects have featured prominently throughout this study, including extended discussions of candles[16] and photographs,[17] as well as the preceding examples of clothing and liturgical space. "Matter matters" not only to occasional practitioners but also to sacramental theologians, to the extent that this phrase has become a common aphorism in the discipline of liturgical studies. As sacramental theologian Louis-Marie Chauvet emphasizes, "What is most spiritual always takes place in the most corporeal."[18] Sacramental theologian Joris Geldhof speaks of the critical potential of the liturgy in the face of modern "spiritualizing tendencies"[19] within the church and broader culture:

> The liturgy's materiality matters: it cannot be imagined and experienced unless the places where it is celebrated, the colors, the vestments, the vessels, incense, etc. are taken into consideration.[20]

These material elements of the liturgy are significant for occasional practitioners as well. However, participants are also invested in matter beyond the official rite. Furthermore, they may interpret official liturgical materials in a diversity of ways, through overlaps with additional ritual systems in addition to connections within the Christian ritual system and, potentially, adjacent texts.

Words

Participants rarely mention *words* spoken during worship in interviews. Scripture readings and prescribed prayers voiced by the presider seldom come up. This is even the case when I provide participants with a printed

---

[16] For more on candles, see Chapter 6.
[17] For more on photographs, see Chapter 8.
[18] Chauvet, *The Sacraments*. Gibler anchors a theology of baptism in a natural history of the central liturgical objects of water, oil, and fire. Linda Gibler, *From the Beginning to Baptism: Scientific and Sacred Stories of Water, Oil, and Fire* (Collegeville, MN: Liturgical Press, 2010). Thomas Long emphasizes the importance of the human body in the context of Christian funerals. Thomas Long, *Accompany Them with Singing: The Christian Funeral* (Louisville, KY: Westminster John Knox Press, 2009).
[19] Joris Geldhof, *Liturgy and Secularism: Beyond the Divide* (Collegeville, MN: Liturgical Press, 2018), 136.
[20] Geldhof, *Liturgy and Secularism*, 136.

order of worship that consists mostly of words. Words are simply not central to the liturgical experience of occasional practitioners. One nonreligious occasional practitioner describes her experience of her mother's funeral:

> At the end of the day, the choice of readings, it was never clear to me what they were really about. Like it didn't resonate for me because I haven't been involved in the church in a long time. I find the language very difficult to follow, what it's supposed to be about. If you're not already familiar with it, it's kind of opaque, I guess. At least it was for me. So, I'm just sort of like, you know, whatever.

Although this participant associates her lack of understanding and appreciation for scriptural and liturgical language with infrequent participation, a routine practitioner expresses a similar sentiment about his weekly attendance, first at a service that uses the *Book of Common Prayer*, and then at one that relies on the *Book of Alternative Services*, neither of which he finds particularly important:

> When we started, we were at 11 o'clock, and so we're using the maroon book, and that was tricky to get used to. You know, there's a lot of page flipping and going through. I didn't mind it, like I didn't have anything really to compare it to. And then when we switched to 9 o'clock, there was a different book. They changed the language a little bit. So fewer "thuses" and "thous" and a little bit more regular language. To be honest, the prayers to me aren't—it's a bad thing to say—aren't the most important thing to me.

In addition, participants are often comfortable speaking words during worship that do not reflect their personal commitments. When words are used that they might resist, they freely reinterpret them. For example, one agnostic participant describes her approach to the commitments made at the baptism of her children:

> I: How do you make sense of the God language and the scripture readings and that kind of thing that happens during the baptism service?
> R: Because I believe there's something, the God language, it's just like, okay, that's your something. That's what your definition of the something is. I'm like, "You can call it God, you can call it whatever you want to call it," but there's something so I'm like, "Okay, that's acceptable. I'm

comfortable with that." A lot of the scripture, I'm also quite comfortable with because, if nothing else, they're a lovely story of trying to impart a principle or a value that I tend to agree with.

Some parents take a similar approach to involving nonreligious godparents in the baptism of their children, as discussed in Chapter 3 and Chapter 5.

The relative insignificance of words for liturgical participants is a challenge to the discipline of liturgical studies. Liturgical scholars have invested more than a century of attention in words. The origin of the discipline is in the comparative study of texts. Liturgical theologians tend to read great significance into the words that are used in worship. In some cases, liturgy is in danger of being reduced to words. However, words for worship, especially prescribed and scripted words, to a large extent simply wash over occasional practitioners—and likely many other participants. This does not mean that words do not matter. For example, it is possible for words to be spoken that participants experience as harmful or lifegiving. However, occasional practitioners' emphasis on the material more than the linguistic presses beyond an emphasis on language. In an address at Yale Divinity School in 2018, Anglican theologian and former Archbishop of Canterbury Rowan Williams emphasized the act of naming as a necessary aspect of human presence in the world, and a transformative naming and being named—notably itself "an irreducibly physical affair"—as central to Christian liturgy.[21] However, in responding to questions, Williams also acknowledged two dangers of this approach. The first is the risk of privileging the articulate over the inarticulate, which prompts him to emphasize that naming must go beyond language.[22] This opens space for liturgical theological dialogue with occasional practitioners through practice. The second, Williams acknowledged, and was unable to resolve, is the critique that any act of naming risks being an act of hegemony in which one group dominates another. Williams asks, "What are the practices that disrupt uncriticized hegemonic thinking?"[23] Openness to doing liturgical theology with those on the liturgical and theological margins, for whom the linguistic and conceptual dimensions of

---

[21] Rowan Williams, "Naming the World: Liturgy and the Transformation of Time and Matter," in *Full of Your Glory: Liturgy, Cosmos, Creation*, ed. Teresa Berger (Collegeville, MN: Liturgical Press, 2019), 36.

[22] Rowan Williams, "Some Highlights from the Question and Answer Session That Followed Rowan Williams's Keynote Address," in *Full of Your Glory: Liturgy, Cosmos, Creation*, ed. Teresa Berger (Collegeville, MN: Liturgical Press, 2019), 40.

[23] Williams, "Some Highlights," 41.

Christian worship are less central, may be one such practice. The occasional practitioners in this research invite all who engage with Christian worship to engage more deeply with the material dimensions of practices and to consider the ways in which liturgical theology is being done without words.

Liturgical Practice as Emotional More than Conceptual

While participants in this research share their reasoning around occasional religious practice, my overall impression of these conversations is that the emotional rather than conceptual content of occasional liturgical experiences is primary for them. As participants reflect on these events, they share their feelings as much as their thoughts—although these dimensions of human experience and cognition cannot easily be differentiated. The emotional content of occasional religious practice tends to be expressed in relation to two areas: the overall mood of the event, and specific moments within the event.

Mood

Mood—the atmosphere, feeling, tone, or spirit of an experience—is a particularly difficult dimension of Christian liturgy to capture. At the same time, reflections on mood run through this research. As discussed in relation to types of occasional practitioners, some long for a spiritual connection in relation to significant life events—a connection that is often associated with a certain mood. As discussed in relation to the overlaps between the Anglican and Roman Catholic ritual systems in Chapter 7, worship may have a "warm" or "cold" mood, and this is central to how participants assess the experience. Liturgical space is closely connected to mood; one participant describes this connection as "the whole ambience of being in the church." Mood is often conveyed in *how* stories are told, as much as through *which* stories are told. Foregrounding the question of mood, each interview and quotation in this entire analysis could be revisited.

Participants often convey mood through words like: "beauty," "comfort," "solemn," "serious," "mystery," "dignity," and "peace." Likely due to how participants were selected for this research, most describe the mood of the events that are the focus of our conversation in largely positive terms, while occasionally making negative comparisons to other contexts. Participants frequently use phrases that evoke emotion to capture their overall sense of the event, as well as the mood they observe through others:

It was just very warm, very—I wouldn't even say that somber was a part of the mood at all.

People had commented that it was just so emotional.

It just left us with such a great feeling.

It is a comfort for me to go into church, to go in there.

It always felt like a safe place. Always very like comfortable.

The baptism was very positive. I felt good about it. I felt good after.

I think I really enjoy going to the Anglican service in the sense that I feel a sense of like, almost like peace.

I just love the feeling that you get when you go to church. I know when my daughter comes home sometimes she'll say, "Oh, Mom, can we go to church on Sunday? I haven't gone for a long time." It's just a peacefulness.

The opening sentences, those readings, just kind of—yeah. You could just kind of let go once that happens. And then it's okay to cry. To be sad.

The ceremony meant more to me than I thought it would have. At first, I was just kind of going through the motions. And then afterwards, like I said, I did feel a little bit more emotional than I—yeah. That's my church.

That was a compelling service because you really felt that you were in the house of the Lord and the Lord was there. At least, that's what—that's the way I always felt at Evensong.

I feel at home and whenever I enter any church, Sarah. We've been all over the world to different churches in Spain and wherever, Portugal, all sorts of places I've been. To me a church is a place of reverence and it's a place where you feel a sense of peace.

I guess it just made them feel—it was a feel-good look on their face. Everybody looked calm, satisfied. I can't even think of the right word, but I hope you understand what I'm trying to say.

These overall impressions are important for how occasional practitioners interpret liturgical experiences. While they often cannot describe specific details months or years later, they know how their participation in a certain baptism or funeral liturgy in a specific congregation made them feel. Most occasional practitioners also express a general sense for what they consider to be a suitable mood for Christian worship on holidays and other occasions when they attend.

Moments

In addition to describing the overall mood of a liturgical event in relation to emotional rather than conceptual content, participants often describe fleeting moments they consider especially significant because they are associated with certain emotions. These moments may also contribute to the overall mood. Because these moments are important for how occasional practitioners understand their religious identities, make choices about religious practice, interpret religious rituals, and do liturgical theology, many stories that have been shared already capture these fleeing instances. Therefore, I include only a few more examples here.

Meaningful moments may be characterized by grief or delight. A widow describes the "amazing calmness" that came over her as she walked into the church, prepared to offer her husband's eulogy:

> When I went into the church, this amazing calmness came over me. I wasn't upset, I wasn't nervous. I was just calm. Part of that I think is because I wrote the eulogy and I practiced it many, many, many, many times. I read it so often I was getting sick of reading, but I thought, "I have got to do this because, if I don't, I'm not sure I'm going to be able get through it." I got up there and I did that and there was just, through, really through the whole service, there was just a calmness.

A participant describes being a child attending church with her family for an Easter service and looking over at her father and seeing him cry for the first time:

> I still remember going there, standing next to my Dad, singing at Easter service and he started crying. I've never seen my Dad cry before. Just the tears were coming down his face and I think I knew at the time he was

remembering his parents. And I thought, wow. It dawned on me, Dad was always so strong, but I realized I guess it was part of growing up that your Dad, he has deep emotions too. He wants to cry. He probably holds it in all the time but this time he couldn't. I just held his hand. So, that was nice. Where were we going with this? Sorry [laughter].

A family and the congregation share an informal moment of laughter as a shorter priest attempts to reach up to anoint the forehead of a taller man during his baptism:

I think it was the unscripted moments that kind of stand out for me. You do have kind of like your traditional baptism and the elements that happened. But what I honestly remember the most are the elements like oh, [the priest] made a little joke when she couldn't reach my head. That made it very comforting. Made it very welcoming. Almost kind of a fun experience.

A mother laughs with delight as she retells the story of her now adult son requesting the role of dinosaur in the annual children's Christmas pageant, one of the few occasions her mother would attend religious services:

[The priest] said, "Okay, everybody come over here. We're going to have the Christmas pageant in about four weeks, and so I want you to choose your parts and then we're going to have rehearsals." Well of course all the children say, "I want to be a shepherd" and "I want to be an angel" and [my daughter] said "I want to be Mary this year, you said I could be Mary next year." And so [the priest] says, "Andrew, what do you want to be?" He says, "I want to be a dinosaur." Everybody just broke up laughing.

Experiencing emotion and witnessing the emotional responses of others are both significant.

Some moments are emotional because they are encounters among participants who relate to religion in different ways. A young mother is moved to tears as she describes her supportive nonreligious partner willingly handing over a child to a priest for baptism:

[My husband] was holding [my son] for the most part, he wanted to take on that role. He's very protective of him in a way but also wanting to protect him and be there for him. He's the man of the household. I'm always there as the mom but I think for him, it was so special to hold him and be that person on his special day. So I think the moment that [my husband] gave him up to [the priest], it was letting him go and having him have his own moment to have his baptism, and to have the water on him and that whole process. So I started tearing up.

A staunchly nonreligious daughter describes the value of her mother's funeral as primarily about community support except for the first hymn, "This Is My Father's World":

And it was just really, I would summarize it by saying it was a hundred percent about the people. Okay, maybe three percent about that first hymn which was fun to sing. Fun, that's the wrong word. It's very comforting to sing a hymn that my mother liked. And it was about nature. And I knew a lot of people at the funeral were nature lovers. And like that would mean a lot to them. So, it was like a connection point.

In both the examples above, part of what makes these moments meaningful is the opportunity to express and receive support across religious difference through participation in religious ritual.

These moments span the mundane to the momentous. These small, emotion-laden stories—preserved in tears and laughter—are what stick with occasional practitioners years after these events take place. They are moments that contribute to the mood and meaning of the event.

Event as Concept

Although emotional rather than conceptual content is central to how many occasional practitioners experience Christian liturgy, there are several instances in which an occasional practitioner engages with the liturgical event itself as an abstract concept rather than as a concrete experience with specific content. The baptism or funeral is a "box to check" rather than a substantive experience. For example, this conceptual understanding of baptism may be what is behind parents calling a church to "get the child done," as clergy report, and as this occasional practitioner describes:

I just love the fact that I had done it. I had done something that I have to admit at one point, I wasn't sure if it was going to get done because having contacted some churches and getting the reception that we did, I wasn't sure if I was going to be able to find somewhere to go, that would let me do it. So that was huge for me.

I encountered a similar dynamic in an interview with an older man about the funeral for his father. In an email exchange the evening before the interview, he asked whether he needed to prepare, and I responded that it would be a very open-ended conversation about the story of his father's funeral. He clearly gave this some thought and spoke for more than twenty minutes uninterrupted at the outset of the phone interview about the meaning and purpose of funerals. However, he seemed shocked when I asked specifically about his father's funeral service:

> But—oh, geez, let me think. I—oh. I'm sorry. I can't—I guess I should have thought about this. I didn't think about the service. [Laughs] I was thinking about everything else, all my other cluttered thoughts going around it.

He was unable to offer any sort of thick description of his father's funeral. It is as if the *idea* of the funeral was more important than the *experience* of the particular funeral itself. This is a rare exception to the emphasis on emotion.

Emotion has long been recognized as a significant aspect of Christian worship.[24] Recent liturgical theology acknowledges the importance of emotion, such as James K. A. Smith's work on how liturgy forms human desires,[25] Susan Ross's feminist sacramental theology that closely links affect and embodiment,[26] and the February 2021 issue of the journal *Liturgy* edited by Edward Phillips, which is on the theme of worship and emotion.[27] Practical theologian Allie Utley's research on liturgy and affect is particularly noteworthy in relation to the lived liturgical theology of occasional practitioners. Drawing on affect theory, Utley claims that religion may not be predicated on language and examines worship as embodied, social, and nonrepresentational.[28] She approaches these themes autoethnographically

---

[24] Dale M. Coulter, *The Spirit, the Affections, and the Christian Tradition* (Notre Dame: University of Notre Dame Press, 2016).

[25] James K. A. Smith, *Desiring the Kingdom: Worship, Worldview, and Cultural Formation* (Grand Rapids, MI: Baker, 2009); James K. A. Smith, *Imagining the Kingdom: How Worship Works* (Grand Rapids, MI: Baker, 2013); James K. A. Smith, *Awaiting the King: Reforming Public Theology* (Grand Rapids, MI: Baker, 2017).

[26] Susan Ross, *Extravagant Affections: A Feminist Sacramental Theology* (New York: Continuum, 1998).

[27] L. Edward Phillips, ed., "Worship and Emotion," special issue, *Liturgy* 36, no. 1 (2021).

[28] Allie Utley, "Sensing Worship: An Autoethnography of Liturgy and Affect" (PhD diss., Vanderbilt University, 2021), https://ir.vanderbilt.edu/handle/1803/16749.

as an intensive practitioner and, while she acknowledges that occasional religious practice impacts the affective experience of all worshipers,[29] hearing directly from occasional practitioners is not central to her project. Nevertheless, Utley's examination of affect resonates with the ways occasional practitioners in this research speak of mood and significant moments in worship. Utley describes her objective: "The white, mainline, Protestant church has overemphasized the role of reason and rationality, and I would like to provide an account in that context of the ways emotion governs the worshiping community."[30] Occasional practitioners' emotional approach to liturgical experience has the potential to contribute to this account.

Liturgical Practice as Relational More than Personal

A third theme that emerges in conversation with occasional practitioners is Christian liturgy as corporate and relational more than individual and personal. A robust understanding of occasional religious practice resists a modern individual Protestant bias toward considering personal belief to be the measure of authentic (or even permissible) practice. In this sense, occasional practice also challenges individualistic consumeristic notions of modern spirituality, such as Robert Bellah's "Sheilaism";[31] the type of personal religious synthesis "imprisoned in the private realm of individual insight" described by Vincent Miller;[32] or Thomas Quartier's focus on individualization in relation to funerals.[33] As demonstrated in Chapters 3 and 4, many Anglican occasional practitioners in Toronto understand their religious identity in relation to their cultural heritage or family background. Many are motivated to initiate religious practices occasionally because of their cultural heritage or relational connections. Many attend liturgies and even take active roles in facilitating participation in religious services to support family members, friends, and acquaintances. Whether and how practice changes over the life course are also affected by relationships. "Believing in belonging" and "collectivistic religion" as ways of understanding

---

[29] Allie Utley, "Hope Emerges? An Exploration of Energy and Power in the Context of Worship," *Liturgy* 37, no. 2 (2022): 49.
[30] Utley, "Sensing Worship," 13.
[31] Bellah et al., *Habits of the Heart*, discussed in Vincent J. Miller, *Consuming Religion: Christian Faith and Practice in a Consumer Culture* (New York: Continuum, 2005), 88–91.
[32] Miller, *Consuming Religion*, 228.
[33] Quartier, *Bridging the Gaps*.

contemporary religiosity are closely tied to occasional practice.[34] As explored in Part II, occasional practitioners intuitively interpret rituals through multiple overlapping ritual systems, including ritual systems associated with family and culture. Here in Part III, I again analyze how occasional practitioners emphasize the corporate dimensions of their liturgical participation, in the opening discussion of photography, and below in terms of how they describe the meaning of baptisms and funerals.

Meaning of Baptism

When I ask about the meaning of baptism in interviews, I frame the question by saying that "baptism is a practice with many layers of meaning" to free participants to offer their personal reflections, rather than attempting to provide "the correct answer." Participants respond by speaking of the meaning of baptism in a diversity of ways. Some describe baptism as a "foundation" or "first step." Some speak of baptism as an opportunity for gratitude and celebration. Some describe baptism as dedicating the child to God or themselves to raising the child in the Christian faith. Some emphasize baptism as blessing the child, which may be associated with divine protection. Some associate baptism with salvation and see it as "a ticket into heaven," although they often question this claim in the same breath. More than any of these layers of meaning, however, participants associate baptism with belonging in the family or in the church: they understand baptism in relational terms.

Some occasional practitioners strongly associate baptism with *family belonging*. Baptism is more about the corporate Christian identity and practice of the extended family than about the specific beliefs or practices of the nuclear family:

> When you look at it, like coming into a family, so it's like a family that is rooted in principles from their faith that should be there to support you and all the parts of your life, that should accept you for who you are. They should also lead by example so that you have something, someone to look up to and model after. It should also be an opportunity for family to celebrate a life. Even though you already have like the baby's already a year or six months, it's a formal way of celebrating that baby.

[34] Day, *Believing in Belonging*; Jakelic, *Collectivistic Religions*.

> I think also baptisms are really nice because it's a way to unite families. I mean I think there's the immediate family. But sometimes, it's just another moment for the extended family to come together in celebration for a new member.
>
> I guess what it comes down to is, for us, our family being present is the most important thing to baptism. So I guess the congregation itself doesn't, we didn't mind, we wanted to have some place where there was meaning, but like you had pointed out like, why travel all that way [to Toronto] while [in our current location in another province] we know some of the parishioners more. I think our family was more important to us.
>
> Maybe it is how you get into heaven. I don't know. But it's certainly a nice coming-together with the family and it's a nice welcoming into a different community within the church and the family that is the church.

Even two of the three participants in this research who were baptized as adults, from whom one might expect a stronger emphasis on personal conviction, interpret the event in relation to family belonging and relationship with the church:

> I guess my feelings afterwards is, I didn't think that I would feel—I don't know if the word's emotional about it, but just a little bit more connected to my family, but I definitely do. It's just that little ceremony has made me feel just a little bit more connected even if it hasn't really changed my religious views or how involved I will be with the church. It just makes me feel like we're a little bit more tied to that.
>
> And I think also, even though I'm not actively religious, I think like the enablement of being part of the church through the baptism, I think, was valuable as well. In the future, I do feel much more inclined to attend a Christmas service or going on Easter or even on a Sunday or just having a bit of a larger role in connection with the church. Like that, I think, has a lot of value in that as well.

As the examples above suggest, belonging in the family and belonging in the church are related for some occasional practitioners.

Belonging in the church is another common theme in how occasional practitioners understand the meaning of baptism. Although baptism takes place in a local congregation, for many participants this sense of ecclesial belonging is broader than a specific parish, as the freedom of movement between the Anglican and Roman Catholic traditions discussed in Chapter 7 suggests. Participants describe this understanding of the meaning of baptism explicitly and, in certain cases, point to how they experience it ritually, and how they expect it to be manifest in the future:

> The baptism is the entrance and acceptance into the Christian community.

> After the baptism, now the child is a member of the church.

> To me, it's the introduction of the children into the church and if that's going to be part of their upbringing and I feel like it's important that they all have the same introduction and the same opportunity to go through that kind of formalized, ritualized process of introduction into that group.

> I think we felt so welcomed in that community and being in front of everyone and just knowing that God will be watching over him, and it was really special.

> I also find it quite special when [the priest] takes [the child] around, she took [my son] around or just, you know, highlights them. And so that everybody understands that "it takes a village." And I find that especially pretty cool.

> For me now the meaning of baptism is being part of a community.... So as a mom of two, I'd like them to be part of that community and able to, if and solely if they're in trouble or they want to go talk to someone that's like me or anybody else, they would have something to talk to that would not judge them, would be there to guide them.

Many occasional practitioners emphasize belonging in the church as central to their understanding of baptism, but do not associate this with personal belief or routine practice. This sense of belonging is broader and more communal than many clergy might desire or require. While the individual remains at the center of the rite, the practice makes sense in the context of relationships, and belonging in the family and church is a corporate, more than individual, approach to the meaning of baptism.

Meaning of Funerals

In a similar approach to baptism, I ask participants to reflect on the meaning and purpose of funerals, as well as on what makes for a "good funeral," in ways that invite a breadth of reflections. Participants describe funerals as being either for the deceased or for the living. Some see funerals as a space for grief and mourning, for closure and saying goodbye, as well as for naming hope. Some emphasize celebrating the life of the deceased with gratitude and recognition of their legacy. Some focus on providing support for the close family of the deceased and one another. Amid this diversity, consistent themes emerge with respect to what is considered a "good funeral."

The starting point for a good funeral for occasional practitioners is that *people gather together* and do so in significant number. Being together on these occasions is important in terms of personal reflection, mutual support, and honoring the deceased:

> It sounds really simplistic, but I think with a lot of the sermons and the words given by the pastor or the priest or whoever, it's very simple stuff about, you know, the passages of life and the next step is death and it's nothing to be afraid of. These are things we all know but somehow when you hear them, when you hear them as a group, it resonates more deeply. You can think them all you want alone in your room and it doesn't have the same effect.

> I know [the deceased] would have been very, very pleased, but she was a people person. And she would have loved to have seen the turnout, and the warmth and the caring especially for [her son], because he's an only child, doesn't have any siblings. I know she would have been very encouraged and happy to see a good turnout that there was and a lovely service.... Well again, a good turnout of people to show that this person was well loved, well known in the community.

A second significant feature is that those who know the deceased speak of their life. This includes *hearing formal eulogies and informal stories* from family members and friends:

> I think, it's good when people that really know the person get up and speak. It's hard to do. Very hard. I understand when people can't do it. Or choose not to. Because it's hard when they break down. It's hard for everybody watching that. But I think that's a big part of it is having somebody get up and speak about who they were to remember them.

> I guess what makes a good funeral is something that you feel represents the person that the funeral is supposed to be for. I thought the actual funeral

service for my dad was wonderful, because the people that spoke knew him very well.

Part of making it a good funeral where you come away feeling—It can be anything that makes it. It can be a six-year-old getting up there and saying how much they're going to miss their grandfather or whatever. It's a personal touch.

Having people who really knew the deceased to speak. I have been to ceremonies where the person was not known by a religious community yet they had a religious funeral and you can all see the discomfort in the pastor's or priest's delivery because they didn't know the person. So that's a really important thing that those who get up to give eulogies actually knew the person.

Just if it's—I think when a funeral—a good sense of the person, if you know the person. Like a good sense of that person comes across. And if you learn something about that person you didn't know. No perfect childhood or something. Like you never knew before. And just chatting with people. And it doesn't even have to be directly about that person. Probably make it a better positive experience.

As an extension of this, participants highly value when there is a meaningful *personal connection between the clergy person and the family*:

There's a clear connection between [my friend] and [my friend's] family and the pastor, so that made a big difference. A lot of funerals it's sort of cliché type, whereas hers was very specific to [my friend] and her family. So that made a really big difference too and it was just a very warm welcoming send-off. It was joyful. It wasn't sad—it wasn't sad because in this event it wasn't, you know, what a horrible loss this was. It was more about what an amazing woman she was.

And it's—as I say, the thing—as far as I'm concerned, is that if the person has a relationship with a minister—because I go to so many, we go to quite a few funerals, as I'm in that demographic—and so many of them you go to, the minister says, "Well, I met the family yesterday and I had to find out who they were," and things like this, "and I hear he's a wonderful person but I have no knowledge myself." And as I say, with my dad's, with knowing [the priest] and knowing the church, and for him it's just like coming home.

Even when [the priest] gave her homily she was speaking as a person who didn't just know him in passing, like she knew him. And I like that because it made her be able to speak a lot more personally in a lot more heartfelt way. I mean, not that it wouldn't be heartfelt if she was talking about someone she didn't know quite as well. It would still be lovely, but there was a personal connection there that was nice.

A big turn-off for me is when the officiant is—is that the right word? The person who's leading the ceremony. The minister. The priest. The pastor. Whatever. And I know it's hard for them, right? When they don't know the person. But it's just somehow it just feels like you're a number, right? This person doesn't really know that person and yet they're expected to say something really meaningful and deep about them. And that's just not possible if they didn't know of them. And then they rely on people to tell them things so they could say something. And it just comes off feeling very fake and not—it's just not, it's not a very genuine experience. It doesn't feel genuine. It doesn't feel like that person really means it. Whatever it is they're saying.

Other ways the funeral may be *personalized* are significant, such as the choice of music, readings, objects, or the incorporation of additional cultural elements such as a bagpiper:

They loved that it was so personal about my mom.... So many said, "Oh, your mother would have loved this. Your mother would have loved these roses. Your mother would have loved this piper." And I said, "Oh God, because she picked it out." But yes, I think everyone felt good about the sendoff, really about the tribute, I think, to my mom. They really enjoyed the funeral. I've had people say that's the best funeral they have attended because it was relaxed. It was warm and friendly and personal. And yes, emotional of course. I don't know what other kinds of funerals they've been to, but they enjoyed this one.

Participants in this research, whether routine or occasional practitioners, understand good funerals to be relational, to reflect the life and the relationships of the deceased. Although this may involve personalization of the funeral to reflect the deceased, it is not ultimately about the personal experience of participants but about their relationships with the deceased and the support they can offer one another.

What participants consider a good funeral is a contrast to how many clergy speak of what makes for a good funeral. Clergy tend to emphasize the funeral as being about God and setting the life of the deceased in a broader Christian narrative of hope anchored in the resurrection of Jesus. This prompts them to focus on managing and minimizing requests for eulogies and personalization to ensure this religious content comes through, although these elements are a priority for participants since they facilitate relational connection.

To conclude, participants in this research make personal choices about religious practice in a religiously diverse context. However, they recognize that these choices are shaped by networks of relationships, past and present, and they understand these events corporately as much as individually. These practices, therefore, are not primarily understood as expressing or forming personal faith commitments, but rather as corporate relational events that emerge from and shape networks of relationships where individuals are valued as part of a family and broader community. This approach resonates with Joris Geldhof's assessment of the liturgy as a critique of individualism since it is "intrinsically social and collective"[35]:

> The liturgy can, and perhaps should, play a role in confronting people with their arrogance and self-deceit, in bringing people together, in sending people out to meet others, in inspiring them to engage with their neighbors and communities, and to reaching people who are otherwise forgotten. Very clearly, the liturgy shows that every human being is unique, worthy, and equal. Nothing less than the image of God, who, unlike human beings, loves everyone without distinction and without imposing conditions, warrants this. This image of God is beautifully reflected in the liturgy.[36]

The occasional practitioners in this research have a deep and intuitive sense for this corporate and relational dimension of the liturgy. They are among those who are brought together by the liturgy and who have the potential to discover and extend love without distinction through the liturgy. This resonates with Cláudio Carvalhaes's eco-liturgical theological emphasis on resisting individualism and instead recognizing the interrelatedness of all beings:

> Thus, subjects of eco-liturgical liberation theologies must move away from the modern notion of emancipation and autonomy. The pretense of

---

[35] Geldhof, *Liturgy and Secularism*, 134.
[36] Geldhof, *Liturgy and Secularism*, 135.

autonomy and emancipation created a notion of self that is divided, centered on an illusion of individual indivisibility and fulness that is marked by economic historical developments. This atomized sense of self dismantled intertwined notions of life and self that are related to the land and all its living beings.[37]

Occasional practitioners embody a relational approach to religious practice that can invite all participants to resist modern notions of individual cognitive assent as the measure of ritual sincerity and liturgical legitimacy.

Theological Contributions of Occasional Practitioners

I have chosen to focus on three liturgical theological themes—the material, emotional, and relational—because they are *deep currents* that flow through the qualitative data. Although I have selected specific examples and quotations in the discussion above, these themes crystallize broader patterns. Furthermore, these three themes are interconnected. As many of the examples indicate, the material, emotional, and relational are bound up with one another in the liturgical experience of participants.

These three themes express liturgical theological insights "from below"—from those whose voices have been silenced or who have simply not spoken—and offer *a critique of theology done "from above."* They challenge theological work that has focused on liturgical texts and theoretical concepts, and on individual participants or personal faith and formation. The dimensions of Christian worship that matter most to many occasional practitioners are strikingly removed from the theologizing of academic theologians. It is baffling to attempt to hold together these conversations with occasional practitioners and a primary theology of liturgy as the "perichoresis of the Trinity,"[38] for example, or even the ubiquitous idea of full, conscious, and active participation.[39] The liturgical theological reflections of occasional practitioners are exquisitely ordinary.

---

[37] Carvalhaes, *Ritual at World's End*, 35.
[38] Fagerberg, *Theologia Prima*.
[39] *Sacrosanctum Concilium*, Constitution on the Sacred Liturgy (1963), http://www.vatican.va/archive/hist_councils/ii_vatican_council/documents/vat-ii_const_19631204_sacrosanctum-concilium_en.html.

At the same time, these themes "throw flashes of light" on a chaotic liturgical landscape through which academic theologians pick their way. These themes emerging from the experience of participants *speak into discussions in academic liturgical theology*, including conversations about sacramentality and secularism, as the brief references throughout suggest. Any one of these themes merits a volume in its own right; my goal here is only to point to possible connections that could fuel further research and reflection. Although occasional practitioners may not have theological vocabulary, their experience can contribute to liturgical theology, and can even bring awareness to how ritual experts and professional theologians experience liturgy as material, emotional, and relational, as in the vignette at the beginning of this chapter.

Finally, the themes of materiality, emotion, and relationship as described by occasional practitioners point to an *inexpressibility of religious experience* that has long been recognized in the Christian tradition. It is not simply that occasional practitioners do not have the theological language to describe their liturgical experience; it is also that their experience is beyond verbal description. They remind ritual experts to exercise caution when making claims about that which cannot be circumscribed by language or concept, or grasped individually. Occasional practitioners invite ritual experts to take seriously intuitive and relational expressions of the inexpressible, of "experiences that are beyond the capacity of speech to mediate."[40]

It is crucial to keep in mind, however, that these three themes are *specific to this case*: this series of interviews, anchored in these three congregations, in the Anglican Church of Canada, in Toronto, in the 2010s. Although echoes in liturgical theological scholarship, as well as in Nancy Ammerman's approach to religion as practice,[41] suggest there might be parallels and comparisons to be made in other settings, I make no claim that this reflects "the liturgical

---

[40] Mitchell, *Meeting Mystery*, xvi.
[41] These three themes reflect central topics in the sociological study of religion as practice, as described by Ammerman, including the materiality of lived religion and the emotional expression of religion. There are also significant resonances with embodiment in religious practice, religious aesthetics, narrative, and, as discussed in the next chapter, morality. In these ways, the liturgical experience and reflection of occasional practitioners have the potential to contribute to research on lived religion and sociology of religion that centers on religion as practice. Ammerman, "Rethinking Religion"; Ammerman, *Studying Lived Religion*.

theology" of occasional practitioners beyond this immediate case study. I do hope that this provides one example of what listening deeply to occasional practitioners looks like and what might be gained from doing theology with occasional practitioners. I hope it inspires similar listening and learning in other settings, especially on the part of ritual experts, including academic theologians and clergy. To return to the image of Jesus and the Samaritan woman—what is being whispered at other wells?

10
Occasional Practitioners and the Concerns of Ritual Experts

Near the end of an interview with a younger priest, I ask what he hopes to learn from my conversations with occasional practitioners, especially those connected to baptisms:

I: Are there questions you would hope that I would ask, or themes that you would want to know more about?

R: Hmm. I'd just be interested to know whether—you know, to what degree they actually sort of understand what's going on. That's kind of my main interest. Like what is happening here? What are the—what is your child or what are you getting yourself into? I guess that's the main thing that I'd want to know.

I: What would be a sign that they know what they're getting themselves into? How would you know that they know?

R: Well, probably that they're coming a bit [attending worship]. Yeah, actually, probably that'd be the best sign that they knew what they were getting themselves into. But also, I mean, if it's a catechetical thing, like creedal thing, that they sort of like—they just have some basic understanding of the Trinity, the Father, Son, Holy Spirit, like what Jesus has done for us, the resurrection of the dead, the Holy Spirit in the church, that kind of stuff. Just like the basics, you know? Like a basic sense of what objectively the Christian faith is.

I: This may seem like a really obvious question, but why would that be important for you, that knowledge?

R: Because I just want some sort of quantifiable understanding of whether I'm doing my job or whether it's having an effect, yeah?

I: Right.

R: Why would that help me?

Occasional Religious Practice. Sarah Kathleen Johnson, Oxford University Press.
© Oxford University Press 2025. DOI: 10.1093/9780197806579.003.0011

I: Or why would you want them to have that knowledge? Or why would it be important for you for them to be able to kind of articulate that in that process?

R: Well, I mean, I want people to have a relationship with Jesus. But I also think that like a lot hangs on whether or not they would get the basics of the Christian faith, because it's sort of the thing that—the thing that helps you persevere against life's troubles. And I think that without it, without the Christian faith, it's hard to—it's hard to stand up under what you're going to live through with any kind of hope. So, it's a hope issue, too.

Although occasional practitioners do at times speak to the questions raised by this priest, I expect that he would be disappointed by responses that often describe God as "something more," tradition in terms of stability and comfort, and the life of faith as being a "good person" rather than the doctrinal specificity he outlines. However, I also expect that he would not find them to be without spiritual resources for persevering in times of struggle, or without hope.

In the previous chapter, the priorities of occasional practitioners were the focus, and I considered possible points of connection to ongoing conversations in liturgical theology. Now, I consider how occasional practitioners address concerns that are central to many liturgical theologians and Christian clergy. These themes include (1) how participants speak of God, (2) how they understand themselves in relation to the Christian tradition, and (3) the ways in which they connect liturgy and ethics, especially in the context of everyday life. Unlike the themes that are central to occasional practitioners, the topics explored here are less pervasive in the qualitative data.

God

In a discussion of liturgical theology, it is reasonable to ask whether and how participants in this research speak of God. Although the priest who raised the question above would likely be discouraged by the lack of "creedal" content in their reflections, occasional practitioners do mention God in interviews. As is clear in Chapter 3, occasional practitioners have diverse religious identities, including identifying as atheist, agnostic, and indifferently nonreligious. Nevertheless, practitioners with a range of religious identities speak of how they understand who God is and what God does.

Many occasional practitioners with a broad range of religious identities affirm that there is "something more" or "some higher power." They speak of this "something" in surprisingly consistent ways:

> We are convinced there's a higher energy, if you want to call it that way. That we know that there is something more than our physical world.

> There is a need in human beings to be able to acknowledge, to be able to feel, to be able to speak to something greater than themselves. And that need has always been there and will always be there. How we do that seems to be up for grabs right now.

> I suppose I believe that somewhere out there is a greater power that is somewhat looking out for us.

> I like to think of the concept of God as being quite broad and open. I don't think about the concept of God as being like this guy, right? So, I like to think that the concept of God is—can be just about anything that helps people, that just helps people. And yeah, I don't—I haven't quite—I kind of feel like, I actually kind of believe in the power of prayer in a kind of the power—the collective power of people to think positively about something. I know I sound like a nutcase [laughter]. . . . I just think that people can help people. And no, we don't need this authoritarian figure, if I can describe the Anglican god that way. Yeah. I kind of resist that idea. So, I don't need to define—I guess I don't need to define for myself what it is.

> I believe in a greater, like greater meaning to life. I believe that there's, like—I don't know—what we can call God.

> Because I believe there's something, the god language, it's just like, okay, that's your something. That's what your definition of what the something is. I'm like, "You can call it God, you can call it whatever you want to call it," but there's something, so I'm like, "Okay, that's acceptable. I'm comfortable with that."

> We'd accept it—the fact that there is something stronger, something out there, something powerful, something that we might not really understand.

> I have maybe a more arm's-length relationship with what God really is.

> There is probably a—I don't know—a spirit, an energy, a force, something out there. But [my husband] would have difficulty trying to describe what that is. But he wouldn't say that there is one God.
>
> I hope that there is a higher being, but I don't believe in any particular theology surrounding that I guess is where I would put myself. . . . Yeah, so that's—I guess why I don't ascribe to any particular faith. I hope that there is something beyond what we can observe and it seems like there should be.
>
> I like the, I guess the idea that God is sort of omnipresence. It's just an energy that comes over time. And also that God is within—it's within and it's without, and if it's all around, it's everything.

Although there are a handful of participants in this research who would confidently claim faith in God, many participants are very honest about their questions about God. There is an underlying sense of humility and uncertainty regarding the existence and nature of God in many of these comments.

Another common sentiment which occasional practitioners express is that God spans religious traditions and is *not particular to Christianity*:

> In the end, I think it's all the same, the same Head Honcho up there, if he is up there, I hope.
>
> So to me, God is God. So, Baptist path, Anglican, Muslim, whatever it is, we all pray to the same God. So, denomination isn't as important to me.
>
> At the end of the day, we all believe in God and we may practice differently but all roads lead to what we believe in and that God, that there is a higher power.

These insights suggest a certain ambiguity and openness. Most occasional practitioners in this research acknowledge "something more," although the specifics are vague and vary.

In keeping with this general sense of God, occasional practitioners rarely mention *Jesus*. This is especially noteworthy in the context of conversations about Christian worship including baptism and funerals, which have strong Christocentric elements, and Christmas and Easter Sunday, which mark the birth and resurrection of Jesus. Nevertheless, most participants do not bring up Jesus and are reticent to discuss Jesus if I ask, as I started to do once I noticed this absence:

I: Back to the question of the place of Jesus or God language. What's the place of that for you either in your own experience and also in the context of the funeral?

R: It's not language that I would ever use, but I'm comfortable with it. We certainly give the answer whenever there's a children's talk. So, you would've seen the children's talk even at 9:00 and often the children's talk involves [the priest] asking the kids a question. And the kind of joke is, if you answered "Jesus," you're pretty safe. The answer is probably "Jesus," if not, maybe "God." Anyways, that's kind of an aside, but I don't know. I'm comfortable with the language. I'm comfortable with the discussions as long as I'm not the one doing it because I'm not comfortable. I'm not very comfortable talking about Jesus and talking about God. Saying a prayer is fine; listening to it is fine and having it, whoever's giving the sermon or whatever, relating things to real life.

I: The cross [jewelry you wear] is a symbol that's connected to Jesus. Is this "something stronger, higher power" connected to Jesus for you and for your family?

R: Sometimes it's nothing physical. Sometimes it's just a feeling, a connection. You could close your eyes and you feel if you're not looking at a cross or you're not in a church, you still have that feeling. I think it just gets stronger as you get older. It's hard to explain. Even if you're not wearing a cross, you can still feel that you can talk or pray and it's still being heard.

Although some participants speak of Jesus as a moral teacher, as in the discussion of ethics below, and some mention Jesus in relation to forgiveness, it is clear that Jesus is not at the center of how they understand God or Christian worship.

The *Holy Spirit* is even more absent. The Holy Spirit is mentioned only seven times in interviews with non-expert participants, and three of these are in the context of the baptismal formula, and one in relation to naming a religious institution. It is also noteworthy that three of the four participants who mention the Holy Spirit are routine practitioners at the time of the interview. At the same time, it seems like speaking of God as Holy Spirit has potential to resonate with those who identify as spiritual and with those more comfortable speaking of God as a mysterious and elusive "something more."

Although they generally describe God as "something more," participants have a sense that this higher power is *invested in their well-being*. They describe God as a "guide," "comfort," and "protector," a constant companion in life's most difficult moments. These ways of thinking of God often come up in the context of discussing what participants hope to pass on to their children:

I'm trying to teach all that [to my children], that there is a God, he's looking out for him or for her, and that he's always with her and he can help you navigate your feelings. He's the inner voice.

And God is always watching and always there and you may not get the answer you're looking for right away, but there is somebody other than Mommy and Daddy, somebody that is always watching over you and helping guide you through life.

It really is just your own personal way of connecting with God and the universe, and this is your way of figuring out how to steer your life in a direction that you want and the direction you've been coming through those obstacles in life, whether they're good, they're bad, they're ugly, whatever it may be.

I think it's important to believe in something other than yourself, especially when you're going through things. And these kids, they're going through a lot more now with social media and with the peer pressures. I mean, I shouldn't say a lot more; it's no different. It's just they're going through a bit different than we were. So I just think whether it be God or whatever, Jesus or whoever they want to, I do think it's important that they understand that they can lean on or pray to or think of someone other than themselves to get them through whatever it is besides their parents.

For [my daughter] I explained like, you know, this is what I believe, "I believe in God and when we pray to God, this is his house [the church], it's like visiting your parents in their house, like paying respect. And God is omnipresent and omnipotent, but we also make that effort to visit him in his house, just like when we visit your grandparents in their house." So she's like, "Oh, okay."

It's a belief. You believe that you came from a bigger power. You believe you're going to go. Having something close to your heart will take care of your heart, your soul, now and in the end. When you're alone and when you feel desperate, if you can speak to this power that you've held close to your heart, you will never be lost. You will always have that thing there.

But there are times where—on a daily basis, I'll have a conversation with God. Just sort of started waiting for him. And in a state of career transition as well. So, always look to him for some guidance and advice.

> I can pray for my child to be protected, but realistically I know that God can't stop a car from hitting my child in the street or a gunman shooting up a concert and I'm at it. Like I don't believe in God has that—like just because I prayed to God, I'm in this specialized bubble that will never be—so in a way I think it's more of a, what's the word I'm looking for? It makes me feel better to have faith as a person, to feel like there's something protecting, or there's something more than just what we have here. I think it's like a personal comfort.

Many participants speak of this potential for an intimate connection with a higher power. Those with evangelical backgrounds tend to speak of God in more personal terms as someone they can engage in personal conversation through prayer.

In addition to this image of God as a comforting companion and guide, several participants describe God as a *judge*, especially in relation to the afterlife:

> I believe there's God. I believe that his son came down to earth and lived amongst us and taught us. And he would be coming back one day. We better be ready. Because I don't think he's going to like what he sees [laughter]. But, yeah, I don't know. I just, I believe. It's just something I've always believed. I can't not believe. I don't know how else to explain it.

> I certainly believe that there's a higher being. I certainly believe that we're judged in order to get into heaven. I think baptism could be part of it, but I think it's also being a good person.

> I believe that there is a God and that there is life after. And that if I do good to people here, then I will be treated good on the other side.

Some occasional practitioners do connect their understanding of God, ethics, and liturgical practice, as discussed further below.

In these comments from occasional practitioners, we can hear echoes of Tomáš Halík's invitation to dialogue with those for whom God is a question:

> The conviction as gradually matured within me that God approaches us more as a question than an answer. Maybe the one whom we mean by the word God is more present to us when we hesitate to say the word too hastily. Maybe he feels better with us in the open space of the question than in the constrictingly narrow gully of our answers, our definitive statements, our

definitions and our notions. Let us treat his Holy Name with the greatest restraint and care.[1]

At the same time, the Anglican liturgy is replete with definitive statements about God known in specificity as the Trinity, not only as "something more." The contrast between the explicit and substantive claims about God made in Christian worship and the gentle theism of occasional practitioners is striking. However, occasional practice readily accommodates this substance, perhaps pointing back to the centrality of the material more than the linguistic, the emotional more than the conceptual, and the relational more than the personal.

The experience of "something more" in connection with Anglican liturgy in Toronto has parallels to theologian and musicologist Hanna Rijken's research on the surprising introduction and warm reception of the practice of Anglican choral evensong in the Netherlands since the 1980s. Dutch participants in choral evensong describe their experience in ways that combine aesthetic and religious metaphors, interpreting it as both beautiful and sacred:[2]

> It seems to us that the participants in the choral evensongs, both believers, ex-believers and non-believers, attend this "new" emerging musical ritual because they look for "something" which they do not find elsewhere. This "something" seems to be profundity, deep experiences, experiences of transcendence evoked by the beauty of the music. For some participants it is encountering "the higher," for other participants it is the encounter with God.[3]

Rijken situates this response to choral evensong in the context of the Dutch religious landscape and draws on the work of Richard Kearney to interpret it as a "returning to God after God," where one is "free to choose between faith and nonfaith."[4] For Kearney and Rijken, this is rooted in a "critical retrieval of sacred things that have passed" that also have "an unrealized potentiality or promise to be more fully realized in the future."[5] The dynamics that Rijken identifies in relation to the Anglican evensong in the Netherlands may also be part of what is behind how occasional participants in Anglican liturgy in Toronto speak about God, as well as about tradition.

---

[1] Tomáš Halík, *I Want You to Be: On the God of Love* (Notre Dame: University of Notre Dame Press, 2016), 3.
[2] Hanna Rijken, *My Soul Doth Magnify: The Appropriation of Choral Evensong in the Netherlands* (Amsterdam: VU University Press, 2020), 30.
[3] Rijken, *My Soul Doth Magnify*, 129.
[4] Richard Kearney, as quoted in Rijken, *My Soul Doth Magnify*, 130.
[5] Kearney, as quoted in Rijken, *My Soul Doth Magnify*, 130.

Tradition

Tradition, the dynamic historic practice of the Christian church lived out today and the distinctive liturgical and theological expression of the Anglican communion, is a central concern for theologians and clergy. As Cláudio Carvalhaes writes, citing prolific and influential liturgist Robert Taft:

> What is at stake here is the engagement of traditions in order to foster and expand it, and not the appeal to dismiss it. This discussion has resonance even in Roman Catholic quarters. When speaking of tradition, Robert Taft says:
> "There is no ideal form of the liturgy from the past that must be imitated. Liturgy has always changed. We don't study the past in order to imitate it. Tradition is not the past. Tradition is the life of the church today in dynamic continuity with all that comes before. The past is dead, but tradition is alive, tradition is now."
> In keeping with the engagement and *aggiornamento* of tradition, we are trying to honor tradition and make it alive to our day.[6]

Occasional practitioners living the tradition in our day speak often of "tradition," although what they mean by tradition may be quite different from the diversity of ways in which liturgical scholars and clergy understand the concept. Concepts of tradition are evident in how occasional practitioners speak of religious identity in relation to cultural heritage and family background in Chapter 4, as well as their motivations in terms of cultural heritage as addressed in Chapter 5, and in the discussion of materiality in Chapter 9.

Participants in this research speak of tradition in several ways. Some associate tradition with a feeling of *history*:

> I actually have a degree in history as well. So, understanding how the church has quite an essential role in education and social activities throughout the past 2000 years or whatever. In understanding how the church is really in many ways thought to be an example of almost like a personification of mankind's attempt to understand existence and how we came to be and

---

[6] Carvalhaes, *Eucharist and Globalization*, 258.

what is knowledge and what is good—all those things that we can't really understand. Church is an excellent way to kind of channel those feelings into something positive and something beautiful. So, I think that's a strong spiritual force in itself even if it does originate kind of within the community or within the people. So, I like that. It appeals to me. And I think it's something good.

R: When you take them up to actually be baptized and that ritual, I guess that part of it. Other parts of the service have changed and become modernized, but that particular part to me feels ancient and you can understand how old that particular physical ritual is within the church. So maybe that feels the most significant. Obviously, it's designed to make it feel significant. That's certainly the part that always stands out is that moment.
I: What feels ancient about it?
R: The words feel ancient and the marking on the forehead is a very physical act with symbolic meaning, I guess. You understand that according to the church teachings that this has always been the way that things have been done. This is how we mark the entrance into the church family. I can see you're always taught that it is or whether it is actually the ancient practice or not. That's certainly the way it's portrayed, I guess.

Some participants use tradition to speak of *worship style*, most often when contrasting experiences of worship in different communities:

Traditional meaning like hymns—when we sing songs it's more like choral and hymns instead of—Because I did attend like, not just baptisms, but also a different church where it's more like rock music and hip and that's really not what I know of worship. Nothing wrong with it. It's just not my type of worship.

So, we ended up going with the Anglican church, which is where I was baptized anyway.... The thing that we like about it is that it's conservative. For me, I like the sort of conservative church services. I have attended some that are a bit more modern. You know, they have like a lot of like the band and the music and all the things. That's nice I think for when you're young. But when I'm bringing up my children in the church, I'd like them to [experience] a little bit more of the ... traditional structure of a church service.

Perhaps related to this use of tradition, some participants set tradition *in opposition to spirituality and religion*:

> [Baptism is] both traditional and spiritual for [my mother-in-law]. Traditional in a sense that baptism, she's gone to many, she baptized her children, so it's definitely a tradition in that way, and then spiritual in that she just believes in the spirit side of things and tapping into that bigger picture of life and that it isn't just what we see and feel.

> Even though the rite of baptism itself doesn't have or doesn't hold as strong of a religious connotation for us, it was still important for us to do it. Part of that is past generations, the tradition of it, and part of it is our own beliefs, needing to make sure the kids are grounded in something as opposed to nothing.

Although tradition is used in different ways by these participants, each captures a sense of continuity and stability across time, in contrast to novelty, and each establishes a notion of tradition existing apart from personal conviction and individual spiritual experience.

Occasional practitioners value the sense of *continuity and stability* that they experience as tradition. Turning to trusted practices, especially in times of loss and disorientation, is a source of comfort. This is especially the case when a loved one dies:

> I think that, well, I think the whole is not having to figure out what to do. When someone dies, there's a lot to put together in a very short period of time. Part of the way I think people get through it is they know what the tradition is. They know they don't have to think up what they're going to do. They know what they're going to do. They know they're going to call in the funeral home and they know they're going to have to get a burial plot or a cremation plot or something. Like they know all those things. If somebody had said to me, "Oh, I'll do a funeral service for you. You tell me what you want, you make up the service, and I'll do it," I would have been beside myself because I don't know what we're going to do here. Whereas you just had to follow along with what the church already has prepared and has done

for centuries. That's a very stress-free way to get through a very stressful situation.

And knowing it's a tradition, right? Yeah, exactly, I know exactly what to expect when my parents pass, I know what that will look like. I know that—my family's been in this area since the early 1800s. We have a really old cemetery where all of—for hundreds of years my family has been buried. So I guess there's something comforting knowing exactly what's going to happen, right? When this happens, I know what the service looks like, I know where to take them. At a time of struggle there's a comfort in familiarity and in not having to make these decisions and discover these things anew, right? It's something you've done before. You can focus on your mourning and your understanding and not have to worry about figuring out where's the cemetery, who do I contact, how does this look, how do we arrange this? And I think that's the comfort in familiarity and tradition for me.

The familiarity of the service, really, it's comforting when you can—yeah. That feeling of—it's ritual, but it's that feeling of, I know what is going to happen and I can rest and not be anxious of what's going to happen. Because actually, I didn't think about it this morning, but the opening sentences, those readings, just kind of—yeah. You could just kind of let go once that happens.

In this sense, the specifics of the Christian or Anglican tradition matter to occasional practitioners primarily because they are what feels familiar and comfortable to them, perhaps because of their family background, or because of overlaps with the Roman Catholic ritual system, or the cultural dominance of Christian practices in Toronto, or other factors. Although this specific tradition suits their needs, certain occasional practitioners describe how any familiar ritual could fulfill the same function:

There's something about the tradition and the ritual of it. I think it's really important. It gives you some kind of—I wouldn't even say control, but just some kind of—I think rituals can be comforting in a time of loss like that. It gives you sort of this is what happens next because it's like your whole world is a bit turned upside down at the time and it gives you some structure to hang onto, I guess?... You kind of need that. Like, I needed that.

> It's the ritual, not the religion. The people need rituals. I think it's a human—I think it's part of who we are as human beings. I don't know the science behind it. But it's very clear to me that human beings like ritual. And if we didn't have it, then we create it, you know?

What is stable and familiar is highly contextual, especially in an increasingly nonreligious and religiously diverse context like Toronto. Nevertheless, Christian practices remain part of this stable and familiar ritual system for many people. Occasional practitioners value tradition for its stability and comfort within their context more than for the theological specificity of its content. In other words, they tend to value the experience and idea of tradition more than the specifics of the Christian tradition. This resonates with an emphasis on the experience of Christian worship as more emotional than conceptual and more relational than personal.

Although the broader emphasis tends to be on stability, there are two participants, both of whom would identify as Christian and one who is a routine practitioner, who emphasize and value *tradition as dynamic* as well as stable:

> I think tradition—I mean there's a lot of nostalgia in tradition. It's comforting because it's familiar. In a world of change, everything's changing. And it's something that evolves more than changes. I think the church is trying to change and evolve. They keep current and relevant. And that's what I like about the Anglican church because—especially our church. My youngest is a lesbian and so, they've been very accepting of that. They're accepting of gay people. They're accepting of a lot of people that in other churches wouldn't be welcomed. Everybody's welcomed, even people from outside the Anglican faith, well, they're welcome to take communion. So, I think when I say tradition, it's not because I don't want change. It's just because it's familiar. But it's nice when they make some changes. I think it's refreshing. You want to stay relevant. You want to say—you know the church has to grow and keep relevant or people will stop going. So, it's traditional and familiar at a time when the world's changing but recognizing that it needs to evolve as well. So, they're always trying to make some changes. But that's hard. People don't like change.
>
> I know that people in my family—my extended family who complain of the Anglican church being old-fashioned or complain about the Christian church as being against gays or against women, whatever, pedophilia, it's

all lumped together. And they only go to church if there's a funeral, if there's a baptism, if there's a wedding. And they say, look at it, it hasn't changed. But those are rituals that don't change because they are needed. Because they are ritual. And if you went on a Sunday when everyone was dancing or when there was a discussion about gay marriage from the pulpit, you might think, oh, I guess it changes just like culture changes and community changes. So, yeah, it's a big problem for the church.

As this participant observes, the dynamism of tradition may be less visible to those who practice only occasionally. At the same time, through their presence, occasional practitioners are also shaping the tradition through the selection of certain practices and the integration of different ritual systems, as discussed in Chapter 6.

With this dynamism in mind, it is worth considering the theological perspectives of occasional practitioners in relation to the definition of tradition offered by philosopher Alasdair MacIntyre:

> A tradition is an *argument extended through time* in which certain fundamental agreements are defined and redefined in terms of two kinds of conflict: those with critics and enemies external to the tradition who reject all or at least key parts of those fundamental agreements, and those internal, interpretive debates through which the meaning and rationale of the fundamental agreements come to be expressed and by whose progress a tradition is constituted.[7]

Through their presence and participation in Christian worship, occasional practitioners as primary theologians are part of the argument as either external or internal participants, depending on the identities and motivations of the individuals and communities involved. However, their experiences and perspectives have often been ignored or marginalized. Including occasional practitioners in the conversation requires learning to converse in new ways—ways that have space for material, emotional, and relational forms of interpretation and expression that challenge the conceptual, verbal, and individual frameworks that have long structured the argument and its effects.

---

[7] Alasdair MacIntyre, *Whose Justice? Which Rationality?* (Notre Dame: University of Notre Dame Press, 1988), 12. Emphasis added.

Ethics

The integral relationship between Sunday worship and everyday life, between liturgy and ethics, is central for clergy and liturgical theologians. This concern is at the heart of Cláudio Carvalhaes's liturgical theology:[8]

> More than just a set of actions carried out within the context of the gathered community worship, at its very core worship speaks to a lifestyle involving every facet of daily living.[9]

Forging connections between occasional practice and daily life is a concern often mentioned in conversations with clergy, specifically a desire that a baptism not be an isolated event but rather manifest in a life of daily discipleship, ideally including routine participation in corporate worship. Occasional practitioners do link their religious practice with daily life, especially to the idea of being a "good person," which they see as shaped in part by occasional liturgical participation.

Many occasional practitioners speak of a desire to be a *good person*, to remember their loved ones with honesty as good people, and especially to raise their children to be good people:

> I want to be a good person. I want to live my life believing in something.

> I just live my life so that I can serve like my family and live in a way that I think is like righteous and good.

> I just hope that [my grandchildren] can do the right thing and they're honest and they're good people, just like their parents. I can only speak for my son because I know he came from a good family and he's always, he's a very giving, kind, loving person, always has been and always will be.

> I just want [my son] to be a good person and be kind to people.

> It sounds a little superficial to say, but just encouraging her to just—[my niece and nephew] to just be good people.

> To be good people, to be caring and kind and respectful. I think that's important.

---

[8] Carvalhaes, *Eucharist and Globalization*; Carvalhaes, *What's Worship Got to Do with It?*
[9] Carvalhaes, *Liturgies from Below*, xiv.

Being a good person involves the types of characteristics already mentioned in the quotations above, and elaborated here:

> Be kind to people. Have a sense of inclusivity and make sure that nobody feels left behind, no matter who they are. That's really important to me.

> Of course, all parents have things that they want them to be. To me the most important things are being kind and being honest. If I could only pass on a couple of things to my children, those would be the two.... I hope they are nice people. If I could only have one thing from my children, it would be that they're nice people.

> Be a kind, loving person. Be a kind person. Don't hurt people. Try and help people. Don't be mean spirited. Be giving, be generous. I think also appreciate things, appreciating the things you have, and the life you have, and the people that are around you. And principles.... At least be a good person. But also make yourself happy. You have to do things that, you know, you have to self-love. You have to love yourself and follow your own inner guidance and find out what that is.

Most of the characteristics that participants associate with being a good person are not necessarily tied to Christianity or religion.

Occasional practitioners are very clear that *nonreligious people can be good people*, as in the examples of nonreligious godparenting discussed in Chapter 5, and that good values can be engaged apart from the specific teachings of Christianity, as these participants describe:

> I think if you're a good person, you're a good person that's just—whatever that form may be. You may not be religious, but if you're good in terms of how you treat other people. Which again is a lot of the tenets of Christianity. You may not be Christian, but you are Christian-like. And that's fine. Everybody can't always be the same.

> But I sometimes think about the—that was my upbringing, right? And if I hadn't had that upbringing, would I be a different person? Because there's a certain kind of moral, sort of substance there, I guess. How you act. If you're good to people. If you help people. Stepping up when you need to. But those aren't necessarily strictly Christian values, right? They're values of many different religions, like helping your neighbors, all that kind of stuff. Like that's just basic stuff.

I know for myself, it's not so much the straight religious teachings I want to pass on, it's the principles behind the religion, so that "do unto others" type of ideas and respecting other people and being good and being kind, not necessarily the story of the Bible. Because again, the ideas are there and it's the ideas I want to pass down, not necessarily the stories that I want to pass down. For me, as long as I'm passing down the principles and the ideas of the church, I feel like that's the way of honoring them being a part of the church without necessarily having to read the specific stories from the Bible to demonstrate the concepts and the behaviors that I want to pass on.

At the same time, there are also a couple of participants who have a sense that *church people are more likely to be good people.* This is partly because of awareness that the church does good things for church members and the broader community, like sponsoring refugees, providing Christmas gifts for families in need, distributing food to those who are hungry, organizing youth programs, speaking up against injustice, and more. However, there is also a sense that there is something formative about connecting with a church community:

> Like I said, there's just many good things that come out of being connected to [the church]. It seems to be a source of good people, right? Yeah, mostly good people, although there are always jerks everywhere you go in life. People go there for different reasons, but I would say 85 percent are there to do good works and to be kind to each other.

> To me it's common sense, right? It's being a good person, right? So it's less about sort of the prayers and the actual lessons. Sometimes the lessons are pretty good, but it's less about the actual lessons that you actually are hearing in the church and more about it helping to develop your understanding of you as a person so that you start thinking about others. It's hard to do, by the way. First and you know you're more kind, considerate, thoughtful. Some of those characteristics that I appreciate and that I saw with my parents and that you get from that community at the church. Because they are, as a group, the people at the church are not a cross section of humanity, I think they're better. I don't know why. Well, part of it is there—I don't know, it's like the attitude and the just being involved in the church helps that and helps people develop, I think.

These quotations begin to point toward the links that occasional practitioners make between religious participation and being a good person.

After exploring how participants reflect on God and tradition in quite general terms, I was genuinely surprised to return to the qualitative data with the question of ethics and discover how often occasional practitioners *anchor being a good person in scripture and the teachings of Jesus*. There are many who point to the "golden rule":

> I think one of the best sayings attributed to Jesus is "do unto others as you would have them do to you." That was the golden rule that we learned in public school. And I wasn't even aware that it was a religious saying or writing until I went to Sunday school. I just thought that's the golden rule and everybody should live by it.

> Oh, my core beliefs and my values. I would have to say lots of mine, my values, were probably from part of my raising: do unto others as you would have others do unto you.

> Well, I guess it's be a good person really, like all the teachings of any religion really is like the do unto others as you want them to do unto you. And which is like the golden rule for I think every religion out there, that's kind of the big one. Just grow up, like be a caring, loving person and that's the rest of it, behave yourself, I would hope. That's how I was brought up.

> I mean like be kind, be kind to all people. Just be a good person. Like treat people the way you want to be treated. Kind of live that way, live in that way.

> I'm okay with the golden rule and just being a kind person in general, helping those who are less fortunate than you are, and not being too high on yourself.

> Love your neighbor as yourself. These are all lovely because even though it's religious in nature here. It's the way you live your life, like being kind to other people, being respectful of other people.

This echoes Nancy Ammerman's sociological work on "Golden Rule Christians"[10] as a pervasive style of religiosity in the United States that needs

---

[10] Nancy Ammerman, "Golden Rule Christianity: Lived Religion in the American Mainstream," in *Lived Religion in America: Toward a History of Practice*, ed. David D. Hall (Princeton, NJ: Princeton University Press, 1997), 196–216.

to be understood on its own terms. Golden Rule Christianity is defined by practice, especially caring for those in need and living out religious values in daily life, rather than by religious ideology. The Golden Rule Christians in Ammerman's research affirm transcendence and participate in congregations, in which they value opportunities to serve those in need, dynamic worship, and activities for children. In 1997, Ammerman argued that Golden Rule Christianity may be the dominant form of religiosity of middle-class suburban Americans across age, race, and gender. This approach to Christian ethics appears alive and well in Toronto, Canada, twenty years later.

The Ten Commandments are another common reference point mentioned in interviews with participants, either generally or in terms of specific commandments:

> That's why and I think even though I don't go to church ... as best as I could I do follow the commandments. I don't go to church, but I do follow the ideals. I pretty well follow the commandments. I haven't killed anybody. Like I don't cheat on my wife. For the most part, I don't break any of the commandments. Thou shall not lie—once in a while.

> Even though my father was not religious and my mother was slightly religious, we've always kind of held those Christian values, like the Ten Commandments and so on. I certainly hope that my daughter takes some values. I think there's a lot to be said for those, the practices of doing good and being part of a community. I think those are great values to have and I'd love to pass those on to my daughter.

> I'm trying to teach all that, that there is a God. . . . And that way [my daughter] has that basic there. And then the next level would be like the teachings of the Bible. Like not to covet your neighbor's things and to like share, to be kind, and to put yourself in someone else's shoes and to think of the poor. All those things are kind of second level to me. And then after that, then she could go into exploration and learn about other religions and other cultures.

> The importance of family, the importance of being nice to each other, and kind to each other, and being a good person—that can be religious or not religious. I think that's the beauty of the teachings like love thy neighbor and the Ten Commandments. It is a religious aspect, but ultimately, it's how you want to live your life and how you want to be as a person. I think that's it. Whether my children go to church every Sunday, I don't know if that really bothers me.

Occasional practitioners reference and value these explicitly religious and specifically Christian sources for understanding what it means to be a "good person."

Furthermore, occasional practitioners consistently see Christian practice, including occasional practice, as a source for this moral teaching for themselves and for their families. In the rare instances when participants reference the scripture text read during a worship service (this only occurs when I share the order of service with the full text printed), it is to make this type of moral connection, in this case citing the Beatitudes:

> I was looking through this again, the gospel from that service, I'm like, "Oh, yeah, that is one of my favorite, that's one of my favorite readings," because it's the idea everybody will eventually be made equal. If you're hungry now, you'll be full later. If you're sick now, you'll be fine later. But then the same thing in reverse, if you've lived a life of wealth at some point, you're going to feel the other end of that. And then again, the point of that being, if someone needs your help, give it to them. If they do something horrible to you, don't turn around and retaliate. Just accept and offer your other cheek because that's what makes you a good person because you don't know if you will, at some point, you might end up on the other side because everything balances out in the end.

Another participant mentions the specific reading at her child's baptism, the Parable of the Good Samaritan, as one of her favorites because of the values it teaches. However, participants are more likely to emphasize practices in general, such as preaching about scripture, space for reflection, and the overall message of Christian worship as forming themselves and their families as good people:

> I want her to be a good person. And that is—from what we were preached about as a child, and what we read, and what my grandparents taught me—is to love one another as you love yourself, to be that good person, to try to understand where people are coming from, why they might have done things. And I always say to my husband, you know, good people make bad choices. It doesn't mean they're bad people. And I think that's an essence, kind of what is being preached in some sermons.

> But to just about anybody if you read the story of Jesus right up to—I think the crucifixion is a bit much—but if you read the story of his life a lot of it is, you could find a lot of analogies for modern living in there that are good for your self-respect: dealing with people, dealing with unpleasant

people, things like that.... So that's still a philosophy that I hold onto is that if you—there are still lessons in there that are good for the modern world. That's why I still continue going to church. The sermons were still good.... You can go in, you can sit down and you get a good story, you get some good community out of it, and it's a good time to sit and just—it's food for thought is what that is. So that's why I still continue going. And now I don't go anymore because my weekends are tied up with family stuff and this, that, and the other thing. But that was, that's why I continued going for the longest time.

We believe that Jesus walked the earth to give us an example of how to live. Those who are ostracized are those that we should embrace first. Those who have made mistakes are the ones that you should learn from, rather than judge those who hurt or are hurting. That if you want to be forgiven, you have to forgive. Like it's very hard to forgive people, I think, who've done or people who have somehow failed in your eyes, but that's what we're called to do. We're supposed to look at Jesus as a metaphor for how to be better people. I hope my kids will always look at that example. Usually the message that we take away, like at the end of most services, is that love is the only thing that can heal. Everything. Hatred cannot heal. Revenge cannot heal. It just leads you to more revenge. It leads you to more anger, leads you to more frustration, but love, if you lead with love, if you lead with forgiveness, then go walk the earth like Jesus, which is the example.

Across generations, religious identities, and ways of relating to religion, there is a shared sense among participants in this research that being a good person matters and that, although it is possible to be a good person without practicing religion, religious practice can help instill these values. Occasional religious participation is part of instilling these values through worship practices that teach them, and through seeing them lived out by other people individually and in community.

Is being a "good person" the robust and subversive solidarity anchored in the ministry and teaching of Jesus Christ and the relationships among all beings that Cláudio Carvalhaes describes? Not necessarily. How occasional practitioners speak of God, tradition, and ethics is more akin to Christian Smith's concept of Moralistic Therapeutic Deism.[11] Nevertheless, it is a

---

[11] Christian Smith, *Soul Searching: The Religious and Spiritual Lives of American Teenagers* (Oxford: Oxford University Press, 2005), 162–163.

step in the direction Carvalhaes depicts, and it has the potential to become common ground. Carvalhaes suggests the following questions as preparation for coming together at the eucharistic table: "What injustices are we fighting together? What healing is needed? How can we engage the gifts of our people? Who should we invite?"[12] Occasional practitioners are engaged in these questions as well, and they may be a starting point for doing theology together in the context of occasional practice.

Occasional Practitioners' Reflections on Themes from Ritual Experts

These three themes, selected due to their centrality for ritual experts in the Christian tradition, including the clergy interviewed for this research, are addressed by occasional practitioners in Anglican liturgies in three congregations in Toronto. While participants certainly do not address these topics in the same manner as ritual experts do, the participants in this research have insights that can enrich the theology and practice of Christian worship. At minimum, a better understanding of how liturgical participants actually think of God, tradition, and ethics can help experts connect with them on the occasions when they do attend Christian liturgies.

Ideally, however, these ways of speaking of God, tradition, and ethics can be valued as liturgical theological perspectives from the margins. Like Halík's seekers, many occasional practitioners encounter God as a question, "something more" just out of reach while also comfortingly present. Tradition is related to connecting with "something more," especially through a sense of continuity and stability beyond oneself, particularly in difficult times, although the specific substance of this tradition is less important. In contrast, being a "good person"—a primary life goal for many for occasional practitioners and often their greatest hope for their children—they anchor in the specific substance of Christianity, which they understand as received in part through occasional practice. The ways in which participants in this research engage these three interconnected themes also reflect their emphasis on materiality, emotion, and relationship.

---

[12] Carvalhaes, *Eucharist and Globalization*, 286.

Doing Liturgical Theology with Occasional Practitioners

In this third part of the book, I have outlined *why*, from a liturgical theological perspective, it is necessary to do theology with occasional practitioners. I have also considered that *how* we do liturgical theology may need to change to incorporate the experiences of occasional practitioners. And I have provided one model of *what* this might look like in practice by drawing on the case of occasional practitioners connected to three Anglican congregations in Toronto. While I highlight the importance of materiality, emotion, and relationships for occasional practitioners in this study, I am not suggesting that these themes are unique to occasional practitioners. Instead, occasional practitioners invite all participants, including ritual experts and liturgical theologians, to greater awareness of the multidimensionality of liturgical experience and the ways in which material, emotional, and relational aspects also inform their liturgical theologies.

I return now to the example of photography from the beginning of Part III of the book. Occasional practitioners have a distinct point of view on Christian liturgical practice. Their vantage point on the margins of ecclesial communities and academic theology allows them to see practices differently. The images they create include elements not found on the printed page or even in the ecclesial space, although the space itself is significant for them. Instead of focusing on texts, concepts, and personal convictions, they depict the materiality of the event—architecture, clothing, objects. More importantly, the images capture relationships—family members, friends, communities. Viewing these images may evoke emotions that echo those experienced at the time, both in significant moments and in the overall mood of the event. These materials, emotions, and relationships may be part of what reveals that "something more" was part of this event, an event anchored in familiar and comforting tradition, that will hopefully contribute to the goal of being a "good person." Of course, God cannot be captured on camera, but even if this were possible, it might not be the most important photograph. Yet, all of these snapshots together tell the story of a liturgical event that matters deeply to participants. The flashes of light that occasional practitioners throw on this occasion can illuminate it in new ways for everyone involved.

Conclusion

In most interviews, participants had few questions for me about who I am or why I am doing this research. However, one interview with an Anglican priest concluded with a lengthy discussion of my motivations and intentions. The priest asked: "Would you like to provide a challenge to pastoral practice?" "Would you like to bring your experiences to Synod?" "Do you think your experience can be shared with other Christian denominations and religious traditions?" "Can you articulate the question as it relates to everybody?" "What is your theological context?" "What is your position and your mission?" "What is your intention?" I am grateful for this priest's questions and the accountability they imply. As this research continued to take shape, my thoughts often returned to those questions and their possible implications: Why *does* this research matter for the church and the world? What difference might it make? While there are clearly practical and pastoral applications associated with occasional religious practice, this book foregrounds the contributions of this research to the academic study of religion and theology. I trust that such academic study has implications for the church and for society.

The central contribution of this study is to introduce and develop the concept of *occasional religious practice*—participation in religious practices occasionally rather than routinely, usually in connection with certain types of occasions, including life transitions, holidays, and times of crisis—to define, describe, and understand a primary way in which people relate to religion in North America and Europe in the twenty-first century. In this Conclusion, I outline key contributions associated with the case study and methodological approach, and summarize what I see as the wide-reaching theoretical implications of this research for the disciplines of sociology of religion, ritual studies, and liturgical studies.

Contributions Related to the Case Study

This study contributes to knowledge of religion in Canada as it relates to occasional religious practice associated with baptisms and funerals that occur in certain Anglican congregations in Toronto. It enriches an understanding of how participants approach and reflect on these baptisms and funerals. It explores Anglican ecclesial and cultural expressions. It offers a window into religious life in Toronto as a multicultural megalopolis. Furthermore, observations and interviews anchored in these particular events initiated conversations that addressed occasional practice broadly and engaged participants from a range of religious backgrounds, traditions, and geographic regions. Although this research will be of special interest to Anglicans, there are substantial connections to Roman Catholicism. Since the Anglican tradition has resonances with numerous other expressions of Christianity, the theory and theology developed in this setting very likely apply elsewhere. However, in order to demonstrate this empirically, comparative research is necessary. I hope this case study inspires reflection on and examination of how occasional practice is present in relation to other practices, in other Christian traditions and non-Christian religions, as well as in other historical, cultural, and geographic contexts.

Methodological Contributions

I employed an interdisciplinary approach at the intersection of liturgical studies and sociology of religion that builds on recent developments in each discipline—the turns toward ethnography as theology and religion as practice, as described in Appendix A. Drawing deeply on the theoretical and theological resources, as well as the methodological tools, associated with both liturgical studies and sociology of religion, alongside the anthropological study of ritual in the discipline of religious studies, I modeled the benefits and future potential of a deeper integration of these disciplines. This research addressed two specific concerns held in common across disciplines: (1) who has a voice in determinations about liturgical theology and practice; and (2) what gaps exist (a) between prescribed practices and observable patterns of worship, and (b) between official teachings on and participants' interpretations of their experiences of those worship practices.

Specifically, in this study I employed qualitative methods and an abductive approach to examine Christian worship in the context of the sociological literature on religious change, such change having been a central concern in the field of sociology since its inception. A focus on religious practice, and public worship in particular, provides a new window into religious change by distinguishing practice from belief and affiliation, and recognizing that frequency of attendance is not the only measure that matters in considering the importance of religious practices for participants. At the same time, this study introduces recent literature on religious change to the discipline of liturgical studies and demonstrates how a nuanced account of this changing social context is crucial for doing liturgical theology. In addition, this study gestures toward the possibility of research at the intersection of liturgical studies and sociology of culture, which has immense potential for further exploration. The interdisciplinary approach demonstrated here makes a methodological contribution that is a starting point for future connection and collaboration across disciplines.

Theoretical and Theological Contributions

The most substantial contributions of this volume relate to theorizing religion and thinking theologically about liturgy. I define occasional religious practice in comparison to routine and intensive religious practice, as well as to the possibility of never participating in religious practices. What is considered routine is determined contextually, and occasional and intensive practice are defined in relation to it. Occasional practice may be associated with holidays, life transitions, personal or communal crises, or incidental circumstances. This understanding of occasional practices builds on sociological definitions of religion as practice. Situated in historical context, occasional religious practice is not a new phenomenon, although the literature on religious change suggests it is a dominant way in which people relate to Christianity in the Global North in the twenty-first century. Although it has parallels in various religious landscape studies, these studies tend to group occasional practice in categories that are also defined by other measures of affiliation and belief. Separating occasional practice from these factors recognizes and examines it as a phenomenon in its own right and as an ordinary and substantial way of relating to religion. It also reveals tremendous internal diversity among occasional practitioners.

Occasional religious practitioners involved in Anglican religious practices claim diverse religious and nonreligious identities. There are those who identify as Anglican because of past or present belief or practice, cultural heritage or family background, or personal choice; notably, many people claim Anglican identity apart from routine practice. There are also people who identify as Roman Catholic for a similar range of reasons who practice occasionally in the Anglican tradition. Some occasional practitioners identify with other Christian traditions, or simply as "Christian," perhaps as a default category among white Canadians or a primary category of identification among racialized Canadians. Occasional practitioners may also identify with non-Christian religious traditions. Occasional practitioners who identify as "spiritual" or "spiritual but not religious" may do so to indicate a sense of spiritual connection in their lives, point to participation in alternative spiritual practices, or simply to suggest they are nonreligious but not anti-religious. There are also explicitly nonreligious occasional practitioners who identify as atheist, agnostic, or indifferent to religion. This research demonstrates that this diversity of participants is present at Anglican liturgies on certain occasions.

Occasional practitioners have diverse motivations for participating in religious practices on certain occasions. I develop a taxonomy of types of occasional practitioners based on situational roles and motivations. Initiators bring about the practice and may be motivated by cultural heritage, specific relational connections, or a desire for spiritual connection. Some initiators may also be invisibly routine, meaning they practice privately rather than publicly and therefore appear to be occasional practitioners. Other initiators may be involuntarily occasional, meaning they desire to practice routinely but barriers beyond their control prevent them from doing so. Supporters include advocates who encourage the practice without being in a position to initiate it, inner-circle supporters who have central roles in enacting the practice although they would not have initiated it, and outer-circle supporters who tend not to have specific responsibilities. Catalysts, such as the infant being baptized or the deceased, bring about the practice but can neither directly initiate nor support it. Occasional practice changes over time for many participants, whether affected by annual cycles or life-course factors including childhood, adolescence, parenthood, and aging. Occasional religious practice is shaped by complex motivations and circumstances, and occasional practitioners occupy various roles. Occasional practice is personal and social, spiritual and cultural, although these dimensions of human experience may be difficult to differentiate. None of these types of occasional religious practice can be easily dismissed. These practices are meaningful and purposeful for participants, most of whom are comfortable with their relationship with religion and who are content to identify as "not very religious."

In addition to providing a close look at occasional practitioners, the concept of occasional religious practice facilitates the re-examination of ritual itself. I extended Catherine Bell's theory of ritual systems, which claims that ritual practices relate to other ritual practices in systems. Relationships within and between systems interpret and reinterpret ritual practices, informing the meaning and practice of rituals for participants as well as how rituals change over time. These relationships of repetition, opposition, and centrality are connections that ritual participants make themselves. However, participants positioned differently within systems, such as occasional practitioners and clergy, may interpret the same system quite differently. This is especially true when attending to the nesting and overlapping relationships between multiple different ritual systems.

In this framework, occasional religious practice is defined as selective participation in a ritual system that some practice routinely. Drawing on cultural sociology, I examined how participants select practices in ways that are highly situational and often strategic, while also being motivated by deeply held internal cultural models. Occasional practice is therefore both a coherent, reasonable, and purposive expression of foundational commitments, and a strategic and flexible response to a specific situation. The selection of specific ritual practices is also influenced by overlaps among ritual systems. This can result in the separation of rituals from certain systems and the interpretation of rituals in relation to other overlapping systems in ways that contribute to the transformation of rituals over time. This approach provides a theoretical framework for ritual systems analysis that could be applied to other cases. It also gestures toward the potential for greater engagement with sociology of culture in liturgical studies. Furthermore, it offers a theoretically anchored social scientific argument for the need to attend to practitioners positioned differently within ritual systems, including occasional practitioners, in order to understand the meaning, function, and development of ritual in contemporary society.

Attention to the liturgical theological insights of occasional practitioners is crucial from a theological perspective as well as a social scientific one. I made three distinct yet interrelated arguments for why it is necessary to do theology with occasional practitioners. The first engaged with scripture, specifically the stories of Zacchaeus and the woman at the well. The second re-examined Mrs. Murphy, the mythical primary theologian in liturgical studies, and introduced her great-granddaughter, who is almost certainly occasionally religious. The third drew inspiration from the liturgical liberation theology of Cláudio Carvalhaes and made a case for attending to those on the liturgical and theological margins as a way to start where it hurts, to think at the border, and to enter into dialogue through praxis. Taking occasional practitioners seriously requires theologians to be open to changing how theology is done and what is considered liturgy. It requires setting aside the false, yet persistent, assumption that liturgical participants are fully believing, actively practicing, morally compliant, and formally affiliated with the Christian tradition. By letting go of this assumption, and attending to the theological and liturgical margins as privileged places of theological insight, additional dimensions of what Christian worship is meaning and doing today can be uncovered.

With this framework in mind, I outlined three themes from participants that are deep currents running through the qualitative data: liturgical experience as material more than linguistic, with a specific focus on space, clothing, and objects; liturgical experience as emotional more than conceptual, with an exploration of overall mood and specific moments; and liturgical experience as relational more than personal, using the example of the meanings of baptisms and funerals for participants. These three themes present a challenge to liturgical studies, which has historically been a text-centered and concept-laden discipline, and which, at times, has considered personal assent to verbalized ideas the measure of authentic practice. I then addressed how participants address themes that are important to ritual experts, including how participants describe God in general terms as "something more"; how participants value "tradition" as a source of history, continuity, and stability; and how participants connect worship and ethics, especially through the desire to be "good people" and through a sense that occasional participation in Christian worship can contribute to this goal. I did not claim that these themes or patterns represent occasional practitioners broadly, only those who connect with the Anglican tradition in Toronto and specifically the congregations at the center of this research. Additional research examining other cases will determine how widespread these emphases are among occasional practitioners in other religious traditions and social settings and what other themes may be central. However, these themes point to how dialogue with occasional practitioners can challenge and enrich liturgical theological reflection in ways that are essential today.

Theoretically and theologically, and drawing on a concrete ethnographic case study, this book has demonstrated that it is crucial to attend to occasional religious practice to understand the contemporary religious landscape, how rituals function and evolve in contemporary contexts, and the benefits of doing liturgical theology in dialogue with participants who relate to religion in a diversity of ways. It is a call to value and learn from the very ordinary religious experience of occasional religious practice.

APPENDIX A

Methodology: Ethnography as Theology, Religion as Practice, and the Relationship between Liturgical Studies and Sociology of Religion

Appendix A outlines the interdisciplinary methodology that anchors and is modeled in this research. "It's complicated" may be the most accurate description of the ambiguous and evolving relationship between theology and sociology and the subdisciplines of liturgical studies and sociology of religion.[1] Over the past century, the relationship between theology and sociology has been characterized by assumed interdependence, deliberate distance, casual dismissal, careful borrowing, and thoughtless appropriation. I propose that developments in both sociology of religion and liturgical studies have the potential to shift this relationship in significant ways, making dialogue between the disciplines not only possible but vital.

Two monographs, *The Promise of Salvation* by Martin Riesebrodt[2] and *Religion* by Christian Smith,[3] propose a turn toward sociological definitions of religion anchored in practices that are both institutionally prescribed and based on premises about superhuman powers. These definitions of *religion as practice*, and empirical research questions associated with them, depend on a robust understanding of the diverse and changing nature and content of religious practices. Therefore, defining religion in this way invites dialogue with liturgical scholars and theologians who specialize in the study of institutionally prescribed practices and superhuman premises.

At the same time, a growing number of theologians, including Christian Scharen,[4] Pete Ward,[5] Natalie Wigg-Stevenson,[6] and Todd Whitmore,[7] make a case for *ethnography as theology*, arguing that qualitative research methods, broadly defined, can be foundational

---

[1] Portions of this Appendix were presented as part of a panel titled "Theology and Sociology: #RelationshipGoals," to which Nancy Ammerman served as a respondent, at the Society for the Scientific Study of Religion in St. Louis in 2019, and in the Critical Theories and Liturgical Studies seminar at the North American Academy of Liturgy in Atlanta in 2020.

[2] Riesebrodt, *Promise of Salvation*.

[3] Smith, *Religion*.

[4] Christian Scharen, "'Judicious Narratives,' or Ethnography as Ecclesiology," *Scottish Journal of Theology* 58, no. 2 (2005): 125–142; Christian Scharen, ed., *Explorations in Ecclesiology and Ethnography* (Grand Rapids, MI: Eerdmans, 2012); Christian Scharen and Aana Marie Vigen, eds., *Ethnography as Christian Theology and Ethics* (New York: Continuum, 2011); Christian Scharen, *Fieldwork in Theology* (Grand Rapids, MI: Baker Academic, 2015); Christian Scharen, *Public Worship and Public Work: Character and Commitment in Local Congregational Life* (Collegeville, MN: Liturgical Press, 2004).

[5] Pete Ward, ed., *Perspectives on Ecclesiology and Ethnography* (Grand Rapids, MI: Eerdmans, 2012).

[6] Wigg-Stevenson, *Ethnographic Theology*.

[7] Whitmore, *Imitating Christ*.

rather than illustrative when speaking of God, the church, Christian ethics, and Christian worship. Intriguingly, in parallel with Smith and Riesebrodt, *practices* are emerging as an important concept in this theological literature.[8] In recent years, liturgical scholars have also employed ethnographic methods to both illustrate[9] and anchor[10] reflection on Christian worship. The successful implementation of ethnography as a way of doing theology requires both the robust research methods and the theoretical tools for understanding social dynamics that are the focus of the social sciences, including sociology of religion.

In the discussion that follows, I focus first on theology, especially liturgical studies, and consider its relationship with the social sciences over the past decades, the turn toward ethnographic methods, and the possible contributions of sociology of religion to liturgical studies at this time in its development. I then consider sociology of religion, examining points of connection with theology in the past, before exploring how practice-based definitions of religion create new possibilities for relationship. I conclude by noting important differences between the disciplines, as well as common goals.

While I aim to strengthen the relationship between liturgical studies and sociology of religion, and while I conduct research at this intersection, I am not arguing that every sociologist of religion needs to engage with theology, especially Christian theology, or that every theologian needs to employ qualitative methods or engage social theory. I am simply suggesting that there are new points of convergence between liturgical studies and sociology of religion, as well as theology and sociology, where important research can be done to further our understanding of religion and its place in the lives of individuals and communities today.

Liturgical Studies

Liturgical studies is a theological discipline concerned with the history, theology, and practice of all dimensions of Christian worship, in the past and present, across confessions and cultures.[11] Although theologians have reflected on and altered expressions of Christian worship since the inception of the Christian tradition, liturgical studies as an academic discipline came into focus at the turn of the twentieth century.[12] Largely motivated by a desire for practical liturgical reform, liturgical historians drew heavily on historical methods to analyze liturgical texts, in part under the influence of comparative

---

[8] Scharen, *Fieldwork in Theology*; Mary McClintock Fulkerson, *Places of Redemption* (Oxford: Oxford University Press, 2007).

[9] Melanie Ross, *Evangelical versus Liturgical?* (Grand Rapids, MI: Eerdmans, 2014); Siobhán Garrigan, *Beyond Ritual: Sacramental Theology After Habermas* (Aldershot: Ashgate, 2004).

[10] Mary McGann, *A Precious Fountain: Music in the Worship of an African American Catholic Community* (Collegeville, MN: Liturgical Press, 2004); Siobhán Garrigan, *The Real Peace Process: Worship, Politics, and the End of Sectarianism* (London: Equinox, 2010); Ricky Manalo, *The Liturgy of Life: The Interrelationship of Sunday Eucharist and Everyday Worship Practices* (Collegeville, MN: Liturgical Press, 2014); Rebecca Spurrier, *The Disabled Church: Human Difference and the Art of Communal Worship* (New York: Fordham University Press, 2020).

[11] Gerhards and Kranemann provide a succinct introduction to the history of the discipline of liturgical studies. Albert Gerhards and Benedikt Kranemann, *Introduction to the Study of Liturgy*, trans. Linda Maloney (Collegeville, MN: Liturgical Press, 2017).

[12] Gerhards and Kranemann, *Introduction to the Study of Liturgy*, 38–39.

anthropology.[13] At the same time, liturgical theologians explored questions of meaning and purpose, found within the liturgy itself and in dialogue with systematic theology. The Second Vatican Council, especially the promulgation of *Sacrosanctum Concilium* in 1963, was a watershed moment that foregrounded liturgical questions for theologians in all areas of study, as well as for social scientists,[14] and fueled wide-ranging shifts in practice within and beyond the Roman Catholic tradition. A desire to better understand and implement liturgical change may in part be what prompted increasing engagement with the social sciences.[15]

Since the 1980s, liturgists have explicitly engaged the work of anthropologists such as Victor Turner, Mary Douglas, and Clifford Geertz,[16] a group that later expanded to include Michel Foucault and Talal Asad, among others.[17] Around the same time, ritual studies emerged as a discipline within religious studies, especially through the work of Catherine Bell[18] and Ronald Grimes,[19] and ritual theory was brought into conversation with both historically and theologically oriented liturgical scholarship.[20] This period also marks the beginning of qualitative research on Christian worship that employed social scientific methods by scholars such as Mark Searle[21] and Margaret Mary Kelleher.[22] Mary McGann published what may be considered the first ethnographic monograph in the discipline of liturgical studies in 2004,[23] and numerous other liturgical scholars have engaged

---

[13] Stringer makes a case for the influence of anthropology on two classic works in the field: Anton Baumstark, *Comparative Liturgy* (London: A. R. Mowbray, 1958); and Gregory Dix, *The Shape of the Liturgy* (London: Dacre Press, 1945). Martin Stringer, "Liturgy and Anthropology: History of a Relationship," *Worship* 63, no. 6 (1989): 503–521.

[14] Stringer observes that social scientists who engaged Christian worship in the mid-twentieth century, including David Martin, Mary Douglas, and Keiren Flanagan, tended to do so in relation to questions of liturgical reform. Martin Stringer, *On the Perception of Worship* (Birmingham: Birmingham University Press, 1999), 6–8.

[15] Mary Collins is an example of this pattern.

[16] Stringer, *On the Perception of Worship*, 4–6; Stringer, "Liturgy and Anthropology."

[17] Nathan Mitchell, *Liturgy and the Social Sciences* (Collegeville, MN: Liturgical Press, 1999).

[18] Bell, *Ritual Theory, Ritual Practice*; Bell, *Ritual: Perspectives and Dimensions*.

[19] Grimes, *Ritual Criticism*; Ronald Grimes, *Beginnings in Ritual Studies* (Columbia: University of South Carolina Press, 1995); Ronald Grimes, *The Craft of Ritual Studies* (Oxford: Oxford University Press, 2013).

[20] Theodore Jennings, "Ritual Studies and Liturgical Theology: An Invitation to Dialogue," *Journal of Ritual Studies* 1, no. 1 (1987): 35–56. Ritual theory has been further developed in relation to liturgical studies in the Liturgica Condenda series published by Peeters, including research by scholars Marcel Barnard, Mirella Klomp, and Cas Wepener, among others. Of note, there is a separate trajectory of ritual theory within sociology that centers on the work of Randall Collins, who builds on the theoretical tradition of Émile Durkheim. Erika Summers-Effler, "Ritual Theory," in *The Handbook of the Sociology of Emotions*, ed. Jan E. Stets and Jonathan H. Turner (New York: Springer, 2006), 135–154.

[21] Mark Searle, "Notre Dame Study of Catholic Parish Life in the United States," The Association of Religion Data Archives, accessed December 11, 2023, https://www.thearda.com/data-archive?fid=NDLTRGY. Stringer's ethnographic research on Christian worship in Manchester takes place during this time, although it is published a decade later and he identifies as a social scientist, not a liturgist. Stringer, *On the Perception of Worship*.

[22] Kelleher issued one of the first calls for ethnographic research in liturgical studies. Margaret Mary Kelleher, "Hermeneutics in the Study of Liturgical Performance," *Worship* 64, no. 1 (1993): 292–318.

[23] McGann, *A Precious Fountain*. McGann also published a brief volume on methodology that integrates ethnography as received from ethnomusicology into liturgical studies. Mary McGann, *Exploring Music as Worship and Theology* (Collegeville, MN: Liturgical Press, 2002).

ethnographic methods in recent years.[24] The use of social scientific theory and qualitative research has blossomed in liturgical studies over the past four decades, although history and theology remain the focus of the discipline.

Ethnography as Theology

Although social scientific approaches to the study of Christian worship are not new, recent developments in the conception of the relationship between theology and ethnography are setting a new direction.[25] Scholars, including Christian Scharen, Todd Whitmore, and Natalie Wigg-Stevenson, among others,[26] go beyond borrowing theory and methods from the social sciences to claim that ethnography *is* theology. While each ethnographic theologian is quick to emphasize the particularity of their contexts and methods,[27] common themes emerge.

Lutheran ethicist Christian Scharen first made the case that "ethnography ought to be a means of doing theology" in 2005, claiming that ethnography is a necessary corrective to idealized ecclesiology that is not "recognizably real."[28] Scharen's frequent collaborator, Pete Ward, also sees ethnography as the antidote for the "disconnection between what we say doctrinally about the church and the experience of life in a local parish."[29] In 2011, Scharen, along with fellow Lutheran ethicist and co-author Aana Marie Vigen, took this a step further and claimed "ethnography *as* Christian theology and ethics," meaning that "the situation or context of study has embedded and embodied within its life substantive contributions to theology and ethics."[30] This expands how ethnography has often

---

[24] Liturgical scholars who engage ethnographic research include Rebecca Slough, Siobhán Garrigan, Thomas Quartier, Melanie Ross, Sharon Fennema, Jennifer Davidson, Rebecca Spurrier, Nathaniel Marx, Audrey Seah, Layla Karst, Ricky Manalo, and Nelson Cowan.

[25] Accounts of this "ethnographic turn" can be found in Scharen and Vigen, *Ethnography as Christian Theology and Ethics*, 28–46, and Elizabeth Phillips, "Charting the 'Ethnographic Turn': Theologians and the Study of Christian Congregations," in *Perspectives on Ecclesiology and Ethnography*, ed. Pete Ward (Grand Rapids, MI: Eerdmans, 2012), 95–106. The most comprehensive exploration of the turn toward ethnographic methods may be Pete Ward and Knut Tveitereid, eds., *The Wiley Blackwell Companion to Theology and Qualitative Research* (Hoboken, NJ: John Wiley & Sons, 2022).

[26] Many of these scholars are associated with the Network for Ecclesiology and Ethnography, founded in 2007. This group expanded to include the Ecclesial Practices Group at the American Academy of Religion several years later, and since 2014 publishes the journal *Ecclesial Practices*: https://brill.com/view/journals/ep/ep-overview.xml.

[27] "The proposal made here is not for how ethnographic theology in general should be done. Rather, I propose that ethnographic theological methods—like sociological or anthropological ethnographic methods—should always be geared to the particular research question(s) at hand. The research question guides both the mode of inquiry and the type of knowledge that inquiry can produce." Wigg-Stevenson, *Ethnographic Theology*, 11. "When I think about anthropological theology as a method or approach, I think of it simply as the appropriation of ethnographic methods to raise theological questions. Someone else doing this in a different context might experience and so highlight quite different moments or modalities in the process." Whitmore, *Imitating Christ*, 28.

[28] Scharen, "'Judicious Narratives,'" 125. "Ethnography, although dominated by the domain of anthropology and sociology today, in fact has been and should be a skill available to the theologian as theologian. . . . By this argument I surely do not mean all theology or all theologians should become ethnographers. But I surely do mean this for those who would speak of the church." Scharen, "'Judicious Narratives,'" 141.

[29] Ward, *Perspectives on Ecclesiology and Ethnography*, 4.

[30] Scharen and Vigen, *Ethnography as Christian Theology*, xxii.

been employed in theology and liturgical studies, making it integral rather than merely a starting point or illustration:

> Rather than pairing ethnographic facts to universal theological truth, the ethnographer—through apprenticeship to the situation/people—aids in the articulation of those embedded theological convictions as primary theology itself. This perspective does not preclude bringing into the conversation other theological or theoretical materials, but the point is that they do not automatically have privilege over the local theological understandings operative in the lives of those studied.[31]

According to Scharen and Vigen, ethnography is foundational and authoritative for theology: "in order to do theology and ethics well, scholars need to explore them through visceral ways, within embodied communities, and in particular contexts."[32] This has implications not only for theological reflection but for how ethnographic methods are employed and understood.[33]

Roman Catholic ethicist Todd Whitmore similarly argues that "ethnography is not simply a method that provides information to plug into our theology; rather, ethnography *is* a way of doing theology."[34] In embracing "anthropological theology," to use his term, Whitmore sets aside the alternative:

> I am here categorically rejecting the idea of theology as a "second-order" form of discourse that reflects *on* the practice of the Christian community as if standing outside of, or at least at a remove from, the activity of that community.[35]

For Whitmore, an ethnographic approach to theology is morally imperative both because it challenges "the untenable view that theology can be done from 'nowhere,'"[36] and because it is one of few ways to access the lives and narratives—that is, the theology—of marginalized peoples and cultures.[37] Whitmore aims to privilege the local theological understandings evident in the lives of those studied.

Baptist practical theologian Natalie Wigg-Stevenson focuses on how ethnographic methods can foster the already organic relationship between everyday and academic theologies in order to bolster the co-creation of theological knowledge:[38]

> Rather than reflecting ethnographically *on* Christian community or *on* Christian practice, the method I construct here seeks to do ethnographic reflection *in* Christian community and *as* Christian practice.[39]

---

[31] Scharen and Vigen, *Ethnography as Christian Theology*, xxii–xxiii. Emphasis added.
[32] Scharen and Vigen, *Ethnography as Christian Theology*, xviii.
[33] Eileen R. Campbell-Reed and Christian Scharen, "Ethnography on Holy Ground: How Qualitative Interviewing Is Practical Theological Work," *International Journal of Practical Theology* 17, no. 2 (2013): 232–259; Christian Scharen, "Interviewing Interpreted as a Spiritual Exercise and Social Protest," *Ecclesial Practices* 4 (2017): 218–236.
[34] Whitmore, *Imitating Christ*, 29.
[35] Whitmore, *Imitating Christ*, 2.
[36] Whitmore, *Imitating Christ*, 11.
[37] Whitmore, *Imitating Christ*, 4–5.
[38] Wigg-Stevenson, *Ethnographic Theology*, 10.
[39] Wigg-Stevenson, *Ethnographic Theology*, 46.

330 APPENDIX A

She does so with lucid awareness of the role of the academic theologian in ethnographic theology:

> Theological fieldwork necessitates being able to map the field of study *and the academic theologian's role within that field*; otherwise we mistakenly imagine ourselves to have a God's-eye view on the action, failing to see our implication in it.[40]

Recognizing the academic theologian as a powerful partner in the ethnographic process is essential. As John Swinton writes, "Ethnography is first and foremost an interpretive exercise. The act of interpretation is necessarily value-laden."[41] Academic theological ethnographers, along with sociological and anthropological ethnographers, enter the field with particular values and questions.

Scharen, Whitmore, and Wigg-Stevenson clearly identify as *theologians* while undertaking substantial multi-year, sometimes multi-site, ethnographic studies. From within three distinct streams of the Christian tradition—mainstream Protestant, Roman Catholic, and Free Church—they claim ethnography *as* theology. While their research engages people, it is *theo*logical, it is *about God*:

> We understand ethnography as a process of attentive study of, and learning from, people—their words, practices, traditions, experiences, memorizes, insights—in particular times and places in order to understand how they make meaning (cultural, religious, ethical) and what they can teach us about reality, truth, beauty, moral responsibility, relationships and the divine, etc. The aim is *to understand God, human relationships, and the world from their perspective*—to take them seriously as a source of wisdom and to de-center our own assumptions and evaluations.[42]

Furthermore, ethnographic theology is invested in making *normative claims* about what ought to be, in addition to describing and explaining what is:

> One area in which anthropological theology goes beyond much anthropology is to move from attention to and thick description of the other to discernment as to whether aspects of the life of the other can inform *us* how to live.[43]

In order to make normative claims about God and the Christian life, ethnography as theology remains *in dialogue with tradition*. For example, Wigg-Stevenson tackles the traditional theological themes of Trinity, Christology, and soteriology;[44] Whitmore engages scripture, especially the story of Zacchaeus;[45] and Scharen focuses on the practice of the

---

[40] Wigg-Stevenson, *Ethnographic Theology*, 11. Emphasis added.
[41] John Swinton, "'Where Is Your Church?' Moving Toward a Hospitable and Sanctified Ethnography," in *Perspectives on Ecclesiology and Ethnography*, ed. Pete Ward (Grand Rapids, MI: Eerdmans, 2012), 81.
[42] Scharen and Vigen, *Ethnography as Christian Theology*, 16. Emphasis added.
[43] Whitmore, *Imitating Christ*, 30.
[44] Wigg-Stevenson, *Ethnographic Theology*, 177–184.
[45] Whitmore's engagement with the story of Zacchaeus is one example. Whitmore, *Imitating Christ*, 15–24.

Eucharist.[46] This is ethnography that is indisputably theological. At the same time, this is theology that is clearly ethnographic.

Sociological Contributions to Ethnography as Theology

The emerging emphasis on *ethnography itself* as theology in practical theology and liturgical studies creates space where dialogue with sociology is not only possible, but necessary, both methodologically and theoretically.

Methodologically, sociology has invested a century in reflecting on and developing methods for accessing human experience through observation of and engagement with the social world. There is no need to reinvent qualitative research methods for ethnographic theology.[47] Furthermore, as ethnography becomes more foundational than illustrative, the methodological stakes rise, increasing the need for more rigorous research methods. This may take the form of theoretical reflection, such as Wigg-Stevenson's engagement with the complex bodily dimensions of ethnography developed by Loïc Wacquant,[48] or simply learning practical skills, such as how to write fieldnotes[49] or use qualitative data analysis software.[50] Calling something "ethnography" does not automatically guard against the "methodological laziness" that Pete Ward describes as plaguing ecclesiology:

> It becomes acceptable to make assertions where there is no evidence. We assume a common perception of contemporary church life between the author and the reader. We base whole arguments on anecdotes and the selective treatment of experience.... The turn to ethnography challenges these conventions by the simple observation that *assertions about the lived reality of church require a kind of discipline and rigor similar to those that pertain in other areas of theological writing*. Taking this disciplinary rigor seriously does not mean that theologians become something they are not, just as theologians do not necessarily compromise what they are and what they are about when they make use of philosophy or history.[51]

Sociologist of religion Gerardo Marti likewise expresses concern regarding how some theologians employ qualitative research methods, while affirming the embrace of ethnography among theologians. In particular, Marti advocates for a distinction between "found theologies" and "imposed theologies," the importance of openness to "surprise," and theoretical and methodological resources that can be borrowed from the social sciences for making these distinctions and discoveries.[52] Ongoing engagement with methodological

---

[46] Christian Scharen, "Ecclesiology 'From the Body': Ethnographic Notes Toward a Carnal Theology," in *Perspectives on Ecclesiology and Ethnography*, ed. Pete Ward (Grand Rapids, MI: Eerdmans, 2012), 56–65.

[47] Although theologians approach ethnographic research with distinct questions and priorities that may at times inform methods, this should be in dialogue with established best practices. Campbell-Reed and Scharen, "Ethnography on Holy Ground."

[48] Wigg-Stevenson, *Ethnographic Theology*, 72–78.

[49] Robert Emerson, Rachel Fretz, and Linda Shaw, *Writing Ethnographic Fieldnotes* (Chicago: University of Chicago Press, 2011).

[50] For example, MAXQDA, NVivo, or ATLAS.

[51] Ward, *Perspectives on Ecclesiology and Ethnography*, 4. Emphasis added.

[52] Gerardo Martí, "Ethnography as a Tool for Genuine Surprise: Found Theologies versus Imposed Theologies," in *The Wiley Blackwell Companion to Theology and Qualitative Research*,

developments and best practices for qualitative research within a social scientific discipline such as sociology is one way for theologians to remain accountable to observing the social world and collaborating with communities in a responsible and rigorous manner.

In addition to method, theory is an important area for dialogue. Theologians necessarily encounter social dynamics that are adjacent to, yet interact with, theological questions in the field. This may include questions of gender, race, class, and the role of institutions or family structures in theological and ecclesial matters, among many other subjects. Theory related to the human dimensions of religious ethnography can enrich the theological aspects of this work, yet theologians are often unfamiliar with recent sociological literature. For example, culture is a pressing concern in both theology and sociology, yet liturgical studies often anchor discussion of culture in older models, most often Geertz,[53] missing more recent developments in sociology of culture, including repertoire theory and culture and cognition.[54] There are significant theoretical contributions which sociology can make to ethnographic theology and liturgical studies.

Furthermore, sociologists of religion and ethnographic theologians engage common philosophical foundations, such as those of Pierre Bourdieu. An emerging focus on Bourdieu's approach to practices in Scharen, Wigg-Stevenson, and McClintock Fulkerson[55] is particularly noteworthy in relation to the sociological definitions of religion as practice. Shared philosophical reference points can establish common ground for dialogue.

Barriers to Sociology in Liturgical Studies

Although there is tremendous potential for sociology of religion to contribute to liturgical studies by enriching both the method and theory involved in ethnographic theology, there are significant barriers to overcome.

First, there is a fear among some theologians that employing social scientific methods may reduce Christian worship to culture and religious experience to social experience. However, Elizabeth Phillips describes how recent trends in the social sciences, including greater appreciation for the situatedness of all knowledge and the emergence of activist social science, mitigate the concern of reductionism.[56] Furthermore, Peter Berger's "methodological atheism"[57] is giving way to a more spacious "methodological agnosticism."[58] Although social science does not aspire to make normative faith claims regarding

---

ed. Pete Ward and Knut Tveitereid (Hoboken, NJ: John Wiley & Sons, 2022), 471–482; Gerardo Martí, "Ethnographic Theology: Integrating the Social Sciences and Theological Reflection," *Cuestiones Teológicas* 49, no. 111 (2022): 1–18; Gerardo Martí, "Found Theologies versus Imposed Theologies: Remarks on Theology and Ethnography from a Sociological Perspective," *Ecclesial Practices* 3, no. 2 (2016): 157–172.

[53] Mark Francis, *Shape a Circle Ever Wider* (Chicago: Liturgy Training Publications, 2000), 15–17.
[54] Swidler, "Culture in Action"; Swidler, *Talk of Love*; Vaisey, "Motivation and Justification"; Smith, Ritz, and Rotolo, *Religious Parenting*.
[55] Wigg-Stevenson, *Ethnographic Theology*; Scharen, *Fieldwork in Theology*; McClintock Fulkerson, *Places of Redemption*.
[56] Phillips, "Charting the 'Ethnographic Turn,'" 101.
[57] Berger, *The Sacred Canopy*, 100.
[58] Douglas Porpora, "Methodological Atheism, Methodological Agnosticism and Religious Experience," *Journal of the Theory of Social Behaviour* 36, no. 1 (2006): 57–75; Smith, *Religion*, 19.

Christian worship or religious experience, it does not preclude theologians who employ ethnographic methods or engage social theory from doing so within the context of theological scholarship.

Second, there is legitimate concern that mastering one discipline, especially an interdisciplinary field like liturgical studies, is challenging enough without attempting to master another. This is certainly a barrier, especially in institutions where firm boundaries are in place between confessional and social scientific approaches to religion. Nevertheless, there is tremendous potential for interdisciplinary learning, which can also take the form of collaborative approaches to scholarship, currently more common in sociology than theology.

These two fears may be amplified in the discipline of liturgical studies as a result of the work of Anglican social scientist Martin Stringer. Stringer has undertaken several ambitious projects over the past decades that aim to bring together liturgical studies and sociology of religion. Stringer's sweeping historical argument, *A Sociological History of Christian Worship*,[59] has been critiqued by liturgical historians;[60] his empirical argument regarding defining religion in *Contemporary Western Ethnography and the Definition of Religion*[61] has been critiqued by social scientists;[62] and his ethnographic account of Christian worship in four congregations, *On the Perception of Christian Worship*,[63] has not received much attention in liturgical studies, which appears to be its target audience. The massive empirical and theoretical scope of these undertakings raises questions about whether mastery of the material without substantial collaboration is possible. Stringer may also be accused of the reductionism that theologians fear, for example, in speaking of the "meaning" of Christian worship while identifying two kinds of reality that are "beyond the scope of the ethnographer": "the inner life of those being studied" and "the possibility of the reality of the Other."[64] In addition, Stringer was an early advocate for dialogue between liturgy and the social sciences, and the perceived constraints and tensions within and between the disciplines informed his approach and its reception. Despite these drawbacks, Stringer raises important questions worthy of attention in liturgical studies, especially his emphasis on the "way in which ordinary members of Christian congregations in England today understand and respond to the worship they experience every Sunday, and often more frequently."[65]

One of the greatest fears associated with social scientific approaches to Christian worship may be their challenge to idealized understandings of the liturgy, both historical and theological, prevalent in the discipline. Observing real worshiping communities and learning more about what worshipers claim is (and is not) part of their experience may threaten professional theologians' claims regarding the nature and power of the liturgy, especially when these claims imply empirically observable outcomes. However, I believe that this challenge is exactly what is needed today in liturgical studies to fuel liturgical

---

[59] Martin Stringer, *A Sociological History of Christian Worship* (Cambridge: Cambridge University Press, 2005).

[60] Bryan Spinks, review of *A Sociological History of Christian Worship*, by Martin Stringer, *Journal of Ecclesiastical History* 57, no. 3 (2006): 542–543.

[61] Martin Stringer, *Contemporary Western Ethnography and the Definition of Religion* (London: Continuum, 2008).

[62] Timothy Fitzgerald, review of *Contemporary Western Ethnography and the Definition of Religion*, by Martin Stringer, *Journal of the American Academy of Religion* 77, no. 4 (2009): 974–982.

[63] Stringer, *On the Perception of Worship*.

[64] Stringer, *On the Perception of Worship*, 210.

[65] Stringer, *On the Perception of Worship*, 17.

theological reflection that engages pressing contemporary questions in meaningful ways. Sociology of religion is a valuable resource for this task, especially due to recent theoretical developments in the field that define religion in terms of practices.

Sociology of Religion

While the study of social order and social change existed in antecedent forms, sociology as an academic discipline emerged around the late nineteenth century.[66] Religion was prominent in the origins of the discipline, with key figures such as Émile Durkheim[67] and Max Weber[68] focusing on matters related to religion (including ritual), and empirical research being conducted alongside the global expansion of the Christian tradition.[69]

Although qualitative methods and the study of religion were central in the early years of the discipline, in the mid-twentieth century the focus of sociologists of religion shifted to secularization, with the underlying assumption that religion would fade from society.[70] Clear lines were drawn between theology and sociology, although certain scholars engaged the intersection between fields.[71] By the late 1990s, however, it became clear that secularization was not a universal narrative and that religion is likely to remain a significant force in global society.[72] In addition to a willingness to regard religion as something other than a remnant of the past, key shifts in the social sciences created greater openness to relationship with theology:

> In general, the social sciences have experienced a turn away from modern, structuralist, and positivist understandings of social sciences and social-scientific objectivity toward post-structuralist, constructivist, and interpretivist understandings of the situatedness of the social sciences themselves as well as of the individuals who conduct social-scientific research.[73]

Sociology is situated and value laden in the choice of subject matter and interpretation of results. Sociologists are no more or less objective than theologians, but simply ask questions within a different frame of reference toward different ends.

---

[66] Alan Sica, "A Selective History of Sociology," in *The Wiley Blackwell Companion to Sociology*, ed. George Ritzer (Malden, MA: John Wiley & Sons, 2012), 25–54.
[67] Émile Durkheim, *The Elementary Forms of Religious Life* (New York: Free Press, 1995). Originally published in French in 1912.
[68] Max Weber, *The Protestant Ethic and the Spirit of Capitalism* (New York: Scribner, 1958). Originally written in German in 1905.
[69] Edward E. Evans-Pritchard, *Witchcraft, Oracles and Magic among the Azande* (Oxford: Clarendon Press, 1976); Bronislaw Malinowski, *Magic, Science and Religion and Other Essays* (New York: Doubleday, 1954).
[70] Berger, *The Sacred Canopy*; Christian Smith and Robert D. Woodberry, "Sociology of Religion," in *The Wiley Blackwell Companion to Sociology*, ed. George Ritzer (Malden, MA: John Wiley & Sons, 2012), 367–384.
[71] David Martin, *Reflections on Theology and Sociology* (Oxford: Oxford University Press, 1997); Robert Bellah, *The Robert Bellah Reader* (Durham, NC: Duke University Press, 2006).
[72] Peter Berger, "Secularism in Retreat," *The National Interest* 46 (1996): 2–12; Smith, *Religion*, 23–60.
[73] Phillips, "Charting the 'Ethnographic Turn,'" 101.

Although religious and nonreligious ritual has been the object of sociological analysis,[74] this has rarely included Christian liturgy. Perhaps influenced by the assumption of secularization, the sociological study of Christian worship has primarily consisted of counting whether or not people attend religious services, with little regard for what they experience when they do. In 1989, Martin Stringer observed:

> There are a large number of sociological studies of churches and "parishes" both in Europe and in the United States. Many of these are very good at determining the social backgrounds of the people who attend the churches and perhaps, in part, eliciting why they might go. However all those that I have read are totally silent on what actually happens when they get inside the church building and begin to worship. It is almost as if the sociologist remains at the church door and waits for the congregation to come out again.[75]

This pattern continues today, with the significant exception of ethnographic congregational studies that pay close attention to many aspects of religious communities, including corporate worship.[76] In addition to philosophical and methodological shifts that open space for dialogue with theology, a turn in recent years toward defining religion in terms of prescribed practices makes dialogue with liturgical studies vital.

Religion as Practice

How best to define religion has long been a subject of debate among social scientists. In recent years, Martin Riesebrodt[77] and Christian Smith[78] have proposed that religion is best defined in terms of practices,[79] an approach that is receiving substantial and largely positive attention.[80] I first outline how Smith and Riesebrodt define religion and then

---

[74] Durkheim, *The Elementary Forms*; Randall Collins, *Interaction Ritual Chains* (Princeton, NJ: Princeton University Press, 2004).

[75] Stringer, "Liturgy and Anthropology," 504.

[76] Nancy Ammerman, *Congregation and Community* (New Brunswick, NJ: Rutgers University Press, 1997); Penny Edgell Becker, *Congregations in Conflict* (Cambridge: Cambridge University Press, 1999); Mary Ellen Konieczny, *The Spirit's Tether* (New York: Oxford University Press, 2013); Nicolette Manglos-Weber, *Joining the Choir* (New York: Oxford University Press, 2018); Omar McRoberts, *Streets of Glory* (Chicago: University of Chicago Press, 2005).

[77] Riesebrodt, *The Promise of Salvation*.

[78] Smith, *Religion*.

[79] Riesebrodt and Smith both aspire to universal definitions of religion. I do not share this aim and instead see their approach as extremely useful for the particular questions at the center of my research, including (1) making space for dialogue with theology, especially liturgical studies; (2) a focus on observable practices that can be accessed through qualitative research; and (3) theoretical tools for engaging questions of Christian worship and religious change, especially what I am calling occasional religious practice.

[80] Mary Ellen Konieczny, Loren D. Lybarger, and Kelly H. Chong, "Theory as a Tool in the Social Scientific Study of Religion and Martin Riesebrodt's *The Promise of Salvation*," *Journal for the Scientific Study of Religion* 51, no. 3 (2012): 397–411; *Religion* by Christian Smith won the Society for the Scientific Study of Religion Distinguished Book Award in 2018 and has been widely reviewed. Nancy Ammerman advocates for an approach to religion as practice that emerges from the study of "lived religion" as a framework for sociological research on religion within and beyond religious institutions and across cultural contexts. While Ammerman critiques the emphasis on structured and prescribed practices and superhuman powers in Smith and Riesebrodt, "spiritual practices" remain at the center of her sociological approach to religion and likewise point to the possibility of dialogue

consider possible contributions from theology and liturgical studies, as well as barriers to these contributions being received.

Christian Smith offers the following definition of religion:

> Religion is *a complex of culturally prescribed practices, based on premises about the existence and nature of superhuman powers*, whether personal or impersonal, which seek to help practitioners gain access to and communicate or align themselves with these powers, in hopes of realizing human goods and avoiding things bad.[81]

Several aspects of this definition are important to highlight for the purposes of this discussion. First, this is a *substantive* definition that is focused on the meanings of a type of action, not functional outcomes. Second, this definition is centered on *practices*—"culturally meaningful behaviors that are intentionally repeated over time"[82]—rather than on beliefs. Third, the meanings of practices that matter for defining religion are *culturally prescribed*. It matters "that *the practice itself* is institutionalized in a complex of repeated actions that are culturally meaningful in religious terms,"[83] not that individual practitioners or communities affirm or are even aware of these meanings. Fourth, what makes prescribed practices meaningful in religious terms is reference to *superhuman powers*. Fifth, an emphasis on institutionally prescribed meanings associated with superhuman powers does not preclude *critique* of established authorities and traditions and may even provide tools for doing so.[84]

Smith's definition of religion relies heavily on Martin Riesebrodt.[85] Smith borrows Riesebrodt's substantive content-based approach to religion as a complex of practices that are culturally prescribed—"liturgies," to use Riesebrodt's word—and that are associated with superhuman powers that "promise salvation," to reference Riesebrodt's language. While Smith intentionally avoids language associated with the Christian tradition in hopes of broader application, when considering dialogue with liturgical studies[86] Riesebrodt's choice of words is helpful. For Riesebrodt, *liturgy* is the key to "how the meaning of religion as a complex of practices can actually be discovered":[87]

> The meaning of religious practices cannot be adequately understood either on the level of intellectual discourses or "theologies" in the broad sense of the word, or on that of subjective interpretations, including the Romantic or phenomenological variants. *They can be properly understood only on the level of institutionalized*

---

with theology and liturgical studies. Nancy Ammerman, "Rethinking Religion: Toward a Practice Approach," *American Journal of Sociology* 126, no. 1 (July 2020): 6–51; Nancy Tatom Ammerman, *Studying Lived Religion: Contexts and Practices* (New York: New York University Press, 2021).

[81] Smith, *Religion*, 22. Emphasis added.
[82] Smith, *Religion*, 26.
[83] Smith, *Religion*, 32.
[84] Smith, *Religion*, 15.
[85] Riesebrodt's definition of religion is very similar: "Religion is a complex of practices that are based on the premise of the existence of superhuman powers, whether personal or impersonal, that are generally invisible. I call this the religious premise. . . . Religious practices normally consist in using culturally prescribed means to establish contact with these powers or to gain access to them." Riesebrodt, *The Promise of Salvation*, 75.
[86] Smith, *Religion*, 13–14.
[87] Riesebrodt, *The Promise of Salvation*, 79.

practices or "liturgies," under which concept I subsume rules and meanings for human intercourse with superhuman powers.[88]

A focus on liturgies is the alternative to an intellectualism that privileges the cognitive conceptions of academics and a subjectivism that focuses on the interpretations of individuals. Riesebrodt defines liturgy broadly:

> By "liturgies" I refer to any kind of institutionalized rules and scripts that guide humans' intercourse with superhuman powers, express its meanings, and are enacted in interventionist practices of worship. Such rules or scripts may be codified in writing or transmitted orally; they may be generally acknowledged and accessible, or secret and reserved for special persons.[89]

"Interventionist practices" include all practices aimed at establishing contact with superhuman powers, especially "symbolic actions such as prayers, chants, gestures, formulas, sacrifices, vows, or divination."[90] It is not a stretch to see how Smith and Riesebrodt's approach to defining religion as practice opens a conversation with theology, and especially liturgical studies.

Contributions of Liturgical Studies to Religion as Practice

Both Smith and Riesebrodt want to provide a definition of religion that rings true with religious insiders, including practitioners and theologians, as well as with social scientists:

> This practice-centered approach to religion is not an alien imposition; it is consistent with the view from inside religions.[91]

> My explanation of religion is not based on an interpretation of religious practices that is imposed from without, but is found in the respective meanings of religious practices and their liturgies themselves.[92]

The primary way to assess whether they have been successful is to engage insiders who specialize in the content and meaning of religious practices.

When religion is defined as a complex of culturally prescribed practices, engaging with theologians, especially liturgical scholars, is valuable for determining whether something is or is not religion and successfully implementing a research agenda centered on religious practices.[93] The focus on institutionally prescribed practices puts liturgical scholarship front and center:

---

[88] Riesebrodt, *The Promise of Salvation*, 72. Emphasis added.
[89] Riesebrodt, *The Promise of Salvation*, 84. Emphasis added.
[90] Riesebrodt, *The Promise of Salvation*, 75.
[91] Smith, *Religion*, 45.
[92] Riesebrodt, *The Promise of Salvation*, 91.
[93] This is the case only for research conducted within or adjacent to the Christian tradition. In other religious and nonreligious contexts, other ritual specialists would need to be engaged. Both Smith and Riesebrodt aspire to craft definitions that speak to religion universally, which is beyond the scope of my argument here—an argument focused on how these definitions are beneficial in the specific case of dialogue between sociology of religion and liturgical studies.

> The meanings of religious practices as conceptualized here, in other words, derive not from the cognitive assent of the people engaged in them at any given time but *from a variety of institutional sources, including historical traditions, sacred texts, and explanations by religious specialists*. Religious practices are social realities irreducible to the beliefs of the people who enact them.[94]
>
> The meaning of religious action is no longer derived from subjectivist interpretations, "worldviews," the interpretations of religious intellectuals, or political discourses. Rather, it is derived from liturgies, that is, from *the meaning of practices as expressed in spoken words, symbolic actions, formulas, gestures, or songs*.[95]

The way to determine whether a practice is religious is through sacred texts, historical traditions, symbolic actions, gestures, formulas, songs, and explanations by religious specialists; in other words, the subject matter that has been the focus of liturgical studies for a century. Liturgical scholars explore and theorize the diverse and changing content of religious practices, including official rites and popular practices, based on rich historical and contemporary source material. Failing to engage this resource is not only a missed opportunity, but risks oversimplification of the contents and meanings of religious practices.

Choosing to define religion in a way that depends on insider, theological, emic perspectives does not diminish the potential for outside, sociological, etic understandings:

> This book offers a social scientific account of religion (what anthropologists call an "etic" approach) that tries to take seriously the "insider" or "native" beliefs, categories, and meanings of religious traditions and people (what is called an "emic" approach) without being bound by them. The latter perspective (emic) concerns how reality is viewed and explained within the social group being studied; the former (etic) concerns how outsiders, like social scientists, define, categorize, understand, and explain the same social group using different, scholarly, "non-native" terminology and explanations. Taking an etic approach without discounting the emic sometimes involves switching between the two perspectives and navigating tricky tensions.[96]

Defining religion in terms of practice allows space for emic and etic perspectives not only to coexist but also to strengthen one another. Smith and Riesebrodt focus on the "human side" of religion and do not make normative theological claims, although their definition requires theologians to do so and leaves space for theological development and dialogue.

Barriers to Theology in Sociology of Religion

Despite the benefits of dialogue with theology in practice-based approaches to the social scientific study of religion, resistance may remain. This may be a lingering fear of supposedly objective science being sullied by subjective confessionalism, or a wariness of appearing to engage scholars who make normative theological claims instead of developing empirical social theory. The larger barrier may simply be a sense that this is not necessary. Although anthropologist Don Seeman makes a case for anthropologists engaging religion and theology, he is clear that this is not the present norm in the discipline: "This

---

[94] Smith, *Religion*, 31. Emphasis added.
[95] Riesebrodt, *The Promise of Salvation*, 87. Emphasis added.
[96] Smith, *Religion*, 16–17.

cachet of ethnography within religion and theology does not, however, typically extend to the reciprocal appreciation of religion and theology within the world of professional anthropology."[97]

Nevertheless, there are important exceptions, including Derrick Lemons and his collaborators in *Theologically Engaged Anthropology*,[98] who agree that "theologians and anthropologists benefit from working together," whether through dialogue around common topics that maintains the distinctives of each discipline, or approaches that blur disciplinary boundaries.[99] Joel Robbins also articulates the value of theology for anthropology, not only in terms of disciplinary self-reflection and as a source of ethnographic data, but also as an encounter that may shape driving questions about theory and action.[100] Although there are certainly many social scientific questions, including questions about religion, that can be engaged apart from theology, certain topics demand mutual engagement, and understanding religion as practice is one of them.

Different Projects and Common Goals

Liturgical scholars and sociologists of religion have different projects. Liturgical scholars are invested in questions of Christian faith and practice, in conversation with scripture, tradition, and religious experience, and often have the objective of concrete intervention in ecclesial contexts in terms of shaping practices and reflection on practices. In contrast, sociologists of religion are invested in empirical and theoretical questions about the role of religion in society, at the micro and macro levels, with the aim of developing better social theory. Most of the time these communities of scholarship participate in separate conversations that engage distinct literatures, within different parameters. These are both worthwhile aims and, for the reasons outlined above, dialogue across disciplines would make each discipline better able to achieve its own goals.

At the same time, there are common goals between liturgical studies and sociology of religion (Table A.1). Both aim to describe and explain present-day religious practices and the experiences of religious practitioners. Both aim to describe and explain how present practices are part of a historical trajectory that is rooted in the past and what types of change can be anticipated in the future. Both aim to better understand how religious practices are related to cultural and social context. The turns toward ethnography as

---

[97] Don E. Seeman, "Does Anthropology Need to 'Get Religion'? Critical Notes on an Unrequited Love," *Practical Matters* 3 (2010): 10–14.

[98] Derrick Lemons, ed., *Theologically Engaged Anthropology* (Oxford: Oxford University Press, 2018).

[99] Lemons, *Theologically Engaged Anthropology*, 5–6.

[100] Joel Robbins, "Anthropology and Theology: An Awkward Relationship?" *Anthropological Quarterly* 79, no. 2 (2006): 285–294. The December 2013 issue of the *Australian Journal of Theology* focuses on the relationship between theology and anthropology and includes an afterword from Robbins. Joel Robbins, "Afterword: Let's Keep It Awkward: Anthropology, Theology, and Otherness," *Australian Journal of Theology* 24, no. 3 (2013): 329–337. Anthropological research that implements this approach includes Eloise Meneses and David Bronkeman, eds., *On Knowing Humanity: Insights from Theology for Anthropology* (New York: Routledge, 2017); T. M. Luhrmann, *When God Talks Back: Understanding the American Evangelical Relationship with God* (New York: Vintage Books, 2012); James Bielo, *Ark Encounter: The Making of a Creationist Theme Park* (New York: New York University Press, 2018); James Bielo, *Words upon the Word: An Ethnography of Evangelical Bible Study* (New York: New York University Press, 2009).

Table A.1 Liturgical Studies and Sociology of Religion: Different Projects and Common Goals

	Liturgical Studies	**Sociology of Religion**
Subject matter	Christian faith and practice	Role of religion in society
Primary methods	Engagement with scripture, tradition, and religious experience	Qualitative and quantitative empirical methods
Goal	Intervention in ecclesial contexts	Developing better social theory
Literature	Theological	Sociological
Common Goals		

Describe and explain present-day religious practices and the experiences of religious practitioners

Describe and explain how present-day religious practices are part of historical trajectories

Describe and explain how religious practices are related to cultural and social context

theology and religion as practice are one starting point for collaborative exploration of these broad common questions.

Two specific research agendas emerge at the intersection of the work of Scharen and Whitmore and Smith and Riesebrodt. First, Whitmore and Riesebrodt share a common concern regarding *who* gets to determine what theology or religion is, including the assertion that it is neither the intellectual elite, nor each person for themselves. Riesebrodt and Whitmore mirror each other in this regard:

> *Intellectual interpretive cultures are no longer privileged as the bearers of "genuine" meaning* and opposed to the philistine superstition of the masses. Religion is not a theologically "pure" tradition but a factual system of religious practices that combines theory and practice.[101]

> Theology as it is practiced today is largely—one could say almost entirely—a discipline of texts. Yet in sub-Saharan African alone there are 200 million people who do not read or write.... How do these and similarly socially located people figure in what and to whom we write? *Not to undertake methodologies that gather the perspectives, judgements, and patterns of life of such people risks—I would even say virtually assures—reinforcing the patterns of political and economic dominance that coincide with the rise of literate culture.*[102]

Although their motivations are distinct, with Riesebrodt anchoring his approach in methodological concerns and Whitmore in Catholic social teaching, the question of who gets to define which religious practices are considered culturally prescribed is both empirical and theoretical, sociological and theological. That question is behind Martin Stringer's question, "To whom exactly should the ethnographer be listening?"[103] It is a question that can best be explored by drawing on the strengths of each discipline, and it is closely connected to the second common concern.

[101] Riesebrodt, *The Promise of Salvation*, 87. Emphasis added.
[102] Whitmore, *Imitating Christ*, 4. Emphasis added.
[103] Stringer, *On the Perception of Worship*, 64.

Second, Smith and Scharen both articulate the need for empirical research that examines the *gaps* between culturally prescribed practices and the experiences, meanings, and intentions of practitioners: "Whether and when gaps may exist between the 'official' intentions of the practices and the subjective purposes of the practitioners in any instance is an *empirical* question, one often worth investigating."[104] This is especially the case when the gaps are wider:

> How do religious communities negotiate dissonances between their official prescriptions and subjective dispositions of practitioners when the latter disagree with or do not fit easily into official standards?[105]

Smith's motivations appear theoretically driven, in contrast to Scharen's framing of the same question, which is more practically oriented:

> In order for scholarship about the church to be most helpful to the church—gathered in community and scattered in daily life—rapprochement between empirical and theological understandings of the church ought to be encouraged in such a way that the actual life of the church is attended to, thought through theologically, and thereby strengthened (one hopes) for more faithful witness.[106]

Again, although the motivations and overarching projects differ, the central research question is the same and is a question best answered in dialogue between those who study institutionally prescribed practices and those who do empirical research on individual and social experience of these practices.

Situating This Study

These two intersecting research agenda are methodological starting points for my research on Christian worship in a changing religious landscape and specifically occasional religious practice (Figure A.1). Echoing Smith and Scharen, I am concerned with a *gap* between both prescribed practices and empirically observable patterns in worship practice, and official liturgical theological interpretations and participants' interpretations of

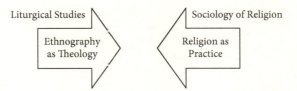

1) *Who* has a voice in determinations about liturgical theology and practice
2) *Gaps* between (a) prescribed practices and observable patterns of worship, and (b) official teachings and participants' interpretations of their experiences

Figure A.1 Interdisciplinary methodology.

---

[104] Smith, *Religion*, 34.
[105] Smith, *Religion*, 15.
[106] Scharen, *Explorations*, 2. Emphasis added.

their worship experiences. Specifically, liturgical theologians and church leaders tend to assume that participants are actively practicing, fully believing, morally compliant, and formally affiliated with the tradition when, in increasingly nonreligious and religiously diverse social contexts, this is clearly not the case (if it ever was). This is particularly true of practices that bring together diverse circles of family and friends, such as baptisms and funerals.

In addition, echoing Riesebrodt and Whitmore, I am concerned with *who* has a voice in determinations about liturgical theology and practice. Most often liturgical leaders, especially clergy, and religiously committed routine practitioners have dominated these conversations, which is understandable. However, attending to a broader range of perspectives is crucial, both sociologically and theologically.

In conclusion, the trajectory in sociology of religion toward a situated understanding of knowledge and the recognition that religion remains a significant force in society together open space for dialogue with theology; and defining religion as a complex of culturally prescribed practices related to superhuman powers makes dialogue vital. The trajectory in liturgical studies toward increasing engagement with the social sciences, especially recent scholarship claiming ethnography as theology, demands increased dialogue with sociology of religion around both method and theory. Although there are ongoing barriers to relationship between the disciplines, and although each discipline is directed toward distinct aims, the common goals and research agenda make research at the intersection of liturgical studies and sociology of religion both possible and desirable, as demonstrated in this research.

APPENDIX B

Research Methods

This interdisciplinary research is situated at the intersection of liturgical studies and sociology of religion, as discussed in Appendix A. While engaging the theological methods of reflection on scripture, tradition, and religious experience, it also relies on qualitative social science research methods, especially participant observation and interviews. The specifics of the interdisciplinary and mixed methods approach employed are outlined in detail below, including the theoretical approach, pilot studies, case selection, and research process.

Theoretical Approach

This specific research project began with a hunch that a "surprising" phenomenon—specifically, that people turn to religious practices to mark significant moments in their lives despite rarely engaging religion at other times—could tell us something about the changing North American religious landscape and the place of Christian worship in it. This is surprising both in the context of liturgical studies literature that tends to assume that participants are formally affiliated, fully believing, actively practicing, and morally compliant, and in the context of sociological literature on religious change that tends to focus either on nonreligion or strong religion, with less attention to the space in between. While this phenomenon is less surprising than one may at first expect (as discussed in Chapter 2), it is a starting point for an abductive approach that moves between empirical research and theory.

An abductive approach[1] to qualitative research aims to hold together empirical observations and theoretical propositions throughout the research process:

> In good research, these two parts of the story not only intertwine but amplify each other. The theoretical account allows us to see things in the empirical that we would gloss over. The empirical description, in turn, pushes the theory in unexpected directions.[2]

I did not bring a specific hypothesis, theory, or theological claim to the field with the aim of illustrating, challenging, or extending it, as in more deductive qualitative methods.[3]

---

[1] Stefan Timmermans and Iddo Tavory, "Theory Construction in Qualitative Research: From Grounded Theory to Abductive Analysis," *Sociological Theory* 30, no. 3 (2012): 167–186; Iddo Tavory and Stefan Timmermans, *Abductive Analysis: Theorizing Qualitative Research* (Chicago: University of Chicago Press, 2014).

[2] Tavory and Timmermans, *Abductive Analysis*, 2.

[3] Michael Burawoy, "The Extended Case Method," *Sociological Theory* 16, no. 1 (March 1998): 4–33; Michael Burawoy, *The Extended Case Method: Four Countries, Four Decades, Four Great Transformations, and One Theoretical Tradition* (Berkeley: University of California Press, 2009).

Neither did I aspire to approach the field inductively as a blank slate, as classical grounded theory would imply.[4] Instead, I employed an abductive approach inspired by Iddo Tavory and Stefan Timmermans, who transparently name the interplay between theory and method in qualitative research with an emphasis on the process of producing theoretical hunches from surprising research findings. They anchor this approach to developing theory—making meaning—in the pragmatist philosophy of Charles Peirce. The application of an abductive approach includes bringing a broad range of theory to the field, in my case drawn not only from sociology but also from religious studies and liturgical studies; recognizing the importance of the position of the researcher and the community of inquiry; and analyzing surprising findings systematically within the context of variation in the collected data. An abductive approach echoes other qualitative methods in terms of making ongoing comparisons within the collected data, selecting additional cases on theoretical grounds, taking detailed fieldnotes, transcribing interviews, coding, and writing memos. The measure of a successful theory is one that *fits* the empirical data,[5] that is more *plausible* than competing theories, and that is *relevant* to the broader intellectual community.[6]

An abductive approach is helpful for addressing issues of normativity that plague qualitative theological research in how it holds together theory and practice: "Theory should not replace or be replaced by empirical research; it is part of the same act."[7] Lived religious experience, accessed through empirical research, and theoretical or theological formulations intertwine with and amplify each other; neither can have the first or the last word. In avoiding the pitfalls of both overly deductive and overly inductive approaches in the social sciences, an abductive approach also makes a way forward for ethnographic theology. This is particularly fruitful when examining *who* has a voice in determinations about Christian theology, with a desire to bring together academic theologians (theory) and everyday theologians (empirical research). It is also generative when exploring *gaps* between prescribed practices (theory) and observable patterns of worship (empirical research), as well as gaps between official teachings (theory) and participants' interpretations of their experiences (empirical research). In this way, an abductive approach is especially suitable for research at the intersection of sociology and theology, as outlined in Appendix A.

Pilot Studies

The questions that this volume addresses and the ways that it frames those questions developed significantly through four pilot projects, two that examine occasional participation in religious practices, and two that explore theological diversity within worshiping communities.

In 2015, I interviewed Protestant clergy in the Midwestern United States from a range of Anglican, Reformed, Methodist, and Anabaptist traditions about their experience

---

[4] Barney Glaser and Anselm Strauss, *The Discovery of Grounded Theory: Strategies for Qualitative Research* (Chicago: Aldine, 1967).

[5] At times, theologians make claims about matters that are not empirically observable and that should not be examined according to this criterion. At other times, theologians make claims that can be subject to empirical observation.

[6] Tavory and Timmermans, *Abductive Analysis*, 104–120.

[7] Tavory and Timmermans, *Abductive Analysis*, 128.

of receiving and responding to requests for infant initiation (both baptism and child blessing) from families whom they see as less connected to the church. While distance from the church is frequently conceived of in terms of less frequent participation in worship, this pilot project expanded the conception of the forms that distance from the church may take: (1) *formal distance* describes those who are not official members of a church; (2) *relational distance* reflects a lack of regular participation in congregational life; (3) *temporal distance* describes past rather than current relationship with a church; (4) *theological distance* is characterized by personal beliefs that push the boundaries of the acceptable diversity of beliefs assumed to be shared by the community; and (5) *moral distance* is associated with life choices or situations that deviate from communal norms.[8] This framework nuances the diverse range of relationships that individuals may have with the church and religion.

Moving from the individual to the congregational level, in 2017, I analyzed the annual statistical returns from the Anglican Diocese of Toronto to consider which of the more than two hundred congregations have a larger increase in attendance on Christmas and Easter than would be expected: If we expect attendance to double on these holidays, what are the characteristics of congregations in which attendance triples or quadruples? The concept of "occasional religiosity" as something that could include participation on both holidays and at life transitions (among other possibilities) began to take shape in the context of this quantitative study, along with a sense that occasional practice varies not only among individuals but also across congregations.[9]

Anchored in a single congregation, in 2016, I conducted a year-long ethnographic study at First Unitarian Church in South Bend.[10] The Unitarian Universalist tradition is openly theologically diverse, with atheists, agnostics, Christians, Buddhists, humanists, and others gathering weekly for "worship" that engages eclectic content within a mainline Protestant format. Relying on participant observation, I explored how ritual practices—especially trusted structures, personal stories, embodied actions, and tangible yet multivalent symbols—foster social solidarity in the context of theological diversity, and specifically in relation to times of crisis.[11]

In addition, in 2016, I conducted a twenty-three-interview study with the Women's Liturgical Choir, an elite group of singers who provide musical leadership for the Roman Catholic mass in the Basilica of the Sacred Heart at the University of Notre Dame.[12] Like First Unitarian Church, the choir is a theologically diverse community that includes singers who are nonreligious, who identify with non-Christian religious traditions, and who are affiliated with a range of Christian traditions, including Orthodox, Episcopal, Lutheran, Methodist, Baptist, nondenominational, and Roman Catholic. Unlike First Unitarian, this theological diversity is largely unacknowledged as this choir moves

---

[8] Sarah Kathleen Johnson, "Poured Out: A Kenotic Approach to Initiating Children at a Distance from the Church," *Studia Liturgica* 49, no. 2 (2019): 175–194.

[9] Sarah Kathleen Johnson and David Sikkink, "Occasional Religious Participation at Christmas and Easter: A Congregational Level Analysis" (paper presented in the Sociology of Religion Unit at the annual meeting of the American Academy of Religion, San Diego, CA, 2019).

[10] I have permission to name First Unitarian Church as the location of this research and express my gratitude for their collaboration.

[11] Sarah Kathleen Johnson, "Crisis, Solidarity, and Ritual in Religiously Diverse Settings: A Unitarian Universalist Case Study," *Religions* 13, no. 7 (2022): 614, https://doi.org/10.3390/rel13070614.

[12] I have permission to name the Women's Liturgical Choir and express my gratitude for their collaboration.

through the uniform practices of providing liturgical leadership in a specific religious tradition: How do theologically diverse participants experience routine participation in Christian worship? This study became a starting point for exploring how individuals who are positioned differently within overlapping ritual systems navigate harmony and dissonance at the intersection of these systems.[13]

Each of these pilot studies established the groundwork for a case study of occasional religious practice in the Anglican tradition in Toronto.

Case Selection

This book has examined what Christian worship is meaning and doing in increasingly nonreligious and religiously diverse social contexts. In so doing, it contributes to our understanding of religion in the twenty-first century, religious ritual, and liturgical theology. At the same time, it is a close examination of how particular individuals experience specific events in certain communities during a narrow window of time. As an ethnographic case study, it claims that "a case study that pays close attention to a specific experience—even an exceptional one—reveals patterns and designs that pervade the larger picture as well."[14] Therefore, as a way into these broad theoretical and theological themes, I examine baptisms and funerals in the Anglican Church of Canada in Toronto, Ontario, between 2017 and 2020.

Anglicans

This study is based in Christian churches affiliated with the Anglican Church of Canada, which is the primary expression of the Anglican Communion in Toronto.[15] Anglican baptisms and funerals are well-established, clearly defined, historically mainstream religious practices in Toronto. At the same time, the Anglican tradition is facing declining membership and participation.[16] Therefore, these rituals may continue to serve as family traditions or cultural defaults for those who are otherwise not especially religious. Certain Anglican churches may also have a role in public life, for example, in performing high-profile funerals, especially for politicians, even if the deceased was nonreligious or was an active participant in another Christian tradition. Furthermore, quantitative studies of religion in Canada suggest that the Anglican tradition is a good place to begin exploring occasional practice.[17]

Theologically, Anglican religious identity is more anchored in ritual practice than in doctrine or ecclesial structure, especially in the *Book of Common Prayer* (1962), which

---

[13] Sarah Kathleen Johnson, "Harmony and Dissonance in Overlapping Ritual Systems: A Religiously Diverse Choir Sings in Roman Catholic Mass" (paper presented in the Ritual Studies Unit at the annual meeting of the American Academy of Religion, Boston, MA, 2017).
[14] Davidman, *Tradition in a Rootless World*, 27.
[15] Anglican Church of Canada, "Welcome to the Anglican Church of Canada." While the Anglican Church in North America also has a small presence in Toronto, it is not a focus in this analysis. The Anglican Church of Canada is the equivalent of the Episcopal Church in the United States and the Church of England.
[16] Elliot, "Statistics Report for House of Bishops."
[17] Bibby, "The Christmas Onlys"; Bibby, *Resilient Gods*.

is named and primarily used for communal rather than personal prayer, and the *Book of Alternative Services* (1985), the latter of which, rather than being an alternative at this stage, has become the primary prayer book in active use in Canada.[18] Grounded in the prayer books, Anglican liturgy is relatively fixed yet also somewhat flexible. This allows a range of institutional actions and interpretations to exist within a recognizable and coherent historical, theological, and liturgical tradition. The liturgical life of the Anglican tradition has both Catholic and Protestant resonances, potentially rendering results that are applicable to a wider spectrum of the Christian tradition. The Anglican tradition is itself internally diverse, with Anglo-Catholic, mainline, evangelical, and intercultural expressions in the city of Toronto.

Baptisms and Funerals

Anglican *infant baptism* and *funeral* practices are at the center of this study as a point of access for reflection on religious ritual and Christian liturgy. Historically and across cultures, religious rituals mark birth and death. At the same time, secular alternatives are readily available in modern urban centers. In contexts that are otherwise seen as highly secular, religious rituals marking life transitions are episodes "in or through which the implicit becomes explicit";[19] they are moments when individuals, families, clergy, and church communities must make concrete decisions about whether and how to engage in religious practices.[20] Studying life transition rituals provides access to people with a range of relationships to a tradition, including those who, apart from participation in these rituals, may consider themselves nonreligious or practice a different religious tradition. As significant family rituals, baptisms and funerals demonstrate how multiple generations experience and interpret the same religious event.[21] Furthermore, there is well-developed liturgical material and theological reflection associated with these practices in the Anglican tradition,[22] which allows for assessment of whether and how official institutional approaches align with the experience and interpretations of participants.

In the Anglican tradition in Toronto, baptism is almost always celebrated using the *Book of Alternative Services*, because the rite for baptism in the *Book of Common Prayer* is for private, infant baptism.[23] The practice of baptism as prescribed in the *Book of*

---

[18] *The Book of Common Prayer* in its various forms is foundational for Anglican identity. The Anglican Church of Canada has two prayer books in active use: the 1962 *Book of Common Prayer* (General Synod of the Anglican Church of Canada, *Book of Common Prayer and Administration of the Sacraments and Other Rites and Ceremonies of the Church According to the Use of the Anglican Church of Canada* [Toronto: ABC Publishing, 1962]) and the 1985 *Book of Alternative Services* (General Synod of the Anglican Church of Canada, *Book of Alternative Services of the Anglican Church of Canada* [Toronto: ABC Publishing, 1985]). Clergy may also borrow liturgical resources from other communities within the Anglican Communion. Anglican Church of Canada, "Liturgical Resources," accessed December 11, 2023, https://www.anglican.ca/faith/worship/resources.

[19] Davie, "Vicarious Religion," 29.

[20] Tavory and Timmermans encourage looking for variation through a focus on situations that "require actors to make their usually implicit forms of meaning-making explicit, both for themselves and for others in the situation." Tavory and Timmermans, *Abductive Analysis*, 74.

[21] Dillon and Wink, *In the Course of a Lifetime*; Voas and Chaves, "Is the United States a Counterexample?"

[22] General Synod of the Anglican Church of Canada, *Book of Alternative Services*; General Synod of the Anglican Church of Canada, *Book of Common Prayer*.

[23] General Synod of the Anglican Church of Canada, *Book of Alternative Services*, 151–166.

Alternative Services includes the presentation of the candidates; the examination of the candidates, including both renouncing evil and accepting Christ; a commitment from the congregation ("Will you who witness these vows do all in your power to support these persons in their life in Christ?"); prayers for the candidates; thanksgiving over the water; the baptismal covenant, which is a question-and-answer form of the Apostles' Creed as well an affirmation of six specific commitments; baptism with water "in the name of the Father, and of the Son, and of the Holy Spirit"; anointing with the sign of the cross; giving of light in the form of a candle; and welcoming the newly baptized into the household of God.[24] In this form, baptism is a profoundly corporate experience. As is written in the *Book of Alternative Services*, "Baptism unites Christ with his people. That union is both individual and corporate.... Christians are not just baptized as individuals; they are a new humanity."[25]

Funeral liturgies in the Anglican tradition take various forms and may draw on either the *Book of Common Prayer* or the *Book of Alternative Services*.[26] These liturgies may take the form of a funeral, at which the body is present, or a memorial service, at which it is not. Cremation is a commonly chosen option in the Anglican tradition in Toronto. Other choices that planners make include which book will serve as the primary source for the service, and whether to celebrate the eucharist as part of the liturgy. Friends and family shaping the liturgy may also make choices about various elements, such as scripture readings, hymns, and prayers, many of which would also be found in Sunday worship. In the Anglican tradition, funerals may include tributes from family members at the outset of the service, and clergy navigate how to accommodate this element in various ways. Preaching from clergy is also usually part of the liturgy. The primary feature of a funeral that would not be found in Sunday worship, apart from distinct thematic content throughout, is the commendation, in which the deceased is handed over to the care of God.

From a liturgical standpoint, baptisms and funerals are integrally connected theologically and within the rites themselves.[27] At the same time, there are notable distinctions between baptisms and funerals. Infants are usually at the center of baptism, and older adults tend to be at the center of funerals, although people in midlife, especially the parents of the infant and the adult children of the deceased, are likely to be involved. In addition, the two rituals may have significantly different emotional tenors, with baptism characterized by a joyful, forward-looking orientation, and funerals potentially characterized by grief, and looking back (or looking forward to a life to come). Baptisms in the Anglican tradition generally take place in the context of Sunday worship, whereas funerals often reflect Sunday worship patterns yet occur at other times. These and other distinctions between the practices yield insights that apply not only to these events, but also to other Christian worship practices.

---

[24] General Synod of the Anglican Church of Canada, *Book of Alternative Services*, 151–166.

[25] General Synod of the Anglican Church of Canada, *Book of Alternative Services*, 146.

[26] General Synod of the Anglican Church of Canada, *Book of Common Prayer*, 591–610; General Synod of the Anglican Church of Canada, *Book of Alternative Services*, 565–605. In some cases, other resources may also be available, such as *Book of Common Prayer* texts with contemporary language replacing archaic language or resources in additional languages.

[27] Morrill, *Divine Worship and Human Healing*.

Toronto

Toronto, Ontario, Canada, is a large, modern, multicultural, pluralistic urban center. Many religious and nonreligious ritual options are available for marking birth and death. At the same time, historically, the Anglican tradition has had a prominent social role in English-speaking Canada, with Toronto being a particularly significant site for Anglicanism.[28] Although Toronto is distinct from other regions in Canada, it holds important symbolic value as a center of national identity and culture. Toronto also has a large population of new Canadians, recent immigrants to Canada, some of whom may participate in Anglican life transition rituals, especially if they have connections to other former British colonies. The religious history of the region, diversity of the population, cultural cachet of the city, and abundance of ritual options make selecting an Anglican ritual a noteworthy choice.

Canada is an excellent national context in which to consider questions of occasional religious practice since occasional practice is clearly widespread,[29] yet understudied. Occasional religious practice appears to be the most common way of being religious in twenty-first-century Canada across age, gender, and geographic categories.[30] Despite the pervasive presence of the occasionally religious in the Canadian religious landscape, those who practice only occasionally have been the subject of very little research.[31] In order to understand religion in Canada better, it is necessary to understand occasional religious practice.

Canada is also a valuable case since there are potential parallels to patterns in both Europe and the United States.[32] For example, David Voas and Mark Chaves argue that religion is declining in Canada, Europe, and the United States according to generational patterns.[33] Mark Noll describes how "Canada, which for so long looked much more Christian than Western Europe, and considerably more Christian than its southern neighbor, now appears in its religious character to resemble Europe much more closely than it does the United States."[34] Grace Davie raises the question of whether vicarious religion—her concept for religion manifest in "continuing requests, even in a moderately secular society, for some sort of religious ritual at the time of a birth, a marriage, and most of all at the time of a death"—is present in some form in the United States as well as in Britain,[35] and, I would add, Canada. What is learned about occasional religious practice in Canada may illuminate these other contexts.

Declining Participation in Anglican Baptisms and Funerals

The number of people in Canada who mark birth and death with Anglican liturgical practices has been in decline since the 1960s:

---

[28] Hayes, *Anglicans in Canada*.
[29] Bibby, *Resilient Gods*, 84.
[30] Bibby, *Resilient Gods*, 65.
[31] Thiessen, *The Meaning of Sunday*, 67.
[32] See Chapter 2.
[33] Voas and Chaves, "Is the United States a Counterexample?"
[34] Mark A. Noll, "What Happened to Christian Canada?," *Church History* 75, no. 2 (June 2006): 273.
[35] Davie, "Vicarious Religion."

350   APPENDIX B

For Anglicans, baptisms rose from 37,557 in 1948 to a peak of 46,681 in 1960, an increase of nearly 25%. A decade later (1970) baptisms had declined to under 30,000 and by 2001 were under 15,000 a year, a 70% fall from the 1960 high point.[36]

Taking into account the Canadian birth rate shows that there are not merely fewer children being born, but fewer children being brought for Anglican baptism.[37] The number of baptisms in the Anglican Diocese of Toronto is also in decline. Over eight years, the number of baptisms in the diocese has been cut almost in half, from 1,055 in 2011 to 597 in 2018. The number of funerals has also decreased significantly, from 1,712 in 2011 to 1,254 in 2018 (Figure B.1).[38] These shifts align with larger changes in the Canadian religious landscape and are part of what make this a suitable case study. There are nevertheless

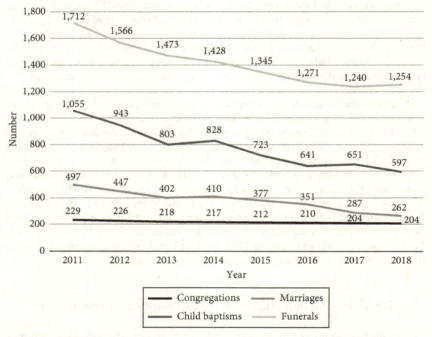

Figure B.1 Decline in baptisms, marriages, and funerals in the Anglican Diocese of Toronto, 2011–2018.

---

[36] Brian Clarke and Stuart Macdonald, *Leaving Christianity: Changing Allegiances in Canada Since 1945* (Montreal and Kingston: McGill-Queen's University Press, 2017), 49.
[37] Clarke and Macdonald, *Leaving Christianity*, 51.
[38] Anglican Church of Canada, Diocese of Toronto, Annual Statistical Returns, 2013–2018. The Statistical Returns may be accessed by contacting the Diocesan Archives.

ample opportunities to observe these practices, and to speak with participants connected to them.

Broader Application

A case study entails focusing on some areas rather than others. In this analysis, the Anglican tradition is not directly compared to other ecclesial traditions, religious traditions, and nonreligious practices, although comparisons are often made by participants during interviews. Individuals and families who choose religious practices are not directly considered alongside families who do not, such as those who have secular funerals at funeral homes. Toronto is not directly compared to smaller cities, suburban, or rural contexts in Canada, or internationally to other world cities. Rituals associated with birth and death are not held alongside rituals associated with adolescence or marriage. Significant limits are necessary in an ethnographic case study that aims for depth in one area rather than comprehensive breadth. There are many comparisons that could be explored in future research.

At the same time, the theory emerging from this research may apply beyond the immediate case in various ways. Results associated with the roles of religion in the multicultural, pluralistic, urban context of Toronto may apply to other similarly diverse urban centers, including those of smaller size, especially in other historically Christian regions, such as the United States and Western Europe. Due to the internal diversity of the Anglican tradition, particularly in terms of the range of theological and liturgical expressions, other Christian traditions—including mainline Protestant denominations, certain expressions of Roman Catholicism, other Christian traditions influenced by evangelical and charismatic liturgical practice, and other intercultural communities—may relate to this research. The established and historically mainstream nature of Anglicanism means that some results may apply more generally to ongoing participation in life-course rituals in other established religious traditions. Furthermore, results associated with rituals related to birth and death may speak into other life-course transition rituals, including those related to adulthood (confirmation in the Anglican tradition), and marriage, as well as into Christian liturgical practice broadly. This research speaks to much more than Anglican baptisms and funerals in Toronto; this case is a way into broader social scientific and theological questions.

Research Methods

As a *qualitative mixed methods* study, this research consists primarily of interviews supported by participant observation and archival research. While existing *quantitative data* regarding baptism and funeral rituals provide valuable context for the study, and *historical background* is necessary for understanding the history of Christian baptism and funeral practices, the Anglican tradition, and religion and nonreligion in Canada, these sources primarily serve the purpose of framing and interpreting qualitative fieldwork. I recognize with gratitude my dependence on congregational leaders welcoming my presence in their communities, clergy being willing to invest time and effort in facilitating connections with families involved in baptisms and funerals, and, most of all, participants in interviews sharing their stories with honesty and vulnerability.

Extended Interviews

Extended *interviews* are necessary to "get beyond the surface description that surveys provide, to get to the important experiences, feelings, contradictions, processes, and complex layers of meaning in most people's lives."[39] Extended interviews are necessary to access personal reflections on religious practices and experiences that cannot be seen by an observer. Through interviews, this research aims to give both non-expert participants and clergy serving congregations a voice in determinations about liturgical theology and practice. Interview guides are included in Appendix C.

The main focus of this research is interviews with *non-expert participants* in baptisms and funerals, including those at the center of the practice, such as the family of the infant or the deceased, as well as others connected to the experience, such as godparents, grandparents, grandchildren, and friends. Interviews with family members focused on inviting narrative description of the liturgical experience—"tell me the story of the baptism" or "tell me the story of the funeral"—as a starting point for exploring the significance of these practices for participants in the context of their lives and relationships with religion.[40] Beginning with an open-ended question allowed participants to identify their own priorities and set an agenda. While there were key themes I aimed to address in each interview, my goal was to understand what participants described as important in their experience and understanding of the event.

This research also includes extended interviews with *clergy* about their experience of baptisms and funerals, with a focus on times when these events involve families who are more loosely connected to the church. Interviews with clergy focus on specific examples of baptisms and funerals and move from these concrete cases to more general theological reflection. Hearing from both liturgical leaders and non-expert participants is a way to explore gaps between participants' interpretations of their experiences and official teaching. However, while clergy represent the Anglican tradition, they may also offer valuable critiques of it, often based on pastoral experience.

Participant Observation

Although the narrative and meaning-centered approach of interviews is important, participant observation of *baptisms and funerals*, preparation processes, and associated events provides crucial access to embodied and expressive dimensions of these practices and situates them in a larger religious and cultural context. Participant observation creates space to value non-cognitive interpretations that are physical and emotional, alongside cognitive meaning-making. Observation of events that involve interview participants can enrich conversations by engaging specific details. Observation can verify or challenge aspects of interviews, potentially pointing to surprising gaps between accounts and actions. Observing baptisms and funerals that are not connected to interviews provides context for how these practices often unfold in specific communities, contributing to an understanding of occasional practice.

---

[39] Smith, *Soul Searching*, 118.
[40] Stout critiques Robert Bellah's problematic push for discursive meaning. Jeffery Stout, *Ethics After Babel: The Languages of Morals and Their Discontents* (Cambridge: James Clark, 1988).

Participant observation of the *larger liturgical context* within which baptisms and funerals are celebrated, including ordinary Sunday worship, is crucial for understanding how these occasions exist within ritual systems. Participant observation is also a way to explore other Christian occasions that may be associated with occasional religious practice, such as Christmas and Easter, as well as cultural events, such as Remembrance Day and Mother's Day. In addition, participant observation is one way to situate specific congregations within the larger Anglican liturgical landscape in Toronto.

Archival Research

Participant observation is limited to events that take place within the time frame of the research, and interviews are limited by who is accessible to me as a researcher. Therefore, for this book I supplemented qualitative fieldwork with archival research.

The *Diocesan Archives* of the Diocese of Toronto preserve copies of the statistical returns submitted annually by each congregation in the diocese.[41] These detailed records have tracked the number of baptisms and funerals (along with a variety of other measures) in each congregation each year for more than a century. The most recent statistics are available online as part of the material provided to participants in Synod, the annual gathering of the lay and clerical members who constitute the governing body of the church. These records offer an overview of baptisms and funerals in the diocese that it would be impossible to construct through participant observation and interviews.

The Nancy Mallett Archives and Museum at Cathedral Church of St. James keeps meticulous records of worship services and events at the Cathedral.[42] I turned to the archives to examine funerals for high-profile Torontonians, such as politicians and business leaders, that were held at the cathedral. Records for these events include orders of service, photographs, newspaper clippings, internal communications, material objects, and more. Additional resources are available from other sources, including archived video footage of the funerals. In this case, the archives were a point of access to events that occurred in the past and that involved families unlikely to participate in this research.

Access to records kept by *specific congregations* provide context for interviews, especially orders of service for baptisms and funerals preserved and shared by parish administrators.[43] Another source of context is online obituaries that often provide a succinct introduction to the deceased and an outline of their family system.

---

[41] The Anglican Diocese of Toronto has kept exceptional records of congregations since before 1900. Every congregation submits annual statistical returns. These returns are compiled and made available for annual Synod meetings, and Synod minutes are preserved by the Diocesan Archives. The annual statistical returns from 2011 through 2018 are also available as PDF documents online. What precisely these numbers track has evolved over the past century, although there is striking consistency in some areas, especially in relation to average Sunday attendance, membership, giving, and records of baptisms, confirmations, marriages, and funerals. The data from the past five years are particularly valuable for estimating the number of baptisms and funerals to expect in congregations that are the focus of the study. Anglican Church of Canada, Diocese of Toronto, "Annual Returns," accessed December 11, 2023, http://www.toronto.anglican.ca/parish-administration/finance/annual-returns.

[42] Many thanks to Nancy Mallett for her gracious support in accessing and navigating the archives.

[43] Many thanks to parish administrators for providing electronic copies of orders of service for many baptisms and funerals.

Research Process

My first visit to Toronto for the purpose of exploring its potential as an ethnographic site took place in June 2017. I moved to Toronto in May 2018, and I concluded the fieldwork engaged in this analysis in June 2020. While the Anglican Diocese of Toronto covers a large geographic region that includes rural areas and small towns, this research is focused on the Greater Toronto Area, including the City of Toronto and its suburbs. The first phase of research focused on building familiarity with the Diocese of Toronto through initial assessment of the annual statistical returns, historical research, informal conversation with Anglican contacts, participant observation of public worship, and obtaining Institutional Review Board (IRB) approval for this study. With this foundation in place, I was able to proceed with qualitative fieldwork: participant observation of worship, interviews with clergy, partnerships with particular congregations, and interviews with non-expert participants involved in baptisms and funerals. While interviews with participants in baptisms and funerals are at the center of this research, participant observation and interviews with clergy situate these conversations within specific congregations and within the broader context of the Anglican Diocese of Toronto.

In March 2020, COVID-19 arrived in Toronto, and on March 13 the Archbishop of Toronto announced the cessation of worship services.[44] The following day, the College of Bishops of the Diocese of Toronto issued the emphatic clarification, "The key principle to follow is: NO CONGREGATION IS TO BE ASSEMBLED, OF ANY SIZE, AT ANY TIME."[45] On March 17, the Premier of Ontario declared a state of emergency,[46] and on March 28, gatherings were limited to five people, with the exception of funerals, when ten people were permitted to gather.[47] Various types of restrictions remained in place for the remainder of this research. Restrictions affected the process of fieldwork itself, with interviews moving to the phone and online, and the potential scope of the study, limiting the number of baptisms, funerals, and interviews included, both because of the restrictions on gathering for these events and the additional pressures facing congregations and clergy required to facilitate these connections. While I considered returning to the field to conduct further research when restrictions were lifted, it was clear that the focus of these conversations would be the impact of the pandemic rather than "ordinary" baptisms and funerals. The purpose of this research was to study occasional religious practice—a widespread and enduring phenomenon—rather than the disruptive impact of the pandemic on liturgy.[48] Therefore, while the pandemic is mentioned

---

[44] Anglican Church of Canada, Diocese of Toronto, "Bishop Announces Cessation of Worship Services," March 13, 2020, accessed December 11, 2023, https://www.toronto.anglican.ca/2020/03/13/bishop-announces-cessation-of-worship.

[45] Anglican Church of Canada, Diocese of Toronto, "Statement from the College of Bishops on Current Restrictions," March 14, 2020, accessed December 11, 2023, https://www.toronto.anglican.ca/2020/03/14/statement-from-the-college-of-bishops-on-current-restrictions.

[46] Government of Ontario, "Ontario Enacts Declaration of Emergency to Protect the Public," March 17, 2020, accessed December 11, 2023, https://news.ontario.ca/opo/en/2020/03/ontario-enacts-declaration-of-emergency-to-protect-the-public.html.

[47] Government of Ontario, "Ontario Prohibits Gatherings of More than Five People with Strict Exceptions," March 28, 2020, accessed December 11, 2023, https://news.ontario.ca/opo/en/2020/03/ontario-prohibits-gatherings-of-five-people-or-more-with-strict-exceptions.html.

[48] I have conducted qualitative research on the impact of the pandemic on Christian worship in Toronto that overlaps with this study. Sarah Kathleen Johnson, "Online Communion, Christian Community, and Receptive Ecumenism: A Holy Week Ethnography during COVID-19," *Studia Liturgica* 50, no. 2 (2020): 188–210; Sarah Kathleen Johnson, "Evolving Practices of Online

in several of the later interviews, it was not a central focus of this study. I was fortunate to have robust data in place prior to the pandemic that provide strong support for the results of this research.

Participant Observation of Anglican Worship in Toronto

Between June 2017 and March 2020, I observed more than eighty Anglican services of worship in the Diocese of Toronto and wrote detailed fieldnotes.[49] These services took place in fourteen different parishes. I selected parishes for two reasons: (1) to explore the breadth of liturgical practice in the diocese, (2) to connect with potential partner congregations, and later to maintain relationships with these congregations. I attended ordinary Sunday worship routinely in partner congregations, including participating in each of the Sunday services offered in each partner parish at least once.

To observe occasional religious practice associated with *holidays*, I prioritized attending more services during certain seasons, including eight services associated with Christmas over two years and eight services that occurred between Good Friday and Easter Sunday in one year. I also attended services on the adjacent Sundays in the same communities for contrast and context.

Over these three years, a high priority for me was attending services that include baptisms, and I was able to attend eleven baptism services in total, including nine in partner congregations. I was also able to observe one preparation meeting that involved several families the day before the baptisms took place. I observed five funerals in partner congregations. Fewer funerals took place than anticipated, and gaining access to attend funerals proved more difficult, with openness to this possibility emerging around the time participant observation of in-person worship ceased because of pandemic restrictions.

Interviews with Clergy

Interviews with twenty Anglican clergy were a preliminary phase and ongoing component of this research (Table B.1). The first interviews with clergy took place in November 2017, and interviews were ongoing throughout the research process until March 2020. I took fieldnotes following each interview. Interviews with clergy were transcribed and coded in MAXQDA. Some clergy provided me with additional materials, such as resources they use to prepare families for baptisms or to plan funerals.

I selected clergy for the same two reasons that I selected congregations for participant observation: (1) to explore the breadth of liturgical practice in the diocese, and (2) to connect with potential partner congregations. In the context of interviews, I asked clergy to recommend others with whom I might speak, especially those who may have a different approach to baptisms and funerals, to facilitate theoretical sampling. These twenty

Communion in Ecumenical Perspective: An Ethnographic Study of Four Pandemic Holy Weeks" (paper presented at the biannual congress of Societas Liturgica, Maynooth, Ireland, 2023).

[49] Emergency measures associated with the COVID-19 pandemic were implemented shortly before Easter in 2020. While I observed twenty-nine Anglican liturgies online, this material is not included in this analysis.

Table B.1 Interviews with Clergy

Interviews with Clergy (20)	
Type	19 in person 1 phone
Role	14 rectors 6 associates
Gender	14 men 6 women
Age	4 under 45 12 over 45 4 unknown
Race	15 white 4 people of color 1 unknown
Character of congregation	5 Evangelical 4 Mainline 4 High Church 4 language of worship other than English 3 Anglo-Catholic

interviews reflect a diversity of liturgical and theological expressions, including Anglo-Catholic, Evangelical, High Church, and Mainline congregations and communities that worship in languages other than English. The parishes are located in a range of social settings, including urban and suburban congregations, and higher and lower income areas. In some cases, I interviewed multiple clergy within a single congregation, especially with potential partner congregations and in partner congregations composed of distinct worshiping communities. Therefore, these twenty interviews represent fifteen different parishes.

All clergy whom I contacted responded positively to the request for an interview and a mutually agreeable time was established in all but one case. Interviews took place in church offices (apart from one conducted in a coffee shop and another in a home) and in some cases interviews included a tour of the church building. The interviews ranged in length from 50 minutes to 2 hours and 20 minutes, with an average length of 1 hour and 20 minutes. The clergy interviewed are diverse in role (14 rectors, 6 associates), gender (14 men, 6 women), age (4 under 45, 12 over 45, 4 unknown), and race (15 white, 4 people of color,[50] 1 unknown). Some had been in ministry for decades and others were just starting out. Some had served several congregations within and beyond the Diocese of Toronto, and others had one primary ministry context. The clergy whom I interviewed take a broad range of approaches to responding to requests for baptisms and funerals and giving leadership to these practices.

---

[50] To protect the privacy of participants, more specific information is not provided.

Partner Congregations

Partnerships with congregations established key sites for observing baptisms and funerals and interviewing family members connected with the observed events, as well as similar events that took place in recent years. I only considered congregations as possible partners if a significant number of both baptisms and funerals were expected to occur during the time frame of the study based on the statistical returns from previous years. Higher numbers of baptisms and funerals were required to ensure enough participants for the study and to maintain anonymity. Therefore, partner congregations tended to be larger. Partner congregations were also selected to contrast with one another in liturgical expression, geographic location, and leadership style. Therefore, I established partnerships sequentially; once a congregation confirmed its participation, I considered various options for theoretical variation. Variation across congregations is intended to mitigate potential idiosyncrasies associated with a single congregation, rather than to allow for direct comparison or to be representative of the diocese, neither of which is possible within this framework. The level of analysis in this study is primarily individual, not institutional: differences between participants are generally more significant than the differences between congregations.

Three congregations are key partners in this research. The Cathedral Church of St. James has given permission to be named. At the time of this research, the Cathedral is composed of several distinct worshiping communities with four English-language services each Sunday, one Mandarin-language service, and one service at St. Bartholomew's Anglican Church, a ministry in collaboration with the Cathedral. While the Cathedral is rooted in and serves its neighborhood in downtown Toronto, it is also the liturgical center of the Diocese of Toronto as the seat of the bishop. It is served by numerous clergy in various roles. There was significant staff turnover during this study, which makes it possible to protect the identities of clergy while acknowledging the Cathedral as a partner in this research.

The second partner congregation is a suburban parish that I will call St. John's Anglican Church. St. John's is located outside the City of Toronto in a suburb within the Greater Toronto Area. This mainline, theologically progressive congregation has a deep history and had a very active congregation at the time of this research, with three Sunday morning services, programming for families with children, and various ministries in the community. St. John's is served by multiple clergy and staff who remain anonymous in this research. Unlike the Cathedral, St. John's does not have a high profile in the Diocese. It is rarely mentioned in interviews with clergy. In many ways, St. John's is much more ordinary, both in its liturgical expression and its focus on connecting with the local neighborhood and families who have a history of relationship with the parish.

The third partner in this research, which I will call Christ Church, is a parish located in a residential neighborhood in the city of Toronto. This high church congregation in a wealthy neighborhood has a long and established history; yet, unlike the Cathedral that is the seat of the Diocese, it focuses on its neighborhood and families with a historic connection to the parish. Christ Church is served by multiple clergy and staff who remain anonymous in this research. The partnership with Christ Church was the final partnership established and did not have as much time to unfold before this research was disrupted by the COVID-19 pandemic. Nevertheless, it was a significant site for participant observation and the source of several interviews.

In addition to the three congregations who generously accepted the invitation to partner in this research, three congregations declined to participate. All three of these congregations would identify, at least in part, with the Evangelical Anglican tradition. Notably, all three have specific expectations for families involved in baptisms, including participation in multiple classes and a sense of personal faith commitment, and primarily conduct funerals for families with a preexisting relationship with the church. Although all three provided understandable reasons for declining the invitation to participate, such as staff transitions or other significant changes in congregational life, the similarities among these congregations made me wonder whether there were other factors involved. For example, each of these congregations sees baptisms and funerals as key moments to draw in families who are more tangentially connected to the church and may consequently be protective of these pastoral relationships. In addition, the possibility of knowing more about the families involved in these events may be threatening, especially if what is learned does not align with the ideals and expectations of leaders.

Interviews with Non-Expert Participants

Forty-one interviews with non-expert participants in baptisms and funerals form the core of this research (Table B.2). Parents, adult children, grandparents, grandchildren, spouses, and friends were willing to speak about these events as significant moments in their lives, which created space for a broader conversation about Christian worship and the place of religion in their lives. This was a unique opportunity to understand religion from the perspective of those who are occasional practitioners and to listen for their lived liturgical theology. This research aspires to give occasional practitioners a voice in determinations about liturgical theology and practice.

When I was able to attend baptisms in person, I approached families afterward to introduce myself briefly and request their contact information. At times, the clergy person had already mentioned my research to them and had made the introduction. I relied on clergy to contact participants involved in baptisms and funerals in the past to request their permission to share their contact information with me. On my behalf, clergy contacted families involved in baptisms in the year prior to the study, and funerals over the past several years. I encouraged clergy to contact as many families as possible, while exercising their pastoral judgement in complex cases when an invitation to participate in this research might put participants at risk. Most families involved in baptisms responded positively to the request to share contact information, although several did not respond at all. Many families involved in funerals responded positively to the request, although some expressed that they were not comfortable speaking about the funeral. Clergy were also more selective regarding participants in funerals.

Once I received contact information from clergy, I reached out to participants with more information about this research and the specific request for an interview. As a small token of appreciation, I offered each participant a $30 gift card to a bookstore with a section of baby gifts, or a $30 memorial donation. Rather than selecting a sample, I contacted all individuals who were willing to share their contact information and, other than a few who never replied despite my repeated attempts, received a positive response from almost every person I contacted. This suggests to me that family members are invested in these

APPENDIX B   359

Table B.2 Interviews with Family Members

Interviews with Family Members (41)		
Type	25 in person 15 phone 1 video conference	
Congregation	31 St. John's 9 Cathedral 1 Christ	
Event	25 baptisms (15 distinct baptisms) 16 funerals (8 distinct funerals)	
Relationship	Baptisms	14 mothers 3 aunts 2 grandmothers 2 fathers 3 adults who were baptized 1 adult partner
	Funerals	6 daughters 4 sons 3 friends 2 wives 1 grandson
Gender	33 women 8 men	
Age	24 under 45 17 over 45	
Race	26 white 10 people of color 5 unknown	
Religious background*	22 Anglican 9 Catholic 8 other Protestant 2 nonreligious	
Religious practice at time of interview	30 occasional 11 routine	

* NOTE: Three participants described a background that includes another religious tradition or Christian tradition alongside one of those listed here.

events and are willing to discuss them. In addition, each of the twenty-four interviews with an initial contact included snowball sampling—requesting participants to connect me with other family members and friends involved in the event. Most participants were happy to make these connections, and many of the people to whom they reached out were willing to speak with me. Recognizing the diverse relationships to religion within family systems and social networks is a contribution of this research. At the same time, to avoid a narrow focus on certain social networks, I conducted no more than four interviews in connection to a single baptism or funeral. Therefore, twenty-five interviews are connected to fifteen distinct baptisms, and sixteen interviews are connected to eight distinct funerals, although many other examples of baptisms and funerals come up during conversations.

I offered to conduct interviews at the times and in the locations that were most convenient for participants. Interviews took me to every corner of the Greater Toronto Area (GTA), despite being anchored in only three congregations. Most of the twenty-five in-person interviews took place in homes or at coffee shops. Fifteen interviews took place on the phone either because participants did not reside in the GTA or because they preferred to be interviewed by phone.[51] Interviews with working participants were often held in the evening or during a break over lunch. In contrast, interviews with retirees and parents on leave to care for children often took place during the day, sometimes with children present. Two interviews took place with pairs rather than individuals. Interviews ranged in length from 48 minutes to 2 hours and 20 minutes, with baptism interviews averaging 75 minutes and funeral interviews 90 minutes. Some participants shared additional materials during interviews, such as photographs and objects connected to the events. I took fieldnotes following each interview. Interviews were transcribed and coded in MAXQDA.

Interview participants were diverse in age (about 24 under the age of 45, and 14 over the age of 45) and ethnicity (about 26 white, 10 people of color, and 5 unknown). I interviewed significantly more women than men (33 women, 8 men), despite recognizing this imbalance early and attempting to recruit male participants whenever possible. This imbalance is unsurprising since women are generally more religious than men in the Christian tradition in North America, and often take the lead on religion in families, especially in terms of facilitating baptisms and funerals. Hearing about the liturgical experience of women is an opportunity to correct for male bias among clergy and academic liturgical scholars whose voices have historically been dominant.

Most significantly, thirty of the participants in this research fall within the parameters of my definition of occasional practitioners at the time of the interview. Only eleven were routine practitioners at the time of the interview. This means that about three-quarters of the sample is occasional, even though I was not specifically sampling for occasional practitioners but instead following up on every contact available through partner congregations. Therefore, despite being occasional practitioners at present, this group is likely still on the more religious end of the spectrum of those participating in events like baptisms and funerals, since they were open to receiving an email from a clergy person, family member, or friend, and to participating in an interview about religion. Participants also appeared to reach out to family members and friends whom they expected would be comfortable with a conversation about religion.

Although the baptisms and funerals took place in the Anglican tradition, participants come from a range of religious backgrounds. Most participants describe being raised in or having some sense of connection to a religious tradition through their families of origin: twenty-two identify as having an Anglican background, nine a background in the Catholic tradition, and eight a sense of connection to other Protestant traditions. Two participants were raised nonreligious. Three participants describe multiple religious traditions in their backgrounds, with families holding Muslim, Jewish, or Eastern

---

[51] Once meeting in person was limited due to COVID-19, all interviews moved to phone or video conference.

Orthodox traditions alongside the Christian traditions more widely represented in this research. Participants also claim a diversity of religious and nonreligious identities at the time of this research. This is a rich body of qualitative data that makes a unique contribution to liturgical scholarship.

Situating Myself

Qualitative research requires *reflexivity* on the part of the researcher. Because this is a study of the range of ways people relate to religious practices, it was crucial for me to examine my own relationship with religion and participation in religious practices and to consider how this impacts my relationships in the field and my interpretation of the qualitative data. It was also important to recognize how this has changed over the course of the research process. I conducted this fieldwork as a theology doctoral student in the liturgical studies area at the University of Notre Dame in Indiana. I prepared this manuscript for publication as Assistant Professor of Liturgy and Pastoral Theology and Director of Anglican Studies at Saint Paul University in Ottawa, Ontario. Furthermore, I was ordained for ministry in Mennonite Church Canada in the time between completing the fieldwork and publishing this monograph.

At the beginning of each interview with family members involved in baptisms and funerals, I situated myself by saying something like this: "I'm not Anglican. I don't work for the church. There are no right or wrong answers here. I am just interested in your honest reflection on your experience." While some participants responded with slight surprise, this statement seemed to put most participants at ease. I framed the interviews in this way to make it clear that I was not a priest and that I was not testing their religious knowledge or judging their religious participation. This statement worked well to build rapport and create a space for conversations that are different from those that participants have with clergy when preparing for a baptisms or funerals. Each of these statements was true. I was not and am not Anglican. At the time, apart from nine months of intensive fieldwork when I attended multiple Anglican liturgies every Sunday, I had been an occasional Anglican practitioner: I attended holiday and baptism services during my first year in Toronto, sporadically attended a contemplative compline liturgy at an Episcopal church as a divinity school student, visited Anglican cathedrals on vacation, and attended Anglican churches with family members or to support friends. This gave me a certain affinity with participants in this research. Like them, I walked into new worshiping communities, navigated less familiar liturgical books, and interpreted obscure Anglican terminology. At the time of the interviews, it was also true that I did not work for the Anglican church.

By the time I was preparing this manuscript for publication, my position has shifted. I am now the Director of Anglican Studies in the Faculty of Theology at Saint Paul University, a Roman Catholic University located in Ottawa, Ontario. I am directly involved in forming future Anglican priests, deacons, and lay leaders for ministry, liaise regularly with multiple Anglican dioceses and Anglican theological schools, and plan a weekly Anglican Eucharist and participate regularly in Anglican morning prayer. Furthermore, I spent a year as a consultant hired to work with the Anglican Diocese of Toronto on their Cast the Net visioning process (2022–2023).[52] I now present this

---

[52] Anglican Church of Canada, Diocese of Toronto, "Cast the Net," accessed December 11, 2023, https://www.toronto.anglican.ca/about-us/cast-the-net.

research at events for Anglican clergy and in public forums. While I hope this research is helpful for congregations, clergy, and religious institutions, my goal was not and is not the flourishing or even survival of specific religious institutions. While I am indebted to the clergy who have supported this research, I am equally accountable to the occasionally religious participants. I am genuinely interested in valuing their honest reflection on their experience.

In certain interviews, I found it was also necessary to clarify that I am not Catholic. I made this statement when participants gestured toward criticizing the Catholic tradition yet appeared hesitant to do so. My affiliation with the University of Notre Dame and indications that I understood what was said about Catholicism may have been the source of this caution. While I am not Catholic, I am very familiar with the Catholic tradition and have been a routine participant in Catholic worship for much of my adult life. I have also studied theology at two Roman Catholic universities and taught theology courses at three. This is an asset when interpreting interviews with those who identify with the Catholic tradition. At the same time, as a non-Catholic who attends Catholic worship, I am also well positioned to interpret the reflections of non-Catholics who experience Catholic practices.

Several times, participants specifically asked me about my religious background. Only in these cases did I share that my tradition of origin and in which I serve in leadership is Mennonite. This information tended to provoke a neutral to curious response, perhaps because the Mennonite tradition is a smaller and lesser-known expression of Christianity that does not have a significance presence in the city of Toronto. Although I was raised in the Mennonite church, my prior family history is in mainstream Protestant traditions. My grandmothers were among the United Church of Canada women of the 1950s, pouring tea, teaching Sunday school, and organizing church bazaars. My academic interest in Christian worship has led me to participate in and study a broad range of Christian communities. Although I was ordained for ministry in Mennonite Church Canada in 2021, I continue to approach this research primarily as an ecumenically minded liturgical scholar, not a Mennonite church leader.

In contrast to how I framed conversations with non-expert participants in religious practices, when I reached out to clergy and parishes about possible research partnerships, I emphasized my theological background and church leadership experience. In addition to meeting in person, I provided a cover letter, curriculum vitae, and one-page research proposal that included the following:

> About Me: I am a doctoral candidate in theology at the University of Notre Dame, where I completed four doctoral seminars in qualitative research methods and three successful qualitative studies with congregations. I have masters degrees in theology from Yale Divinity School and Conrad Grebel University College, and I completed CPE. My tradition of origin and ministry is Mennonite. I served as a full-time pastor at Ottawa Mennonite Church and currently serve as the worship resources editor for a new hymnal and worship book for Mennonite Church Canada and Mennonite Church USA. Originally from Waterloo, Ontario, I am based in Toronto for three years for the purpose of this research.

In interviews with clergy, especially when they were oriented toward possible research partnerships, I presented myself as a colleague—a pastor, theologian, liturgical leader, and experienced qualitative researcher. My ministry experience was part of what demonstrated my capacity to conduct research interviews that address difficult subjects in pastorally appropriate ways. My obvious investment in the life of the church was a point of connection and foundation for building relationships of trust. I have certain affinities with the clergy who participated in this research. My experience in congregational leadership is valuable for interpreting interviews with clergy and understanding the challenges they face.

While my own relationship with religion is essential to consider because of the focus of this research, other aspects of my identity also influenced conversations with participants and my interpretation of the qualitative data. As a white woman under the age of forty-five, I share central identity markers with many participants, the majority of whom are white, women, and under forty-five. I acknowledge that each of these characteristics contributed to participants experiencing me as non-threatening. Identifying as a student also made me more approachable; there were clearly participants who chose to be interviewed in order to help a student. My ethnicity, educational background, and middle-class economic status also allowed me to move freely in white Anglican cultural spaces. As a Canadian citizen who has spent most of my life in Ontario, my knowledge of the geography of the province was an asset in conversations that frequently mentioned other cities and small towns. A lifetime of familiarity with religion and culture of the Canadian religious landscape was extremely valuable. At the same time, studying in the United States challenged taken-for-granted assumptions in ways that helpfully clarify the distinctiveness of religion in Canada. These aspects of my positionality are largely outside of my control and are crucial to be aware of, both in the field and when interpreting qualitative data.

There are also ways that I intentionally positioned myself. I approached this research as a scholar primarily formed in liturgical studies, with sociology of religion and religious studies as additional areas of specialization. As I prepared to enter the field, I aimed to cultivate "ways of seeing" and "habits of thought"[53] associated with each of these disciplines in order to "explicitly foster" my ability to look at the data from "different theoretical vantage points,"[54] not just within the social sciences but across disciplines. Diverse communities of inquiry have been part of this process, in classrooms, at conferences and seminars, and in writing. Exploring the ongoing roles of Christian ritual practices in increasingly nonreligious and religiously diverse social context requires interdisciplinary research, an interdisciplinary researcher, and an interdisciplinary community of inquiry.

---

[53] Tavory and Timmermans, *Abductive Analysis*, 40.
[54] Tavory and Timmermans, *Abductive Analysis*, 123.

APPENDIX C

Interview Guides

These were semi-structured extended qualitative interviews. While interviews covered many of the themes outlined in the interview guide, participants rarely addressed them in the sequence outlined. Instead, themes emerged in the context of a narrative shaped by interview participants.

Baptism Interview Guide

Questions about the Baptism

1. Tell me the story of N's baptism.
2. Could you share a bit about the conversations you had as a family as you were *making plans* for the baptism?
    a. How did you decide to baptize N?
    b. How did you decide to celebrate the baptism at this church?
    c. Who was involved in decisions about the baptism (parents, grandparents, godparents, etc.)?
3. How did you experience the *process of preparing* for the baptism?
    a. What was involved in terms of classes, meetings, rehearsals, or other contact with the church?
    b. What type of personal or family preparation was part of the process?
4. How would you describe the *church service* itself?
    a. Were there certain moments that were especially significant for you?
    b. How were you feeling during the service?
    c. Were these aspects of the experience that stood out to you?
    d. Could you walk me through some of the different elements that you remember?
    e. Here is a copy of the order of service. As you look back on the service, what are your reflections on the different parts?
    f. Who was present especially for the baptism (godparents, family, friends, etc.)?
    g. What have you heard about the church service from others who were there?
    h. How was the baptism different for you from other church services you have attended?
5. Could you describe *another baptism* that you have attended?
    a. How was this similar or different from N's baptism?
    b. What surprised you about N's baptism?
6. Baptism is a practice with many *layers of meaning*. Could you share a bit about what baptism means to you?
    a. How does baptism relate to personal faith?
    b. How does baptism relate to belonging in the church?
7. Are there things that you would do differently if you had another opportunity to baptize a child?
8. Were there other practices or events that were part of the birth of N?

Background Questions

1. How did you become connected *with this church* C?
2. Could you describe another *worship service you attended* at C?
    a. About how often do you attend worship at C?
    b. Do you ever attend elsewhere?
    c. Are there certain occasions when you are more likely attend church services?
    d. Are there certain aspects of worship that are especially important to you?
3. How would you tell the story of how *faith or religion have been part of your life* over the years?
    a. Were you raised in a religious tradition?
    b. How has your relationship with that and other traditions changed over time?
    c. How have religious practices been part of significant moments in your life (such as marriage, loss of loved ones, times of crisis, etc.)?
4. Are there certain *practices* connected to your faith or values that you hope to pass on to N?
    a. Are there important family traditions?
    b. Are there personal spiritual practices?
5. I know it can be hard to summarize, but how would you describe the *core beliefs or values* that you hope to pass on to N?
    a. How would you describe your understanding of God? How certain are you about God?
    b. How would you describe your understanding of the core of the Christian faith?
    c. Is there anything distinctive about the Anglican tradition that is important to you?
6. What are some of the words that you would use describe your religious *identity*?
    a. If it is helpful, here is a list. You can choose as many as you want. [nonreligious, spiritual, religious, questioning, spiritual but not religious, religious but not spiritual, indifferent about religion, curious about religion, agnostic, atheist, theist, other description ____, Christian, culturally Christian, non-practicing Christian, Roman Catholic, Protestant, mainline Protestant, Black Protestant, Orthodox, Evangelical, Pentecostal, other Christian denomination ____, Muslim, Sikh, Jewish, Buddhist, Indigenous practices, other religious tradition ____]
    b. How important to you is religion?

Making Connections

1. How would describe how your religious *background* shaped your experience of the baptism service (or other worship services)?
    a. Are there certain aspects of the worship service that resonate with you?
    b. If there are points of tension, how do you experience those differences?
2. How would you describe how your *practices* shape your experience of the baptism service (or other worship services)?
    a. Are there certain aspects of the worship service that resonate with you?
    b. If there are points of tension, how do you think about those differences?

3. How would you describe how your *beliefs and values* shape your experience of the baptism service (or other worship services)?
   a. Are there certain aspects of the worship service that resonate with you?
   b. If there are points of tension, how do you think about those differences?
4. Based on your experience, how do you know you have had a *"good" worship* experience?
   a. What would a "bad" worship experience be like?

Concluding Questions

1. Is there anything else you would like to add?
2. Are there other family members, godparents, or friends you would recommend I speak with about the baptism?
   a. Would you be open to putting me in touch with [a specific person]?
3. I am at the beginning stages of speaking with families about their experiences of baptisms. Do you have any suggestions for the most important questions to ask or themes to address?
4. Do you have any questions for me?

Funeral Interview Guide

Questions about the Funeral

1. Tell me the story of the funeral for N.
2. Could you share a bit about the conversations you had as a family as you were *making plans* for the funeral?
   a. What kind of guidance did N provide?
   b. How did you choose to have the funeral at this church?
   c. How did you decide what would be part of the funeral for N?
   d. Who was involved in decisions about the funeral (family, friends, clergy, etc.)?
3. How did you experience the *process of preparing* for the funeral?
   a. What was involved in terms of meetings with the church and funeral home?
   b. What type of personal or family preparation was part of the process?
4. How would you describe the *funeral service* itself?
   a. Were there certain moments that were especially significant for you?
   b. How were you feeling during the service?
   c. Were these aspects of the experience that stood out to you?
   d. Could you walk me through some of the different elements that you remember?
   e. Here is a copy of the order of service. As you look back on the service, what are your reflections on the different parts?
   f. Who was present for the funeral (family, friends, etc.)?
   g. What have you heard about the funeral service from others who were there?
   h. How was the funeral different for you from other services you have attended?
5. Could you describe *another funeral* that you have attended?
   a. How was this similar or different from N's funeral?
   b. What surprised you about N's funeral?

368   APPENDIX C

6. Funerals have so many *layers of meaning*. Could you share a bit about what funerals are about for you?
    a. How does a funeral relate to remembering or celebrating the life of the deceased?
    b. How does a funeral relate to caring for the family and community of the deceased?
    c. How does a funeral relate to the Christian faith?
7. Are there things that you would do differently if you were planning another funeral?
8. Were there other events that were part of marking N's death?

Background Questions

1. How would you tell the story of how *faith or religion has been part of N's life* over the years?
    a. Was N raised in a religious tradition?
    b. How did N's relationship with that and other traditions change over time?
    c. What is your sense for how religion was part of N's everyday life?
    d. How have religious practices been part of significant moments in N's life (birth of a child, marriage, loss of loved ones, times of crisis)?
    e. Do you have a sense for how N would have described his/her/their religious identity?
2. How did N and your family become connected *with this church* C?
3. Could you describe another *worship service you attended* at C?
    a. About how often do you attend worship at C?
    b. Do you ever attend elsewhere?
    c. Are there certain occasions when you are more likely to attend church services?
    d. Are there certain aspects of worship that are more important to you?
4. How would you tell the story of *how faith or religion has been part of your life* over the years?
    a. Were you raised in a religious tradition?
    b. How has your relationship with that and other traditions changed over time?
    c. How have religious practices been part of significant moments in your life (such as marriage, loss of loved ones, times of crisis, etc.)?
5. Are there certain *practices* connected to your faith or values?
    a. Are there important family traditions?
    b. Are there personal spiritual practices?
6. I know it can be hard to summarize, but how would you describe some of your *core beliefs or values*?
    a. How would you describe your understanding of God? How certain are you about God?
    b. How would you describe your understanding of the core of the Christian faith?
    c. How would you describe your understanding of what happens after death, if anything?
    d. Is there anything distinctive about the Anglican tradition that is important to you?

7. What are some of the words that you would use to describe your religious *identity*?
    a. If it is helpful, here is a list. You can choose as many as you want. [nonreligious, spiritual, religious, questioning, spiritual but not religious, religious but not spiritual, indifferent about religion, curious about religion, agnostic, atheist, theist, other description ___, Christian, culturally Christian, non-practicing Christian, Roman Catholic, Protestant, mainline Protestant, Black Protestant, Orthodox, Evangelical, Pentecostal, other Christian denomination ___, Muslim, Sikh, Jewish, Buddhist, Indigenous practices, other religious tradition ___]
    b. How important to you is religion?

Making Connections

1. How would describe how your religious *background* shaped your experience of the funeral (or other worship services)?
    a. Are there certain aspects of the service that resonate with you?
    b. If there are points of tension, how do you experience those differences?
2. How would you describe how your *practices* shape your experience of the funeral service (or other worship services)?
    a. Are there certain aspects of the worship service that resonate with you?
    b. If there are points of tension, how do you think about those differences?
3. How would you describe how your *beliefs and values* shape your experience of the funeral service (or other worship services)?
    a. Are there certain aspects of the worship service that resonate with you?
    b. If there are points of tension, how do you think about those differences?
4. I know this is a bit of a strange question when it comes to a funeral. Based on your experience, how do you know you have had a *"good" worship* experience?
    a. What would a "bad" worship experience be like?

Concluding Questions

1. Is there anything else you would like to add?
2. Are there other family members or friends you would recommend I speak with about the funeral?
    a. Would you be open to putting me in touch with [a specific person]?
3. I am at the beginning stages of speaking with families about their experiences of funerals. Do you have any suggestions for the most important questions to ask or themes to address?
4. Do you have any questions for me?

Clergy Interview Guide

Introduction

1. Can you tell me a bit about yourself and the congregation you serve?

Funerals

1. As you know, the focus of our conversation today is baptisms and funerals. Let's begin at the end. As an example, could you walk me through the most recent funeral you celebrated in this parish?
   a. What was typical about this experience and what was unusual?
2. As I mentioned, I am especially interested in instances when the deceased or the family are unconnected or very loosely connected to the church community.
   a. Could you tell me a story about a time when you conducted a funeral for someone who was less connected to the church?
   b. How did the family from beyond the community end up in this parish?
   c. How was the process of preparation, the funeral itself, and any follow-up different with a family from beyond the church community?
   d. What is your sense for how the family experienced the event?
   e. What is it like for you to perform funerals for families at a distance from the church? How do you understand your role and the purpose of these liturgies?
3. Additional funeral questions
   a. Are there *theological or pastoral approaches* to funerals you find especially compelling?
   b. Are funerals more often held at the *church or a funeral home*? How does the space change the experience?
   c. What *proportion of funerals* are for families at a distance from the church?
   d. What is the role of *the Christian faith and life of the deceased*? For example, what if the deceased appears to have been largely not religious?

Baptisms

1. Let's turn our attention from the end of life to the beginning of life. As an example, could you walk me through the most recent child baptism you celebrated in this parish?
   a. What was typical about this experience and what was unusual?
2. As you know, I am interested in instances when the family requesting child baptism is unconnected or very loosely connected to the church community.
   a. Could you tell me a story about a time when you performed baptism for a family less connected to the church?
   b. How did the family from beyond the community end up in this parish?
   c. How was the process of preparation, the baptism itself, and any follow-up different with a family from beyond the church community?

d. What is your sense for how the family experienced the event?
   e. What is it like for you to perform baptisms for families at a distance from the church? How do you understand your role and the purpose of these liturgies?
3. Additional baptism questions
   a. Are there theological or pastoral approaches to baptism you find especially compelling?
   b. Do baptisms sometimes take place apart from the primary worship gathering on Sunday?
   c. What *proportion of baptisms* are for families at a distance from the church?
   d. Could you talk a bit about the relationship between *baptism and membership* in the church?
   e. Could you say a bit about how you understand the role of the *faith and life of participants*, especially parents or sponsors?

General

1. Do you have *general rules* for how to respond to requests for baptisms and funerals, especially from those who are more loosely connected to the church?
   a. What guidance, if any, have you received from the wider church or in preparation for ministry?
   b. How would you respond if someone with no personal connection to the tradition or in the parish expressed the desire to baptize their child or to hold a funeral for a loved one?
2. I know this is a challenging question since there are so many ways of looking at it, but I am wondering if you could talk about *who you see as part of this church community* and who you would see as coming from beyond the church community?
   a. Active involvement? Regular attendance? Formal membership? Geographic proximity? Historic connection? Christmas and Easter? Baptisms, weddings, funerals? Personal beliefs? Financial support?
3. Baptisms and funerals are often *family* events. How do you approach these practices when family members have a range of relationships with the church, such as interfaith families or families that include religious and nonreligious members?
4. Although the Anglican tradition in anchored in the *Book of Common Prayer* in its various forms, there is still some flexibility. Are there ways you adapt the liturgy depending on the relationship of the participants to the church?
   a. How does the Prayer Book help and hinder marking these significant life moments with families who are more loosely connected to the church?
5. The *internal diversity* of the Anglican tradition is part of what attracts me to studying Anglican baptisms and funerals. How does the distinct (Evangelical/Anglo-Catholic/Intercultural/Progressive/Traditional) character of this parish relate to the celebration of baptisms and funerals for families at a distance?
6. The historic role of the Anglican tradition in *public life* in English-speaking Canada is another reason why I am drawn to study the Anglican tradition (for example, Anglican funerals for prominent figures). How have you witnessed this, either in this parish or elsewhere?

7. Two related practices that we are not focusing on today are *marriage and confirmation*. Could you speak briefly about how marriage and confirmation compare to baptisms and funerals in terms of participants who are more loosely connected to the church?

Conclusion

1. I am in early stages of this research. Are you aware of any church communities or clergy who may be good to connect with around these questions?
2. My hope is to move toward connecting with families who are choosing Anglican baptisms and funerals, to hear about their experiences and, in some cases, to witness the process of preparation, the liturgy itself, and to speak with them more extensively afterward. Do you have any advice as I consider moving toward listening to families?

Bibliography

Ammerman, Nancy. *Congregation and Community*. New Brunswick, NJ: Rutgers University Press, 1997.

Ammerman, Nancy, ed. *Everyday Religion: Observing Modern Religious Lives*. Oxford: Oxford University Press, 2007.

Ammerman, Nancy. "Golden Rule Christianity: Lived Religion in the American Mainstream." In *Lived Religion in America: Toward a History of Practice*, edited by David D. Hall, 196–216. Princeton, NJ: Princeton University Press, 1997.

Ammerman, Nancy. "Rethinking Religion: Toward a Practice Approach." *American Journal of Sociology* 126, no. 1 (July 2020): 6–51.

Ammerman, Nancy. *Sacred Stories, Spiritual Tribes*. New York: Oxford University Press, 2014.

Ammerman, Nancy. "Spiritual but Not Religious? Beyond Binary Choices in the Study of Religion." *Journal for the Scientific Study of Religion* 52, no. 2 (2013): 258–278.

Ammerman, Nancy Tatom. *Studying Lived Religion: Contexts and Practices*. New York: New York University Press, 2021.

Anglican Church of Canada. "Liturgical Resources." Accessed December 11, 2023. https://www.anglican.ca/faith/worship/resources.

Anglican Church of Canada. "Welcome to the Anglican Church of Canada." Accessed December 11, 2023. http://www.anglican.ca.

Anglican Church of Canada, Diocese of Toronto. "Annual Returns." Accessed December 11, 2023. http://www.toronto.anglican.ca/parish-administration/finance/annual-returns.

Anglican Church of Canada, Diocese of Toronto. Annual Statistical Returns, 2013–2018.

Anglican Church of Canada, Diocese of Toronto. "Bishop Announces Cessation of Worship Services." March 13, 2020. Accessed December 11, 2023. https://www.toronto.anglican.ca/2020/03/13/bishop-announces-cessation-of-worship.

Anglican Church of Canada, Diocese of Toronto. "Cast the Net." Accessed December 11, 2023. https://www.toronto.anglican.ca/about-us/cast-the-net.

Anglican Church of Canada, Diocese of Toronto. "Statement from the College of Bishops on Current Restrictions." March 14, 2020. Accessed December 11, 2023. https://www.toronto.anglican.ca/2020/03/14/statement-from-the-college-of-bishops-on-current-restrictions.

Angus Reid Institute. "Faith and Religion in Public Life." November 16, 2017. Accessed December 11, 2023. http://angusreid.org/wp-content/uploads/2017/11/2017.11.15-Cardus-Wave-3.pdf.

Angus Reid Institute. "Faith Continuum Groups Release Tables." April 10, 2017. Accessed December 11, 2023. http://angusreid.org/wp-content/uploads/2017/04/2017.04.10_FaithContinuumGroups_releasetables.pdf.

Angus Reid Institute. "A Spectrum of Spirituality." April 13, 2017. Accessed December 11, 2023. http://angusreid.org/wp-content/uploads/2017/04/2017.04.12_Faith_Wave_1_Part_1.pdf.

Angus Reid Institute. "Spirituality in a Changing World." May 17, 2017. Accessed December 11, 2023. http://angusreid.org/wp-content/uploads/2017/05/2017.05.17-Faith-Wave-1-Part2.pdf.

Astley, Jeff. *Ordinary Theology: Looking, Listening and Learning in Theology*. London: Routledge, 2002.

Astley, Jeff, and Leslie Francis, eds. *Exploring Ordinary Theology: Everyday Christian Believing and the Church*. London: Routledge, 2013.

Aune, Michael. "Liturgy and Theology, Part I." *Worship* 81, no. 1 (2007): 46–68.
Baker, Joseph, and Buster Smith. *American Secularism: Cultural Contours of Nonreligious Belief Systems*. New York: New York University Press, 2015.
Baumstark, Anton. *Comparative Liturgy*. London: A. R. Mowbray, 1958.
Becker, Penny Edgell. *Congregations in Conflict*. Cambridge: Cambridge University Press, 1999.
Belcher, Kimberly Hope. "Ritual Systems: Prostration, Self, and Community in the Rule of Benedict." *Ecclesia Orans* 27, no. 2 (2020): 321–356.
Belcher, Kimberly Hope. "Ritual Systems, Ritualized Bodies, and the Laws of Liturgical Development." *Studia Liturgica* 49, no. 1 (2019): 89–110.
Bell, Catherine. *Ritual: Perspectives and Dimensions*. New York: Oxford University Press, 1997.
Bell, Catherine. *Ritual Theory, Ritual Practice*. New York: Oxford University Press, 1992.
Bellah, Robert. *The Robert Bellah Reader*. Durham, NC: Duke University Press, 2006.
Bellah, Robert N., Richard Madsen, William M. Sullivan, Ann Swidler, and Steven M. Tipton. *Habits of the Heart: Individualism and Commitment in American Life*. Berkeley: University of California Press, 1985.
Berger, Peter. "Secularism in Retreat." *The National Interest* 46 (1996): 2–12.
Berger, Peter. *The Sacred Canopy: Elements of a Sociological Theory of Religion*. New York: Anchor, 1969.
Bibby, Reginald. "The Christmas Onlys: A Wakeup Bell for Canada's Religious Groups." Project Canada Surveys, December 23, 2013. Accessed March 18, 2021. http://www.reginaldbibby.com/images/Release_2013_Christmas_Onlys_Dec_23_2013.pdf.
Bibby, Reginald. "A Research Note: The Christmas Onlys Revisited." Project Canada Surveys, December 22, 2014. Accessed March 18, 2021. http://www.reginaldbibby.com/images/Release_2014_Christmas_Onlys_Revisited_Dec_24.pdf.
Bibby, Reginald. *Resilient Gods: Being Pro-Religious, Low Religious, or No Religious in Canada*. Vancouver: UBC Press, 2017.
Bielo, James. *Ark Encounter: The Making of a Creationist Theme Park*. New York: New York University Press, 2018.
Bielo, James. *Words upon the Word: An Ethnography of Evangelical Bible Study*. New York: New York University Press, 2009.
Bradshaw, Paul. *The Search for the Origins of Christian Worship*. 2nd ed. Oxford: Oxford University Press, 2002.
Bradshaw, Paul, and Maxwell Johnson. *The Origins of Feasts, Fasts, and Seasons in Early Christianity*. Collegeville, MN: Liturgical Press, 2011.
Bramadat, Paul, and David Seljak, eds. *Christianity and Ethnicity in Canada*. Toronto: University of Toronto Press, 2008.
Bramadat, Paul, and David Seljak, eds. *Religion and Ethnicity in Canada*. Toronto: University of Toronto Press, 2009.
Brown, Peter. *The Cult of the Saints*. Chicago: University of Chicago Press, 1981.
Burawoy, Michael. "The Extended Case Method." *Sociological Theory* 16, no. 1 (March 1998): 4–33.
Burawoy, Michael. *The Extended Case Method: Four Countries, Four Decades, Four Great Transformations, and One Theoretical Tradition*. Berkeley: University of California Press, 2009.
Campbell-Reed, Eileen R., and Christian Scharen. "Ethnography on Holy Ground: How Qualitative Interviewing Is Practical Theological Work." *International Journal of Practical Theology* 17, no. 2 (2013): 232–259.
Carvalhaes, Cláudio. *Eucharist and Globalization: Redrawing the Borders of Eucharistic Hospitality*. Eugene, OR: Pickwick Publications, 2013.
Carvalhaes, Cláudio. *How Do We Become Green People and Earth Communities? Inventory, Metamorphoses, and Emergenc(i)es*. York: Barber's Son, 2022.
Carvalhaes, Cláudio. *Liturgies from Below*. Nashville, TN: Abingdon Press, 2020.

Carvalhaes, Cláudio. *Praying with Every Heart: Orienting Our Lives to the Wholeness of the World*. Eugene, OR: Cascade, 2021.

Carvalhaes, Cláudio. *Ritual at World's End: Essays on Eco-Liturgical Liberation Theology*. York: Barber's Son, 2021.

Carvalhaes, Cláudio. *What's Worship Got to Do with It? Interpreting Life Liturgically*. Eugene, OR: Cascade, 2018.

Chauvet, Louis-Marie. *The Sacraments: The Word of God at the Mercy of the Body*. Collegeville, MN: Liturgical Press, 2001.

Church of England Research and Statistics. "Statistics for Mission, 2018." 2019. Accessed December 11, 2023. https://www.churchofengland.org/sites/default/files/2019-10/2018StatisticsForMission_0.pdf.

Clarke, Brian, and Stuart Macdonald. *Leaving Christianity: Changing Allegiances in Canada Since 1945*. Montreal and Kingston: McGill-Queen's University Press, 2017.

Collins, Randall. *Interaction Ritual Chains*. Princeton, NJ: Princeton University Press, 2004.

Cornelissen, Louis. "Religiosity in Canada and Its Evolution from 1985–2019." Insights on Canadian Society. Statistics Canada, October 28, 2021. Accessed December 11, 2023. https://www150.statcan.gc.ca/n1/en/pub/75-006-x/2021001/article/00010-eng.pdf?st=sIvWsSbM.

Coulter, Dale M. *The Spirit, the Affections, and the Christian Tradition*. Notre Dame: University of Notre Dame Press, 2016.

Cowan, Nelson Robert. "Liturgical Biography as Liturgical Theology: Co-Constructing Theology at Hillsong Church, New York City." PhD diss., Boston University School of Theology, 2019.

Cox, Jeffrey. *The English Churches in a Secular Society: Lambeth, 1870–1930*. Oxford: Oxford University Press, 1982.

Davidman, Lynn. *Tradition in a Rootless World: Women Turn to Orthodox Judaism*. Berkeley: University of California Press, 1991.

Davie, Grace. "Believing Without Belonging." *Social Compass* 37, no. 4 (1990): 455–469.

Davie, Grace. *Religion in Modern Europe: A Memory Mutates*. Oxford: Oxford University Press, 2000.

Davie, Grace. "Vicarious Religion: A Methodological Challenge." In *Everyday Religion: Observing Modern Religious Lives*, edited by Nancy Ammerman, 21–36. Oxford: Oxford University Press, 2007.

Day, Abby. *Believing in Belonging: Belief and Social Identity in the Modern World*. Oxford: Oxford University Press, 2011.

Day, Abby, and Mia Lövheim. *Modernities, Memory, Mutations*. New York: Routledge, 2015.

Dillon, Michele, and Paul Wink. *In the Course of a Lifetime: Tracing Religious Belief, Practice, and Change*. Berkeley: University of California Press, 2007.

Dix, Gregory. *The Shape of the Liturgy*. London: Dacre Press, 1945.

Drescher, Elizabeth. *Choosing Our Religion*. Oxford: Oxford University Press, 2016.

Durkheim, Émile. *The Elementary Forms of Religious Life*. New York: Free Press, 1995.

Edgell, Penny, Joseph Gerteis, and Douglas Hartmann. "Atheists as 'Other': Moral Boundaries and Cultural Membership in American Society." *American Sociological Review* 71, no. 2 (2006): 211–234.

Elliot, Neil. "Statistics Report for House of Bishops." *Anglican Samizdat*, October 5, 2019. Accessed December 11, 2023. https://www.anglicansamizdat.net/wordpress/latest-anglican-church-of-canada-membership-and-attendance-statistics.

Emerson, Robert, Rachel Fretz, and Linda Shaw. *Writing Ethnographic Fieldnotes*. Chicago: University of Chicago Press, 2011.

Evans-Pritchard, Edward Evan. *Witchcraft, Oracles and Magic Among the Azande*. Oxford: Clarendon Press, 1976.

Fagerberg, David. *Theologia Prima: What Is Liturgical Theology?* Chicago: Liturgy Training Publications, 2004.

Finke, Roger, and Rodney Stark. *The Churching of America, 1776–2005*. New Brunswick, NJ: Rutgers University Press, 2005.
Fitzgerald, Timothy. "Review of *Contemporary Western Ethnography and the Definition of Religion*, by Martin Stringer." *Journal of the American Academy of Religion* 77, no. 4 (2009): 974–982.
Ford, Rob, and Doug Ford. *Ford Nation: Two Brothers, One Vision—The True Story of the People's Mayor*. New York: HarperCollins, 2016.
Francis, Leslie, and David Lankshear. "Asking About Baptism: Straw Polls and Fenced Fonts." *The Modern Churchman* 34 (1993): 88–92.
Francis, Leslie, Keith Littler, and T. Hugh Thomas. "Fenced Fonts or Open Doors? An Empirical Survey of Baptismal Policy Among Clergy in the Church in Wales." *Implicit Religion* 3 (2000): 73–86.
Francis, Mark. *Shape a Circle Ever Wider*. Chicago: Liturgy Training Publications, 2000.
Fuller, Robert. *Spiritual, but Not Religious: Understanding Unchurched America*. Oxford: Oxford University Press, 2001.
Garrigan, Siobhán. *Beyond Ritual: Sacramental Theology after Habermas*. Aldershot: Ashgate, 2004.
Garrigan, Siobhán. *The Real Peace Process: Worship, Politics, and the End of Sectarianism*. London: Equinox, 2010.
Geertz, Clifford. *The Interpretation of Cultures*. New York: Basic, 1973.
Geldhof, Joris. *Liturgy and Secularism: Beyond the Divide*. Collegeville, MN: Liturgical Press, 2018.
General Synod of the Anglican Church of Canada. *Book of Alternative Services of the Anglican Church of Canada*. Toronto: ABC Publishing, 1985.
General Synod of the Anglican Church of Canada. *Book of Common Prayer and Administration of the Sacraments and Other Rites and Ceremonies of the Church According to the Use of the Anglican Church of Canada*. Toronto: ABC Publishing, 1962.
Gerhards, Albert, and Benedikt Kranemann. *Introduction to the Study of Liturgy*. Translated by Linda Maloney. Collegeville, MN: Liturgical Press, 2017.
Gibler, Linda. *From the Beginning to Baptism: Scientific and Sacred Stories of Water, Oil, and Fire*. Collegeville, MN: Liturgical Press, 2010.
Glaser, Barney, and Anselm Strauss. *The Discovery of Grounded Theory: Strategies for Qualitative Research*. Chicago: Aldine, 1967.
Government of Ontario. "Ontario Enacts Declaration of Emergency to Protect the Public." March 17, 2020. Accessed December 11, 2023. https://news.ontario.ca/opo/en/2020/03/ontario-enacts-declaration-of-emergency-to-protect-the-public.html.
Government of Ontario. "Ontario Prohibits Gatherings of More than Five People with Strict Exceptions," March 28, 2020. Accessed December 11, 2023. https://news.ontario.ca/opo/en/2020/03/ontario-prohibits-gatherings-of-five-people-or-more-with-strict-exceptions.html.
Grimes, Ronald. *Beginnings in Ritual Studies*. Columbia: University of South Carolina Press, 1995.
Grimes, Ronald. *Ritual Criticism*. Columbia: University of South Carolina Press, 1990.
Grimes, Ronald. *The Craft of Ritual Studies*. Oxford: Oxford University Press, 2013.
Guardini, Romano. *The Sacred Signs*. St. Louis, MO: Pio Decimo Press, 1956.
Halík, Tomáš. *I Want You to Be: On the God of Love*. Notre Dame: University of Notre Dame Press, 2016.
Halík, Tomáš. *Patience with God: The Story of Zacchaeus Continuing in Us*. New York: Doubleday, 2009.
Hayes, Alan. *Anglicans in Canada: Controversies and Identity in Historical Perspective*. Urbana: University of Illinois, 2004.

Hermkens, Anna-Karina. "Clothing as Embodied Experience of Belief." In *Religion and Material Culture: The Matter of Belief*, edited by David Morgan, 231–246. New York: Routledge, 2010.

Hiebert, Paul G. "Conversion, Culture and Cognitive Categories." *Gospel in Context* 1, no. 4 (1978): 24–29.

Hines, Dick. *Dressing for Worship: A Fresh Look at What Christians Wear in Church*. Cambridge: Grove Books, 1996.

Hoondert, Martin, Paul Post, Mirella Klomp, and Marcel Barnard, eds. *Handbook of Disaster Ritual: Multidisciplinary Perspectives, Cases and Themes*. Leuven: Peeters, 2021.

Jakelic, Slavica. *Collectivistic Religions: Religion, Choice, and Identity in Late Modernity*. New York: Routledge, 2016.

Jasper, R. C. D., and G. J. Cuming. *Prayers of the Eucharist: Early and Reformed*. 3rd ed. Collegeville, MN: Liturgical Press, 1987.

Jennings, Theodore. "Ritual Studies and Liturgical Theology: An Invitation to Dialogue." *Journal of Ritual Studies* 1, no. 1 (1987): 35–56.

Jesudason, Peniel, Rufus Rajkumar, and Joseph Prabhakar Dayam, eds. *Many Yet One? Multiple Religious Belonging*. Geneva: WCC Publications, 2016.

Johnson, Lawrence. *Worship in the Early Church*. Vol. 4. Collegeville, MN: Liturgical Press, 2009.

Johnson, Maxwell. *The Rites of Christian Initiation: Their Evolution and Interpretation*. Rev. ed. Collegeville, MN: Liturgical Press, 2007.

Johnson, Sarah Kathleen. "Crisis, Solidarity, and Ritual in Religiously Diverse Settings: A Unitarian Universalist Case Study." *Religions* 13, no. 7 (2022): 614. https://doi.org/10.3390/rel13070614.

Johnson, Sarah Kathleen. "Evolving Practices of Online Communion in Ecumenical Perspective: An Ethnographic Study of Four Pandemic Holy Weeks." Paper presented at the biannual congress of Societas Liturgica, Maynooth, Ireland, 2023.

Johnson, Sarah Kathleen. "Harmony and Dissonance in Overlapping Ritual Systems: A Religiously Diverse Choir Sings in Roman Catholic Mass." Paper presented in the Ritual Studies Unit at the annual meeting of the American Academy of Religion, Boston, MA, 2017.

Johnson, Sarah Kathleen. "Online Communion, Christian Community, and Receptive Ecumenism: A Holy Week Ethnography during COVID-19." *Studia Liturgica* 50, no. 2 (2020): 188–210.

Johnson, Sarah Kathleen. "Poured Out: A Kenotic Approach to Initiating Children at a Distance from the Church." *Studia Liturgica* 49, no. 2 (2019): 175–194.

Johnson, Sarah Kathleen, and David Sikkink. "Occasional Religious Participation at Christmas and Easter: A Congregational Level Analysis." Paper presented in the Sociology of Religion Unit at the annual meeting of the American Academy of Religion, San Diego, CA, 2019.

Jojko, Bernadeta. "At the Well: An Encounter Beyond the Boundaries (Jn 4:1–42)." *Gregorianum* 99, no. 1 (2018): 5–27.

Jones-Carmack, Joy. "Relational Demography in John 4: Crossing Cultural Boundaries as Praxis for Christian Leadership." *Feminist Theology* 25, no. 1 (2016): 41–52.

Karst, Layla. "Reimagining Pilgrimage." PhD diss., Emory University, 2019.

Kavanagh, Aidan. *On Liturgical Theology*. Collegeville, MN: Liturgical Press, 1981.

Kelleher, Margaret Mary. "Hermeneutics in the Study of Liturgical Performance." *Worship* 64, no. 1 (1993): 292–318.

Kieckhefer, Richard. *Theology in Stone: Church Architecture from Byzantium to Berkeley*. New York: Oxford University Press, 2008.

Kilde, Jeanne Halgren. *Sacred Power, Sacred Space: An Introduction to Christian Architecture and Worship*. New York: Oxford University Press, 2008.

Konieczny, Mary Ellen. *The Spirit's Tether*. New York: Oxford University Press, 2013.

Konieczny, Mary Ellen, Loren D. Lybarger, and Kelly H. Chong. "Theory as a Tool in the Social Scientific Study of Religion and Martin Riesebrodt's *The Promise of Salvation*." *Journal for the Scientific Study of Religion* 51, no. 3 (2012): 397–411.
Kuha, Mila. "Popular Religion in the Periphery: Church Attendance in 17th Century Eastern Finland." *Perichoresis* 13, no. 2 (2015): 17–33.
Larson-Miller, Lizette. *Sacramentality Renewed: Contemporary Conversations in Sacramental Theology.* Collegeville, MN: Liturgical Press, 2016.
Lathrop, Gordon. *Holy Things: A Liturgical Theology.* Minneapolis, MN: Fortress Press, 1993.
Lemons, Derrick, ed. *Theologically Engaged Anthropology.* Oxford: Oxford University Press, 2018.
Lévi-Strauss, Claude. *Structural Anthropology.* New York: Basic Books, 1963.
Lizardo, Omar, and Michael Strand. "Skills, Toolkits, Contexts and Institutions: Clarifying the Relationship between Different Approaches to Cognition in Cultural Sociology." *Poetics* 38, no. 2 (2010): 205–228.
Lizardo, Omar, Robert Mowry, Brandon Sepulvado, Dustin S. Stoltz, Marshall A. Taylor, Justin Van Ness, and Michael Wood. "What Are Dual Process Models? Implications for Cultural Analysis in Sociology." *Sociological Theory* 34, no. 4 (2016): 287–310.
Long, Thomas. *Accompany Them with Singing: The Christian Funeral.* Louisville, KY: Westminster John Knox Press, 2009.
Luhrmann, T. M. *When God Talks Back: Understanding the American Evangelical Relationship with God.* New York: Vintage Books, 2012.
Lukken, Gerard. "Infant Baptism in the Netherlands and Flanders: A Christian Ritual in the Dynamic of the Anthropological/Theological and Cultural Context." In *Christian Feast and Festival: The Dynamics of Western Liturgy and Culture*, edited by P. Post, G. Rouwhorst, L. van Tongeren, and A. Scheer, 551–580. Leuven: Peeters, 2001.
MacIntyre, Alasdair. *After Virtue: A Study in Moral Theology.* Notre Dame: University of Notre Dame Press, 1981.
MacIntyre, Alasdair. *Whose Justice? Which Rationality?* Notre Dame: University of Notre Dame Press, 1988.
Malinowski, Bronislaw. *Magic, Science and Religion and Other Essays.* New York: Doubleday, 1954.
Manalo, Ricky. *The Liturgy of Life: The Interrelationship of Sunday Eucharist and Everyday Worship Practices.* Collegeville, MN: Liturgical Press, 2014.
Manglos-Weber, Nicolette. *Joining the Choir.* New York: Oxford University Press, 2018.
Manning, Christel. *Losing Our Religion: How Unaffiliated Parents Are Raising Their Children.* New York: New York University Press, 2015.
Marsh, Charles. "Introduction: Lived Theology—Method, Style, and Pedagogy." In *Lived Theology: New Perspectives on Method, Style, and Pedagogy*, edited by Charles Marsh, Peter Slade, and Sarah Azaransky. Oxford: Oxford University Press, 2016.
Marsh, Christopher. *Popular Religion in Sixteenth-Century England.* New York: St. Martin's Press, 1998.
Martí, Gerardo. "Ethnographic Theology: Integrating the Social Sciences and Theological Reflection." *Cuestiones Teológicas* 49, no. 111 (2022): 1–18.
Martí, Gerardo. "Ethnography as a Tool for Genuine Surprise: Found Theologies versus Imposed Theologies." In *The Wiley Blackwell Companion to Theology and Qualitative Research*, edited by Pete Ward and Knut Tveitereid, 471–482. Hoboken, NJ: John Wiley & Sons, 2022.
Martí, Gerardo. "Found Theologies versus Imposed Theologies: Remarks on Theology and Ethnography from a Sociological Perspective." *Ecclesial Practices* 3, no. 2 (2016): 157–172.
Martin, David. "Canada in Comparative Perspective." In *Rethinking Church, State, and Modernity: Canada Between Europe and America*, edited by Marguerite Van Die and David Lyon, 23–33. Toronto: University of Toronto Press, 2000.
Martin, David. *Reflections on Theology and Sociology.* Oxford: Oxford University Press, 1997.

Mayer, Wendy. *The Homilies of St. John Chrysostom: Provenance—Reshaping the Foundations.* Rome: Pontificio Istituto Orientale, 2005.
Mayer, Wendy, and Pauline Allen. *John Chrysostom.* London: Routledge, 2000.
McClintock Fulkerson, Mary. *Places of Redemption.* Oxford: Oxford University Press, 2007.
McFague, Sallie. *Life Abundant: Rethinking Theology and Economy for a Planet in Peril.* Minneapolis, MN: Fortress Press, 2001.
McGann, Mary. *A Precious Fountain: Music in the Worship of an African American Catholic Community.* Collegeville, MN: Liturgical Press, 2004.
McGann, Mary. *Exploring Music as Worship and Theology.* Collegeville, MN: Liturgical Press, 2002.
McRoberts, Omar. *Streets of Glory.* Chicago: University of Chicago Press, 2005.
Meneses, Eloise, and David Bronkeman, eds. *On Knowing Humanity: Insights from Theology for Anthropology.* New York: Routledge, 2017.
Mercadante, Linda. *Belief Without Borders: Inside the Minds of the Spiritual but Not Religious.* Oxford: Oxford University Press, 2014.
Miller, Vincent J. *Consuming Religion: Christian Faith and Practice in a Consumer Culture.* New York: Continuum, 2005.
Mitchell, Nathan. *Liturgy and the Social Sciences.* Collegeville, MN: Liturgical Press, 1999.
Mitchell, Nathan. *Meeting Mystery: Liturgy, Worship, Sacraments.* Maryknoll, NY: Orbis Books, 2006.
Mitchell, Nathan. *The Mystery of the Rosary: Marian Devotion and the Reinvention of Catholicism.* New York: New York University Press, 2009.
Morrill, Bruce. *Divine Worship and Human Healing: Liturgical Theology at the Margins of Life and Death.* Collegeville, MN: Liturgical Press, 2009.
National Church Life Survey. "Infographics: Religion and Spirituality in Australia, 2016 Australian Community Survey." December 2016. Accessed March 18, 2021. https://www.ncls.org.au/news/2016-acs-religion-spirituality-infographics.
National Church Life Survey. "Infographics: Religion and Spirituality in Australia, 2018 Australian Community Survey." July 2018. Accessed March 18, 2021. https://www.ncls.org.au/news/2018-acs-religion-spirituality-infographics.
National Church Life Survey. "Research." Accessed December 11, 2023. https://www.ncls.org.au/research.
Noll, Mark A. "What Happened to Christian Canada?" *Church History* 75, no. 2 (June 2006): 245–273.
Parsons, Talcott. *The Social System.* Glencoe, IL: Free Press, 1951.
Parsons, William, ed. *Being Spiritual but Not Religious.* New York: Routledge, 2018.
Petrin, Anna. "Insights from Mrs. Murphy: Caryll Houselander as Liturgical Theologian." *Worship* 94 (2020): 206–227.
Pew Research Center. "The Gender Gap in Religion Around the World." March 22, 2016. Accessed December 11, 2023. https://www.pewresearch.org/religion/2016/03/22/the-gender-gap-in-religion-around-the-world.
Pew Research Center. "The Religious Typology: A New Way to Categorize Americans by Religion." August 29, 2018. Accessed December 11, 2023. https://www.pewforum.org/wp-content/uploads/sites/7/2018/08/Full-Report-01-11-19-FOR-WEB.pdf.
Phillips, Elizabeth. "Charting the 'Ethnographic Turn': Theologians and the Study of Christian Congregations." In *Perspectives on Ecclesiology and Ethnography*, edited by Pete Ward, 95–106. Grand Rapids, MI: Eerdmans, 2012.
Phillips, L. Edward, ed. "Worship and Emotion." Special issue, *Liturgy* 36, no. 1 (2021).
Porpora, Douglas. "Methodological Atheism, Methodological Agnosticism and Religious Experience." *Journal of the Theory of Social Behaviour* 36, no. 1 (2006): 57–75.
Post, Paul, and Arie Molendijk, eds. *Holy Ground: Re-inventing Ritual Space in Modern Western Culture.* Leuven: Peeters, 2010.

Post, Paul, Ronald L. Grimes, Albertina Nugteren, Per Pettersson, and Hessel Zondag. *Disaster Ritual: Explorations of an Emerging Ritual Repertoire*. Leuven: Peeters, 2003.

Post, Paul, and Louis van Tongeren. "The Celebration of the First Communion: Seeking the Identity of the Christian Ritual." In *Christian Feast and Festival: The Dynamics of Western Liturgy and Culture*, edited by P. Post, G. Rouwhorst, L. van Tongeren, and A. Scheer, 581–598. Leuven: Peeters, 2001.

Power, David, and Luis Maldonado, eds. *Liturgy and Human Passage*. New York: Seabury Press, 1979.

Quartier, Thomas. *Bridging the Gaps: An Empirical Study of Catholic Funeral Rites*. Münster: LIT Verlag, 2007.

Quartier, Thomas. "Liturgy Participant's Perspective: Exploring the Attitudes of Participants at Roman Catholic Funerals with Empirical Methods." *Liturgy* 21, no. 3 (2006): 21–29.

Riesebrodt, Martin. *The Promise of Salvation*. Chicago: University of Chicago Press, 2010.

Rijken, Hanna. *My Soul Doth Magnify: The Appropriation of Choral Evensong in the Netherlands*. Amsterdam: VU University Press, 2020.

Robbins, Joel. "Afterword: Let's Keep It Awkward: Anthropology, Theology, and Otherness." *Australian Journal of Theology* 24, no. 3 (2013): 329–337.

Robbins, Joel. "Anthropology and Theology: An Awkward Relationship?" *Anthropological Quarterly* 79, no. 2 (2006): 285–294.

Ross, Melanie. *Evangelical Versus Liturgical?* Grand Rapids, MI: Eerdmans, 2014.

Ross, Melanie. "New Frontiers in American Evangelical Worship." *Studia Liturgica* 51, no. 2 (2021): 159–172.

Ross, Susan. *Extravagant Affections: A Feminist Sacramental Theology*. New York: Continuum, 1998.

Rowell, Geoffrey. *The Liturgy of Christian Burial: An Introductory Survey of the Historical Development of Christian Burial Rites*. London: Alcuin Club, 1977.

Rutherford, Richard, and Tony Barr. *The Death of a Christian: The Order of Christian Funerals*. Collegeville, MN: Liturgical Press, 1980.

Sacrosanctum Concilium, Constitution on the Sacred Liturgy. 1963. http://www.vatican.va/archive/hist_councils/ii_vatican_council/documents/vat-ii_const_19631204_sacrosanctum-concilium_en.html.

Schaff, Philip, ed. *Nicene and Post-Nicene Fathers*. Ser. 2, Vol. 11. Edinburgh: T&T Clark, 1889.

Scharen, Christian. "Ecclesiology 'From the Body': Ethnographic Notes Toward a Carnal Theology." In *Perspectives on Ecclesiology and Ethnography*, edited by Pete Ward, 56–65. Grand Rapids, MI: Eerdmans, 2012.

Scharen, Christian. *Explorations in Ecclesiology and Ethnography*. Grand Rapids, MI: Eerdmans, 2012.

Scharen, Christian. *Fieldwork in Theology*. Grand Rapids, MI: Baker Academic, 2015.

Scharen, Christian. "Interviewing Interpreted as a Spiritual Exercise and Social Protest." *Ecclesial Practices* 4 (2017): 218–236.

Scharen, Christian. "'Judicious Narratives,' or Ethnography as Ecclesiology." *Scottish Journal of Theology* 58, no. 2 (2005): 125–142.

Scharen, Christian. *Public Worship and Public Work: Character and Commitment in Local Congregational Life*. Collegeville, MN: Liturgical Press, 2004.

Scharen, Christian, and Aana Marie Vigen, eds. *Ethnography as Christian Theology and Ethics*. New York: Continuum, 2011.

Searle, Mark. "Notre Dame Study of Catholic Parish Life in the United States." The Association of Religion Data Archives, 1983. Accessed December 11, 2023. https://www.thearda.com/data-archive?fid=NDLTRGY.

Seeman, Don E. "Does Anthropology Need to 'Get Religion'? Critical Notes on An Unrequited Love." *Practical Matters* 3 (2010): 10–14.

Sica, Alan. "A Selective History of Sociology." In *The Wiley-Blackwell Companion to Sociology*, edited by George Ritzer, 25–54. Malden, MA: John Wiley & Sons, 2012.

Smith, Christian. *Religion: What It Is, How It Works, and Why It Matters*. Princeton, NJ: Princeton University Press, 2017.

Smith, Christian. *Soul Searching: The Religious and Spiritual Lives of American Teenagers*. Oxford: Oxford University Press, 2005.

Smith, Christian, and Michael Emerson. *American Evangelicalism: Embattled and Thriving*. Chicago: University of Chicago Press, 1998.

Smith, Christian, Bridget Ritz, and Michael Rotolo. *Religious Parenting: Transmitting Faith and Values in Contemporary America*. Princeton, NJ: Princeton University Press, 2020.

Smith, Christian, and Robert D. Woodberry. "Sociology of Religion." In *The Wiley Blackwell Companion to Sociology*, edited by George Ritzer, 367–384. Malden, MA: John Wiley & Sons, 2012.

Smith, James K. A. *Awaiting the King: Reforming Public Theology*. Grand Rapids, MI: Baker, 2017.

Smith, James K. A. *Desiring the Kingdom: Worship, Worldview, and Cultural Formation*. Grand Rapids, MI: Baker, 2009.

Smith, James K. A. *Imagining the Kingdom: How Worship Works*. Grand Rapids, MI: Baker, 2013.

Smith, Jonathan Z. *To Take Place: Toward Theory in Ritual*. Chicago: University of Chicago Press, 1987.

Spinks, Bryan. "Review of *A Sociological History of Christian Worship*, by Martin Stringer." *Journal of Ecclesiastical History* 57, no. 3 (2006): 542–543.

Spurrier, Rebecca. *The Disabled Church: Human Difference and the Art of Communal Worship*. New York: Fordham University Press, 2020.

Stevenson, Kenneth. *The Mystery of Baptism in the Anglican Tradition*. Norwich: Canterbury Press, 1998.

Storm, Ingrid. "Halfway to Heaven: Four Types of Fuzzy Fidelity in Europe." *Journal for the Scientific Study of Religion* 48, no. 4 (2009): 702–718.

Stout, Jeffrey. *Ethics After Babel: The Languages of Morals and Their Discontents*. Cambridge: James Clark, 1988.

Stringer, Martin. *A Sociological History of Christian Worship*. Cambridge: Cambridge University Press, 2005.

Stringer, Martin. *Contemporary Western Ethnography and the Definition of Religion*. London: Continuum, 2008.

Stringer, Martin. "Liturgy and Anthropology: History of a Relationship." *Worship* 63, no. 6 (1989): 503–521.

Stringer, Martin. *On the Perception of Worship*. Birmingham: Birmingham University Press, 1999.

Summers-Effler, Erika. "Ritual Theory." In *The Handbook of the Sociology of Emotions*, edited by Jan E. Stets and Jonathan H. Turner, 135–154. New York: Springer, 2006.

Summerson, Andrew. "The Church on Parker's Back: A Primer in *Theologia Prima* for the 'Nones.'" *Worship* 96 (2022): 319–335.

Swidler, Ann. "Culture in Action: Symbols and Strategies." *American Sociological Review* 51, no. 2 (1986): 273–286.

Swidler, Ann. *Talk of Love: How Culture Matters*. Chicago: University of Chicago Press, 2001.

Swinton, John. "'Where Is Your Church?' Moving Toward a Hospitable and Sanctified Ethnography." In *Perspectives on Ecclesiology and Ethnography*, edited by Pete Ward, 71–94. Grand Rapids, MI: Eerdmans, 2012.

Tanner, Norman, and Sethina Watson. "Least of the Laity: The Minimum Requirements for a Medieval Christian." *Journal of Medieval History* 32, no. 4 (2006): 395–423.

Tavory, Iddo, and Stefan Timmermans. *Abductive Analysis: Theorizing Qualitative Research*. Chicago: University of Chicago Press, 2014.

Taylor, Barbara Brown. "Identity Confirmation: John 4:5–42." *Christian Century*, February 12, 2008.

Taylor, Charles. *A Secular Age.* Cambridge, MA: Harvard University Press, 2007.
Thiessen, Joel. *The Meaning of Sunday: The Practice of Belief in a Secular Age.* Montreal and Kingston: McGill-Queen's University Press, 2015.
Thiessen, Joel, and Bill McAlpine. "Sacred Space: Function and Mission from a Sociological and Theological Perspective." *International Journal for the Study of the Christian Church* 13 (2013): 133–146.
Thiessen, Joel, and Sarah Wilkins-LaFlamme. *None of the Above: Nonreligious Identity in the US and Canada.* New York: New York University Press, 2020.
Timmermans, Stefan, and Iddo Tavory. "Theory Construction in Qualitative Research: From Grounded Theory to Abductive Analysis." *Sociological Theory* 30, no. 3 (2012): 167–186.
Utley, Allie. "Hope Emerges? An Exploration of Energy and Power in the Context of Worship." *Liturgy* 37, no. 2 (2022): 48–54.
Utley, Allie. "Sensing Worship: An Autoethnography of Liturgy and Affect." PhD diss., Vanderbilt University, 2021. https://ir.vanderbilt.edu/handle/1803/16749.
Vaisey, Stephen. "Motivation and Justification: A Dual-Process Model of Culture in Action." *American Journal of Sociology* 114, no. 6 (2009): 1675–1715.
Voas, David. "The Rise and Fall of Fuzzy Fidelity in Europe." *European Sociological Review* 25, no. 2 (2009): 155–168.
Voas, David, and Mark Chaves. "Is the United States a Counterexample to the Secularization Thesis?" *American Journal of Sociology* 121 (2016): 1517–1556.
Walker, David. "You Don't Have to Go to Church to Be a Good Christian: The Implicit Religion of the Cathedral Carol Service Congregation." *Mental Health, Religion and Culture* 16 (2013): 903–908.
Ward, Pete, ed. *Perspectives on Ecclesiology and Ethnography.* Grand Rapids, MI: Eerdmans, 2012.
Ward, Pete, and Knut Tveitereid, eds. *The Wiley Blackwell Companion to Theology and Qualitative Research.* Hoboken, NJ: John Wiley & Sons, 2022.
Weber, Max. *The Protestant Ethic and the Spirit of Capitalism.* New York: Scribner, 1958.
Weber, Max. "The Social Psychology of the World Religions." In *From Max Weber: Essays in Sociology,* edited by H. H. Gerth and C. Wright Mills, 267–301. Abingdon: Routledge, 1991.
White, James. *Protestant Worship.* Louisville, KY: Westminster John Knox Press, 1989.
Whitmore, Todd. *Imitating Christ in Magwi: An Anthropological Theology.* London: T&T Clark, 2019.
Wigg-Stevenson, Natalie. *Ethnographic Theology.* New York: Palgrave Macmillan, 2014.
Wilkins-Laflamme, Sarah. *Religion, Spirituality and Secularity Among Millennials: The Generation Shaping American and Canadian Trends.* London: Routledge, 2022.
Williams, Rowan. "Naming the World: Liturgy and the Transformation of Time and Matter." In *Full of Your Glory: Liturgy, Cosmos, Creation,* edited by Teresa Berger, 23–37. Collegeville, MN: Liturgical Press, 2019.
Williams, Rowan. "Some Highlights from the Question and Answer Session That Followed Rowan Williams's Keynote Address." In *Full of Your Glory: Liturgy, Cosmos, Creation,* edited by Teresa Berger, 38–44. Collegeville, MN: Liturgical Press, 2019.
World Council of Churches. *Baptism, Eucharist and Ministry.* Geneva: World Council of Churches, 1982.

Index

For the benefit of digital users, indexed terms that span two pages (e.g., 52–53) may, on occasion, appear on only one of those pages.

Tables and figures are indicated by an italic *t* and *f* following the page number.

100% Anglican, 67–68, 86–87
9/11. *See* September 11, 2001

abductive, 319, 343–44
abortion, 29–30, 197
adolescence, 26, 36–37, 119–20, 320–21, 351
advocates, 4, 92*f*, 109–11, 112–13, 124, 129, 203–4, 205, 212, 320–21
affect theory, 172–73, 188, 246, 277–83
agency, 101, 139–40, 158–59, 209–10, 271–72
agnosticism, 53, 66–67, 80–85, 89–90, 89*f*, 112–13, 207–8, 275, 295–301, 320, 332–33, 345
altar, 108, 136, 219, 254, 263
Ammerman, Nancy, 54–55, 256n.2, 292–93, 311–12, 335n.76, 335n.80
Anglican Cathedral. *See* Cathedral Church of St. James
Anglican Church of Canada, 7–10, 346–51
Anglican identity, 67–70, 89–90, 320
Anglican ritual system. *See* ritual system, Anglican
Anglo-Catholic Anglicans, 8, 201, 202, 346–47, 355–56
Angus Reid Institute, 26, 46*t*, 46–43, 49–50, 53, 88–89, 89*f*, 105
anthropological theology, 329, 330
Apostles' Creed, 66, 347–48
architecture. *See* space
archival research, 11, 351, 353
atheism, 46–47, 46*t*, 53, 66–67, 80–85, 89–90, 115–16, 163, 206–7, 227–30, 237, 295–96, 320, 332–33, 345
Australia, 3, 38–39, 58–63

Baker, Joseph, 53–54, 100, 129–30
baptism, 9, 10, 18–19, 26–29, 35–36, 45, 47–48, 57, 58–59, 66, 91, 92–93, 133–36, 139–40, 148, 150–51, 152–53, 158–64, 169–70, 203–13, 217–18, 219–23, 225–26, 232, 251–52, 272–73, 280–81, 284–86, 294–95, 347–48, 349–51
  adult, 68–69, 100–1, 209, 211–12, 269–70, 280, 285
  garment, 151, 206–7, 217, 222, 269–70, 271–72
  preparation, 114, 144, 148, 153–54, 207–8, 217, 220, 222, 269–70, 271–72, 352, 355, 358, 361
  promises, 66, 144, 158–60
  rite of baptism, 9, 66, 133, 134–35, 147, 150–51, 153–54, 158–59, 168, 347–48
Baptism, Eucharist and Ministry (BEM), 9, 150–51
behavior regulating practices, 35
Belcher, Kimberly Hope, 136–37, 138, 146, 148–51, 155, 156, 157, 166–67, 168–69, 170, 173–74, 184n.43, 185–88, 213, 255*f*, 255
believing without belonging, 56
Bell, Catherine, 5, 136–37, 138, 140, 146–48, 153, 154–58, 164, 167–68, 174–75, 181, 182–83, 186, 187–88, 192, 213, 321
Bibby, Reginald, 23–24, 26, 44–45, 49–50, 85
Bible, 50–51, 71, 79, 85, 86, 87, 88, 105, 107, 108, 123, 190–91, 310, 311–14. *See also* scripture reading during worship
Book of Alternative Services (1985), 8–10, 147, 150–51, 159, 168, 275, 346–48
Book of Common Prayer (1962), 8–9, 10, 94, 275, 346–48
borderless borders, 244–45
bounded and centered sets, 149–50, 160
Bourdieu, Pierre, 332
bread. *See* communion elements
Britain/British. *See* United Kingdom
Buddhism, 75–78, 345
building. *See* space

Caesarius of Arles, 41
calendrical practices, 35–37, 140, 166, 173n.2

384   INDEX

candles, 21, 35–36, 133–37, 146, 148, 170–71, 254, 263, 272, 274, 347–48
Carvalhaes, Cláudio, 226, 237–38, 240, 243–50, 252, 290–91, 302, 308, 314–15, 321–22
casket, 111, 217–18, 268, 273
catalysts, 4, 92f, 93, 111, 116, 265–66, 268, 271–72, 320–21
Cathedral Church of St. James, 1–3, 2f, 17, 133, 153, 353, 357–58, 359t
cathedrals, 1–3, 2f, 17, 21, 33, 35–36, 133, 135, 153, 174, 175, 263, 353, 357, 361
centered and bounded sets. See bounded and centered sets
charismatic, 75, 351
Chaves, Mark, 59–60, 60f, 349
childhood, 119, 157–58, 207–8, 266–67, 320–21
Christ. See Jesus
Christian ritual system. See ritual system, Christian
"Christian, not included elsewhere," 70–73, 89–90, 320
Christmas, 1–3, 18–19, 22–26, 35–36, 42, 45, 48–49, 53–54, 55–56, 57, 58–59, 85, 92–93, 95, 99, 104, 112, 116, 117, 121–22, 124, 126, 130, 143, 172, 174, 225–26, 238–39, 260, 265–66, 280, 285, 297, 310, 345, 353, 355
church building. See space
church shopping, 121, 194, 241–42
Clarke, Brian, 39nn.5–6, 43n.22, 48–50, 70–73, 350n.36
class, economic/social, 42–43, 142, 179, 237–38, 248, 311–12, 332, 363
classical theories of culture, 176–77
clergy, 6–7, 21, 23, 39, 65, 91, 101–2, 130, 140–42, 148, 149–50, 158–64, 167–68, 169–71, 184, 198–99, 200, 201–3, 206–8, 211–13, 217, 223–24, 232, 238–39, 244–45, 246, 270–72, 286, 288–90, 294–95, 302, 308, 315, 321, 342, 344–45, 347, 348, 352, 355–56
clothing, 6, 66, 148, 151, 206–7, 217, 223, 261, 265–72, 274, 316, 322–23. See also dressing up; vestments
cognitive science, 178
collectivistic religion, 57–58, 64, 68, 100, 209–10, 283–84
colonial period in the United States, 43
colonialism, 43, 95–97, 156, 248
communion elements, 189–90, 196, 199, 248n.69, 273
communion. See eucharist
confirmation, 26, 28–29, 35–37, 70, 99, 119–20, 139, 143, 202, 239, 351, 353n.41

conservative Protestants, 70–71, 73, 88, 89–90, 100–1, 169–70, 194, 199–200, 256–57, 271, 300
Constitution on the Sacred Liturgy. See Sacrosanctum Concilium
cottage, 18–19, 117, 248
COVID-19, 11, 254, 354–55, 357–58
Creed. See Apostles' Creed
cremation, 103, 104, 304–5, 348
crisis
  communal, 3, 32, 183, 239, 345
  personal, 3, 29–32, 166–67, 183, 212, 239, 240–43
crying. See tears
cultural believer/culturally religious, 47–48, 53–54, 64–65, 68, 100, 238
cultural models, 5, 177, 179–80, 182, 183, 185, 187–88, 205, 207, 208–10, 212, 213, 321
"cultural turn," 176–83, 319, 321, 334–39

Davie, Grace, 56–57, 184–85, 347n.19, 349
Day, Abby, 57, 68, 284n.34
default religious laxity, 43–44, 143
definitions of religion, 3, 7, 19–22, 35–37, 49, 53, 137–39, 325, 335–37, 342
diagnosis. See medical crisis
dialogue, 6, 7, 12–13, 21, 90, 213–14, 224–25, 227–32, 234, 245–47, 250–53, 276–77, 321–23, 325–26
diffusive Christianity, 43, 49, 129
disability, 107–9, 122, 239, 248
discursive practices, 35
Drescher, Elizabeth, 54
dressing up, 27, 66, 206–7, 217, 265–72, 274
dual-process models of culture, 176, 178–79

early modern period, 8, 42, 94
Easter, 18–19, 22–26, 33, 35–36, 40–41, 45, 48, 53–54, 57, 85, 92–93, 95, 99, 104, 112, 117, 126, 130, 133, 134–35, 136, 143, 172, 174, 184–85, 238–39, 254, 255f, 266–67, 279–80, 285, 297, 345, 353, 355
Easter Vigil, 134–35, 136, 184–85, 254, 255f
Eastern Christian. See Orthodox
ecumenism, 12–13, 150–51, 212–13, 225–26, 362
emotion, 6, 30, 31–32, 34, 77, 109–10, 125, 127, 172–73, 178–79, 198–200, 221, 223, 241–42, 243–44, 254–55, 258–59, 263, 277–83, 285, 289, 291–93, 298, 299, 301, 306, 307, 315, 316, 322–23, 348, 352
England. See United Kingdom

ethics, 6, 58–59, 167, 177, 179, 237–45, 308–15, 322–23, 325–26, 328–29, 344–45
ethnicity, 13, 57, 70–73, 74–75, 89–90, 94–100, 142, 157–58, 179, 205–6, 209–10, 212, 213, 231–32, 237–38, 243–44, 249–50, 311–12, 320, 332, 356, 360, 363
ethnography as theology, 7, 224–25, 318, 325
eucharist, 1, 10, 18–19, 42, 76, 84, 99, 108, 119, 139, 150–51, 188, 189–91, 193, 194–95, 196, 199, 202, 225–26, 248n.69, 256–57, 273, 306, 314–15, 330–31, 348
eulogy, 111, 217–18, 223, 279, 287–88, 289–90
Europe, 3, 10, 33, 38–39, 42, 55–58, 59–60, 68, 72, 95, 125, 187, 225–26, 301, 317, 349, 351
evangelical Anglicans, 8, 270, 346–47, 351, 355–56, 358
evangelicalism. *See* conservative Protestants
evangelism, 12–13, 238

Fagerberg, David, 226, 234, 235–36, 291n.38
family ritual system. *See* ritual system, family
Father's Day, 25
feeling. *See* emotion
female clergy. *See* women in liturgical leadership
first communion, 99, 119, 139, 202, 225–26
flowers, 108, 111, 217–18, 223, 273, 289
font, 66, 77, 145, 217, 221–22, 223, 232
food, 25–26, 106, 150–51, 166–67, 189–91, 217, 220–21, 273, 310
Ford, Rob, 17, 20, 32, 36–37
"formally affiliated, fully believing, actively practicing, and morally compliant," 5–7, 90, 130, 224, 229, 231–32, 234, 235–36, 321–22, 341–42, 343
Francis of Assisi, 263
fringe Catholics, 48–49, 64–65, 238
frontier worship, 43
funerals, 7–11, 17, 26–29, 35–36, 45, 47–48, 55–56, 57, 58–59, 92–93, 95–96, 102, 103–4, 111, 115, 123–24, 217–19, 225–26, 240–43, 268–69, 273, 286–91, 347–48, 349–51
  funeral rite, 10, 348
  preparation, 26, 39, 92–93, 111, 265–66, 268–69, 271–72, 279, 304–5, 348, 352, 355, 361
fuzzy fidelity, 55–56, 64–65, 238

Geertz, Clifford, 176–77, 327–28, 332
Geldhof, Joris, 274, 290
gender, 27, 45, 77, 81–82, 113, 142, 147–48, 170, 195–97, 201, 206–7, 230–32, 236, 237–38, 249–50, 282–83, 306–7, 311–12, 332, 349, 356, 360, 363

general practices, 35–37
generational religious change, 59–63, 119, 235–36, 349
gifts, 108, 133–34, 150–51, 154, 163, 204–6, 219, 220, 269, 272, 273, 310, 358–60
God, concepts of, 6, 13, 80–83, 150–51, 180, 229, 256–57, 275–76, 295–301, 311, 315, 322–23, 330–31
godparents, 27, 66, 77, 84, 111, 113–14, 151–53, 154–55, 158–64, 167–68, 185, 196, 203–13, 217, 219, 220–21, 265–66, 269, 309, 352
"good person," 82, 84, 113–14, 295, 300, 308–15, 316
grandparents, 1, 18–19, 25, 27, 28, 29, 33, 34, 39, 57, 59–63, 68, 76, 84, 92–93, 96–97, 98–102, 109–11, 123–24, 139, 142–43, 146–47, 196, 204–5, 206–8, 217, 218–19, 220, 221, 234–35, 248, 260, 263–64, 269, 271, 272, 288, 299, 308, 313, 352, 358
graveside service, 10
Great Britain. *See* United Kingdom
Grimes, Ronald, 149–50, 327–28

Halík, Tomáš, 227–30, 236–50, 300–1, 315
high church Anglicans, 355–56, 357–58
Hinduism, 33, 75–78
Holy Spirit, 9, 13, 77, 232, 261, 270–71, 294–95, 298, 347–48
homily. *See* preaching
hurt by the church, 107, 189–91, 194–201, 202–3, 239, 240–43, 248, 252–53
hymns. *See* music

immigration, 72–73, 94–100, 124, 202, 210–11, 238, 349
inactive believers/nonbelievers 54
incense, 138, 193, 274
incidental circumstances, 3, 22, 23f, 33–36, 61, 79, 128–29, 174, 319
indifferent, 53, 83–85, 89–90, 320
individualism, 68, 102, 129, 174, 258–64, 283–91, 304, 307, 347–48
infertility. *See* reproductive loss
initiators, 4, 92–109, 111, 112–13, 115, 116, 129, 157–58, 175, 196, 211–12, 273, 320–21
  cultural heritage, 4, 92f, 93–100, 102, 109, 111, 129, 146–47, 174, 175, 204–6, 207, 209–10, 213, 232, 273, 283–84, 302, 320–21
  invisibly routine, 4, 92f, 93–94, 105–7, 108, 126, 129, 163, 241, 320–21

initiators (*cont.*)
  involuntarily occasional, 4, 92*f*, 93–94, 107–9, 122, 126, 129, 239, 320–21
  relational connection, 4, 92*f*, 93–94, 100–2, 109, 111, 129, 206–7, 209–10, 283–84, 320–21
  spiritual connection, 4, 92*f*, 93–94, 102–4, 109, 111, 116, 129, 265, 277, 320–21
inner-circle supporters. *See* supporters, inner-circle
intensive practitioners, definition of, 17–19, 173
intercultural Anglicans, 8, 346–47, 351, 357
interdisciplinarity, 7, 11–12, 137–38, 246, 318–19, 325, 343–44
interventionist practices, 35–36, 337
invisibly routine. *See* initiators, invisibly routine
involuntarily occasional. *See* initiators, involuntary occasional
involved seculars, 54
Islam, 71, 75–78, 116, 174, 297, 360–61

Jakelic, Slavica, 57–58, 68, 100, 284n.34
Jesus, 9–10, 71, 78, 86, 95, 104, 133, 144–45, 151, 159, 189–90, 197–98, 199, 203, 227–32, 236–37, 239–40, 249, 250–51, 289–90, 294–95, 297–98, 299, 311–12, 313–15, 347–48
John Chrysostom, 38, 40–41, 65
Judaism, 26, 53–54, 71, 75–78, 116, 360–61
juxtaposition, 148, 244

Kavanagh, Aidan, 233–34
kneeling, 169–70, 193

language, liturgical, 66, 158–59, 168, 170, 193, 199–200, 223, 251, 254–55, 274–77, 282–83, 292, 296, 298, 303
languages other than English, 97, 193, 355–56, 357
lapsed, 75, 80–81
Larson-Miller, Lizette, 264–65
last rites, 10, 202
late antique period, 38, 40–41, 65
Lemons, Derrick, 339
LGBTQ, 104, 197, 201, 202, 204–5, 209, 237–38, 248n.69, 306–7
liberation theology, 6, 203, 226, 236–51, 290–91, 321–22
life course/life cycle, 35–37, 118–22, 126, 134–35, 320–21, 351
liturgical books, 8–9, 10, 108, 147, 169–70, 193, 199–200, 275, 346–48, 361
liturgical language/texts. *See* language, liturgical

liturgical margins, 6–7, 13, 142–43, 145, 224, 227–32, 236–40, 247–53
liturgy, definition of, 20, 42, 251–52, 321–22, 326–34
lived liturgical theology, 235, 250–53, 254–93, 294–316, 358
lived religion, 256–57, 335–36n.80
lived theology, 256–57
Lord's Prayer. *See* Prayer Jesus Taught
Lord's Supper. *See* eucharist
low religious, 26n.14, 44–45, 50, 64–65, 85, 128
Lutheran, 42, 75, 328–29, 345–46

Macdonald, Stuart, 39nn.5–6, 43n.22, 48–50, 70–73, 350n.36
maid of honor, 77–78
mainline Anglicans, 8, 45, 351, 355–56, 357
mainline/mainstream Protestants, 39, 45, 48, 282–83, 330, 345, 346–47, 351, 362. *See also* United Church; Presbyterian; Methodist; Lutheran; mainline Anglicans
Manning, Christel, 53, 81, 83–84, 105
marginal affiliates, 45–46, 64–65, 85, 128, 257–58
marriage. *See* wedding
Marsh, Charles, 42, 256–57
Marti, Gerardo, 331–32
Mary, mother of Jesus, 95, 197, 251n.74, 280
materiality, 6, 133–36, 169–70, 217–23, 251, 254–56, 257–77, 291–93, 301, 302, 307, 316, 322–23, 353, 360
meals with family, 99, 150–51, 152, 166–67, 189–91, 207, 217, 220–21, 273
medical crisis, 29, 30–32, 240–41, 242–43, 260–61, 270–71. *See also* reproductive loss
medieval period, 41–42, 184–85
memorial service, 10, 348
memory, 24, 25, 39, 61, 119, 133–36, 168–69, 178–79, 193, 199–200, 207–8, 217–24, 250, 258–61, 266–67, 273, 279–80, 286–91, 308
Methodist, 71, 344–46
mid-twentieth-century religion, 39, 49, 334
millennials, 47*f*, 47–48, 50, 100
ministers. *See* clergy
Mitchell, Nathan, 243, 292n.40
mood, 6, 34, 177, 198–201, 207–9, 277–81, 282–83, 316, 322–23
Moralistic Therapeutic Deism (MTD), 314–15
morals. *See* ethics
Mother's Day, 23, 25, 174, 239, 353
moving to a new home, neighborhood, city, or country, 29, 92–93, 97–98, 108, 120, 124–25, 194. *See also* immigration
Mrs. Murphy, 6, 232–36, 321–22
Mrs. Murphy's great-granddaughter, 6, 232–36

multiple religious practice/belonging, 116, 210–11, 360–61
multi-speed system, 41–42, 184–85
music, 1, 10, 17, 67, 80, 108, 111, 117, 125, 137, 169–70, 174, 184, 193–94, 199–200, 204–5, 207–8, 217–18, 246, 248n.69, 259, 261, 278, 279–80, 281, 289, 301, 303–4, 338, 345–46, 348
Muslim. *See* Islam

National Church Life Survey, 58–59
nominal, 48–49, 57, 64–65, 68, 238
nonaffiliated believers, 53
nonreligion, 3, 4, 7–8, 19–20, 26, 47, 49–50, 51*f*, 53–54, 61, 64, 66–67, 78–85, 89–90, 100, 104, 113, 114, 115–16, 122–23, 129–30, 136, 137, 151, 152–53, 158–64, 168–69, 188, 196, 204–5, 214, 224, 229, 238, 248, 262, 264, 274–75, 276, 280, 281, 295–96, 306, 309–10, 320, 335, 341–42, 343, 345–46, 347, 349, 351, 360–61, 363
normative claims, 330–31, 332–33
nostalgia, 39, 306
"not very religious," 4, 11, 85–89, 128, 145, 192, 320–21

objects, 6, 133–36, 223, 251, 254–57, 272–74, 289, 316, 322–23, 353, 360
occasional religious practice, definition of, 3, 5, 17–22, 63–65, 128–30, 173, 317, 319, 321
oil, 66, 272, 274n.18
ordinary theology, 256n.3
Orthodox, 57–58, 69, 75, 135, 207–9, 241, 345–46, 360–61
Our Father. *See* Prayer Jesus Taught
outer-circle supporters. *See* supporters, outer-circle

pall, 273
pandemic. *See* COVID-19
parenthood, 118, 120–22, 179–80, 320–21
Parsons, Talcott, 176
participant observation, 3, 11, 23, 107, 116, 140, 203–4, 225–26, 235, 251, 318, 331–32, 333–34, 343, 345, 350–51, 352–53, 354, 355, 357–58
pastors. *See* clergy
Pentecostal. *See* charismatic
Petrin, Anna, 226, 232–33, 234, 236
pews, 1, 258–59, 260–62, 263–64
philosophical secularist, 53, 81, 83–84
photography, 6, 24–25, 77, 111, 134, 217–24, 246, 251, 254–55, 255*f*, 269, 273, 274, 283–84, 316, 353, 360

pictures. *See* photography
pilot studies, 343, 344–46
Pope, 197, 248–49
popular culture ritual system. *See* ritual system, popular culture
popular religion, 20, 42, 134–35, 196, 251–52, 338
power, 21–22, 130, 142, 156, 224–25, 239, 244–45, 252–53
prayer
 in church, 10, 30, 35–36, 66, 96, 135, 159, 169–70, 193, 199–200, 258, 263, 274–75, 296, 298, 310, 347–48
 Prayer Jesus Taught, 21, 106, 199
 private, 18–19, 21, 30, 61, 78–79, 105–7, 155, 159, 242, 300
preaching, 1, 23, 33, 38, 40–41, 101–2, 193, 197, 223, 271, 287, 288–89, 298, 313–14, 348
preparation for baptism. *See* baptism, preparation
preparation for funerals. *See* funeral preparation
preparation for marriage. *See* wedding, marriage preparation
Presbyterian, 48, 73, 75, 97, 125, 237
priests. *See* clergy
primary liturgical theology, 233–36, 250–51
privately faithful, 46*t*, 46–47, 48, 89*f*, 105

queer. *See* LGBTQ

race. *See* ethnicity
reflexivity, 11–12, 361–63
Reformation era. *See* early modern period
religion, definitions of. *See* definitions of religion
religious change,
 Anglican Church of Canada, 8, 44–50, 349–51, 350*f*
 Australia, 17, 58–63
 Canada, 3, 44–50, 59–63, 88–89, 89*f*, 349–51
 Europe, 3, 10, 55–58, 59–63
 Great Britain, 56–57, 59–63
 United States, 3, 10, 50–55, 59–63
religious middle, 26, 44–45, 49–50
remember. *See* memory
Remembrance Day, 25, 28–29, 239, 353
repertoire theory, 176, 177, 178–79, 181–83, 208–9, 332
reproductive loss, 29–30, 241–42
retirement, 122
Riesebrodt, Martin, 19–20, 21, 35–37, 137–39, 325–26, 335–38, 340, 342

388 INDEX

Rijken, Hanna, 301
ritual need, 212, 239, 243
ritual system
   Anglican, 5, 136–37, 153, 170, 174, 188, 189–214, 277
   Christian, 134–35, 136–37, 142, 146–47, 151, 152–54, 155, 158–64, 168–69, 183–85, 187, 208–9, 212, 213–14, 274
   family, 151, 152–53, 154–55, 157–64, 207, 208–10, 213, 269
   popular culture, 136, 205–6, 207, 208–9, 212
   Roman Catholic, 5, 188, 189–214, 254, 277, 305
ritual system relationships
   centrality, 146, 148–51, 164, 165–66, 170, 184, 185, 205–6, 207, 213–14, 222, 223, 254, 265, 272, 286, 295, 321
   nesting, 151–54, 164, 165–66, 170, 321
   opposition, 146, 147–48, 149, 164, 165–66, 167, 170, 184, 185, 190–91, 194–201, 205–6, 207–9, 212, 213–14, 244, 271–72, 321
   overlapping, 5, 136–37, 151–53, 154–64, 165–68, 170–71, 173, 185–88, 189–214, 243, 244, 251–52, 274, 277, 283–84, 305, 321, 345–46
   repetition, 146–47, 161, 164, 165–66, 167, 170, 181, 182–83, 184, 185, 190–91, 192–94, 205–6, 207, 208–9, 211, 212, 213–14, 222, 271–72, 321
   separation of practices, 5, 36–37, 183–87, 321
   transformation of practices, 5, 136–37, 147, 156–57, 164, 165, 168–71, 186–87, 188, 214, 302, 321
ritual systems, definition of, 5, 137–39
Ritz, Bridget, 179–81, 183, 205
Robbins, Joel, 339
Roman Catholic
   baptism, 28, 62, 97–100, 101, 139, 182, 196, 202, 203–11, 225–26
   funeral, 194–95, 202, 225–26, 240–41
   identity, 48–49, 60–61, 69, 72, 74–75, 81–82, 89–90, 116, 320, 360–61
   mass, 112, 116, 173, 192–94, 198–201, 263–64
   ritual system. *See* ritual system, Roman Catholic
   school, 62, 97–98, 112, 119, 139, 172, 173, 188, 189, 190–91, 199, 210–11
   wedding, 28, 60–61, 139, 189–91, 194–95, 196, 202, 241
Roman Catholicism, 8, 13, 318, 326–27, 329, 330, 346–47, 351, 362
Rotolo, Michael, 179–81, 183, 205
routine practitioners, definition of, 17–19, 173

sacred canopy, 44
sacred umbrellas, 44
Sacrosanctum Concilium, 291, 326–27
Samaritan woman. *See* woman at the well
Scharen, Christian, 224n.2, 325–26, 328–29, 330–31, 332, 340, 341–42
Scotland. *See* United Kingdom
scripture reading during worship, 10, 193–94, 256–57, 274–75, 313
seasons of the year, 18–19, 107–8, 117, 320–21
seekers, 47, 53, 64, 227–29, 236, 315
semi-structured interviews, 11, 365
September 11, 2001, 32
sermon. *See* preaching
settled culture, 177, 181–82
Sheilaism, 283–84
Sikhism, 116
Smith, Buster, 53–54, 100, 129–30
Smith, Christian, 19, 21–22, 35, 43, 44n.28, 130n.11, 137–38, 143, 179–81, 183, 205, 314–15, 325–26, 332n.58, 334n.70, 334n.72, 335–38, 340, 341–42, 352n.39
Smith, James K. A., 282–83
Smith, Jonathan Z., 140–42
sociology of culture, 5, 173, 176–83, 319, 321, 332
soft de-churched, 48, 64–65, 128, 238
"something more," 6, 78–80, 82–83, 180, 295–301, 315, 316, 322–23
songs. *See* music
space, 1, 2f, 6, 46, 94–95, 116, 133, 145, 149, 150–51, 166–67, 209, 217, 223, 251–52, 254–55, 257–65, 274, 277, 316, 356
spiritual but not religious (SBNR), 26, 54–55, 58–59, 64, 72, 78–80, 83–84, 242, 320
spirituality, 20, 54–55, 78–80, 102–4, 283–84
spiritually uncertain, 46t, 46–47, 89f
stained-glass windows, 220, 261–62
Storm, Ingrid, 56
Stringer, Martin, 333, 335, 340
style of worship, 199–201, 303–4
supporters, 4, 92–93, 92f, 109–16, 129, 157–58, 175, 196, 320–21
   inner-circle, 4, 92–93, 92f, 109, 111–14, 115, 116, 129, 158, 203–4, 205, 211–12, 273, 320–21
   outer-circle, 4, 92–93, 92f, 109, 115–16, 129, 174, 320–21
survey questions exclude occasional practice, 46–47, 53, 65
Swidler, Ann, 176, 177, 181–83
Swinton, John, 330

Taft, Robert, 302
Tavory, Iddo, 343–44, 347n.20, 363nn.53–54

Taylor, Charles, 41–42, 184–85
tears, 219, 221–22, 223, 242, 254–55, 256–57, 260–61, 272, 278, 279–81
theologia prima. See primary liturgical theology
theological margins, 6–7, 13, 145, 224, 227–40, 247–53
Thiessen, Joel, 45–46, 49–50, 54, 81n.9, 85, 257–58, 260, 349n.31
Timmermans, Stefan, 343–44, 363nn.53–54
toolkit theory. *See* repertoire theory
Toronto, 1, 3, 7–10, 17, 23–24, 32, 44, 64, 68, 78, 89–90, 95, 130, 187, 191, 212–13, 248, 255–56, 263, 292–93, 305–6, 318, 345, 346–51, 353–55, 357–58, 360
tradition, 6, 21–22, 46, 55–56, 96–97, 98–100, 101–2, 103–4, 146–47, 164, 167–68, 174–75, 180, 181, 192, 199–200, 233–34, 261–63, 267, 270, 302–7, 311, 314–15, 316, 322–23
Trinity, 9, 150–51, 180, 184, 256–57 291, 294–95, 301, 330–31
Trump, Donald, 71

unchurched, 43, 53, 105, 235n.40
United Church, 17, 45, 48, 67, 75, 80–81, 123, 194, 362
United Kingdom, 8, 42–43, 56–57, 58–59, 67, 94–100, 206–7, 225–26, 248, 333, 349
United States, 3, 10, 17, 38–39, 43, 47–48, 50–55, 59–63, 118, 179–80, 271, 311–12, 344–45, 349, 351, 363
unsettled culture, 177, 181–83
Utley, Allie, 282–83

Vaisey, Stephen, 176, 178–79
variable practices, 35–37
vestments, 148, 270–72, 274
vicarious religion, 56–57, 64, 184–85, 349
Victorian England, 42–43, 49
Vigen, Aana Marie, 224n.2, 328–29, 330n.42
Voas, David, 55–56, 59–60, 60*f*, 349

Ward, Pete, 328–29, 331
water, 9, 66, 150–51, 198–99, 209, 221–22, 223, 230–32, 272–73, 280–81, 347–48
Weber, Max, 176–77, 334
wedding, 18–19, 26–29, 35–37, 45, 46–48, 53, 54, 55–56, 57, 58–59, 60–61, 65, 76–78, 93–94, 96, 97, 98, 111, 115, 120, 128, 144, 172, 174, 175, 181–82, 189–91, 194–95, 196, 201, 202, 206–7, 241–43, 263–64, 269, 306–7, 349, 350*f*, 351
  marriage preparation, 28, 60–61, 202, 209, 241–42, 262
Whitmore, Todd, 226, 229–30, 325–26, 328, 329, 330–31, 330n.43, 340, 342
Wigg-Stevenson, Natalie, 325–26, 328, 329–31, 332
Wilkins-Laflamme, Sarah, 47*f*, 47–48, 49–50, 54, 68, 100
wine. *See* communion elements
woman at the well, 6, 230–33, 292–93, 321–22
women in liturgical leadership, 195–96, 198–99, 201, 206–7

Zacchaeus, 6, 227–30, 232–33, 236–37, 321–22, 330–31